Peter Mattock

# Visible Maths

## Using representations and structure to enhance mathematics teaching in schools

Crown House Publishing Limited
www.crownhouse.co.uk

First published by
Crown House Publishing Limited
Crown Buildings, Bancyfelin, Carmarthen, Wales, SA33 5ND, UK
www.crownhouse.co.uk

and

Crown House Publishing Company LLC
PO Box 2223, Williston, VT 05495, USA
www.crownhousepublishing.com

First published 2019. Reprinted 2019 (twice).

British Library Cataloguing-in-Publication Data

A catalogue entry for this book is available from the British Library.

Print ISBN 978-178583350-2
Mobi ISBN 978-178583407-3
ePub ISBN 978-178583408-0
ePDF ISBN 978-178583409-7

LCCN 2019938145

Printed in the UK by
Stephens & George, Dowlais, Merthyr Tydfil

# Acknowledgements

This book is dedicated to:

All the maths teachers and education professionals I have worked with; you have all shaped my practice in some way that has led me to this point.

All of the maths teachers and education professionals I converse with on Twitter; you are a constant source of inspiration that challenges me to keep getting better. I am not going to try and list you all (we all know how that goes, Julia @TessMaths), so just know that I value our conversations and debates.

My mum, Lesley Mattock, who has been one of the greatest sources of support to me throughout my life and without whose help I would never have reached this point.

But mostly this book is dedicated to my loving partner Rowan. Her understanding and support throughout my career and throughout this project has been beyond what any man could hope for. She has put up with so much whilst I have worked to get to where I am in my career, and even more as I balanced leading a mathematics department with writing this book. Without her love this book would never have been written.

I also wish to offer my sincere thanks to:

Jonathan Hall (@StudyMaths) for his excellent website mathsbot.com and in particular for allowing me to use his virtual manipulatives as the basis with which to create the vast majority of the images used in this book.

Jan Parry, Dr Mark McCourt, Professor Anne Watson, Professor John Mason, Pete Griffin and Steve Lomax, all of whom between them have taught me the importance of actually having a personal pedagogy and opened my eyes to the importance of ensuring that pedagogy is well informed, as well as influencing my knowledge of representation, structure, variation theory and a host of other important approaches in an array (no pun intended!) of different ways.

David and Karen Bowman at Crown House Publishing for agreeing to publish this book and their encouragement throughout the process, as well as the support of their staff – particularly Louise Penny and Emma Tuck, who managed to take my ramblings and prompt me to create something coherent from them, Tom Fitton for the excellent illustrations, Rosalie Williams and Tabitha Palmer for dealing with all the marketing, and Beverley Randell for helping me navigate the process of actually taking a book from a collection of thoughts and ideas to something worthy of publication.

# Contents

# Introduction

There is a great mathematics story that I was told in a lecture at university. It involves two donkeys and a fly. The problem goes that two donkeys are 100 metres apart and walking directly towards each other at 1 metre per second. A fly starts on the nose of the first donkey and buzzes between the noses of the two donkeys at 10 metres per second. The question is, how long before the fly is crushed between the two donkeys?

One of the ways to solve this problem is summing an infinite series (i.e. summing the terms of a sequence that continues forever). On its way to the second donkey the fly is travelling for $\frac{100}{11}$ seconds, then on the way back $\frac{900}{121}$ seconds, then another $\frac{8100}{1331}$ seconds, and so on. The $n$th term of the geometric series is given by $\frac{100}{11} \times \left(\frac{9}{11}\right)^{n-1}$ and so the sum to infinity of the series is $\frac{100/11}{1-9/11} = \frac{100/11}{2/11} = \frac{100}{2} = 50$ seconds.

The other way to solve the problem is to ignore the fly completely. Each donkey is walking at 1 metre per second. This means that they will meet halfway at 50 metres. If they travel 50 metres at 1 metre per second it will take 50 seconds.

The story goes that a group of university students were told that a natural mathematician would automatically try to solve the problem using an infinite series and a natural physicist would solve it using the simpler approach. The problem therefore sorted mathematicians from physicists: if a student were able to solve it in a few seconds they were a physicist and if not they were a mathematician. The undergraduates were posing the problem to various students passing through the university library when the famous mathematician Leonhard Euler walked by. They presented the problem to Euler and were amazed when he answered the problem within a few seconds, as they had automatically expected him to begin considering the infinite series. When one of the students explained that a natural mathematician would have begun by forming the infinite series for the motion of the fly, Euler replied, 'But that is what I did ...'

A very similar story exists about the eminent mathematician and computer scientist John von Neumann and trains, which makes me suspect that this is at best a parable about Euler and at worst a case of Chinese whispers. However, the point of the story is not to show how good at mathematics Euler (or von Neumann) was, but instead to show that sometimes in mathematics the way you think about the calculation or problem you are solving has a great impact on how simple the problem is or how much sense it makes. Only the best A level mathematics students would be able to form the infinite series necessary to solve the problem, whereas most early secondary school pupils would be able to work out the simpler solution.

The importance of having different ways to view even the most simple mathematics, in order to build up to more complicated ideas, cannot be overstated. Some ways of thinking about numbers make some truths self-evident, whilst simultaneously obscuring others. In the same way in physics that it is sometimes better to view elementary matter as particles and at other times as waves, so in mathematics it is sometimes better to view numbers as **discrete** and at other times as **continuous**, as counters or bars, as tallies or **vectors**. Crucially for teachers, being explicit about how we are thinking about numbers and operations, and encouraging pupils to think about them in different ways, can add real power to their learning.

Much has been made of the effectiveness of metacognition in raising the attainment of pupils. For example, John Hattie lists metacognitive strategies as having an effect size of 0.6 in the most recent list of factors influencing student achievement.[*] Ofsted also recognises the importance of the use of manipulatives and representations to support flexibility in pupil thinking. In their *Mathematics: Made to Measure* report from 2012, it is noted that schools should choose 'teaching approaches and activities that foster pupils' deeper understanding, including through the use of practical resources, [and] visual images'.[†] In *Improving Mathematics in Key Stages Two and Three*, the Education Endowment Foundation lists 'Use manipulatives and representations' as one of its key recommendations.[‡] It is therefore important that we give the pupils the tools they need in order to think about the mathematics they are working with in different ways.

The use of representations and structure is also an important part of teaching for mastery approaches. The National Centre for Excellence in the Teaching of Mathematics (NCETM) lists representation and structure as one of the 'Five Big Ideas' in teaching for mastery.[§] The NCETM make clear that using appropriate representations in lessons can help to expose the mathematical structure being taught, allowing pupils to make connections between and across different areas of maths. They also emphasise that the aim in using these representations is that pupils will eventually understand enough about the structure such that they do not need to rely on the representation any more. This is often summarised as employing a concrete-pictorial-abstract (or CPA) approach to teaching mathematics.

Recently re-popularised in the UK following the focus on teaching approaches imported from places such as Shanghai and Singapore, the CPA approach actually has at least some of its roots in the 1982 Cockcroft Report, which reviewed the teaching

---

[*]  See https://www.visiblelearningplus.com/sites/default/files/250%20Influences.pdf.

[†]  Ofsted, *Mathematics: Made to Measure* (May 2012). Ref: 110159. Available at: https://www.gov.uk/government/publications/mathematics-made-to-measure, p. 10.

[‡]  See P. Henderson, J. Hodgen, C. Foster and D. Kuchemann, *Improving Mathematics in Key Stages Two and Three: Guidance Report* (London: Education Endowment Foundation, 2017). Available at: https://educationendowmentfoundation.org.uk/public/files/Publications/Campaigns/Maths/KS2_KS3_Maths_Guidance_2017.pdf, pp. 10–13.

[§]  See https://www.ncetm.org.uk/resources/50042.

of maths in England and Wales.[*] The Cockcroft Report advocated (among many other things) the need to allow pupils the opportunity of practical exploration with concrete materials before moving towards abstract thinking.

There are several studies on the use of manipulatives across the age and ability range, with most showing that mathematics achievement is increased through the long-term use of concrete materials. The most comprehensive of these is Sowell's 'Effects of Manipulative Materials in Mathematics Instruction', a meta-analysis of 60 individual studies designed to determine the effectiveness of mathematics instruction with manipulative materials.[†] Those surveyed ranged in age from pre-school children to college-age adults who were studying a variety of mathematics topics. Sowell found that 'mathematics achievement is increased through the long-term use of concrete instructional materials and that students' attitudes toward mathematics are improved when they have instruction with concrete materials provided by teachers knowledgeable about their use'.[‡]

The aim of this book is to explore some of the different concrete materials available to teachers and pupils, ways of using these concrete and pictorial approaches to represent different types of numbers as discrete or continuous, how certain operations work when viewing numbers in these ways, and how these various representations can help to support the understanding of different concepts in mathematics. The book will look at the strengths of each representation, as well as the flaws, so that both primary and secondary school teachers of mathematics can make informed judgements about which representations will benefit their pupils. I will draw on my own experience of using the representations, as well as experiences shared by others, and appropriate research in order to support teachers in understanding how these representations can be implemented in the classroom.

## How to use this book

I have often noticed that one of the difficulties pupils have in acquiring new mathematical understanding is that we introduce new ways of representing or thinking about mathematics at the same time as we try to teach a new mathematical concept or skill. I will take an alternative approach here, which is to explore all of the representations first and then, once they are secure, examine how more complicated calculations and concepts can be developed.

---

[*]   W. H. Cockcroft (chair), *Mathematics Counts: Report of the Committee of Inquiry into the Teaching of Mathematics in Schools* [Cockcroft Report] (London: HMSO, 1982). Available at: http://www.educationengland.org.uk/documents/cockcroft/cockcroft1982.html.

[†]   E. J. Sowell, Effects of Manipulative Materials in Mathematics Instruction, *Journal for Research in Mathematics Education*, 20(5) (1989), 498–505. Available at: http://www.jstor.org/stable/749423?read-now=1&seq=7#references_tab_contents.

[‡]   Sowell, Effects of Manipulative Materials in Mathematics Instruction, 498.

I wouldn't introduce all of these representations at once with pupils; instead I would introduce two or three. Importantly, though, I would ensure that pupils are comfortable with the representation before trying to use the representation to explore a new concept. This generally involves introducing the representation to pupils within a concept they are comfortable with, and modelling with them how the representation fits with what they already know. This then allows the teacher to develop the concept into something new, using the representation as a bridge.

As this book is aimed at teachers, Chapter 1 will set out all of the representations within the secure concept of whole numbers, and Chapter 2 will then extend these representations to include fractions and decimals. The basic operations of addition and subtraction of whole numbers will be introduced in Chapter 3, followed by multiplication and division of whole numbers in Chapter 4, and powers and roots of whole numbers in Chapter 5. Chapter 6 then explores these ideas as applied to fractions and decimals. Chapter 7 examines the use of representations to illustrate the fundamental laws of arithmetic, and then in Chapter 8 we look at how these combine to define the correct order of operations in calculations involving multiple operations. Chapter 9 covers the concepts of accuracy, including **rounding**, significant figures and bounds, before we move on to **irrational numbers** in Chapter 10.

Chapter 11 sees the introduction of different representations applied to algebra, after which we progress to manipulating algebraic expressions by simplifying expressions (Chapter 12), multiplying expressions (Chapter 13) and expanding and factorising expressions (Chapter 14). In Chapter 15 we look at how representations can support with illustrating the solutions of **equations**, and then Chapter 16 examines some particular algebraic manipulations not covered in Chapters 12 to 14 – in particular, the difference of two squares and completing the square. Finally, Chapter 17 seeks to answer some of the questions about the use of representations in the classroom that may arise from the reading of the book.

You will notice while reading the book that some key mathematical terms are presented in **bold** – for your convenience these terms are defined in a glossary, found at the back of the book.

The fact that the book spans almost the complete breadth of primary and secondary school mathematics might make some question the usefulness of covering everything in one text. One reason I have chosen to do so is that I feel it is important that teachers understand not just the stage they are teaching, but also how this builds on what has been taught before and how this is built on in the stages after. This ensures that teachers see how what they are teaching fits into the wider pupil journey, and can support pupils no matter where they are along the way. Pupils will enter and leave stages of schooling at many different points, and just because we might teach in a secondary school doesn't mean we won't need to support pupils who haven't secured concepts from primary school, or similarly that teachers in primary schools won't need to provide depth in a topic by allowing pupils to explore a concept to a point that would normally be taught in secondary school. In this, all-through (3–18) schools have an advantage as they can design their curriculum to build all the way through the school. Those working in separate primary and secondary schools, or other school models, must use strong transition links to make this happen. So, for primary school teachers, this book showcases the mathematics you will teach and show you how it extends into secondary school. For secondary teachers, this book will provide some insight into approaches that might be used in feeder primaries and how you can develop them in secondary school.

I hope this book will support teachers in choosing suitable representations for use in their classrooms by making them much more secure in their own understanding of the strengths and weaknesses of each representation, but also, importantly, of how the representations highlight different interpretations of the concepts we explore with pupils. Some of the examples in the book will be suitable for direct use with pupils in the classroom, whilst some will be of more benefit to teachers in developing their own understanding. Pupils will very often need more than the one or two examples illustrated at each stage; in many cases, they will need to experience careful modelling with multiple examples as well as have the opportunity to explore concepts with the different manipulatives and representations provided. Only in this way will pupils eventually move beyond the representations.

The true aim of this book is for teachers to feel sufficiently confident in the use of the representations that they can explain enough about the underlying structures of the different concepts so that pupils no longer need to rely on the representations to see these structures. This is an important end goal for teachers to keep in mind – pupils should be aiming to move beyond the representation. Representations are tools that provide a window into the underlying structure of a concept. They are a window that pupils can keep coming back to look into, but they are not a window they should continually have to stare through. There is a danger that representations become another procedure that pupils have to remember and apply without understanding; this must be avoided at all costs if pupils are going to work towards mastery of mathematical concepts. This is why multiple representations are used for each concept, and why the literature makes clear the need for multiple representations to ensure pupils have a range of ways of thinking about concepts.

# Chapter 1

# Different representations of whole numbers

Many people believe that counting was the earliest mathematical concept to emerge. Whilst counting can be traced back several thousands of years, the first mathematical idea was actually the one-to-one relationship – relating a number of objects with an equal number of different objects. According to Kris Boulton, ancient shepherds would allow their sheep out to graze during the day, and for every sheep that went out they would put a stone into a pot. At the end of the day, the shepherds would bring the sheep back into the pens to keep them safe from predators. As each animal returned, the shepherds would remove a stone from the pot. When the pot was empty, all the sheep were safely back.[*] Interestingly, it seems that no concept was required for how many sheep there were, just that the number of sheep was equal to the number of stones.

The earliest example of counting itself is thought to be the Ishango bone, which bears scratch marks grouped in 60s. Discovered in Africa in 1960, the bone is believed to be more than 11,000 years old and is seen by many as the earliest example of a mathematical structure.[†] There is still not complete consensus about what these scratch marks represent, but one theory is that they are related to some form of lunar calendar. This would make sense given the prevalence of the number 60 in ancient time-keeping; indeed, our own 60-minute hour and 60-second minute can be traced back to the ancient Babylonians and their **base** 60 number system.

Both of these approaches treat numbers as discrete objects: you have one sheep, two sheep or three sheep (even though the shepherds weren't actually counting them); you have one scratch, two scratches or three scratches. These earliest occurrences of numerical relationships are still relatable to a mathematical representation that we use today to show and track discrete values – tallying.

---

[*]   Kris recounted this story in his presentation 'The Stories of Mathematics – Part 1' at the Complete Mathematics Conference 5, Sheffield, 26 September 2015.

[†]   See http://www.math.buffalo.edu/mad/Ancient-Africa/ishango.html.

# Tallying

Tallying is probably one of the most basic representations of discrete number. In the English national curriculum, tally charts are introduced in Year 2 (age 6–7), although they could be used as a pictorial representation of number in Year 1 or earlier. Children are often taught to count before entering any statutory stage of education, and in the Early Years Foundation Stage statutory framework it is required for pupils to 'improve their skills in counting, understanding and using numbers, [and] calculating simple addition and subtraction problems'.[*]

The use of one mark per item to count harks back all the way to the earliest one-to-one relationships, and is a representation of number that nearly all mathematics students can grasp. The basic tenet of the representation is that a vertical line is used to represent a discrete value (normally 1) and these are grouped together in 5s or 10s when counting large numbers:

$$| = 1 \quad || = 2 \quad ||| = 3 \quad |||| = 4 \quad \cancel{||||} = 5 \quad \cancel{||||}\, | = 6$$

It is very unusual for a tally mark to stand for anything other than 1, although theoretically it is possible (e.g. using pictograms to represent data takes advantage of this idea to represent large numbers). Tallying is severely deficient as a representation of number for anything other than the counting of a small discrete number of objects. Representing negative numbers is also problematic, to the point where no one would really consider using it. However, it is a valid representation of discrete number that can support young children to master counting and create a semi-permanent record, so its value should not be underestimated. Indeed, much medieval accounting was done using tallying – marks representing the value of goods or items traded or borrowed would be carved onto a piece of wood using large tally marks. The wood would then be split along its length so the notches appeared on each half. This provided both parties with a record of the trade that couldn't be altered, and only those two pieces of wood could fit together to confirm they were records of the same trade. Students of mathematics should definitely be aware of tally marks as a representation for counting small discrete values, and possibly some of the history around them, but they should also be aware of the limitations of this representation in moving mathematics forward.

It wasn't until the emergence of complex civilisations that more sophisticated views of numbers developed. As early as 4000 BC, the ancient Sumerians lived in cities, some of which may have had up to 80,000 residents. This required proper

---

[*] Department for Education, *Statutory Framework for the Early Years Foundation Stage: Setting the Standards for Learning, Development and Care for Children from Birth to Five* (March 2017). Available at: https://www.gov.uk/government/publications/early-years-foundation-stage-framework--2, p. 8.

administration and consequently more sophisticated mathematics. Taxes needed to be collected and recorded, resources counted and measured, wealth calculated and compared. It is here that we see the birth of one of the more versatile discrete number representations – tokens, or counters.

# Counters

Counters certainly have many advantages as a representation of discrete numbers when compared to tallying. It is much easier to assign different values to counters (think of the number of different value coins that have existed in various world currencies) and so take relationships beyond the one-to-one relationships that were a hallmark of very early mathematics and counting systems. The fact that counters can be removed, as well as added to, allows for the development of arithmetic, which was crucial in developing the mathematics required to manage the complex financial calculations needed to administrate a city.

In the mathematics classroom, counters can be used in a variety of ways to support pupils' understanding of different types of numbers. At a simple level, counters can be used to represent positive **integers** in the same way that tallies do:

$$\bigcirc = 1 \qquad \bigcirc\bigcirc = 2 \qquad \bigcirc\bigcirc\bigcirc = 3$$

However, the versatility of counters more readily allows for them to hold different values, either by using different colour counters or ones that can be written on. For example, place value counters can be used to support an understanding of large numbers:

$$\textcolor{red}{\bigcirc 1} \quad \textcolor{yellow}{\bigcirc 10} \quad \textcolor{green}{\bigcirc 100} \quad \textcolor{blue}{\bigcirc 1000}$$

This allows large numbers to be represented without needing thousands of counters – for example:

$$= 263$$

In addition to representing larger numbers, counters also have an advantage over tallies in that they can simultaneously represent positive and negative numbers, which is done using either two different colours or, if available, double-sided counters:

The ability to use counters to simultaneously represent positive and negative numbers means that counters are an excellent way to develop directed number arithmetic. Crucial to this is the understanding that a '1' counter plus a '-1' counter results in 0. Indeed, a pair of these together (like the pair below) are often called a zero-pair.

Both tallies and counters have one crucial drawback, however: they only represent numbers as discrete quantities. In both cases it isn't clear that there are numbers between 1 and 2, and whilst it is possible to represent fractions and decimals using counters once these concepts are well defined, it is very difficult to introduce the idea of either fractions or decimal numbers using solely counters or tallies. The first representation that begins to show numbers as both discrete and continuous is one very familiar representation – the number line.

# The number line

As a discrete number representation, the number line shares many of the advantages that counters have over tallies, along with a few others. By representing numbers as positions along a line, we can build in 1s to any number without the need for an excessive number of counters to represent large numbers (assuming each counter has a value of 1).

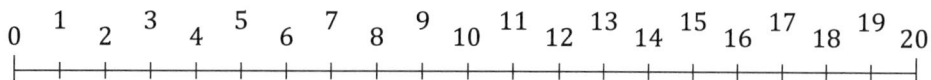

It is also possible to represent numbers of different sizes simultaneously, as with place value counters, but with the added advantage that the relative sizes of the numbers are also shown clearly:

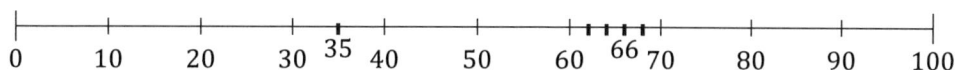

As they are not limited to place value divisions, the divisions on a number line (like counters) can take any discrete value:

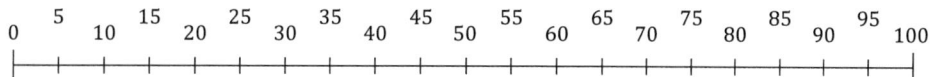

This includes allowing for both positive and negative values simultaneously:

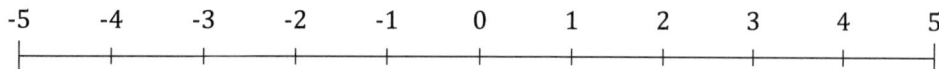

One of the major benefits of the number line representation is that it motivates the 'between' discussion (i.e. What is between 0 and 1? What is between 1 and 2?). Although using position on a number line is still a discrete view of number (we can only be in one position at a time), it begins to hint at the continuous nature of number – which is akin to the particle/wave duality in physics.

There are also drawbacks to the number line. The first is that it doesn't actually develop the concept of number terribly well. Pupils need to have a relatively secure understanding of number to begin to work with a number line. It offers no secure reason why the symbol '2' would have to follow the symbol '1' or why '0' represents nothingness. Pupil understanding of these concepts needs to be secure before the number line is introduced. However, we should consider carefully whether to wait to introduce the number line until we absolutely need it. As we saw in the introduction, introducing a representation at the point of need can be a major stumbling block for pupils. It may benefit learners if we were to first teach them about the concepts of **ordinality** and **cardinality** using counters, and only then explain how we can structure these numbers on a number line.

# Ordered-pair graphs

A slight variation on the number line is to represent **ordered-pairs** on a two-dimensional graph. Although it is a bit more cumbersome than the number line, one advantage of the ordered-pair graph is that it shows the multiplicative relationships between pairs of values. For example, the graph below shows the number 2:

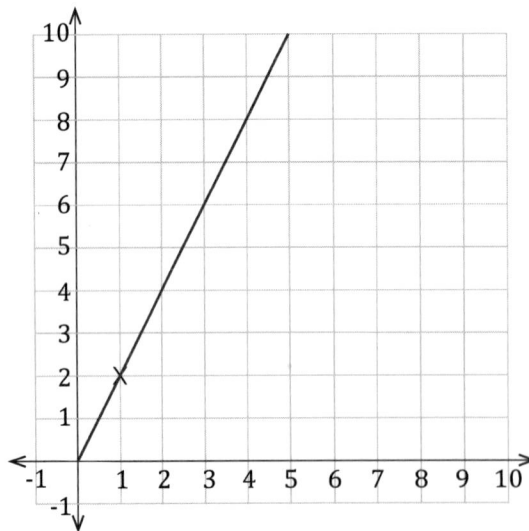

By plotting the point (1, 2) to show the number 2, and then drawing a line, it is possible to show that the multiplicative relationship between 1 and 2 is the same as the relationship between 2 and 4, 3 and 6 and so on, as all of these coordinates appear on the same line. This has obvious benefits when it comes to exploring division and fractions, as well as linking well to the concept of gradient.

Negative values can be represented in a similar way:

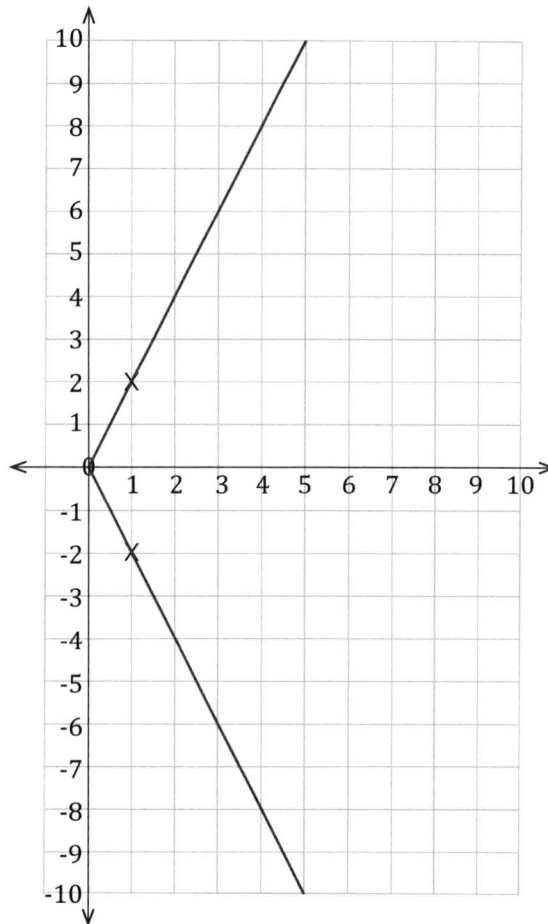

Like the number line, ordered-pair graphs show the duality of number – with a lean more towards the continuous in this example: although the number can be thought of as the plotted coordinate, it can also be considered as the whole line.

This representation does have its limitations, but it also allows for a different view of number which can highlight the properties of numbers that other representations often struggle to capture. The English national curriculum suggests that coordinates should first be introduced in Year 4, with full four-quadrant coordinate plotting in Year 6, although it would be understandable if this specific interpretation of numbers wasn't introduced until secondary education.

# Proportion diagrams

Another way of representing the multiplicative relationships between numbers is to use a **proportion** diagram. Many different forms of this diagram are used, but I prefer the one from the excellent 'Improving Learning in Mathematics' materials from the Department for Education and Skills (often known as the Standards Unit).[*]

Proportion diagrams are not, in fact, a true representation of number. They take the multiplicative relationships between numbers and highlight them, providing a straightforward way to demonstrate and develop proportional reasoning.

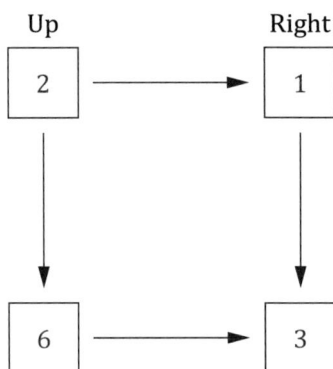

This diagram does not so much represent the number 2 as allow easy manipulation of the relationship between 2 and 1 – for example, to demonstrate that the relationship is the same as that between 6 and 3. Whilst this is not a representation of number as such, it is how ancient Greek mathematicians, such as Pythagoras, considered the universe – as being built out of the relationships between whole numbers (I doubt they used this exact diagram!). It was by considering these types of relationships that they were able to explain things like harmonies in music. One of Pythagoras' many mathematical discoveries was that by fixing a string at simple ratios along its length, it was possible to create notes that were in harmony with the note produced by the original string. However, fixing a string at a point not corresponding to a simple ratio would produce a note out of harmony with the original note.

The proportion diagram will be useful later on when we come to explore fractions, decimals and operations between numbers.

---

[*]    See http://webarchive.nationalarchives.gov.uk/20110505180928/https://www.ncetm.org.uk//resources//1442.

# Bar models

There are several approaches that attempt to capture the continuous nature of number that a number line begins to show, and perhaps the most well-known of these is the bar model:

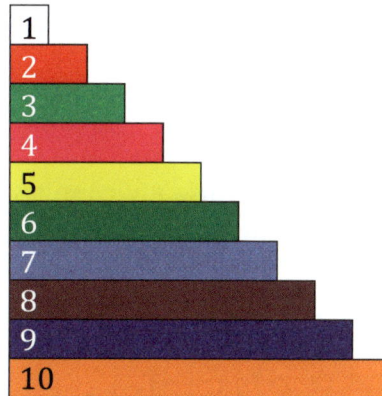

One of the most familiar concrete tools for bar modelling are Cuisenaire rods. Cuisenaire is built on 10 different colour length rods, nominally having the values from 1 to 10. Other numbers can be built out of combinations of these rods. Due to their standard unit width, the rods can be combined end to end in order to represent numbers or combined along their length to create rectangles representing different numbers. They can also be stacked to create cuboids, which then use volume to represent numbers (although this is difficult to show visually when drawing bars).

Like counters, bars can take on different values. This can lead to some problems when using Cuisenaire rods to work with bars – for example, if the white rod represents the number 2 instead of 1, then only even numbers can be represented. This doesn't happen when drawing bars. Teachers need to be aware of this limitation if they are working concretely with pupils to develop their most basic number concepts.

Bars are a very versatile representation as numbers can be represented using their length, area and volume. This allows us to combine bars in different ways, and makes them an ideal representation to explore many of the more developed concepts from the secondary maths curriculum. However, one difficulty with using bars is that it can be problematic to represent positive and negative values simultaneously. This can be dealt with, in part, by superimposing the bars onto a number line:

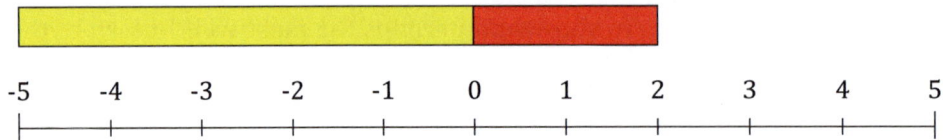

This bar shows 2 compared to -5, but without the number line it would probably be interpreted as 7 (5 and 2 added together).

When working concretely, the bars are usually compared side by side in order to show the relative values of the different bars (as in the diagram above or the left-hand diagram below). When working pictorially it can be beneficial to use a grid to break up the bars as in the right-hand diagram below.

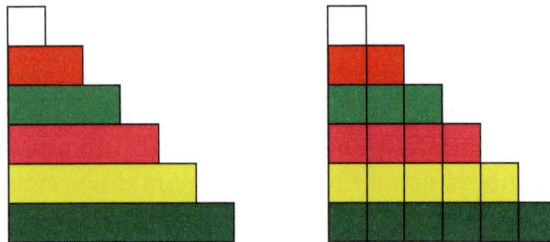

# Base ten blocks

Base ten blocks are a concrete mathematical manipulative designed to show place value and the power of 10 on which our decimal number system is built. For example, the blocks below combine to represent the number 134:

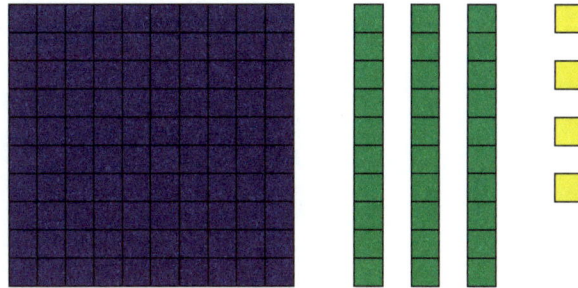

Like Cuisenaire rods, base ten blocks are designed to simultaneously show a discrete and continuous view of number, particularly highlighting the relationships in a base 10 number system. They can be used to represent numbers as length, area or volume (with the concrete version) across four different powers of 10 by combining 1s and 10s end to end, along edges to create area or stacking to create volume. The idea of an area and a length having the same numerical value is a very useful one when generalising properties and operations of number. The ability to use base ten blocks to show this by treating them in a similar way to place value counters makes them a beneficial, if not crucial, representation of number.

Like bars, one way this representation falls down is the simultaneous representation of both positive and negative numbers. Using blocks on a number line can help to overcome this problem in the same way that it does for Cuisenaire rods and bars, but this limits the representation to length only, because area and volume cannot show direction in the same way that displacement can.

This diagram shows the bars as a displacement away from 0, with the '10' bar showing positive 10 and the three '1' bars showing -3:

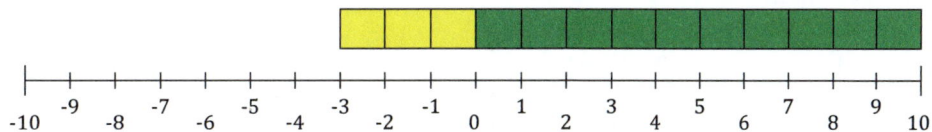

Here, the use of the number line limits us to using length, as the two-dimensional nature of the '100' tile is not compatible with the one-dimensional number line:

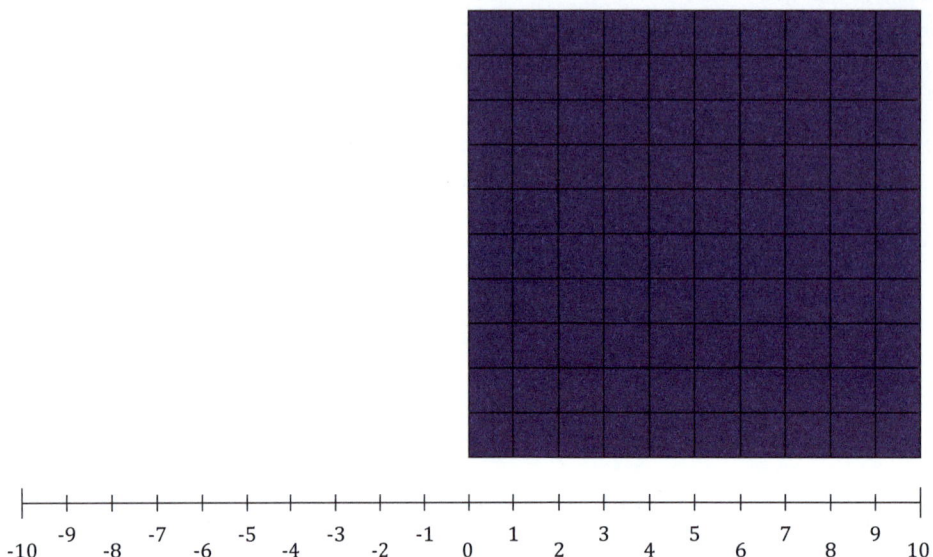

A representation that can show the simultaneous representation of positive and negative numbers using a continuous rather than discrete view of number is vectors.

# Vectors in one dimension

Whilst readers may be familiar with vectors in two or even three dimensions, many people may have never contemplated the parallels between directed number and one-dimensional vectors. However, if we consider a basic definition of a vector as an arrow representing a quantity with both magnitude and direction, then it is very quickly possible to discern their usefulness in representing numbers. Indeed, if you regularly work with complex numbers in an **Argand diagram**, you will recognise that these are simply complex numbers with no imaginary part.

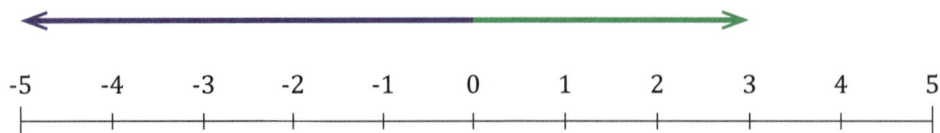

This diagram shows the numbers 3 and -5.

Although losing the area and volume interpretations afforded by bars (Cuisenaire) and base ten blocks, this representation captures the duality of discrete numbers and continuous numbers perfectly – for example, the number 3 can be thought of simultaneously as the point at the end of the arrow and as the length of the arrow. This makes a vector representation ideal for demonstrating nearly all directed number calculations.

Whilst officially (according to the English national curriculum) the geometrical interpretation of vectors is not introduced until Key Stage 4 (when pupils are about 14 years old), I have found that pupils in Year 7 are comfortable with this representation due to their familiarity with number lines. Therefore, I suspect that vectors could be introduced even earlier than Year 7, often just changing jumps for arrows in the earlier stages. In fact, it is entirely possible that we could introduce this representation alongside number lines, so that rather than showing jumps on a number line, we show arrows doing the same job.

# Chapter 2

# Representing fractions and decimals

Now that we have a clear understanding of the different representations that will be useful in exploring different facets of numbers and numerical relationships, it is time to begin developing the number system beyond the integers.

At this point, it is important to draw a distinction between representing a *number* and developing a *concept*. In the counters representation in Chapter 1, we saw that it was possible to represent negative integers using counters of different colours (or suitably labelled counters). However, this requires pupils to have developed the concept of negative integers. Using counters to represent positive integers doesn't motivate the need for negative integers; it simply allows us to manipulate them once we already know they are there. It is important that any representations we use make the introduction of the concept a natural consequence.

The number line is a good example. When representing positive integers (and 0) on a number line like the one below, it is quite natural to consider questions like, 'Is there anything to the left of 0?' and so develop the concept of negative integers.

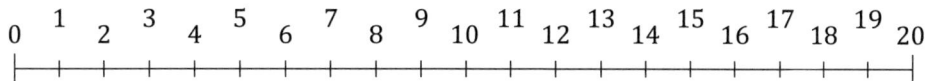

```
0   1   3   5   7   9   11   13   15   17   19
      2   4   6   8   10   12   14   16   18   20
├──┼──┼──┼──┼──┼──┼──┼──┼──┼──┼──┼──┼──┼──┼──┼──┼──┼──┼──┼──┤
```

Another instinctive question to ask is, 'What is in the space between 0 and 1?' This allows teachers to introduce the concept of fractions and develop learners' understanding of numbers that are less than 1. In England, according to the national curriculum, this process begins as early as Year 1 (when pupils are 5 or 6) and continues throughout primary school.

Whilst the number line on page 21 is useful for motivating a discussion about what is between 0 and 1, it is perhaps not the best representation to answer the question. A closer look at the space between 0 and 1 would appear to be in order:

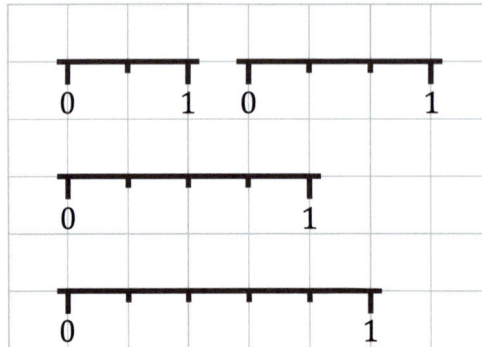

Each of these separate number lines prompts the need for different fractions by breaking the space between 0 and 1 into a different number of equal sized parts. In the first case, the number line shows $\frac{1}{2}$, in the second $\frac{1}{3}$ and $\frac{2}{3}$, in the third $\frac{1}{4}$, $\frac{2}{4}$ and $\frac{3}{4}$, and in the fourth $\frac{1}{5}$, $\frac{2}{5}$, $\frac{3}{5}$ and $\frac{4}{5}$. Other properties of fractions can also be discerned – for example, that $\frac{1}{2} = \frac{2}{4}$ or that $\frac{5}{5} = 1$.

Whether using the positions on a number line or the vector representation, the same 'zooming' of the number line is required:

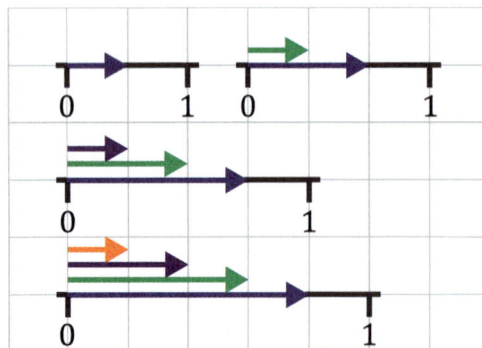

A similar approach is used when representing fractions using a bar model or physically using Cuisenaire rods:

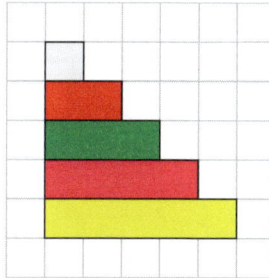

When representing integers, the white block would normally be valued as 1, the red 2, the green 3 and so on (although if we wish we can say that the white block is 2, so the red is 4, the green 6, etc.). An obvious question to ask is, 'What if the red block is 1?' Similarly, the green, pink, yellow or any other block can also be considered as 1, leading to the other blocks representing different fractions.

Whilst the Cuisenaire rods can be placed next to each other (as in the diagram above), a pictorial representation for modelling fractions as bars would normally have overlapping bars:

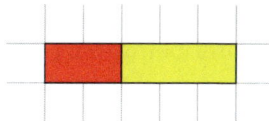

Or even have the squares filled in:

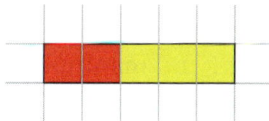

This leads to the typical 'part-shaded' representation of fractions, such as these diagrams:

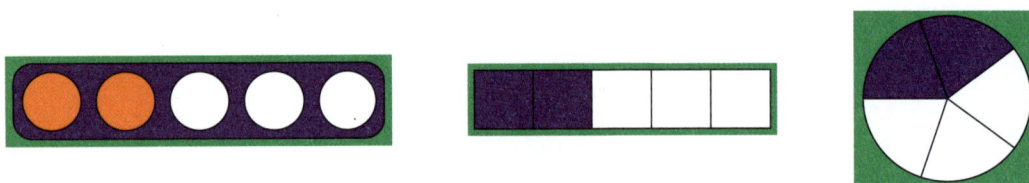

The part-shaded representation is very particular to fractions, which is why it didn't appear in the section on counters in Chapter 1. I realise that this breaks my self-imposed approach of introducing representations before they are needed. However, I justify this in two ways: first, I cannot really see how this representation would be introduced in the classroom before this point; and, second, it develops directly from the bar model and so the representation itself isn't a big conceptual leap.

I find this an interesting representation from the point of view of the mathematics classroom. It is typically the first representation that is used with pupils in primary schools when developing the concept of fractions, and I suspect that this may be part of the reason why many pupils go on to find fractions difficult. The representation does highlight a valid interpretation of fractions, the relative counter, which is a way of counting how much is being selected out of a larger total. In the diagrams above, this would be '2 selected out of 5 in total' or simply '2 out of 5'. The idea of a relative counter links to the idea of fractions being part of one whole, which both the bar model and number line are also designed to show. However, the language that both pupils and instructors tend to use around fractions suggests that this link is often not made explicit.

In my experience, many pupils internalise an early view of fractions as two separate values rather than a number in its own right (i.e. '2 out of 5' rather than 'two-fifths'). An unintended consequence of this early internalisation is the difficulty that some older pupils have in calculating with and manipulating fractions. As part of developing operations and reasoning with fractions, it is important that pupils understand fractions as being single quantities. Cuisenaire rods, bar models and placing fractions on a number line seem to develop this understanding much more clearly, and so I would advocate waiting to introduce the relative counter representations of fractions and working exclusively with bar models and number lines until pupils' understanding of fractions as single values is well embedded. The 2014 English national curriculum suggests that in Year 1 pupils should be taught to represent numbers on a number line and also be familiar with simple fractions such as halves and quarters, so there would appear to be scope here to combine these to develop the interpretation of fractions as single values rather than as separate **numerators** and **denominators**.

A particular case that arises from working with Cuisenaire rods is using the '10' bar to represent 1, leading to the family of fractions $\frac{1}{10}$, $\frac{2}{10}$, $\frac{3}{10}$ and so on:

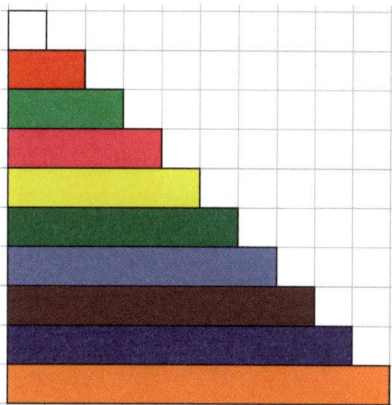

The diagram above shows the link between fractions and decimals (normally introduced in Year 3): the white bar can be seen as $\frac{1}{10}$ or 0.1, the red bar as $\frac{2}{10}$ or 0.2 and so on. The bars/rods or the number line/vector representation can be used to develop the concept of fractions or decimals as parts of a whole as a natural result of subdividing a single unit into smaller chunks of varying sizes:

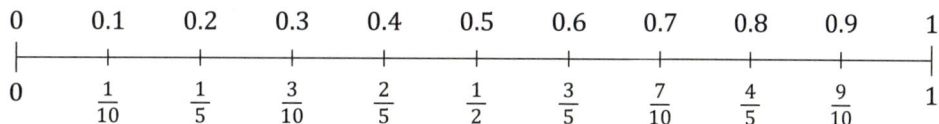

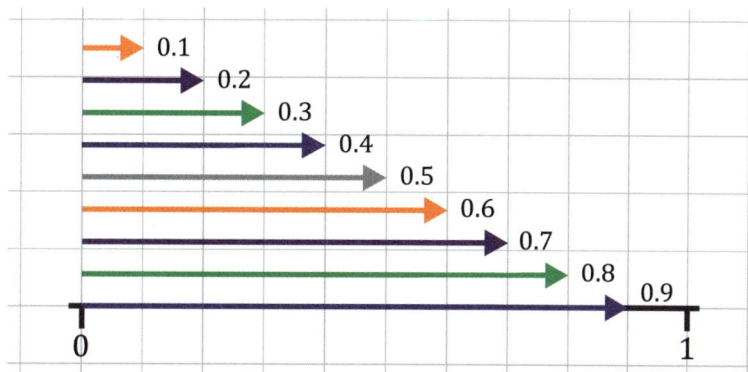

Two properties of the bars/rods and number lines/vectors make them unsuitable for the deeper development of certain concepts around fractions/decimals. The first of these is that it is much more difficult to proceed beyond a single decimal place. Unless we draw a very long number line, we are going to struggle to actually model the meaning of decimals such as 0.02, particularly if we want to retain the relative size compared to a single unit. Whilst it is possible to zoom in further on the number line (as in the diagram below) or ask the question, 'What if the orange bar becomes 0.1?' I would suggest that a consistent reference back to 1 is beneficial as these concepts begin to be formed and explored.

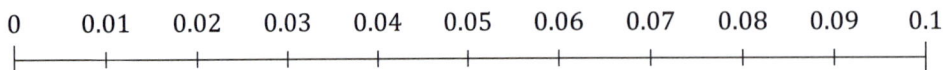

The representation that allows us to explore multiple powers of 10 whilst maintaining this reference back to the size of one whole is, of course, base ten blocks. When looking at integers we have the following progression:

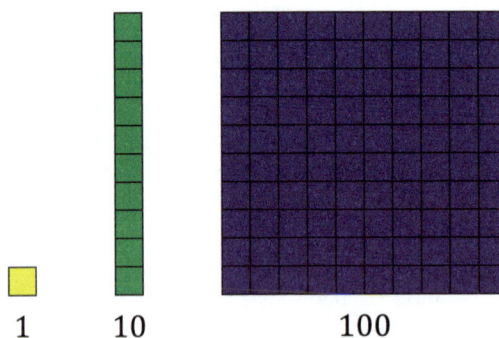

1          10                    100

A natural question to ask is, 'What if the blue square represents 1?' This allows us to extend decimals right down to the hundredths layer (or even to the thousandths layer if using the cube as 1 with the concrete resource), which means pupils can use the different sized blocks to explore patterns like 0.01, 0.02, 0.03, 0.04, 0.05, 0.06, 0.07, 0.08, 0.09, 0.1 or to show that 0.4 is greater than 0.36, which can be a major stumbling block as pupils develop an understanding of place value for numbers between 0 and 1.

2.37

The second issue around using bars, number lines and base ten blocks is that we can only represent a certain family of fractions/decimals in the same diagram. For example, if using the yellow bar below to represent 1, all the other bars can only represent fractions in the family of fifths, or on a number line with four partitions between 0 and 1, we can only represent fractions in the family of quarters.

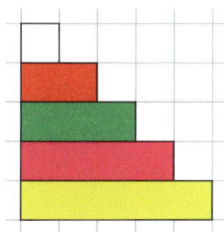

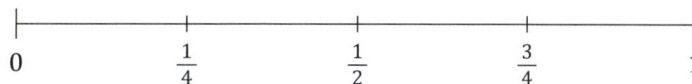

We can begin to solve this problem by exploring the idea of equivalence. In the number line above, we can see that two quarters is halfway along the line between 0 and 1. Both the number line and the bar model can be used to develop the concept of equivalent fractions. Teachers will need to decide whether the introduction of equivalent fractions should follow on immediately from the introduction of fractions or whether to wait a while before we revisit equivalence. What is certain is that the equivalence of fractions has to be fully understood before we move on to concepts such as addition and subtraction with fractions. The English national curriculum suggests that equivalence of fractions should be first taught in Year 2, with pupils expected to recognise the equivalence of $\frac{1}{2}$ and $\frac{2}{4}$.* With bars this may go something like this:

If the pink bar is 1, the red bar is $\frac{1}{2}$.

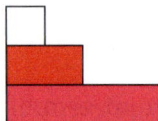

If the pink bar is 1, the white bar is $\frac{1}{4}$ – which means the red bar is $\frac{2}{4}$.

So $\frac{2}{4} = \frac{1}{2}$.

On a number line this may look something like this:

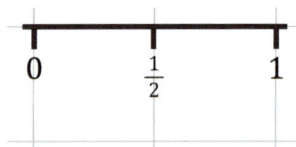

The zoomed number line above shows $\frac{1}{2}$.

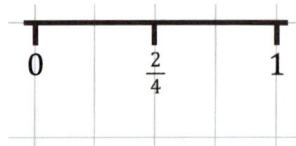

This second zoomed number line shows $\frac{2}{4} = \frac{1}{2}$.

---

\*   Department for Education, National Curriculum in England: Mathematics Programmes of Study. Statutory Guidance (July 2014). Available at: https://www.gov.uk/government/publications/national-curriculum-in-england-mathematics-programmes-of-study/national-curriculum-in-england-mathematics-programmes-of-study. All future references to national curriculum guidelines (from Key Stage 1 onwards) refer to this publication.

This doesn't only work with halves. The diagrams below use bars to show the same idea with thirds and ninths:

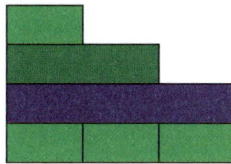

If the blue bar is 1, the light green bar is $\frac{1}{3}$ and the dark green bar is $\frac{2}{3}$.

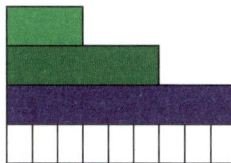

If the blue bar is 1, the white bar is $\frac{1}{9}$, so the light green bar is $\frac{3}{9}$ and the dark green bar is $\frac{6}{9}$. So $\frac{3}{9} = \frac{1}{3}$ and $\frac{6}{9} = \frac{2}{3}$.

If we want to represent many different families of fractions in the same diagram, then we will need a representation that is designed to show multiplicative relationships – namely the ordered-pair graph.

The ordered-pair graph could be seen as overly complicated for integers as it requires the use of two values to represent what is, in essence, just a single quantity – for example, the coordinate (1, 2) to represent 2. But when used as a tool to conceptualise and represent **rational numbers** it is supremely powerful. The conceptualisation comes from questions such as, 'If the coordinate (1, 2), and therefore the straight line from (0, 0) to (1, 2), represents the number 2, what does the coordinate (2, 1) represent?'

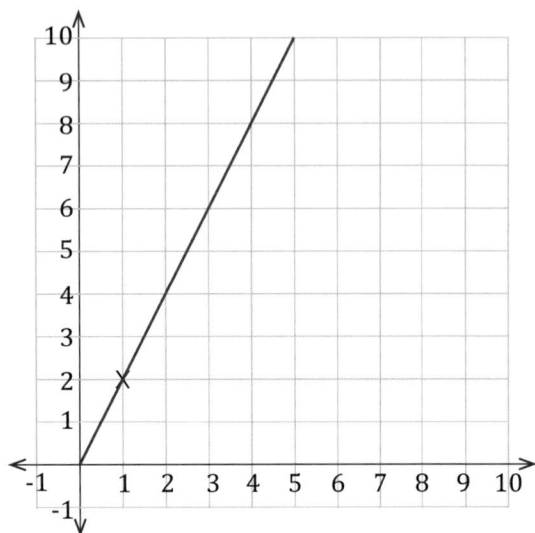

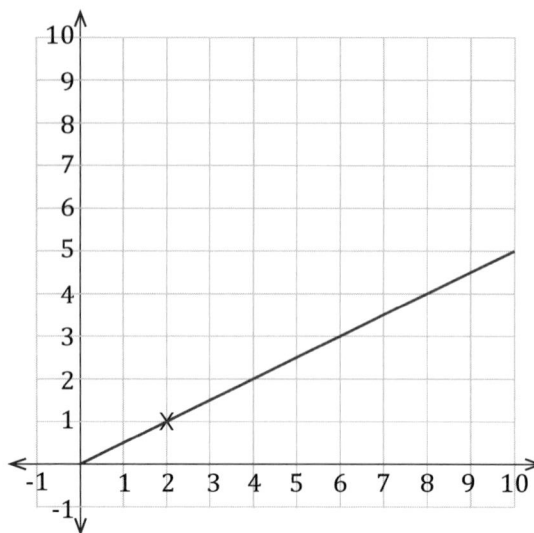

This approach doesn't necessarily capture the 'part of a whole' view of fractions; instead, it is much more like the ancient mathematicians who viewed fractions more as the ratio of two integer values rather than numbers in their own right. Indeed, when Pythagoras exclaimed 'All is number', he was referring to ratios between integers that he believed governed everything from the Music of the Spheres (the movement of the stars and planets) to actual musical harmony (which he showed was actually the case). The famous story of the drowning of Hippasus of Metapontum was a direct result of this belief.

Hippasus was a philosopher from around the year 500 BC. He was an early follower of Pythagoras and part of the Pythagorean Brotherhood, the group of philosophers who worshipped number and believed that the root of all reality lies in mathematical truth. The story goes that Hippasus was working with another of Pythagoras' famous results, Pythagoras' theorem. Hippasus knew that the values of 1, 1 and $\sqrt{2}$ satisfied Pythagoras' theorem, but he was trying to find the integer ratio (fraction) that was equal to $\sqrt{2}$. It dawned on Hippasus that the reason he was unable to find the correct ratio was that it didn't exist. At this point the most popular versions of the story diverge. The first version I came across (in Simon Singh's *Fermat's Last Theorem*[*]) was that Hippasus, rightly proud of this discovery, shared it with his mentor Pythagoras. Unfortunately, it didn't fit with Pythagoras' view of the universe being governed by integer ratios. When Pythagoras couldn't refute Hippasus' argument through logic, he resorted to drowning his student rather than admit he was wrong. The second version is that Hippasus shared his discovery that $\sqrt{2}$ is irrational outside of the

---

[*]    S. Singh, *Fermat's Last Theorem* (London: Fourth Estate, 1997).

Pythagorean Brotherhood, which was strictly forbidden, and for breaking his solemn vow not to reveal the secrets of the sect he was drowned.

Of course, since the time of the ancient Greeks humans have discovered that not only do we have to go beyond the rational numbers to form a complete number system, but even beyond the irrational numbers like $\sqrt{2}$. We will explore the representation of values like this in Chapter 10, but for now we will return to fractions and decimals.

The ordered-pair graph extends beyond the coordinates (1, 2) to represent the number 2 and (2, 1) to represent the number $\frac{1}{2}$ to all other ratios. The coordinate (4, 3) can represent the number $\frac{3}{4}$, whilst the coordinate (3, 4) represents the number $1\frac{1}{3}$.

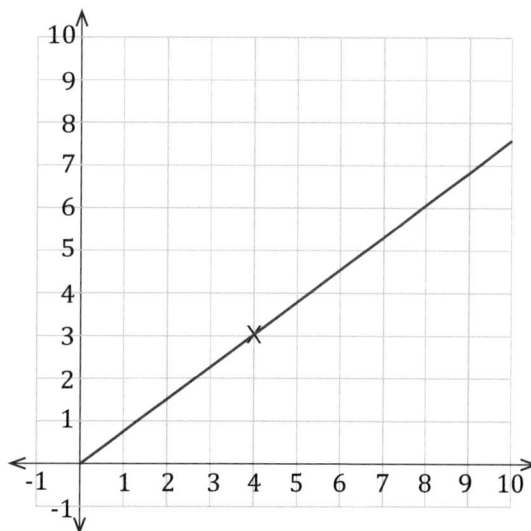

The diagram above shows $\frac{3}{4}$ on an ordered-pair graph.

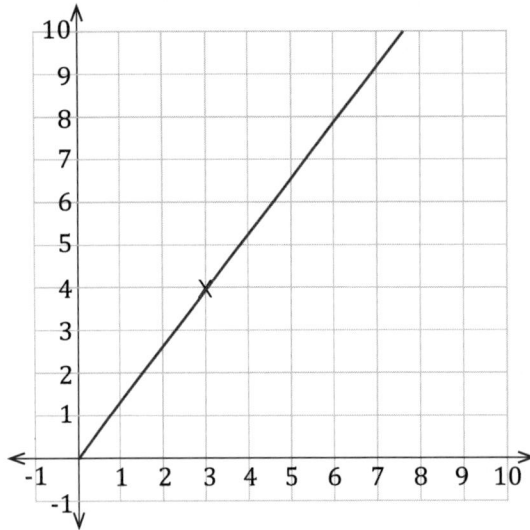

This second diagram shows $1\frac{1}{3}$ on an ordered-pair graph ($\frac{4}{3}$).

One of the major strengths of this representation is that it makes very clear the relative sizes of different fractions, with steeper lines representing bigger values.

The proportion diagram can also be a useful tool for representing the multiplicative relationships within fractions. When introduced with integers in Chapter 1, this diagram was shown using the language of 'up' and 'right' to make the link between the diagram and the ordered-pair graph. When beginning to work with fractions, we change this to the standard language of 'numerator' and 'denominator':

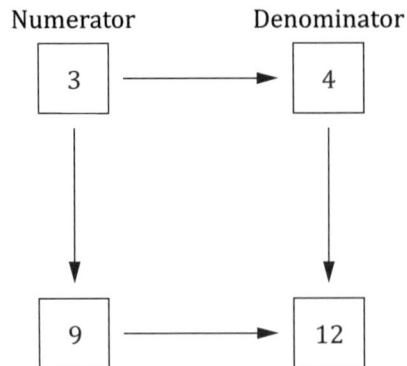

As with the use of this representation for whole numbers, the proportion diagram doesn't so much represent the numbers themselves as it does the similarity in the relationship between the numbers – literally, '3 is to 4 as 9 is to 12'. Of course, in order to see this, pupils will need to have developed a clear concept of multiplication from being taught using different representations – at least, the basic concept of a fraction through working with the ordered-pair graph. As such, the proportion diagram isn't the best representation for introducing rational numbers or developing an early conceptual understanding of fractions. However, once this understanding is in place, this representation can be very powerful in manipulating proportional relationships, like the relationship between the numerator and denominator of a fraction.

Another representation that has its uses once the concept of fractions and decimals is well developed is counters. The versatility of counters to represent different values can be useful when working with whole numbers, but they are particularly valuable when developing certain operations with fractions and decimals. For this reason alone, it is well worth finishing off our development of rational numbers by exploring how pupils understand the way these numbers look when represented as discrete objects.

When using counters to represent fractions, it is necessary to assign a value to a counter. This could be simply taking all counters to have a certain value – in the example below this is $\frac{1}{2}$.

What this representation does not make clear are some fairly basic truths about fractions – an obvious example being the fact that two halves are equal to one whole. It is important to develop the concept of fractions in a way that makes these fundamental truths more self-evident (e.g. using the bar model, number line or ordered-pair graph) before using counters as a representation of fractions. Another conceptual difficulty here is using a 'whole' counter to represent one half or any other fraction. Pupils who can't make this leap don't really understand counting and struggle to see counting as applying to anything other than 1s. In the case above, it may be useful to explore the old half penny and other pre-decimal coins in order to help pupils develop the understanding of counters having fractional values.

To further support the understanding of counters taking anything other than integer values, we can also revisit place value counters. There is a strong link here with pounds and pence; if £1 is 1, then 10 pence is 0.1 and a penny is 0.01. This can be shown pictorially or using plastic coins if available.

**1** = one    **0.1** = one-tenth    **0.01** = one-hundredth    **0.001** = one-thousandth

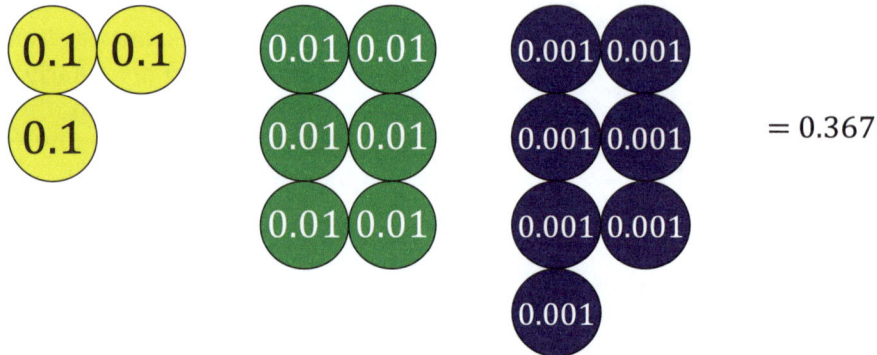

0.1  0.1    0.01  0.01    0.001  0.001
0.1          0.01  0.01    0.001  0.001      = 0.367
             0.01  0.01    0.001  0.001
                           0.001

At this point it is useful is to embed, or re-embed, the concept of **exchange**. Pupils will be comfortable with this idea for whole numbers – that twelve '1' counters can be exchanged for a '10' counter and two '1' counters – but may not naturally transfer this idea to decimal place value counters or to fractional equivalence. Making the idea clear when introducing decimals through bars or number lines helps, but it is still worth getting pupils used to the idea with counters.

Some teachers are tempted to wait until exploring addition/subtraction to broach the idea of exchange. However, this means that two important concepts are introduced at the same time, which can be troublesome. Once pupils are familiar with the use of counters to represent decimals, the concept of exchange can be explored directly, in a similar way to the concept of equivalence in fractions. We might present pupils with situations like the one that follows and ask them what number is represented.

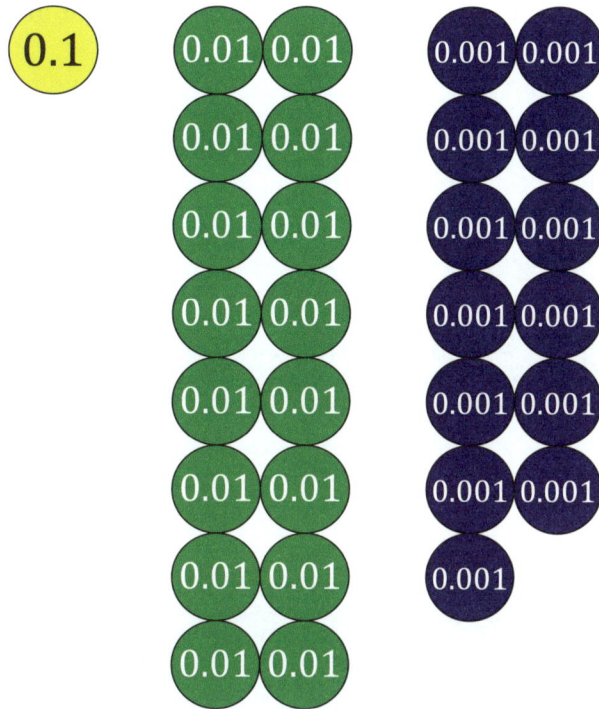

By using the understanding of place value that pupils have already developed, they should be able to see that 10 of the blue counters can be exchanged for 1 green counter, and that 10 of the green counters can be exchanged for 1 yellow counter. This leads to the result below:

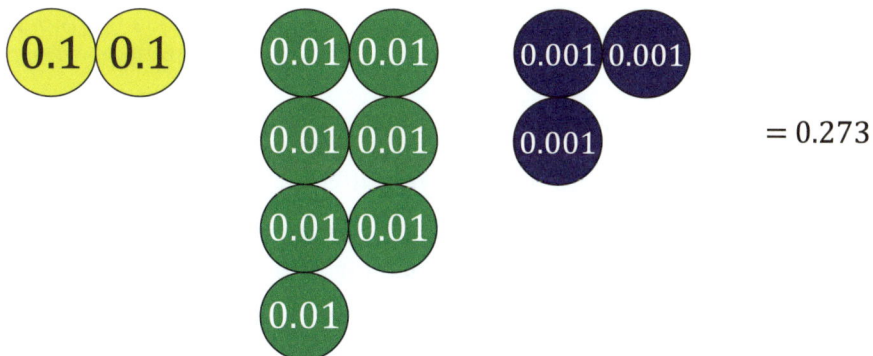

$= 0.273$

Exchange can also be explored using other representations, particularly base ten blocks, where:

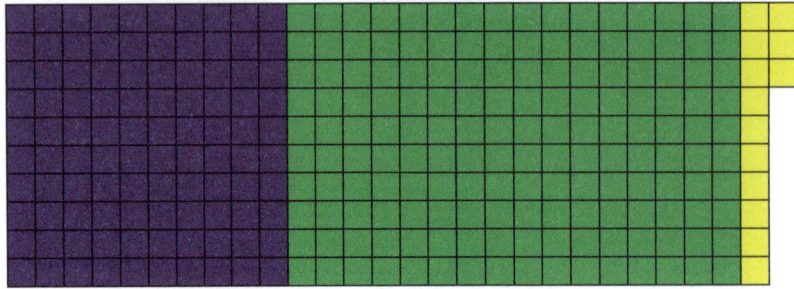

exchanges for:

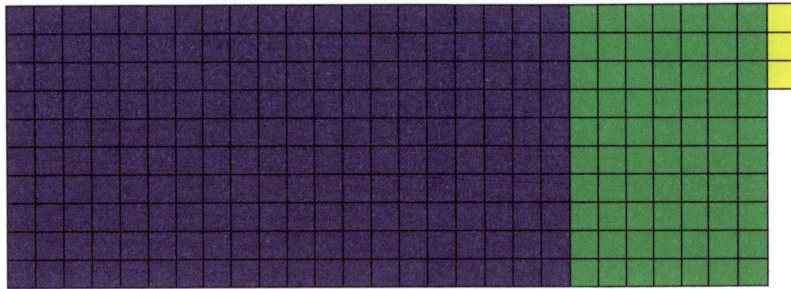

In fact, it would be beneficial to explore exchange with base ten blocks before counters (although, again, I wouldn't wait to explore exchange with base ten blocks before introducing counters). Ideally, the sequence would be something like:

1   Introduce decimals with base ten blocks, defining different shapes as 1.

2   Introduce the use of counters to represent different place values.

3   Explore the idea of exchange using base ten blocks, where it can be physically seen that 10 single cubes can be exchanged for a line, 10 lines for a square and so on.

4   Explore the idea of exchange with counters standing for different place values.

Of course, exchange can also be used with subtraction when we need to 'exchange down' (e.g. exchange a base ten block or counter for 10 unit blocks/counters). This situation does not naturally arise before beginning to examine subtraction, so this form of exchange should probably be left until we are teaching pupils about subtraction.

The representations outlined in the first two chapters should provide pupils with a deeper understanding of both integers and rational numbers and how these relate to each other. The next stage is to look at combining these values using different operations.

Chapter 3

# Addition and subtraction with integers

The different representations of numbers explored in the first two chapters are crucial for providing useful structures to allow us to explore different operations. Without secure concepts – such as place value, exchange and fractions – learners will struggle to comprehend how numbers combine with operations.

We begin by developing the basic operations of addition and subtraction, which are first seen by pupils in Years 1 and 2 under the English national curriculum. Indeed, the national curriculum makes specific reference to Year 2 pupils being able to 'add and subtract numbers using concrete objects, pictorial representations, and mentally'.[*]

## Positive integers

There are a few different interpretations of addition, although they are all linked in some way. The difference between these interpretations arises from the distinction between treating numbers as discrete (by representing them as counters or positions on a number line) or continuous (by treating them as bars or vectors). The most straightforward of these is the idea of addition as the collecting or combining of similar objects, which can be effectively demonstrated using counters to represent discrete numbers:

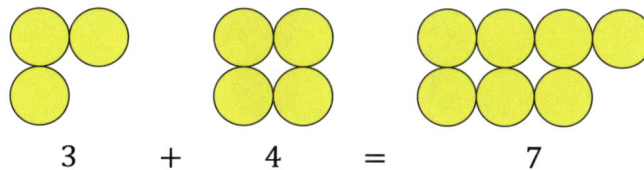

3     +     4     =     7

---

[*] See https://www.gov.uk/government/publications/national-curriculum-in-england-mathematics-programmes-of-study/
national-curriculum-in-england-mathematics-programmes-of-study.

39

By using place value counters, this can be combined with the concept of exchange to allow the addition of larger numbers, bridging gaps over 10s or 100s:

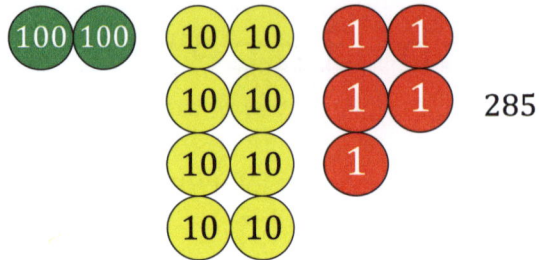

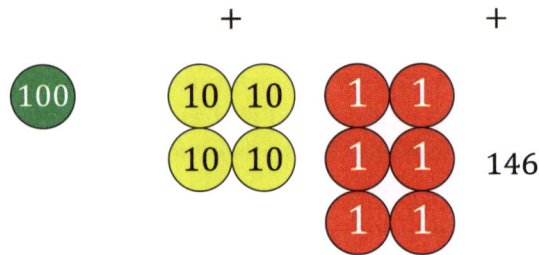

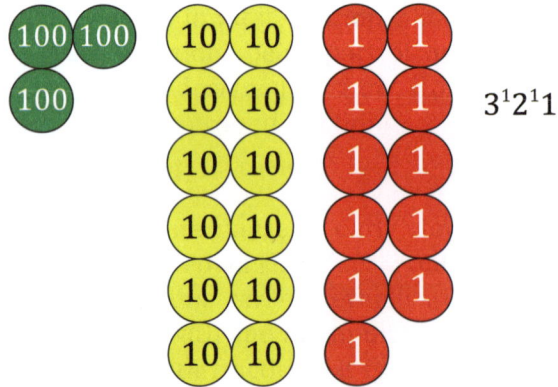

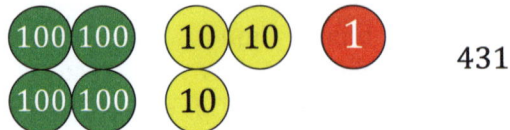

285

+          +

146

3¹2¹1

431

The addition and subtraction of larger numbers would normally be introduced in Year 3.

In Chapter 2, we saw that it was preferable to use base ten blocks before place value counters to explore the concept of exchange. A similar argument could be made for additions requiring exchange. Using base ten blocks before place value counters to model the addition of larger numbers requiring exchange can help pupils to understand how the addition of the separate columns is being carried out and why we start adding from the 1s column (in case the number of 10s changes as a result of exchanging 1s).

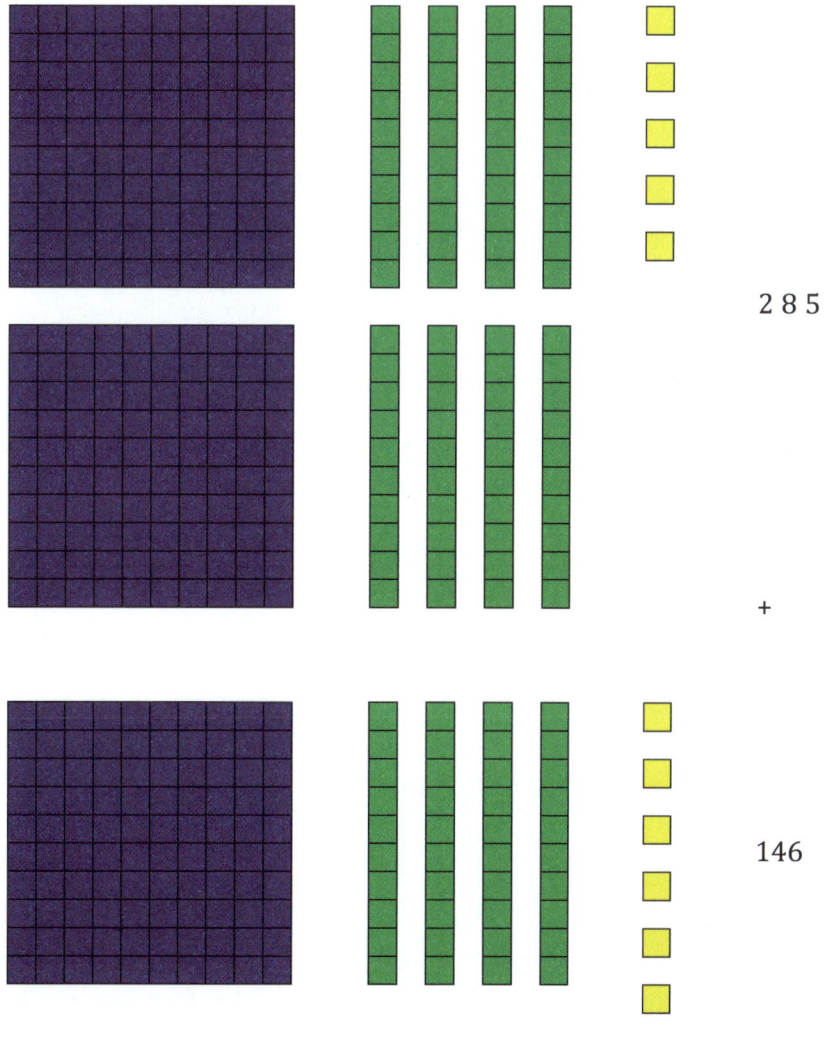

2 8 5

+

146

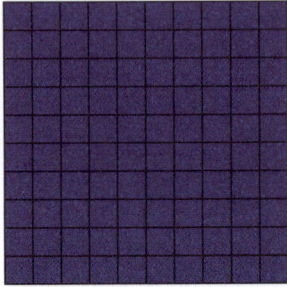 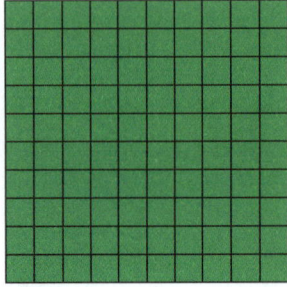 

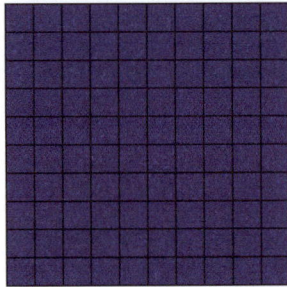 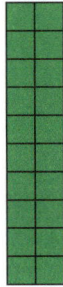

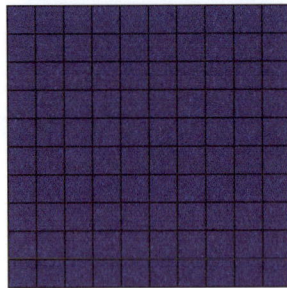

$3^1 2^1 1$

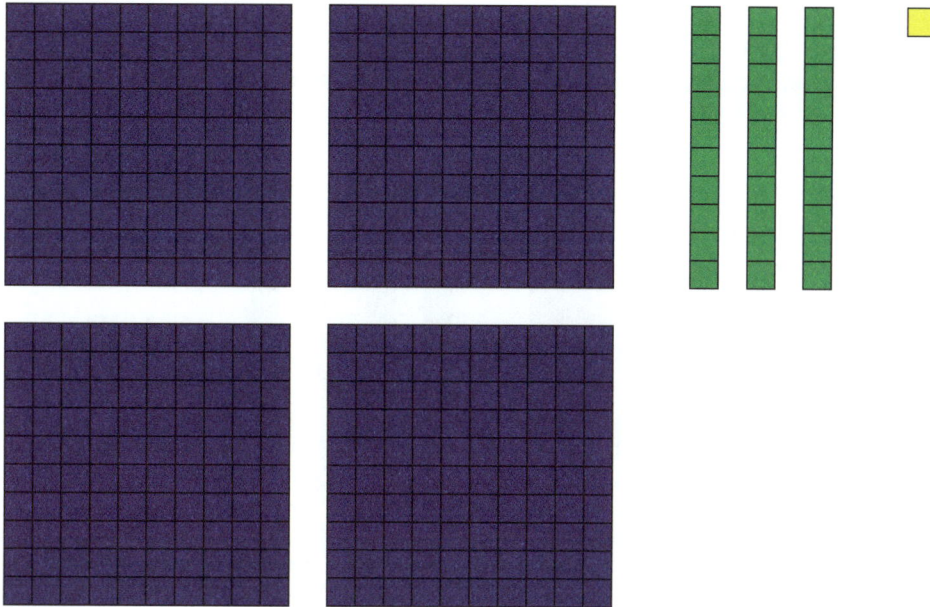

431

Subtraction in both of the representations is best interpreted as the physical 'taking away' of blocks, where necessary using exchange in the reverse way that was alluded to at the end of the last chapter.

247

− 125

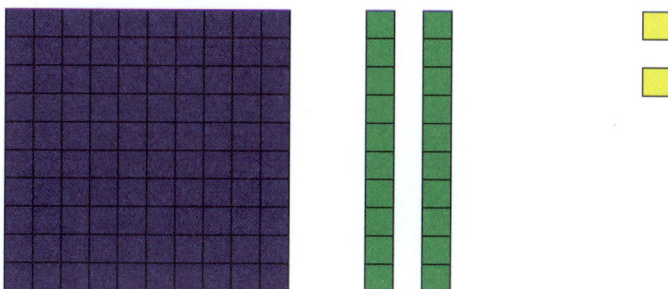

122

Whilst this can be done physically, it is harder to represent visually. The best approach is to use dynamic images or virtual manipulatives where blocks can be physically removed; alternatively, images can be drawn with a dry-wipe marker and rubbed out and removed.

Using exchange in reverse would look something like this:

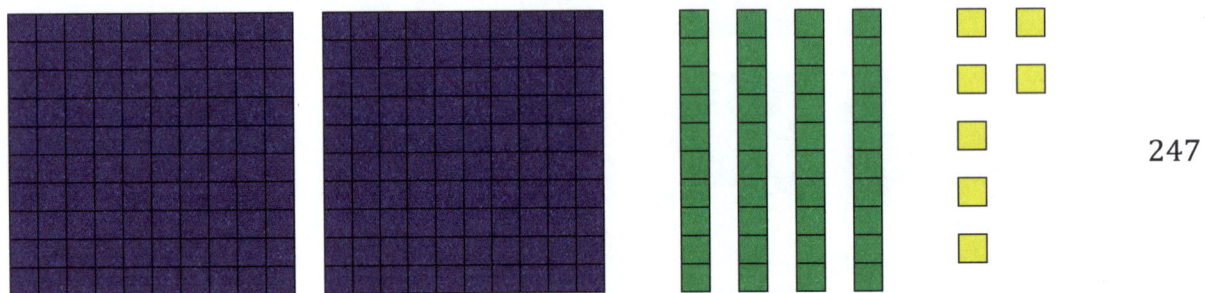

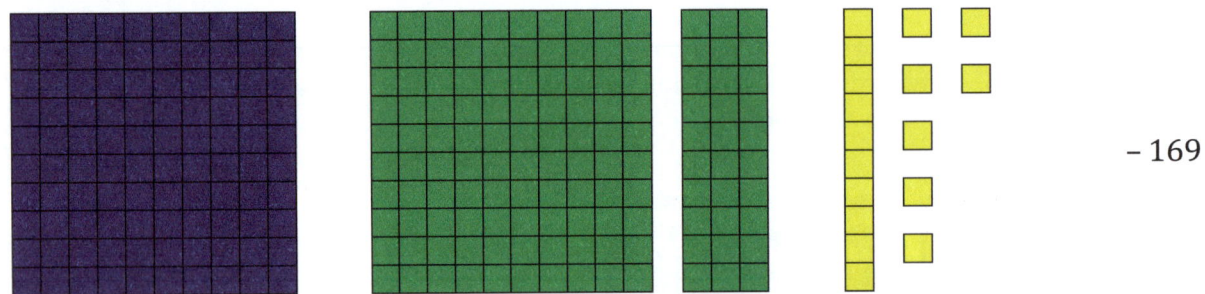

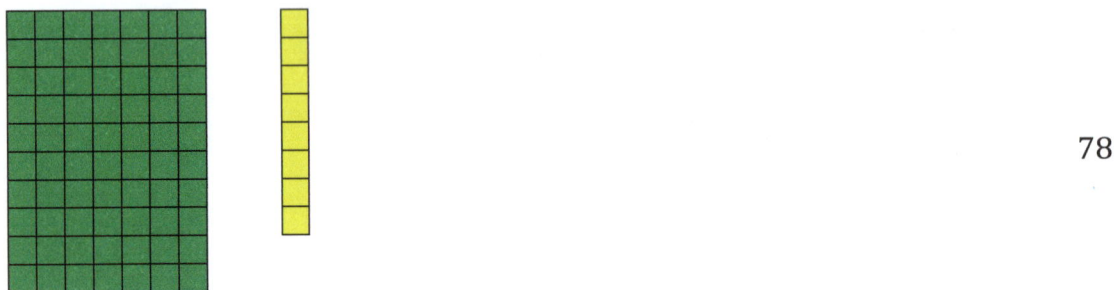

247

− 169

78

We can see in the first and second diagram on page 44 that one of the blue '100' blocks has been exchanged for ten of the green '10' blocks, and that one of the green '10' blocks has been exchanged for ten of the yellow '1' blocks. This enables the removal of six of the '10' blocks and nine of the '1' blocks as well as the blue '100' block, leaving seven '10' blocks and eight '1' blocks.

As well as subtraction being the physical act of taking away, another way of viewing subtraction is as the 'difference between' two numbers. This has an advantage in that it can be interpreted both discretely (i.e. the physical difference between two sets of objects) and continuously. It is also important as this idea of difference or 'additive comparison' has a direct relationship with division using a 'multiplicative comparison' (which we will explore in Chapter 4). When using base ten blocks or counters this would appear as a comparison between two numbers:

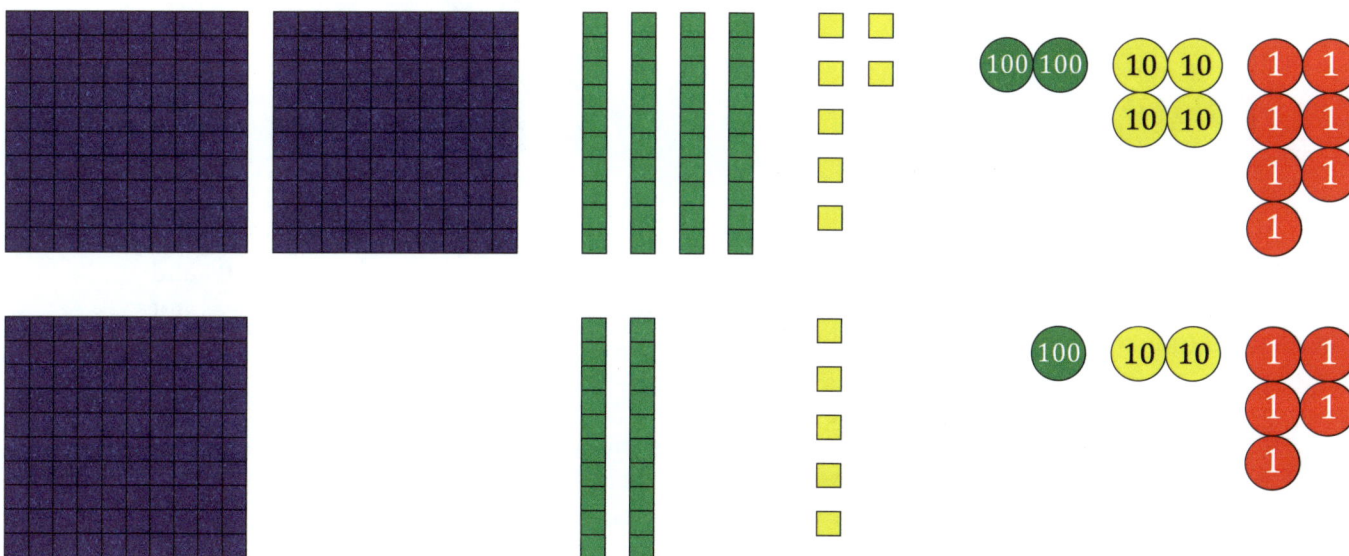

A comparison in both cases shows that the first number (247) has one extra 100, two extra 10s and two extra 1s when compared to the second number (125), so the difference is 122 (hence 247 – 125 = 122).

This is slightly more difficult to see as a difference when exchange is required, either with base ten blocks (shown on page 46) or counters.

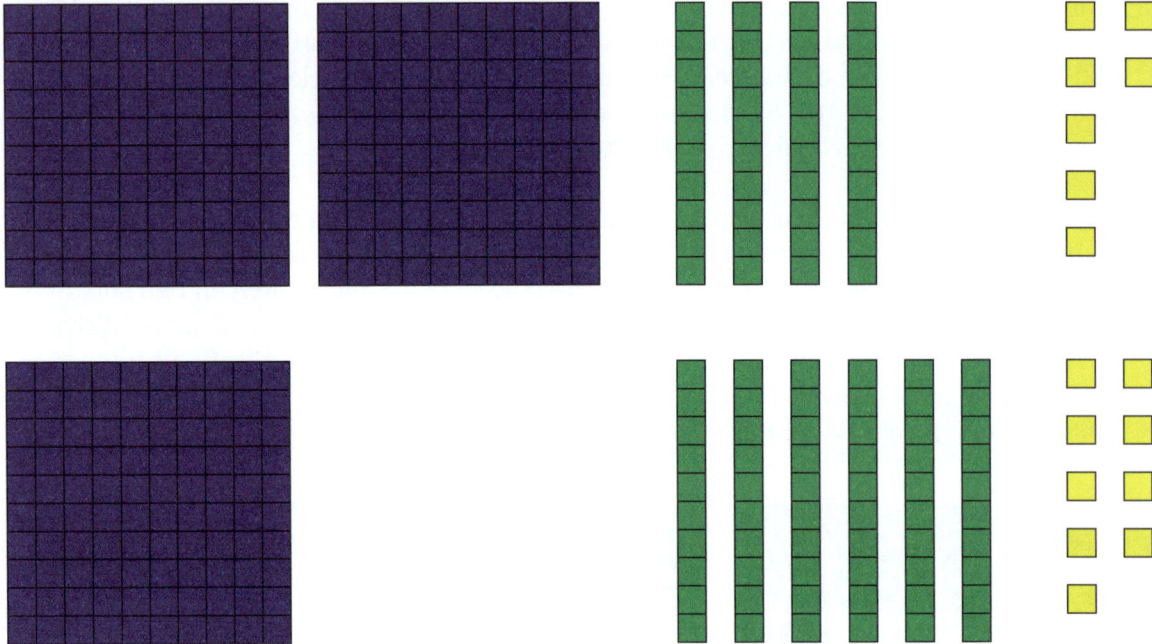

Here the idea of difference is somewhat more muddled. The first number (247) has one more 100 than the second number (169), but the second has two more 10s and two more 1s. Physically, this can be interpreted as 100 – 20 – 2 = 78, but this is not immediately evident.

The answer of 78 is more obvious once the exchange in 247 has taken place (as in the diagram below). It is now easier to see that there is no difference in the 100s, but there are seven extra 10s and eight extra 1s:

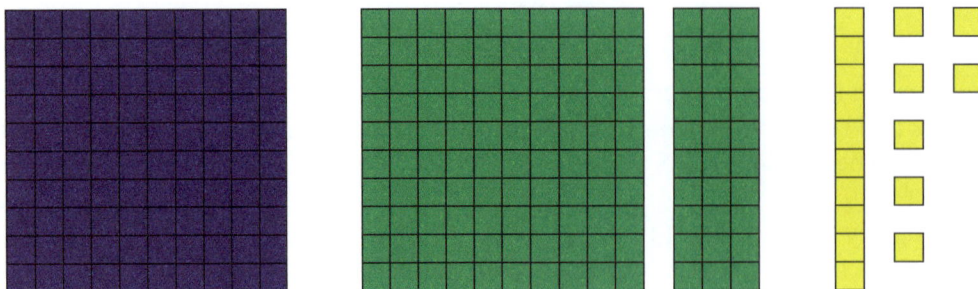

Whilst subtraction can be viewed in this way, it is perhaps not the best approach to introduce the idea of subtraction as difference – other representations can make this clearer.

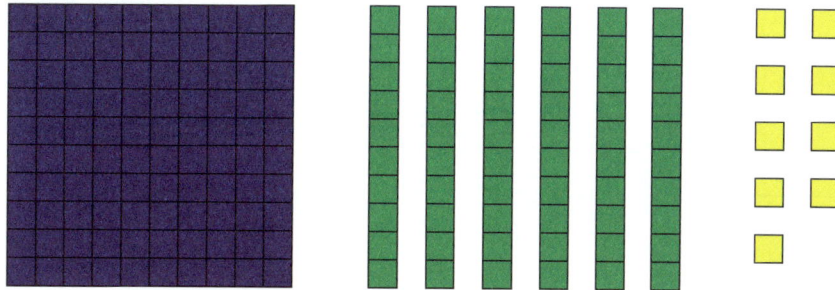

Another view of addition, as well as being a collection of similar objects, is that of 'counting on' from a start value. For example, the sum 5 + 4 can be interpreted as starting with 5 on a number line and then counting on 4:

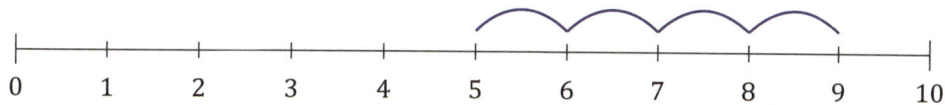

This is still a view of addition that applies to discrete numbers, but it can provide a bridge into other representations. The idea of collection doesn't really apply to number lines; however, by using number lines with different scales we can mirror the collection of counters with different values, thus showing that the idea of a collection of objects and counting on are both different views of the same concept:

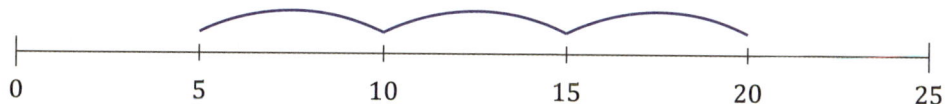

$$5 + 15 = 20$$

The idea of addition for continuous numbers is linked to this idea of counting on. Of course, you cannot truly count on continuous numbers as there is no 'next number' to jump to. When switching to a continuous view of numbers, it is the length of the representation (e.g. the bar) that signifies the number, so the lengthening/connecting of numbers becomes the view of addition. This can be seen on the number lines below for different representations:

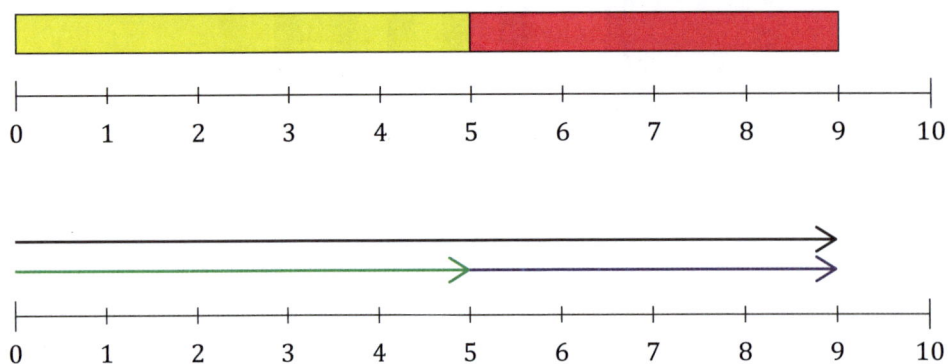

One representation that can allow pupils to see all three aspects of addition (i.e. counting on, collection and lengthening) – and understand that they are three facets of the same operation – is bar modelling and its concrete manipulative, Cuisenaire rods.

This bar model shows that starting with 5 and then connecting another 4 leads to a result of 9 (using the values assigned to these bars if the white bar is considered to have a value of 1). Ideally, when modelled concretely this would be demonstrated by starting with the '5' bar, attaching the '4' bar to the end and showing that this is equal in length to the '9' bar.

To show counting on, we can exchange the '4' bar for four '1' bars. This makes the addition appear like this:

Again, ideally we start with the '5' bar before adding the single bars one at a time, counting aloud as we do – '6, 7, 8, 9' – and then showing that the result has the value of 9.

The approach to addition that is probably the most contrived in this representation is addition as the collection of like objects, as the '5' bar and the '4' bar are not like each other. To model addition as the collection or combination of like objects, we use a version of exchange as modelled below:

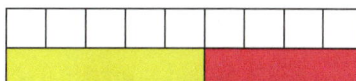

This shows the '5' bar being exchanged for five 1s and the '4' bar being exchanged for four 1s, meaning the 1s can be collected to give nine 1s. Alternatively, when drawing bars (and so using a visual rather than concrete representation), this can be adapted as follows:

By physically breaking the '5' bar and '4' bar into 1s, the collection of 1s can be seen directly.

This representation can also be used to show subtraction as both a difference between two numbers and also as the physical act of taking away, although it is more suited to the first than the second:

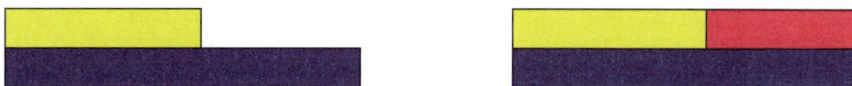

The first diagram here shows a comparison between 5 and 9 – literally, 'How much longer than the "5" bar is the "9" bar?' or 'What is the additive difference between the "9" bar and the "5" bar?' The diagram shows the result – that the difference between the '9' bar and the '5' bar is the '4' bar, so 9 – 5 = 4.

It is interesting to note that the second diagram is identical to the result showing that 5 + 4 = 9. Indeed, bar modelling is a great visual (or concrete) introduction to what is commonly termed the 'part-part-whole' relationship, which aims to highlight the

**inverse** nature of addition and subtraction. The second diagram can be actually be interpreted as 5 + 4 = 9, 9 – 5 = 4, or 9 – 4 = 5.

It is important for pupils to develop a fluent conceptual understanding of addition, and this is one of the reasons why bar modelling is used so heavily in primary schools. In order to foster this fluency, we should give pupils plenty of time to look at bar model examples, like those on page 49, asking them to verbalise and write down the different calculations they can see. For example, in the diagram below, pupils should be encouraged to write the relationship as 2 + 4 = 6, 6 – 4 = 2, and 6 – 2 = 4.

In order to use bars to show the physical act of taking away, an exchange is necessary, which can represented in one of two ways:

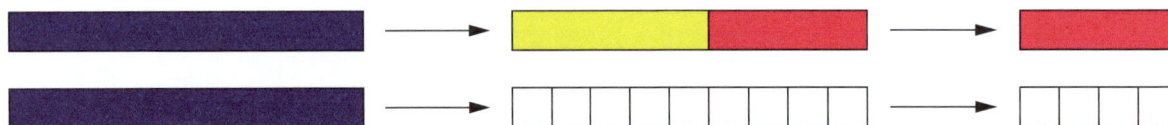

Both of these diagrams illustrate 9 – 5 = 4 as a physical takeaway. The first diagram shows exchanging a '9' bar for a '5' bar and a '4' bar, and then taking away the '5' bar to leave the '4' bar. The second diagram shows the '9' bar being exchanged for nine '1' bars. Five of these bars are then removed to leave four '1' bars. In contrast to base ten blocks, this time it is the physical takeaway that is harder to show, and perhaps more contrived.

Concrete resources can be very effective in helping pupils to understand addition as the physical act of collection and subtraction as the physical act of removal. Pictorial representations such as number lines don't provide the same insight; however, they do have other advantages. In particular, the number line can support pupils with counting on addition and also with counting back and difference interpretations of subtraction.

The number line is a very powerful tool for subtraction, especially when viewed as the inverse of addition (in the form of counting back) and as the difference between two values. The subtraction 9 – 4 can be seen in these two different ways.

9 count back 4 = 5:

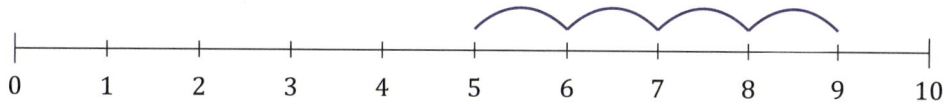

The difference between 9 and 4 = 5:

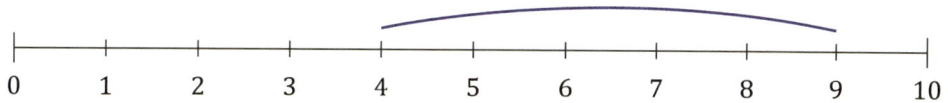

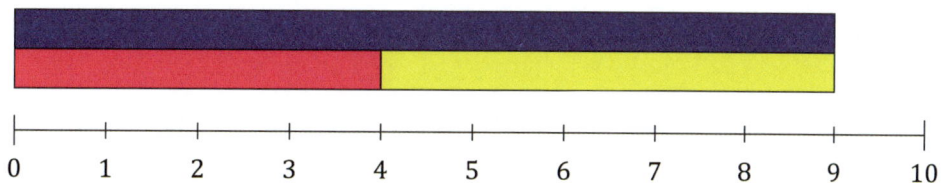

This can also be represented with bars.

Start with 9 and count back 4 = 5:

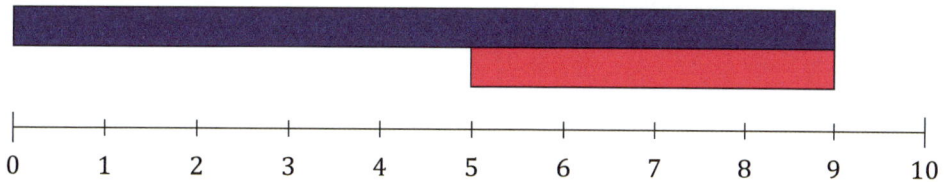

Of course, in the diagram above we could replace the '4' bar with four '1' bars, which might perhaps be a better way to show counting back. This diagram is more 'forward 9 and then backwards 4', which can be seen as opposite to the lengthening of continuous numbers we saw earlier.

The difference between 9 and 4 = 5:

A vector representation can show the same interpretations of subtraction but with an interesting twist. Many people would think that the count back/move backwards approach to 9 – 4 would look like the diagram below:

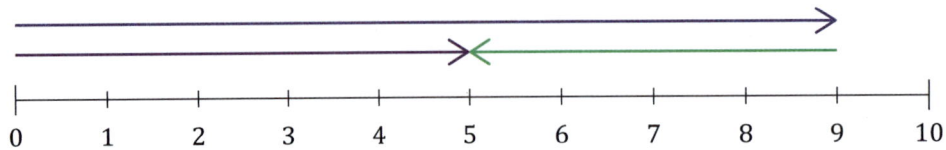

At first glance this does seem to be correct – we start with 9 then move back 4 to get to 5. However, there are a couple of problems with this diagram: the green arrow shows the number -4 rather than 4, and the act of joining vectors (so the tail of one starts at the head of another) is how we add vectors rather than subtract them (this is how we represented 5 + 4 earlier in this chapter).

We will see the above diagram again when we look at addition and subtraction applied to negative integers. In the meantime, the correct diagram for '9 move back (or shorten by) 4' would look like this:

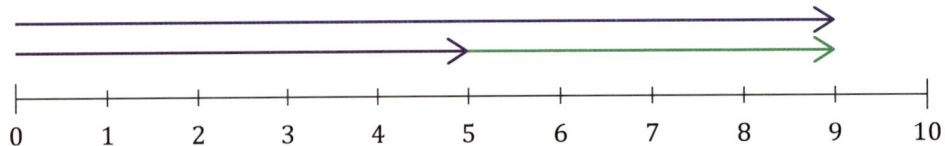

An alternative diagram to show the difference between 9 and 4 would look something like this:

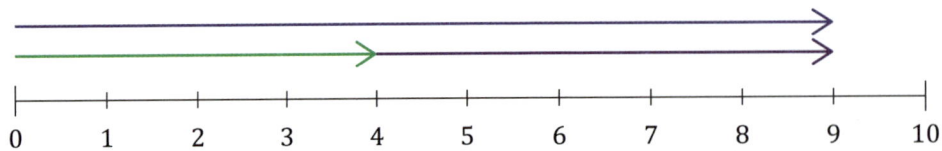

This shows that the difference between 9 and 4 is 5 (as well as showing that 9 count back 5 is 4).

This may seem a little convoluted, but those familiar with vector addition and subtraction will recognise this as the way two vectors are subtracted in two or three dimensions – either head linked to head or tail linked to tail. If we teach pupils now that this is how vector subtraction appears, and get them to practise drawing subtractions in this way, then when they progress to secondary school and begin to work with two- and three-dimensional vectors they will be at a distinct advantage. We will also find that the head-linking-to-head view of subtraction becomes particularly valuable when we examine the subtraction of negative integers later in this chapter.

At this point we have neglected to examine three of our representations: tallying, ordered-pair graphs and the proportion diagram. Clearly, tallying can exemplify the counting on approach to addition:

|||| + ⊪ = ⊪ ||||  ⟶  4 + 5 = 9

It can also illustrate the difference interpretation of subtraction:

⊪ |||| – |||| = ⊪  ⟶  9 – 4 = 5 (the difference between 9 and 4 is 5)

However, as it is difficult to physically remove tallies or to count back, both counting on and difference are far more effectively dealt with using a number line or counters. As suggested earlier, tallies may be a useful approach to the early introduction of number, but their usefulness in developing more advanced calculation is limited. I wouldn't advise using tallies when exploring operations with numbers at all, and would limit their use to the early introduction to number and as a means of counting data when finding frequency (which pupils look at in Year 2).

Turning to the ordered-pair graph and the proportion diagram, these are probably the least suited to the exploration of addition and subtraction. As both are designed to exemplify multiplicative relationships, their utility in developing addition and subtraction is extremely limited. Indeed, rather than using these representations to develop an understanding of addition and subtraction, pupils will need a good sense of addition and subtraction (from working with counters, bars, etc.) before being shown how these apply to proportion diagrams and ordered-pair graphs. For example, if we examine how we complete the calculation 4 + 5 on an ordered-pair graph, it would perhaps look something like this:

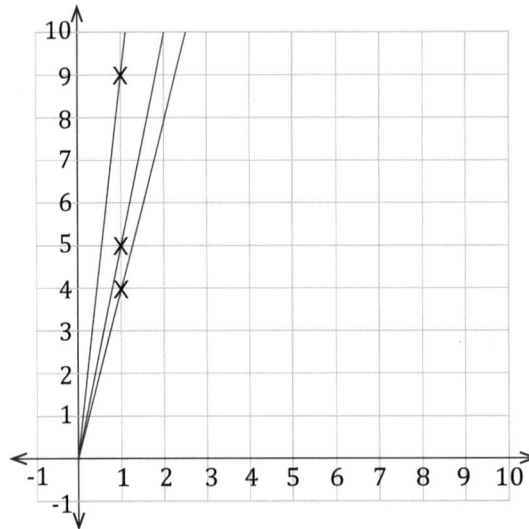

I have emphasised the need for representations to support the natural development of a concept, rather than just being applied when a concept is already well defined. It is certainly true that the ordered-pair graph is not a representation that allows for the natural development of addition in the same way as, say, collecting counters. However, there are certain situations where a representation might not immediately develop the concept but may then become useful later on.

For example, we might define the addition in the diagram above as 'the combined height of the two numbers, when the horizontal distances are equal'. The second part of this definition is very important, and perhaps gives the only justification for examining addition and subtraction using this representation: if we are clear with pupils that the horizontal distances need to be the same, then this can help when it comes to the addition and subtraction of fractions.

The same diagram can also be used for the subtractions 9 – 4 and 9 – 5, again by considering the difference in heights between the points when the horizontal distances are equal.

A similar approach can be applied with the proportion diagram:

| Numerator | Denominator |
|:---:|:---:|
| 4 | 1 |
| + | |
| 5 | 1 |
| = | |
| 9 | 1 |

In this case, the idea is that numerators are added when denominators are the same. However, I would advise caution when applying these additive approaches to what is designed to be a multiplicative structure. Using the proportion diagram for addition is likely to become confusing for pupils, and perhaps prevent them from using the proportion diagram effectively when it is useful (i.e. when examining multiplicative relationships). Personally, I would not use the proportion diagram with addition and subtraction of numbers in any context.

So far, we have only dealt with the addition and subtraction of positive integers. The next area we will look at is the addition and subtraction of negative integers.

# Negative integers

The important idea here is that having defined our representations for negative integers, and also our interpretations of addition and subtraction, these should come together to allow the natural development of the concepts of addition and subtraction of negative integers.

We will start with the addition of a negative value. This would be introduced towards the end of primary school, but it wouldn't normally be dealt with in an abstract way until secondary school.

In this exploration we will look at three slightly different types of calculation:

1   The addition of a negative value to a positive value where the result is positive.

2   The addition of a negative value to a positive value where the result is negative.

3  The addition of a negative value to a negative value.

A good early set of examples could be 5 + (-3), 3 + (-5), and (-5) + (-3). With counters this might look something like this:

5 + (-3)

3 + (-5)

(-5) + (-3)

The final diagram of the three is the easiest to understand. If we are thinking about addition as the collection of like objects, then it seems perfectly reasonable to combine the five '-1' counters and three '-1' counters to create eight '-1' counters, giving a result of -8.

In the other two diagrams, the idea of a collection of like objects doesn't immediately seem to apply. What does apply, however, is an idea we saw back in Chapter 1 when first introducing a counter as a 'negative object' – the idea of a positive and negative counter combining to make a zero-pair. If we apply this idea to the first diagram, we have three 0s which can be removed altogether to leave the two positive counters, or 2. Similarly, if we remove the zero-pairs from the second diagram we are left with two negative counters, or -2. The full demonstration would then look something like this:

5 + (-3) = = 2

3 + (-5) = = -2

(-5) + (-3) = -8

Admittedly, these are not technically the collection of like objects (with the exception of the last diagram), but nonetheless they do adequately show the idea of adding a negative value from a discrete number point of view.

One interpretation of addition that pupils struggle to apply to negatives is the idea of counting on. This is for a very good reason – it makes no sense to consider counting on a negative value! Consider the calculation 5 + (-3) on a number line using the idea of counting on. We can start at 5, but then 'counting on' a negative value can seem confusing. At a push, pupils might end up with a diagram like this:

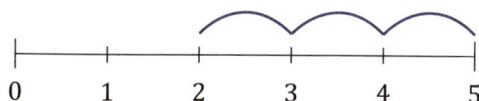

However, this is really 5 count back 3, or 5 – 3. Whilst most people would consider these to be the same thing (myself included), we should be careful about how early we blur the lines between the addition of negatives and subtraction. This is particularly important as we have not yet considered the subtraction of negatives or the ideas of subtraction applied more generally (e.g. to algebra or vectors).

The fact that one of our interpretations of addition doesn't apply well at this point shouldn't be too worrying for us. All of these representations are simply models of numbers and arithmetic with numbers, and much like models in other arenas (e.g. models of the universe in physics or coastal erosion in geography), there will be times when they don't quite fit. Indeed, as we saw in Chapter 1, there are always ways of looking at mathematics that will obscure certain truths whilst illuminating others – in this case, viewing addition as counting on, whilst considering the second **addend** as negative, obscures the truth of what is happening.

A much better way of viewing this process is to use vector notation. This representation supports a great deal of negative arithmetic, and we see that when we consider the addition of a negative value, no matter what the result. Recall that addition with vectors results in the vectors being 'lengthened' by combining them head to tail. The diagrams that follow illustrate how the three calculations we explored earlier with counters look using vectors.

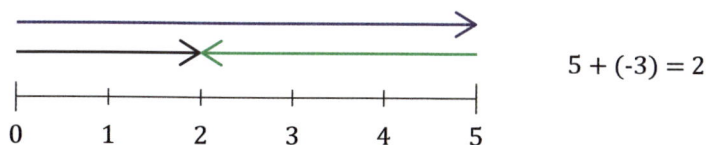

$$5 + (-3) = 2$$

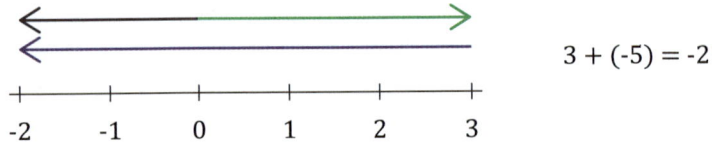

$$3 + (-5) = -2$$

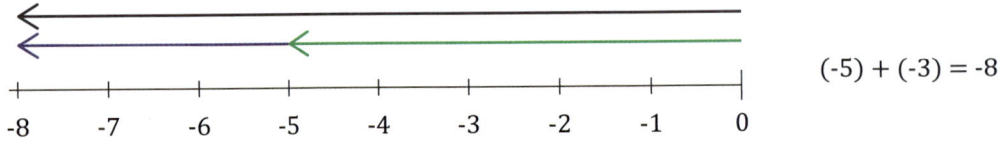

$$(-5) + (-3) = -8$$

Whilst bars can be very powerful when introducing the concept of addition with positive integers, they turn out to be a poor representation when exploring the addition of negative integers. Together with the idea of 'counting on' on a number line, most approaches that attempt to use bars to explore the addition of a negative end up being indistinguishable from the subtraction of a positive. For example, take the calculation 5 + (-3) = 2:

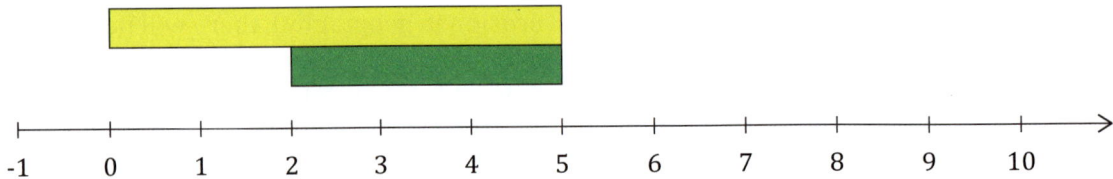

Pupils may be able to see the above diagram as showing 5 + (-3); however, it is very similar to the way 5 – 3 would appear in the subtraction of positive integers, as we saw earlier.

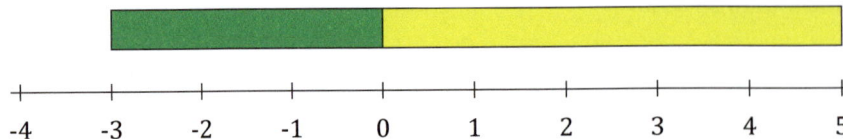

It is entirely possible that pupils will misinterpret the addition in this second representation (it is, of course, 5 and -3 connected together as bars to show addition).

It turns out (perhaps not surprisingly) that if we are going to add and subtract continuous directed numbers, some sense of the direction is important. In using undirected length (some would say distance rather than displacement), bars will always be unsuited to enabling pupils to see what is happening when we work with directed numbers. For this reason, I would not model the addition and subtraction of negative values using bars or Cuisenaire rods.

At this point you may be thinking, 'But I want my pupils to see that adding -3 is the same as subtracting 3', and therefore that the use of bars or counting on a number line is ideal. I am suggesting otherwise for two important reasons:

1   In these representations, it is not self-evident what the addition of negative values should look like. Pupils almost have to take it on faith that it looks the same as subtraction. Indeed, try to come up with a convincing argument as to why the second diagram shouldn't represent 5 + (-3) and you will see the difficulty.

2   Addition and subtraction are different operations with different properties. We will see in Chapter 7 how the correct representation can show why addition is commutative and associative, and why subtraction is not. Although I believe that subtraction is an unnecessary operation (because every subtraction can be replaced by an appropriate addition), I am committed to the idea that, for pupils, subtraction should appear different to addition. I prefer to see the addition of a negative and the subtraction of a positive as two different things that have the same effect, and so the representations we choose to exemplify the addition of a negative should look different to the subtraction of a positive.

For the same reason, I argue that base ten blocks, tallies, ordered-pair graphs and proportion diagrams are all equally unsuitable for exploring the addition of negative numbers, so we will not try. Our aim is to choose representations that make these concepts transparent. It would seem that, properly introduced and understood, counters and vectors are the best representations we have to explore the addition (and subtraction) of negatives.

We will now examine what the subtraction of negatives looks like in these two representations.

When we looked at subtraction as it applies to discrete values, using counters and base ten blocks, we considered two particular interpretations of subtraction: the physical act of taking away counters/blocks to a certain value and the examination of the difference between two different sets of counters/blocks. Both of these can be stretched to the subtraction of negatives using counters; however, neither are without their difficulties. We will again examine three types of calculation:

1   A positive subtracting a negative: 5 – (-3).

2　A negative subtracting a negative, where the result is positive: (-3) – (-5).

3　A negative subtracting a negative, where the result is negative: (-5) – (-3).

All of these need a bit of explaining, so we will proceed with each slowly. First, we will look at subtraction as the physical act of taking away.

If we consider (-5) – (-3), which is probably the most straightforward, we start with five negative counters and we physically take away three of them. The diagram below shows this subtraction:

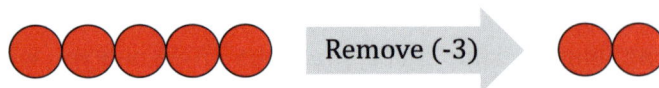

It is slightly harder to illustrate the reverse of this calculation – that is, (-3) – (-5). Obviously, the difficulty is that if we start off with -3 we don't have five negative counters to remove. The approach here is to introduce further negative counters until we have five to remove, using the idea of zero-pairs. The diagram below makes this clearer:

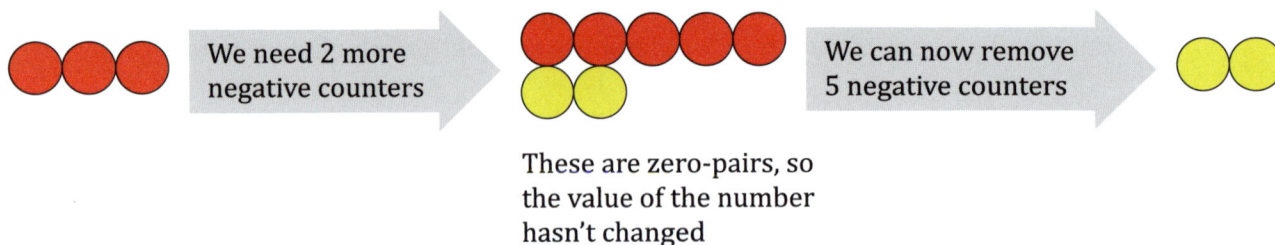

These are zero-pairs, so the value of the number hasn't changed

This demonstrates that (-3) – (-5) = 2.

When we explore 5 – (-3) we proceed in a similar way, by introducing the counters we need to remove using zero-pairs:

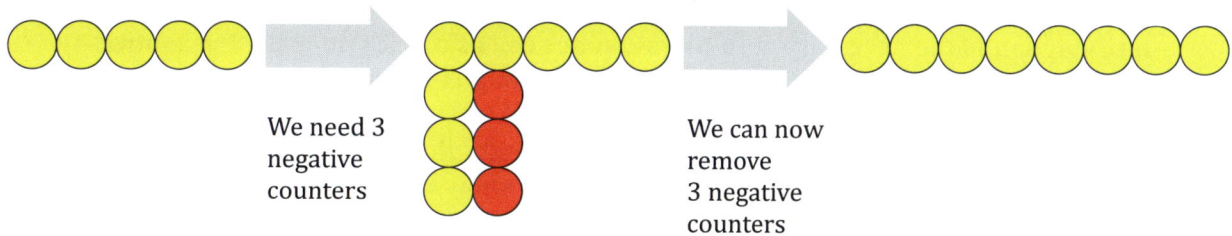

We need 3 negative counters

We can now remove 3 negative counters

This demonstrates that 5 – (-3) = 8.

Examining the differences between two sets of counters is done in a similar way, again using zero-pairs where necessary (in the same way that we used exchange when completing comparisons in subtractions of positive integers). The diagrams below show the same three calculations:

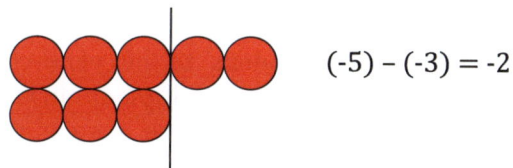

(-5) – (-3) = -2

Literally the difference between (-5) and (-3) is an extra (-2).

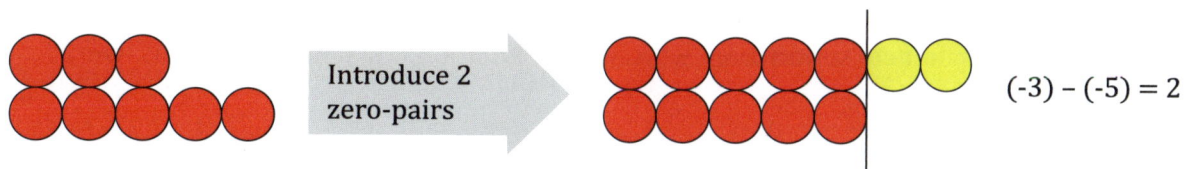

Introduce 2 zero-pairs

(-3) – (-5) = 2

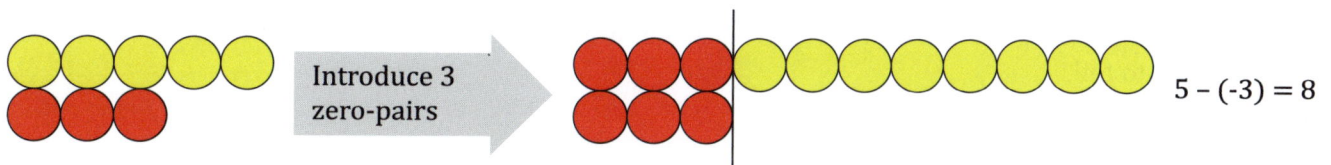

Introduce 3 zero-pairs

5 – (-3) = 8

Whilst these diagrams demonstrate the idea of subtraction of a negative, they both require pupils to have a well-developed understanding of the concept of subtraction and be comfortable with the representation of discrete negative values using counters (particularly the idea of a positive and negative counter forming a zero-pair). The introduction of the necessary zero-pairs can be seen as a 'trick' to make the subtraction work, and it certainly isn't usually something pupils will see for themselves.

However, I would argue that it is not a trick – it simply allows us to apply a concept of subtraction which has already been developed. We know that subtraction can be seen as removal/comparison, so we need the counters to remove/compare. It is no more a trick than the exchanging of one '100' counter for ten '10' counters so that we have enough '10' counters to remove/compare.

In a parallel development in the physical universe (we have already seen the discrete/ continuous view of number mirroring the particle/wave view of matter and energy), physicists are happy with the concept of introducing a particle and anti-particle pair under certain conditions. According to renowned physicist Stephen Hawking, models of this ever-elusive phenomenon show that black holes radiate energy through the creation of particle–anti-particle pairs, where the anti-particle gets drawn into the black hole and the normal particle escapes as energy.[*] Our introduction of zero-pairs can be seen in a similar light.

The subtraction of negative integers needs to be very carefully modelled and explained if pupils are going to see this as a development of their concept of subtraction, rather than just a procedure to provide the answer to negative subtraction problems. We should take our time when explaining and exploring examples like those above, making it clear why the steps indicated are necessary. We should also give pupils plenty of time to work with both concrete and visual representations before expecting a great fluency in calculation from them.

The same calculations can be examined using the vector approach. Remember that when we examined subtraction with vector notation, two interpretations were applicable:

1   The moving back from, or shortening, of a continuous number by connecting the arrows head to head (which is seen as the opposite of the lengthening/ connecting idea of addition).

2   Examining the difference between two numbers by connecting the arrows tail to tail.

---

[*]   S. Hawking, Particle Creation By Black Holes, *Communications in Mathematical Physics*, 43(3) (1975), 199–220.

Both of these representations require care in the approach, particularly the second one – in which the direction of the resultant vector can be ambiguous.

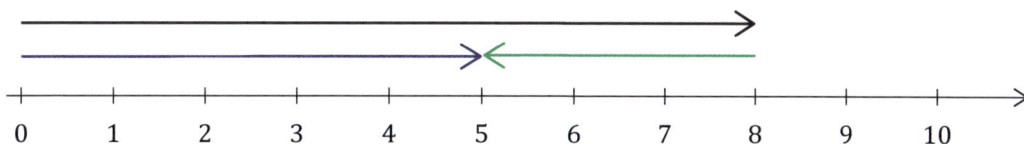

In the diagram above we see the '5' arrow joined head to head with the '-3' arrow, resulting in a length of 8, so 5 – (-3) = 8.

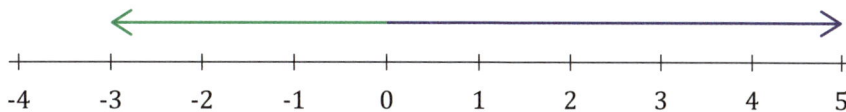

In this second diagram we see the same subtraction but with the arrows joined tail to tail. This shows that the difference between 5 and -3 is 8. However, the same diagram could also stand for the calculation (-3) – 5, which creates the ambiguity alluded to earlier.

Whilst these two diagrams look the same when depicting 5 – (-3) and (-3) – 5 using arrows from tail to tail, the way they are drawn is different. In the first diagram the 5 is drawn first and then the -3, which can be interpreted as '5 is 8 above -3' giving the answer of 8. In the second diagram the -3 is drawn first, followed by the 5, which can be interpreted as '-3 is 8 below 5' leading to the answer of -8. However, this subtlety can be hard to communicate effectively with pupils, so it may well be simpler to ignore the view of subtraction that joins vectors tail to tail and instead stick with the head-to-head approach.

Using head-to-head vector subtraction to complete the other calculations produces diagrams that look something like the two that follow:

(-3) – (-5)

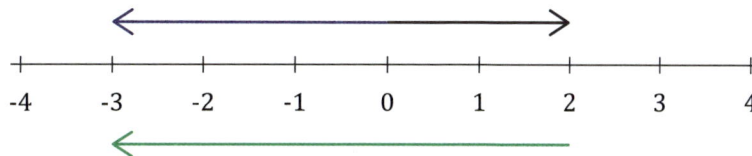

63

Ideally the blue and green arrows are drawn overlapping, as in the diagram at the foot of page 63, with the blue drawn first and the green drawn head to head with the blue, showing the black resultant.

(-5) – (-3)

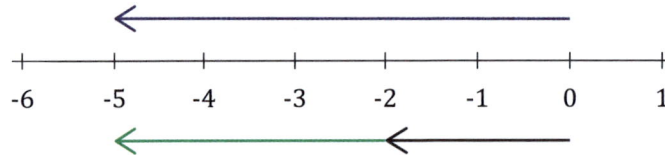

Again, ideally the blue and green arrows are drawn overlapping, with the blue drawn first and the green drawn head to head with the blue, showing the black resultant.

Tallies, ordered-pair graphs and proportion diagrams are unsuitable for examining the concepts of addition and subtraction, so I will not attempt to include them here. In the rest of the book, I will continue in the same way, using only those representations that provide a deeper understanding of a concept, unless I am aiming to draw a distinction between those that make concepts self-evident and those that do not.

Having now explored the ideas of addition and subtraction for positive and negative integers, we can switch to looking at multiplication and its partner and opposite, division.

# Chapter 4

# Multiplication and division of integers

## Multiplication

Multiplication, in common with addition, has different interpretations, all of which can be made clear using one or more of the representations already developed. This time we will focus on four interpretations which can be summarised as:

1  Repeated addition.

2  An increase in dimension.

3  A change in the counting unit (possibly leading to an exchange).

4  Scaling of a value.

We begin with the simple multiplication of positive integers, which is introduced very early in primary school.

If we take a relatively straightforward example, such as 3 × 5, this appears as follows:

3 × 5 = 3 + 3 + 3 + 3 + 3 = 15

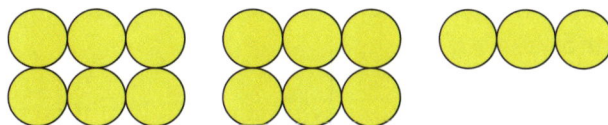

3 × 5 = 5 + 5 + 5 = 15

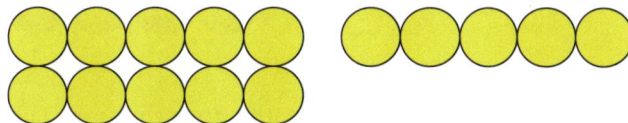

This is the idea of multiplication as repeated addition: we take groups of '3' counters and repeat them five times, or vice versa.

Alternatively, the same collection of counters can be arranged in what is commonly termed (particularly in primary schools) an **array**:

$3 \times 5 = 15$

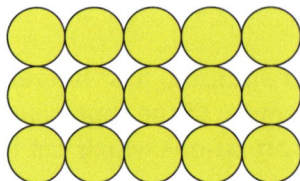

This begins to show an increase in dimension, as a line of counters becomes a two-dimensional array of counters, and will eventually lead to multiplication as a complete area when pupils begin to view numbers as continuous.

A third view of multiplication can be encapsulated by changing the value of a counter, from 1 to either 3 or 5. In this interpretation, $3 \times 5$ can be viewed as:

$3 \times 5 = 15$

This shows the multiplication as a change in the counting unit; instead of counting in 1s, we count in 3s or 5s.

This last interpretation may seem somewhat circular, but in fact it is pretty fundamental to our place value system. Indeed, it is important that numbers like 367 can be seen as $3 \times 100 + 6 \times 10 + 7 \times 1$, literally:

This treats each multiplication as a change in the counting unit (i.e. we are counting three 100s, six 10s and seven 1s). Ideas like writing numbers in **standard index form** are based around this view of multiplication – we change the counting unit from 1s to whatever the largest power of 10 is, so a number like 30,000 becomes $3 \times 10^4$. In fact, even a sum as simple as $3 \times 100 = 300$ can be seen as a form of exchange – we start with three 100s (picture three '100' counters) and exchange them for three hundred 1s. Other multiplications can be interpreted in the same way (e.g. $4 \times 7 = 28$ can be seen as the exchange between four '7' counters, seven '4' counters and twenty-eight '1' counters). The language we use around multiplication even hints at this interpretation: when we learn our times tables we talk about having 'four 7s makes 28' – we are counting how many 7s we have.

Multiplication in other representations generally follows one of these three interpretations. For example, tallies can multiply through repeated addition (although I wouldn't recommend developing the concept of multiplication in this way). Multiplication on a number line can be interpreted as repeated addition or as a change of unit:

$3 \times 5$ as 3 repeated 5 times:

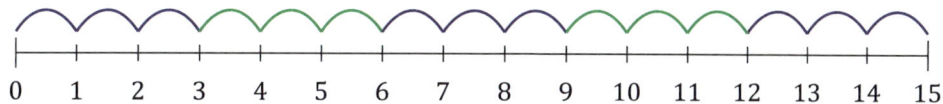

Note: when modelling with pupils, the colour change is unnecessary as the jumps are repeated in sets of 3 or 5.

$3 \times 5$ as 5 repeated 3 times:

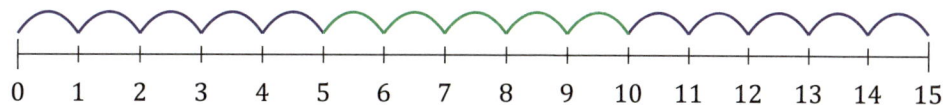

$3 \times 5$ as a change of the counting unit from 1s to 3s:

3 × 5 as a change of the counting unit from 1s to 5s:

The diagrams are similar when using a vector representation of the numbers:

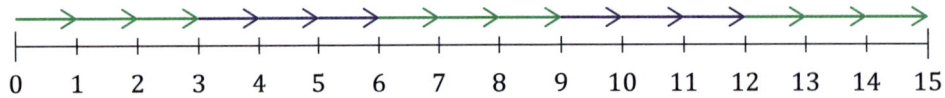

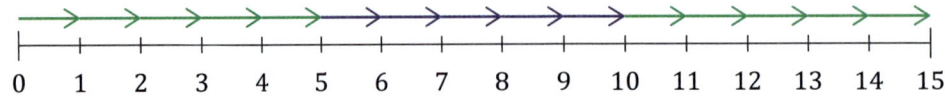

One interpretation of multiplication that neither of these representations shows is the change of dimension. As a number line is a one-dimensional object it is difficult to illustrate a change in dimension. The addition of a second number line, at right angles to the first, could feasibly be used. This could look something like this:

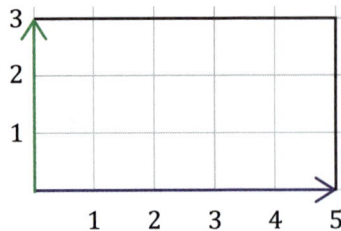

However, this development is probably not necessary and could perhaps be confusing for pupils. A particular confusion can arise with the use of the ordered-pair graph, where the pair of values links to division, whilst in the previous diagram the values are multiplied.

A better representation to explore more deeply the interpretation of multiplication as an increase in dimension is the bar model, especially its concrete version, Cuisenaire rods.

Cuisenaire rods, and bar models in general, provide an excellent structure to show multiplication and multiplicative relationships, particularly the repeated addition and increase in dimension – the latter leading to what is often called the area model of multiplication (and division).

In this representation, $3 \times 5$ can be thought of as the repeated connection of bars (a repeated addition):

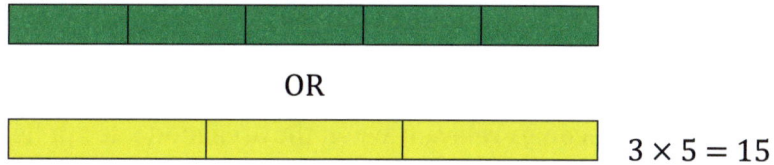

OR

$3 \times 5 = 15$

Of course, this is also a change of the counting unit – instead of counting in 1s we are counting in 3s (or 5s). A simple rearrangement of these blocks can show the change of dimension:

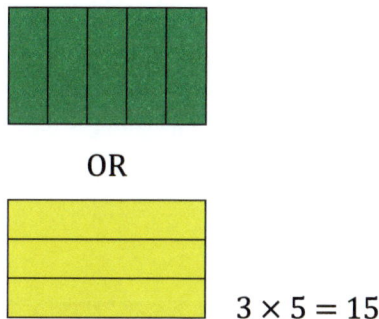

OR

$3 \times 5 = 15$

Alternatively, this can be seen in the diagram below (it is similar to the extension of the number line to two dimensions but without the confusion with ordered-pair):

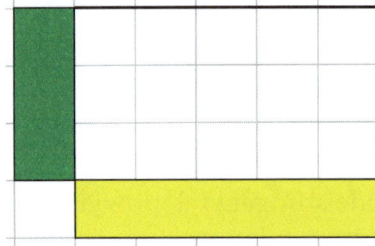

It is the area model of multiplication that ultimately gives rise to one of the standard approaches to multiplying large numbers, namely the grid method. The fact that these two **factors** create an area is also important when we begin to consider algebra and the factorisation of algebraic expressions (as we will see in Chapter 14). This makes the area model view of multiplication and division, and the language of factor, indispensable. Pupils should be intimately familiar with this representation of multiplication by the time they tackle higher algebra.

The grid method becomes relevant when the area model is applied to the multiplication of numbers larger than 10. For example, if we examine the multiplication of 16 x 7, this would look something like this:

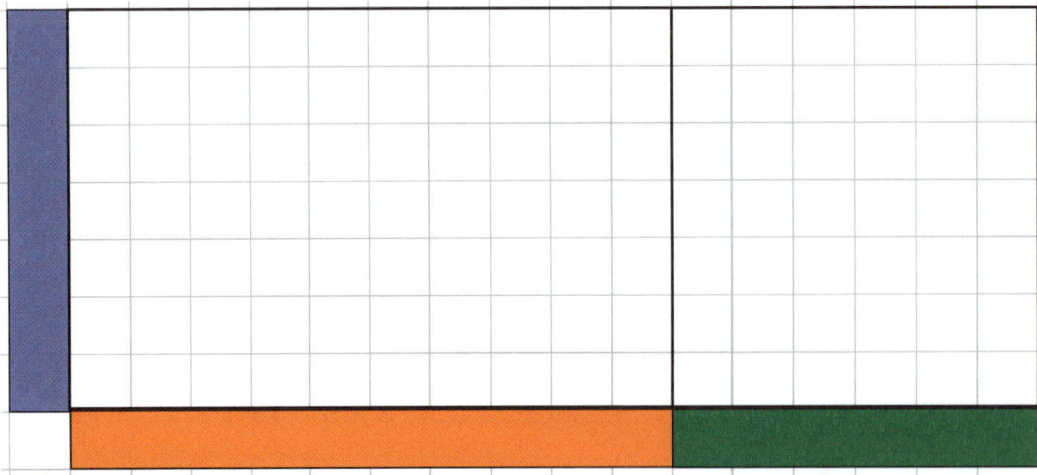

In this diagram the value of 16 has been split into 10 and 6, which results in the two separate rectangles, each with an area that is a result of multiplying by 7. If you are familiar with the grid method of multiplication you will be used to seeing a similar diagram for multiplication, but with the bars replaced by numbers and the rectangles no longer scaled to show the squares:

|   | 10 | 6 |
|---|----|---|
| 7 |    |   |

A further alternative that is not open to pupils when working with concrete resources, but can be demonstrated pictorially, is the bar model already broken into parts. Again, this is a precursor to the grid method for multiplication of large numbers.

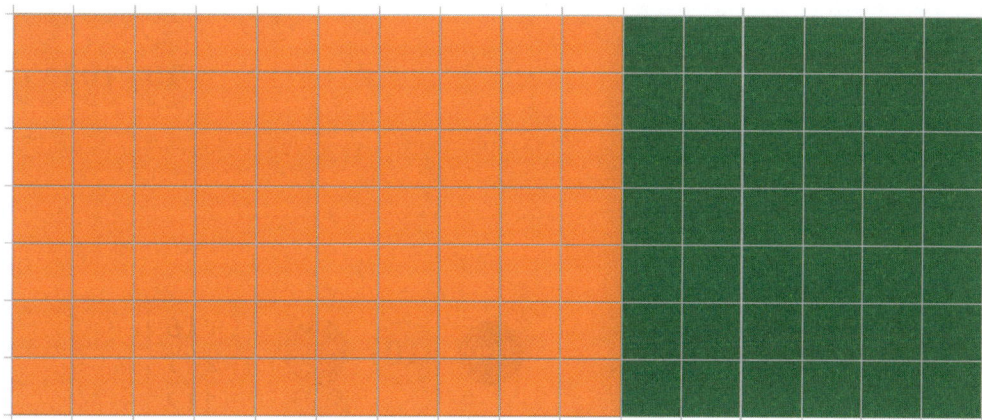

This is the same calculation (16 × 7) shown with the '10' bars and '6' bars rearranged to create an area, but the bars have been broken down into their unit parts to show the result of the multiplication.

It is natural at this stage for us to consider the other most common approaches to multiplying larger numbers, namely the formal column multiplication **algorithm** and the lattice method (also known as Gelusia, Chinese multiplication and as a variant on Napier's bones).

When examining the column multiplication algorithm, it is best to go back to our place value counters where we can explore the same example, 16 × 7:

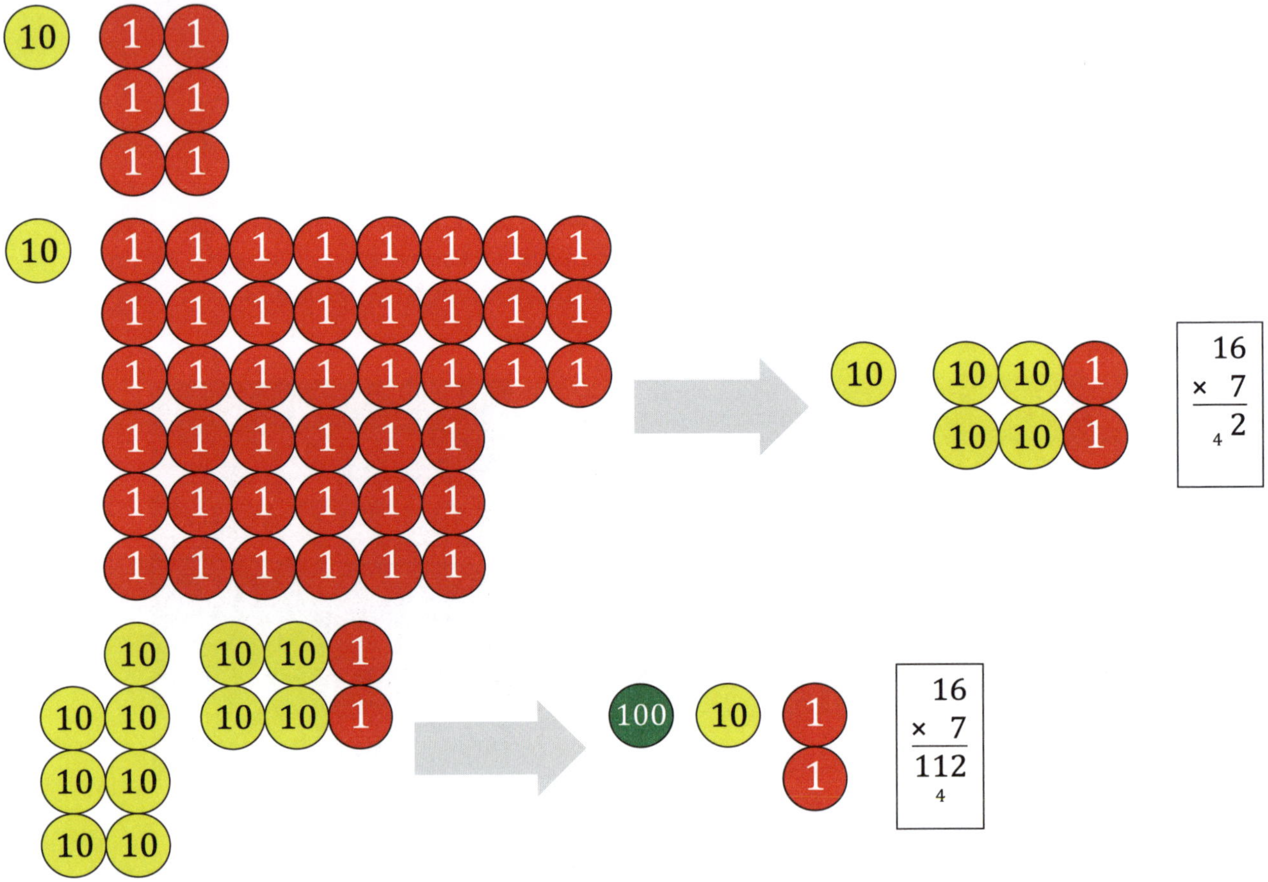

The lattice method works in a similar way:

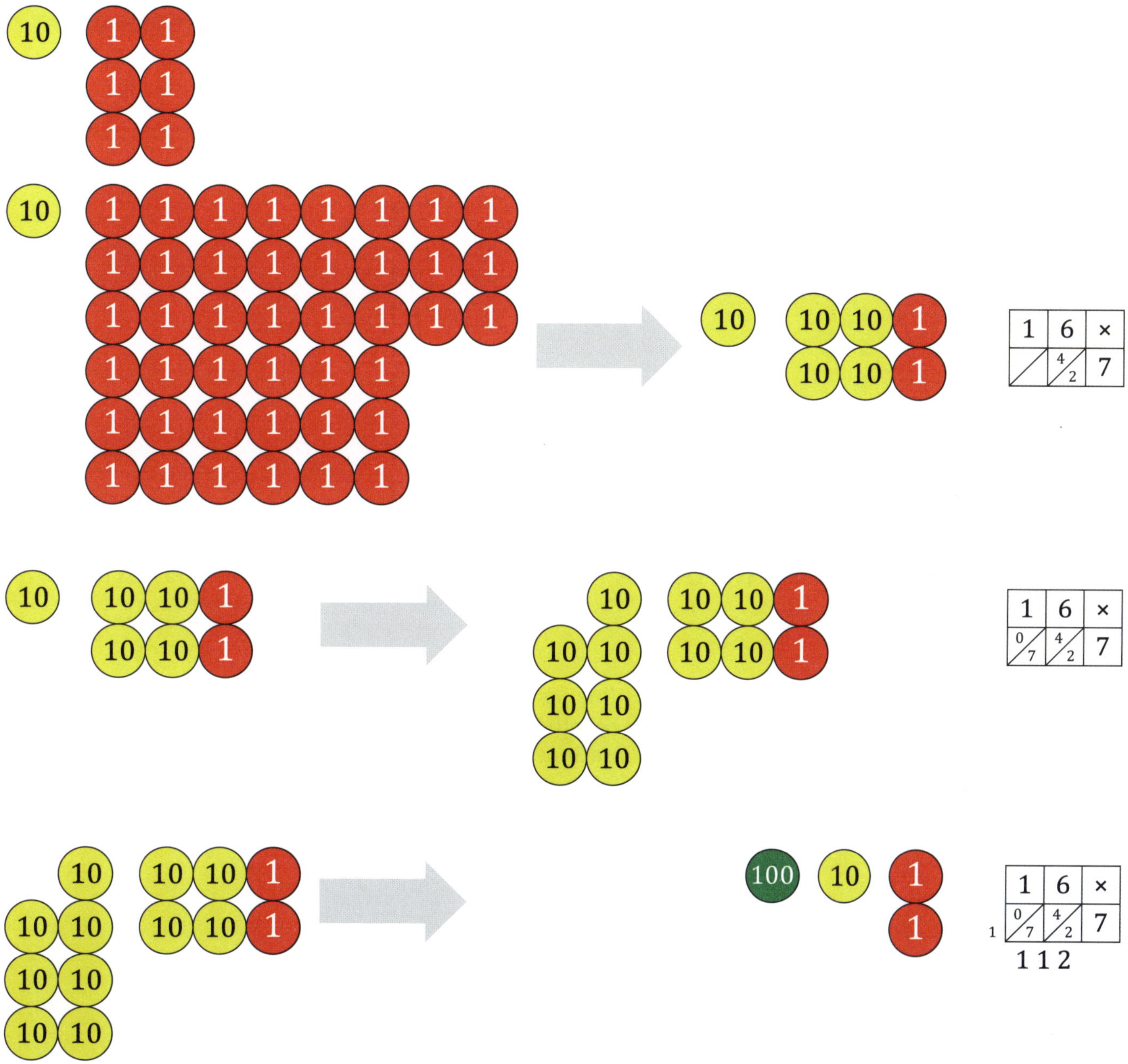

As multiplicative structures, the ordered-pair graph and proportion diagram are clearly well suited to exploring multiplication. Whilst they cannot be used to show interpretations such as change of counting unit or repeated addition, they do make very clear the scaling interpretation of multiplication.

Going back to the multiplication 3 × 5, this could appear as either of the following ordered-pair graphs:

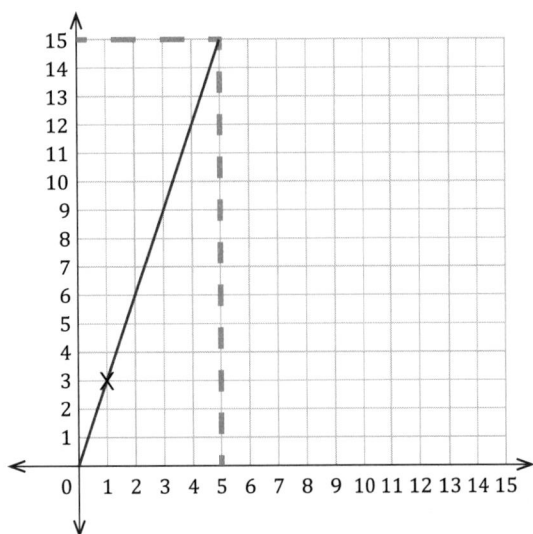

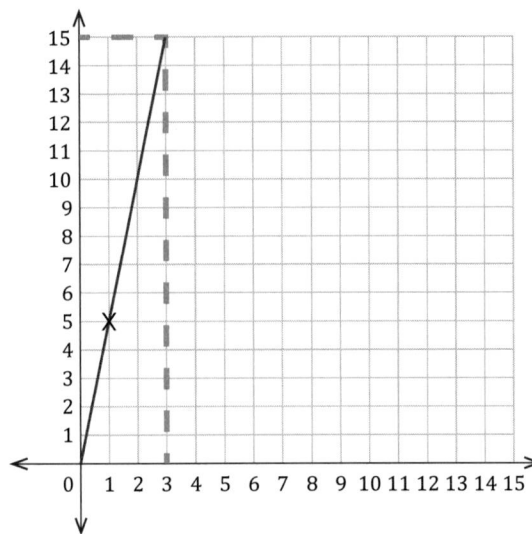

In the left-hand diagram we plot the line for the number 3 and read off from a horizontal value (**divisor**/denominator) of 5 to give a **dividend** of 15. In the right-hand diagram we reverse the divisor and **quotient**, so we now draw the number 5, and use a divisor of 3 to give a dividend of 15. This is the scaling interpretation of multiplication: 5 scaled up by a factor of 3, or 3 scaled up by a factor of 5, results in 15.

A similar idea can be expressed in a proportion diagram:

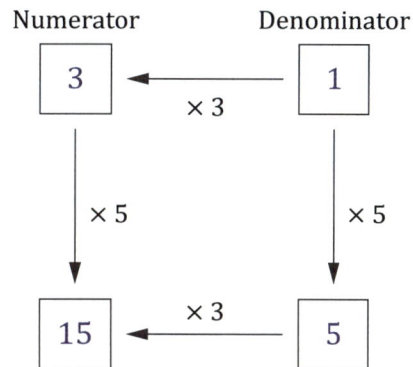

Having developed the concept of multiplication through counters, number lines, bars and multiplicative structures with our pupils, we can now turn our attention to the related concept of division.

# Division

Traditionally, division is seen in two different ways:

1 Grouping – if dividing by a number we create groups of that number.

2 Sharing – if dividing by a number we share out our total into the given number of shares.

Both of these are discrete views of division and can be represented using counters. The example we will look at is 15 ÷ 3:

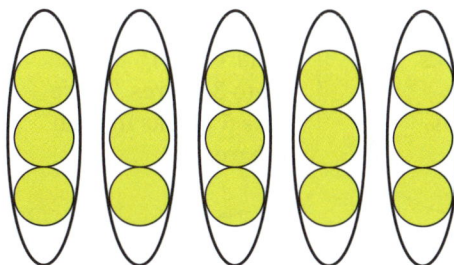

The diagram shows 15 ÷ 3 as 'start with 15 and create groups of 3'. We find we can create 5 groups of 3, and so 15 ÷ 3 = 5.

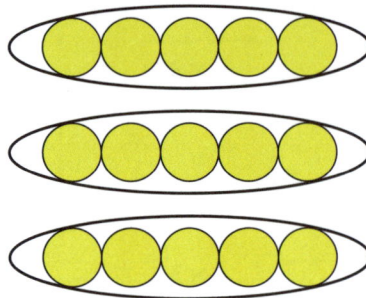

This second diagram shows 15 ÷ 3 as 'start with 15 and share it into three different shares'. We find that each share has 5, and so 15 ÷ 3 = 5.

It is worth noting that we would arrive at precisely the same diagrams if we looked at the calculation 15 ÷ 5. For this calculation, each diagram would take on the opposite meaning, so the first diagram would show 5 shares and the second diagram would show groups of 5. This expresses the idea that if 15 ÷ 3 = 5, then 15 ÷ 5 = 3.

A similar idea can be used to illustrate division using base ten blocks. In this case, however, an exchange would be necessary before the division could begin (the same exchange is required when using place value counters, as shown above, rather than just 15 single counters):

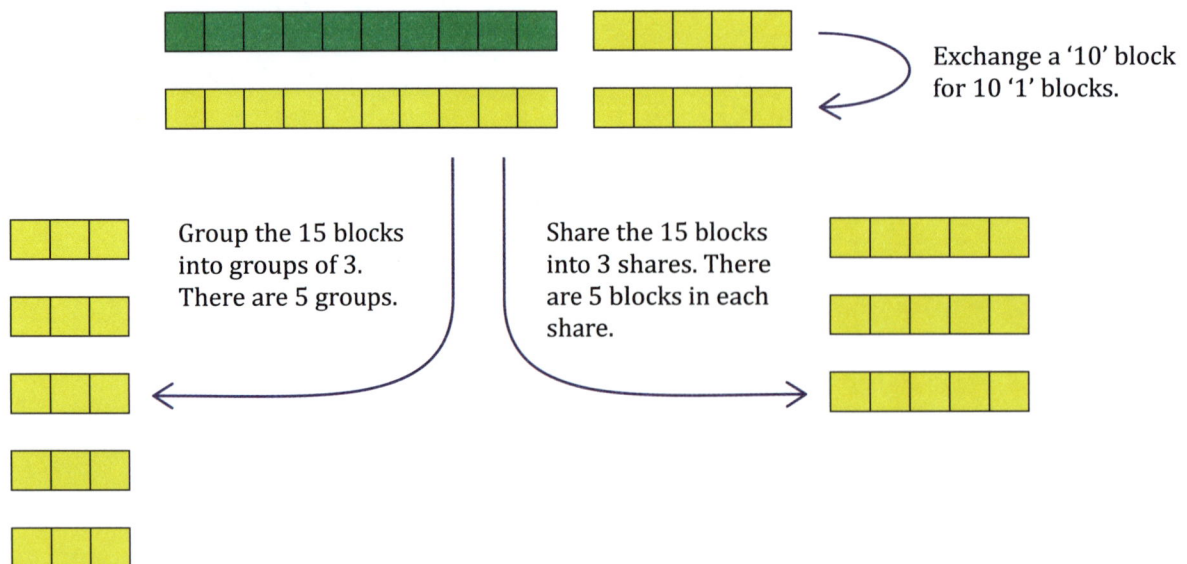

Exchange a '10' block for 10 '1' blocks.

Group the 15 blocks into groups of 3. There are 5 groups.

Share the 15 blocks into 3 shares. There are 5 blocks in each share.

Of course, the same exchange would be required had we used place value counters (rather than 15 separate counters) when first exploring division.

Whilst this exchange might seem to overly complicate something that pupils already tend to find challenging, it is actually a crucial part of them coming to understand formal approaches to the division of larger numbers. Indeed, one way of viewing the formal division algorithm comes from sharing place value counters (or base ten blocks), with the idea of exchange used when necessary.

The calculation 738 ÷ 6 is a good example to make this clear:

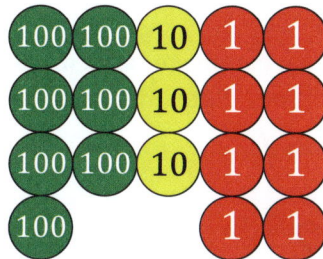

This is the beginning of the formal division algorithm using place value counters. We are creating six shares from our 738. We can put one of our '100' counters into each share, leaving 138:

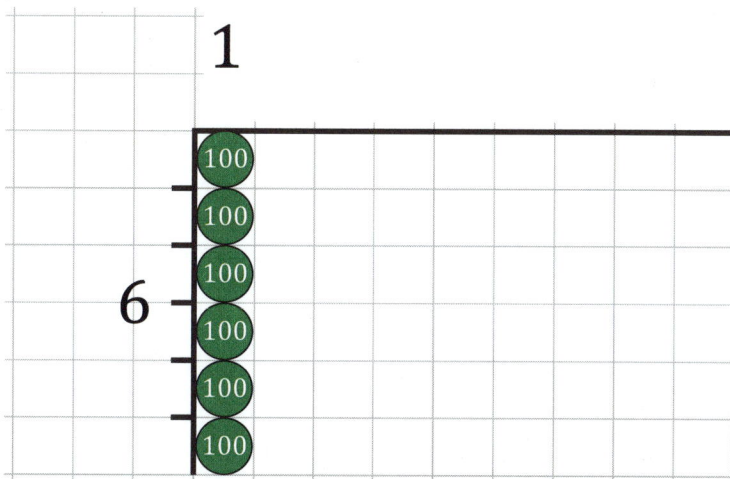

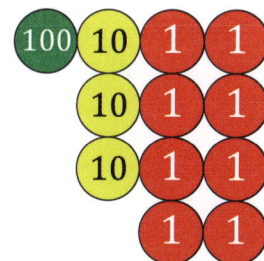

We cannot put the remaining '100' counter into one of the shares, so we exchange it for ten '10' counters. These can then be shared into the six shares:

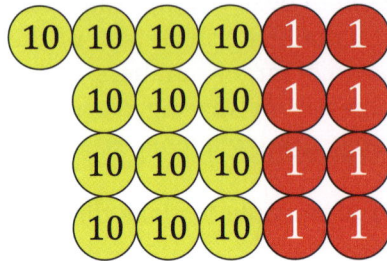

Having thirteen '10' counters, we can place two counters into each of our six shares leaving a single '10' counter and our eight '1' counters:

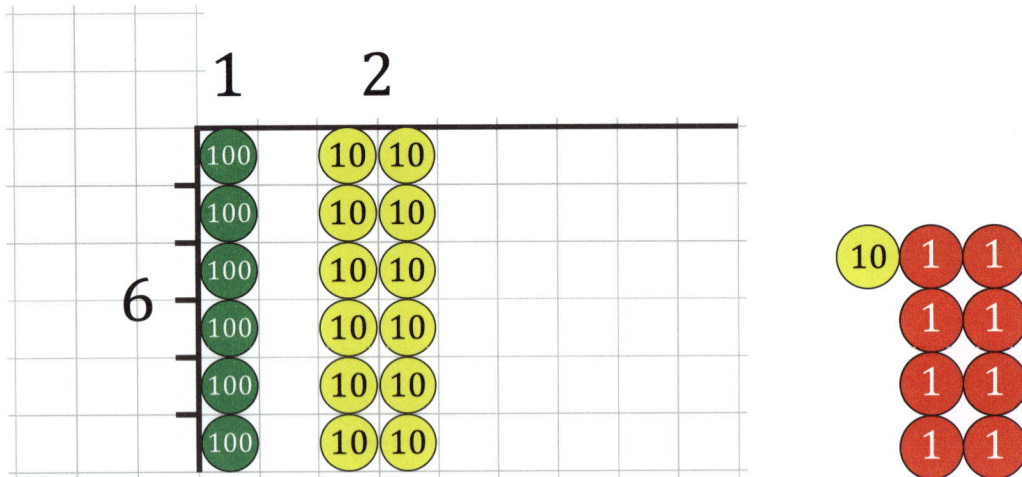

We cannot put the remaining '10' counter into one of the shares, so we exchange it for ten '1' counters. These can then be shared into the six shares:

Having eighteen '1' counters, we can place three counters into each of our six shares. We now have no counters left. Each of our six shares now has a '100' counter, two '10' counters and three '1' counters. So 738 shared into six shares (738 ÷ 6) equals 123:

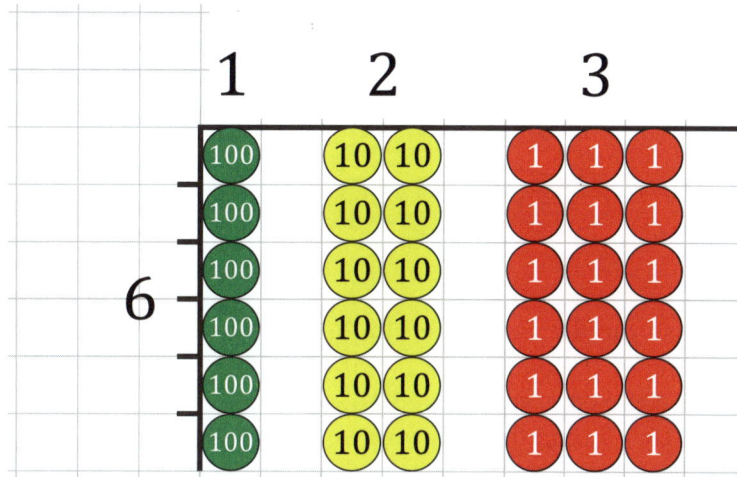

Both of these examples are exact divisions that lead to whole number values. However, it shouldn't be too hard to extrapolate to divisions that do not lead to integer quotients. For example, if we look at the division 16 ÷ 3, we can see where the idea of a 'remainder' following division comes from:

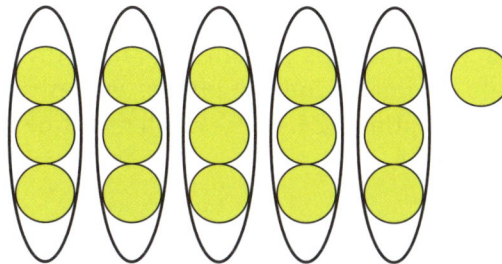

We can see that having 16 counters allows us to create five groups of three, with a remainder of one. In this case it is also possible to see the idea of $16 \div 3 = 5\frac{1}{3}$ – we create five whole groups and have $\frac{1}{3}$ of the next group. Notice that if we use a sharing (rather than grouping) approach to the division, the fraction of $\frac{1}{3}$ is not apparent, although a remainder of one still is:

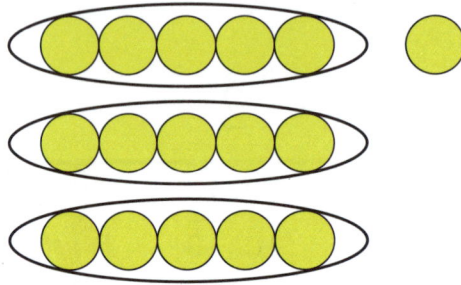

In this case, because the divisor is the number of shares (shown here by ellipses), rather than the number of counters, it is not possible to see the spare counter as a fraction. Of course, if the diagram showed 16 ÷ 5 then we would be able to see this as $3\frac{1}{5}$, but if it shows 16 ÷ 3 then the only way to interpret this is as 5 remainder 1.

Clearly, this is a possible source of misconceptions for pupils. It would be very easy to see the second diagram above as 16 ÷ 5 = $3\frac{1}{5}$, or even $5\frac{1}{5}$ if pupils aren't clear on how the separate parts of the division are manifested in the representation. I suggest that teachers first show pupils a lot of divisions that do not lead to remainders/fractions. They should know how to properly identify the dividend, divisor and quotient, and be familiar with the idea that, when sharing, the divisor represents the number of shares rather than the number of counters within each share.

Place value counters can also allow us to continue these divisions into the realm of decimals, and even divide decimal values by integer values with minimal extra challenge. We start with the calculation 524.4 ÷ 6, which might be attempted by a pupil in Year 6:

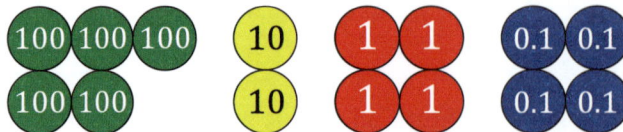

Immediately we can see that if we are going to create six shares, we cannot share the five '100' counters equally into six shares, so we will exchange these for fifty '10' counters. This gives us fifty-two '10' counters, which we can start sharing:

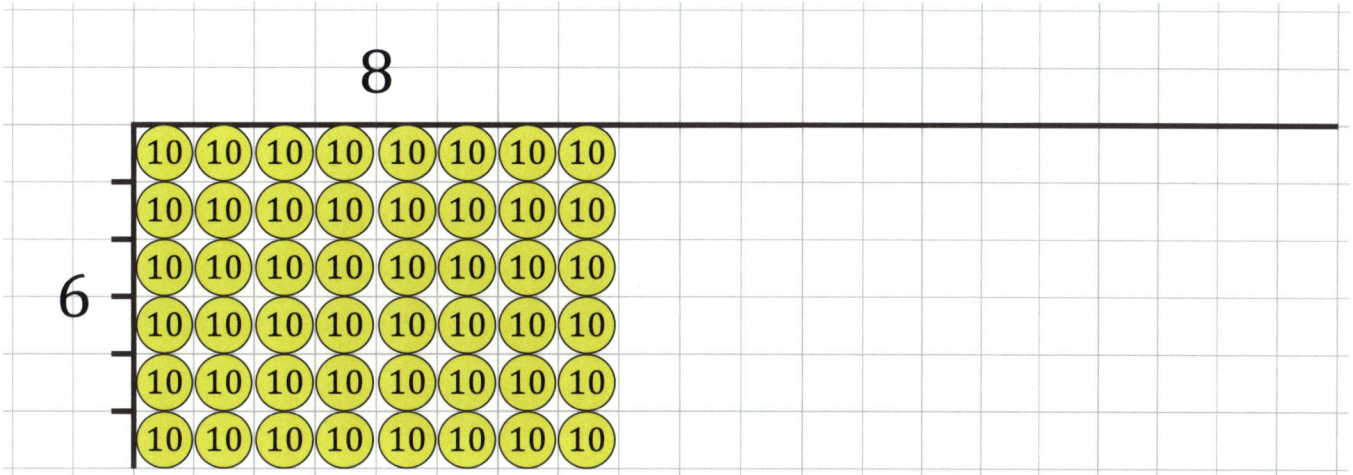

This leaves:

We cannot, of course, share the remaining four '10' counters into six shares, so we exchange these for forty '1' counters, which can be shared into the six shares:

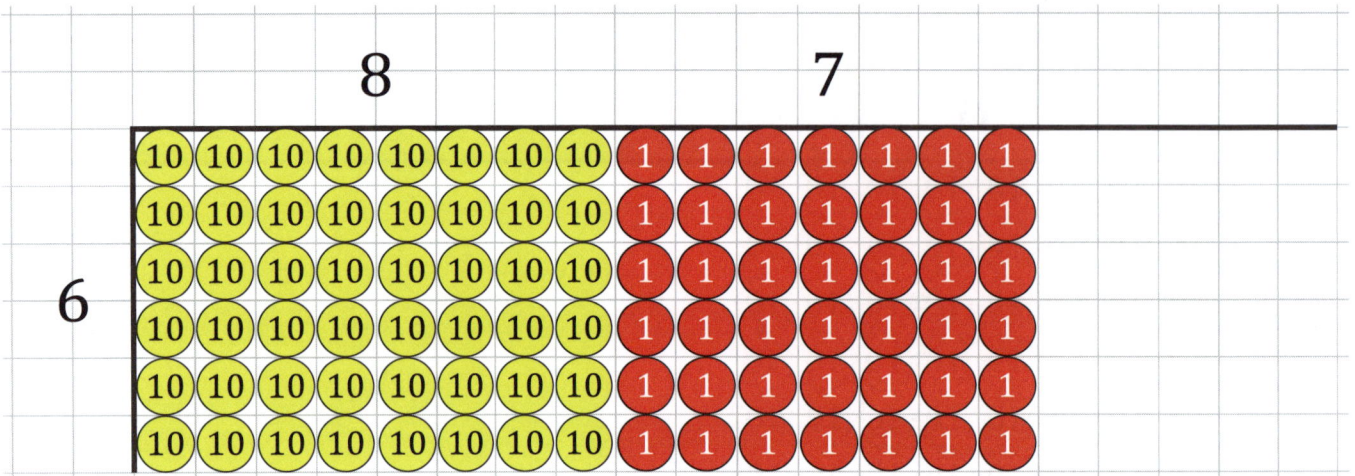

This leaves:

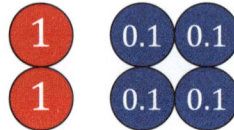

Finally we exchange the two '1' counters for twenty '0.1' counters, which can be shared into the six shares:

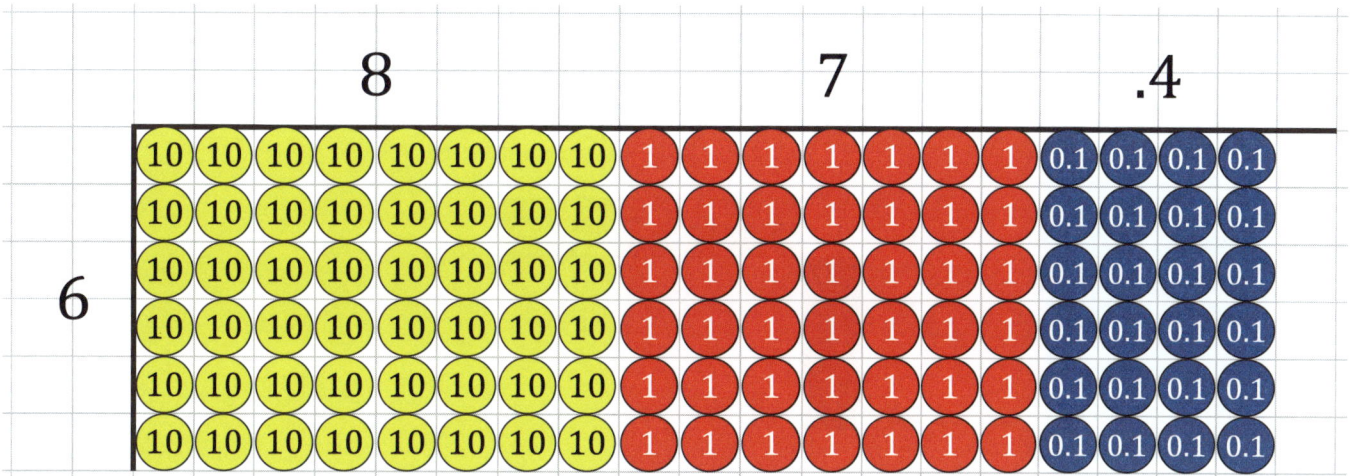

So we have 524.4 ÷ 6 = 87.4.

So far, these are all discrete views of division. We cannot 'group' a continuous number and we cannot create 'shares' of a continuous number, so what does division look like for continuous numbers? Well, despite being a discrete representation, the division diagram above gives us a clue as to how we might interpret the division of a continuous number – because the process of division has created an array.

As you will recall from multiplication, the array is a precursor to an area model of multiplication which uses the interpretation of multiplication as an increase in dimension. This would suggest that the area model of multiplication could perhaps support a view of division for continuous numbers.

Let us start again with our simple example of 15 ÷ 3. Using Cuisenaire rods, we can create an array out of the '3' rod that uses the equivalent of fifteen 1s:

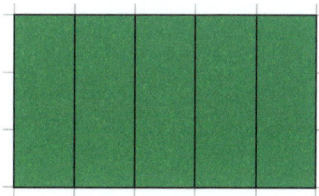

We can see that five of the '3' rods are needed to create this area (alternatively, the length across the top is five). This shows a further interpretation of division, which is the decrease of dimension. In particular, this shows clearly that multiplication and division are the opposite of each other – multiplication increases dimension, whilst division decreases it.

A slightly different view of the same idea which will prove useful is the one below:

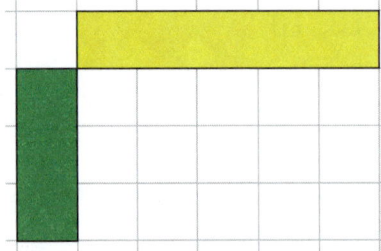

This is still based on the area model of multiplication and highlights that the length across the top is the quotient. This can be read as, 'We need an area of 15 squares with one side of 3. How long is the other side?' This reinforces the division fact that if 15 ÷ 3 = 5, then 15 ÷ 5 = 3, as it is relatively straightforward to rotate the diagram and make three the horizontal length and five the vertical length.

The same idea can be used with larger number divisions, even as far as division by multi-digit numbers. We can see this using the example 518 ÷ 14.

We know the divisor is 14, so one of the lengths of the area we are looking for is 14. This can be modelled using a bar of length 14 or using Cuisenaire rods with a '10' bar and a '4' bar (as shown):

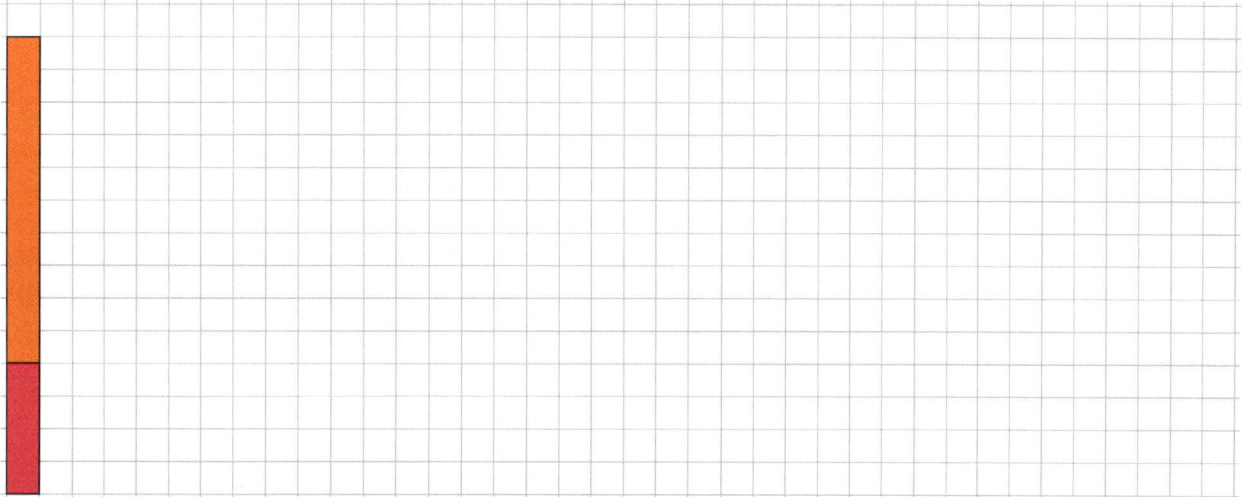

We need to find the other length of the rectangle to create an area of 518. To start with, we know that if we use a '10' bar, this will generate 140 squares of area. We can subtract this from our total of 518 to give a new total of 378 squares:

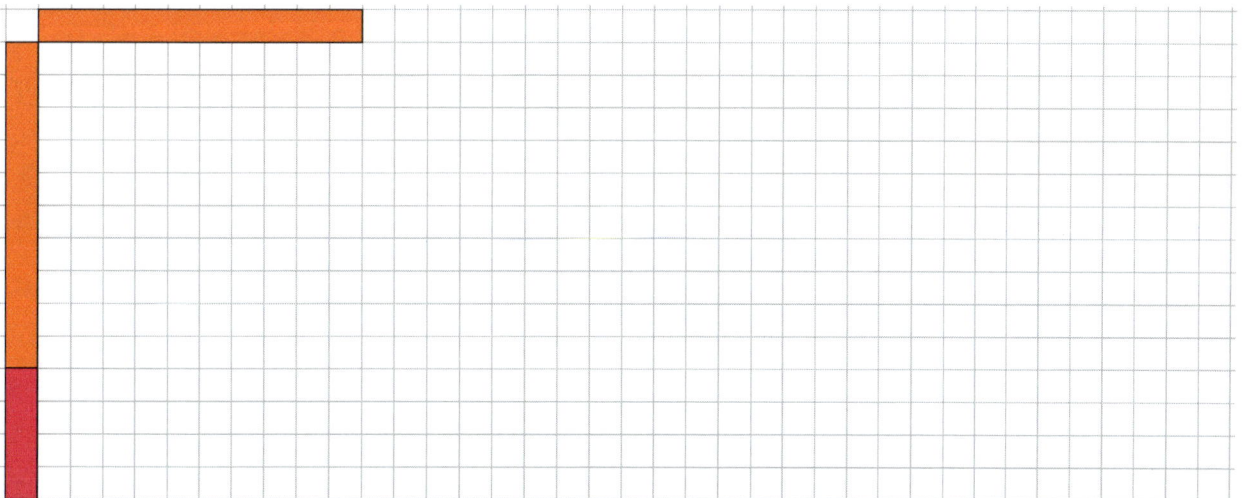

We can do this two more times, which gives us another 280 squares to subtract, leaving 98 squares:

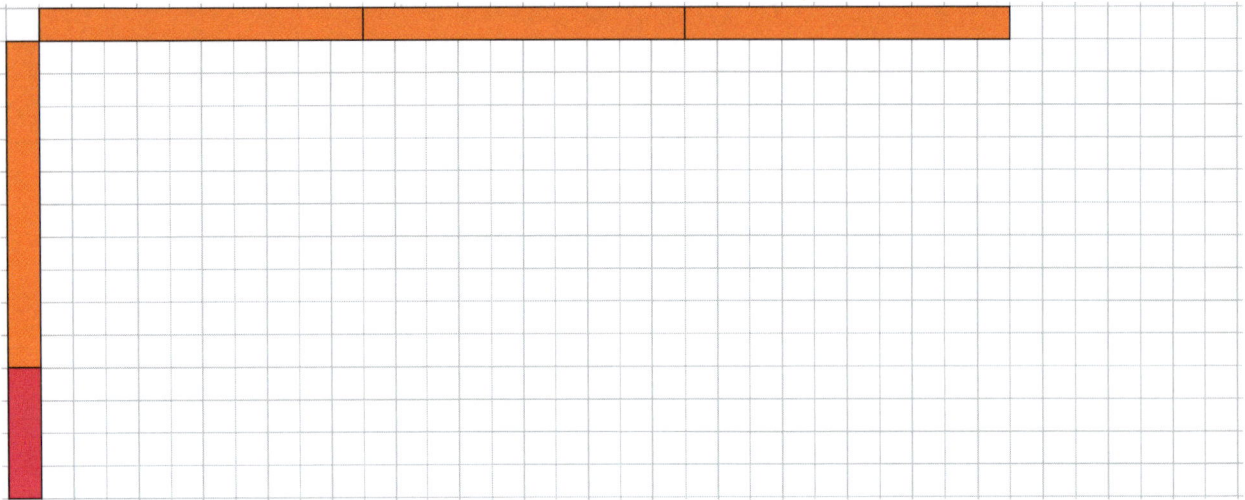

The use of a '5' bar will give another 70 squares that we can remove, which will leave 28 squares worth of area still to find:

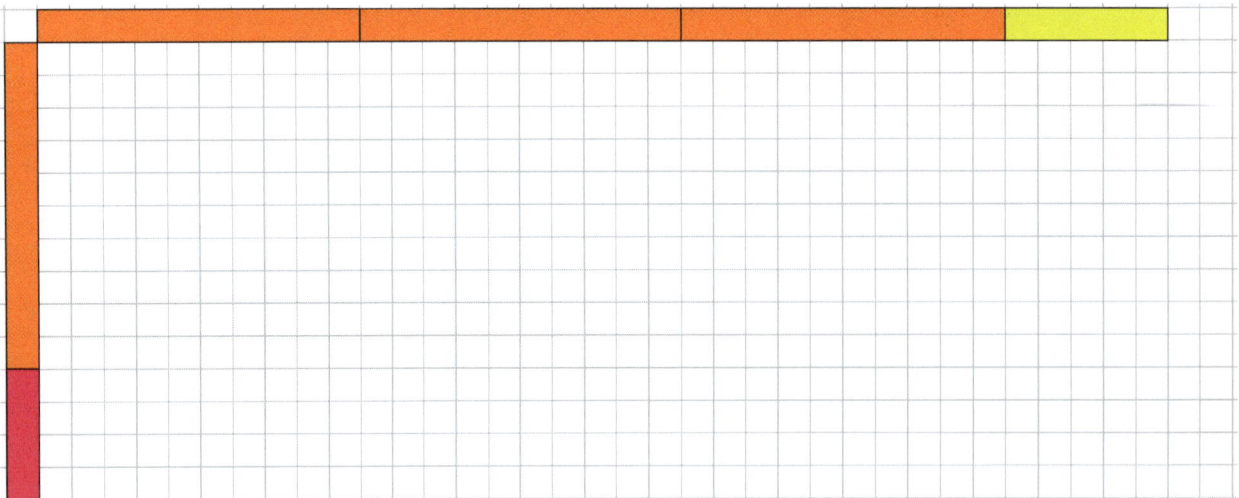

Finally, we can create the remaining 28 squares worth of area using a '2' bar:

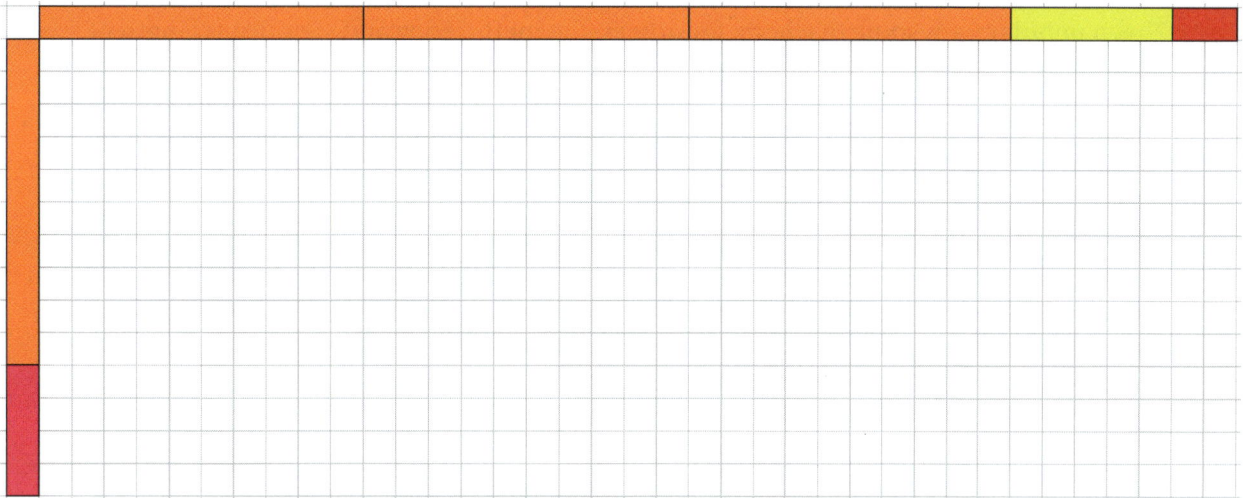

This gives the required 518 squares of area:

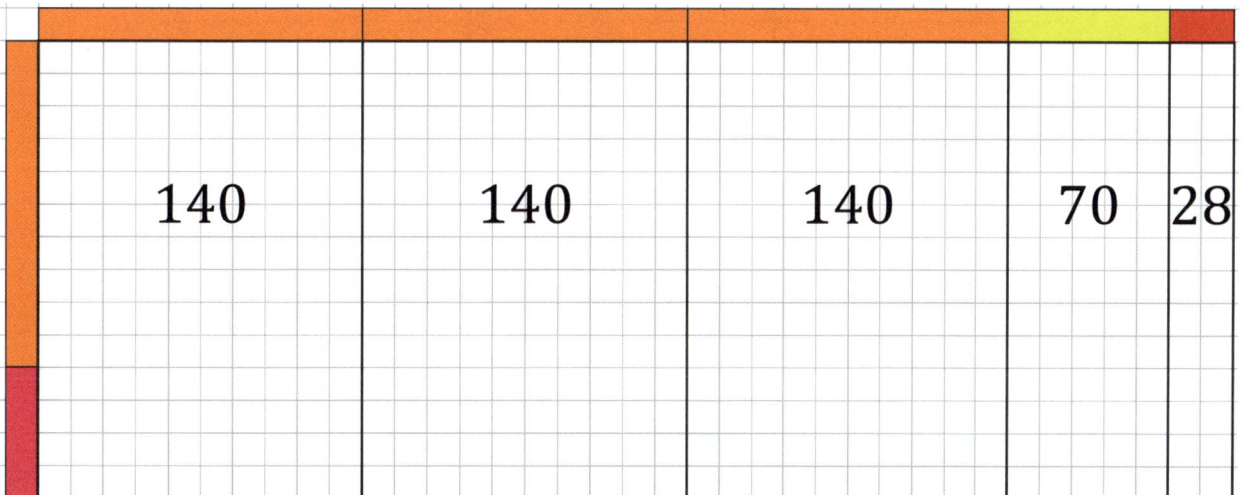

| 140 | 140 | 140 | 70 | 28 |

Whilst this approach mirrors the grid method of multiplication, which derives from the area model, it actually follows more closely the approach to larger number division known as **chunking**. Chunking is a process of repeated subtraction, which can therefore be seen as the opposite of the repeated addition interpretation of multiplication. In repeated addition, we repeatedly add away from a start point of 0, and in chunking division we repeatedly subtract back until we reach 0 (or as close to it as we can, in the case that the division leaves a remainder). Chunking reinforces the important multiplication facts, such as multiplication by 10, 5 and so on, and as such has been popular with some teachers; for others, the inefficiency and significant length of the process can make chunking unattractive. However, the area model of multiplication leads to both chunking *and* the formal division algorithm, so it is important for pupils to understand both (and the views of multiplication to which they link) when securing the concept of division.

The area model of multiplication allows us to cover both of the most used approaches to division (chunking and the formal algorithm), but there are other interpretations of division that can be made clear by using our other representations. One of these is the idea of splitting (which is similar to sharing with discrete objects) which can be seen on a number line or using the vector form of a number:

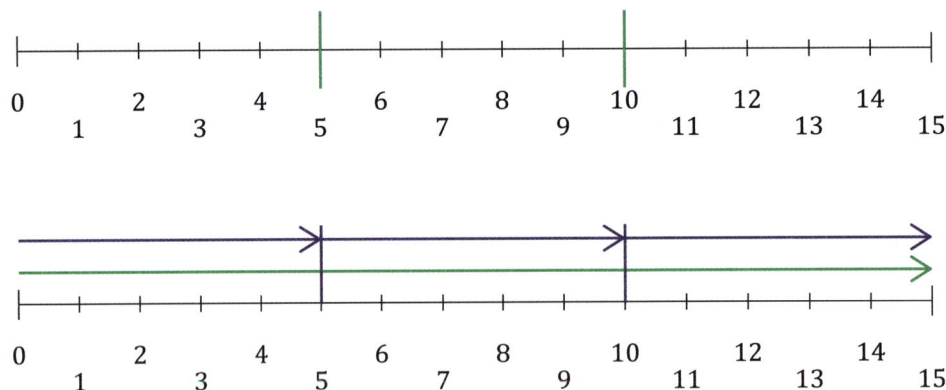

Both of these divisions show 15 ÷ 3.

A big advantage of this representation of division is the ease with which it translates to divisions that do not result in integer answers, particularly where we wish to give the result as a fraction. If we examine 10 ÷ 3, using a number line that has three hatchmarks per unit, we can see the following:

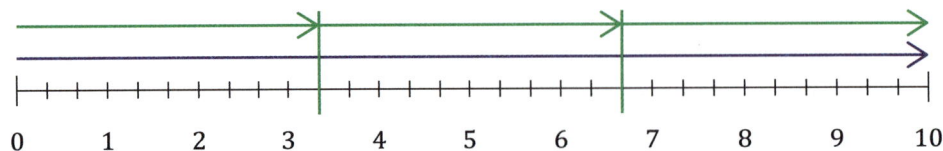

If pupils are familiar with fractional representation on a number line, the use of 3 squares to represent a unit when dividing by 3 (or when using a denominator of 3) should be familiar. Indeed, it is through this representation that pupils can recognise that division leading to non-integer solutions is akin to the conversion from an improper fraction to a mixed number. In the diagram at the foot of page 88, $10 \div 3 = 3\frac{1}{3}$, which is also the same as saying that the improper fraction $\frac{10}{3}$ is equivalent to the mixed number $3\frac{1}{3}$ (in the diagram, each hatch-mark is one-third and the division occurs at 10 squares – i.e. ten-thirds).

Another way of considering division is as the inverse of the multiplication we saw on the ordered-pair graph earlier. Again, pupils need to understand that division is the inverse of multiplication and how the multiplication looks on an ordered-pair graph. Although representing division in this way might seem pointless at this stage, it is worth it later on for the ease with which this extends to multiplication and division with negative integers.

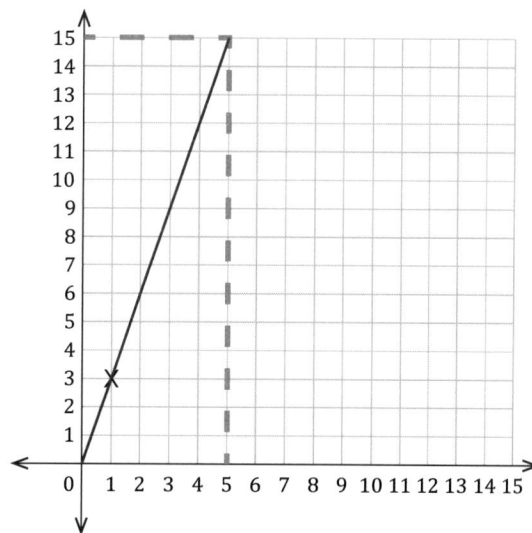

In the diagram above we are completing the division $15 \div 3$, so we have plotted the divisor of 3 and read off the dividend of 15, which produces the quotient of 5.

As an alternative to this, we could plot the point (3, 15) and read down the line to find the value with a horizontal value of 1:

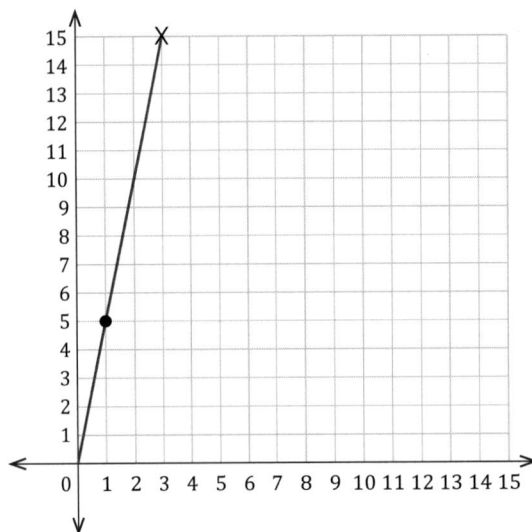

The point (1, 5) lies on the same line as (3, 15). This shows that 3 is to 15 as 1 is to 5, and so 15 ÷ 3 = 5.

This interpretation of division is known as *multiplicative comparison.* It is perhaps the least familiar way of looking at division, but provides the most fundamental view of what division is – that is, a comparison of the multiplicative relationship between two values. In the calculation 15 ÷ 3 = 5, we are literally saying, 'How many times bigger is 15 than 3? 15 is 5 times bigger than 3.'

Multiplicative comparison is a far-reaching idea for division. It can be depicted in virtually all our representations. Multiplicative comparison can be seen as the inverse of the scaling interpretation of multiplication. It can support a wide variety of proportional reasoning problems, particularly when paired with a suitable structure. However, the proportion diagram really comes into its own with multiplicative comparison (which can be seen in the diagram that follows), but it will also become increasingly useful in fractional division and proportional problems later on.

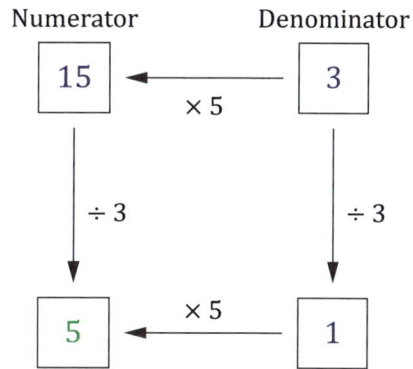

This same comparison can be seen in many different representations:

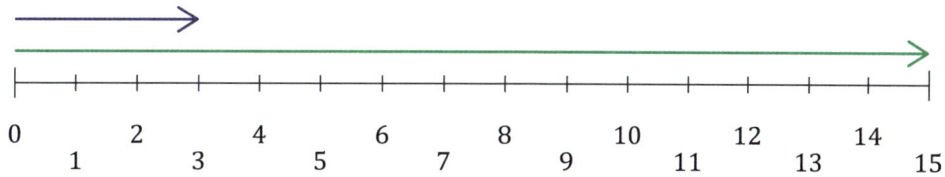

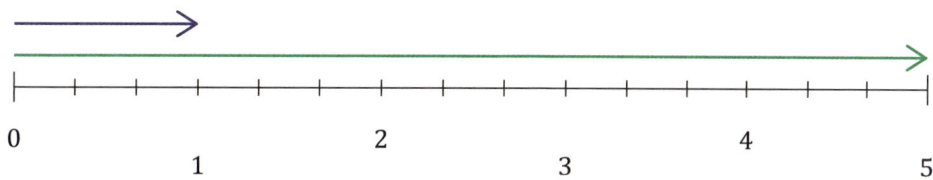

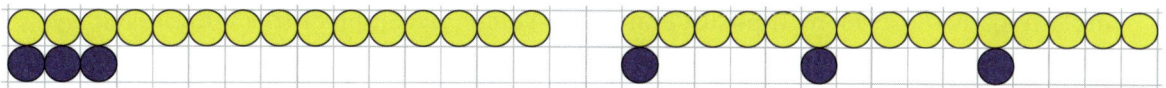

This idea of multiplicative comparison can also be a powerful interpretation of division when it comes to negative integers. Many of the other interpretations of division cannot be applied to negative values, but the idea of comparison can be applied equally to positive and negative numbers. This was described when we looked at the difference approach to subtraction because difference is the additive comparison to this multiplicative comparison. However, this means that we need to take care with these comparisons as they can look very similar.

Pupils need to be clear that when we are examining the difference or additive comparison we are thinking about *how much more* is one number compared to another. Literally this means asking, 'If the end of the first number is 0, where is the end of the second?' When considering the multiplicative comparison, we are thinking about *how many* of one number does it take to make the other, or literally, 'If one number had a value of 1, what would the value of the other be?'

Before we explore negative division, we must first look at multiplication including negative integers (both of which are normally taught in Key Stage 3). We will consider two cases:

1    The result of multiplying a positive integer by a negative integer.

2    The result of multiplying together two negative integers.

The first of these types of calculation is relatively straightforward in terms of our interpretations of multiplication. We start by examining 5 × -3 (or -3 × 5):

5 × -3 = (-3) + (-3) + (-3) + (-3) + (-3) = -15

This is the idea of repeated addition, of course, but it is equally applicable to multiplying a negative integer by a positive integer. We can accomplish the same result by treating each counter as -3, rather than -1:

5 × -3 = -15

Alternatively, we can use a number line/vector representation:

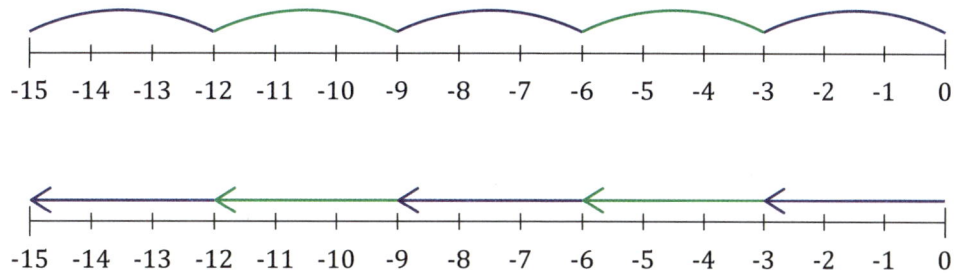

The only representation of multiplication that is not readily accessible when we consider the multiplication of a negative and a positive integer is change in dimension. It is not necessarily the concept of changing dimension that is problematic, rather it is the idea of having a length with a negative value. Consider making an array from the negative counters (recall that the array is the precursor to the full area model of multiplication):

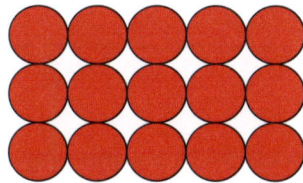

It would be very easy to embed the misconception that if one 'length' is -3, then the other length is -5 and so wrongly conclude that -3 × -5 = -15. This needs to be seen as -3 repeated 5 times, and therefore should have no generalisation to negative lengths. It is for this reason that bar modelling is a poor representation to use for negative multiplication. With bar models and Cuisenaire rods numbers are represented by the length of the bar, so to consider these lengths as negative could lead to misconceptions.

The ordered-pair graph multiplication, properly defined with positive integers, will extend well to multiplication including negative integers. Let's look again at the multiplication 5 × -3:

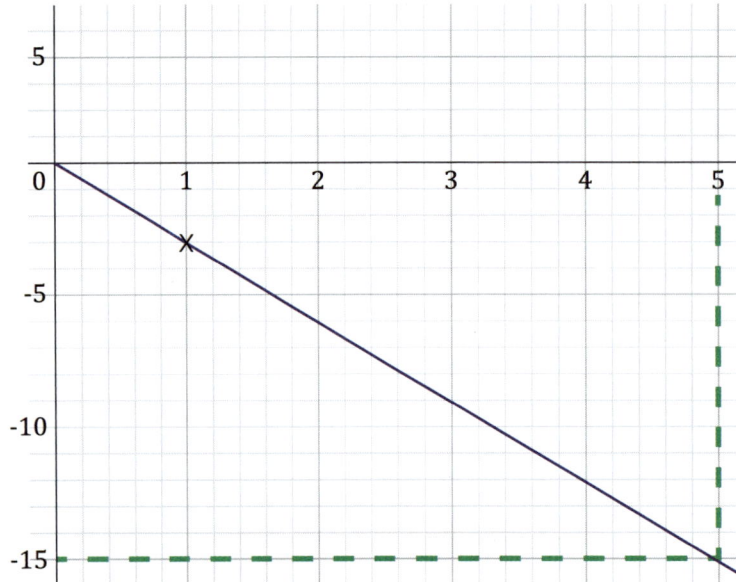

This multiplication works in precisely the same way as the positive integer version. The number -3 has been drawn as the line through (0, 0) and (1, -3). To multiply -3 by 5 we read off 5 from the horizontal axis, leading to -15 on the vertical axis. So -3 × 5 = -15.

As an alternative we could use this diagram:

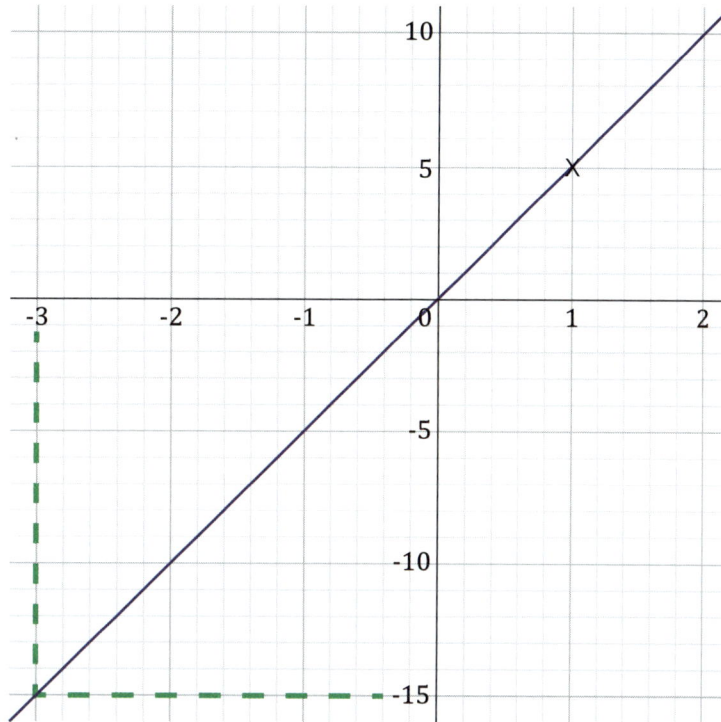

Here the line for 5 has been drawn in and then the multiplication by -3 has been completed, yielding the same result of -15. The great benefit of this representation is that it allows the multiplication of two negative integers in a way that is no more complicated than any other multiplication.

We will now look at the example -5 × -3:

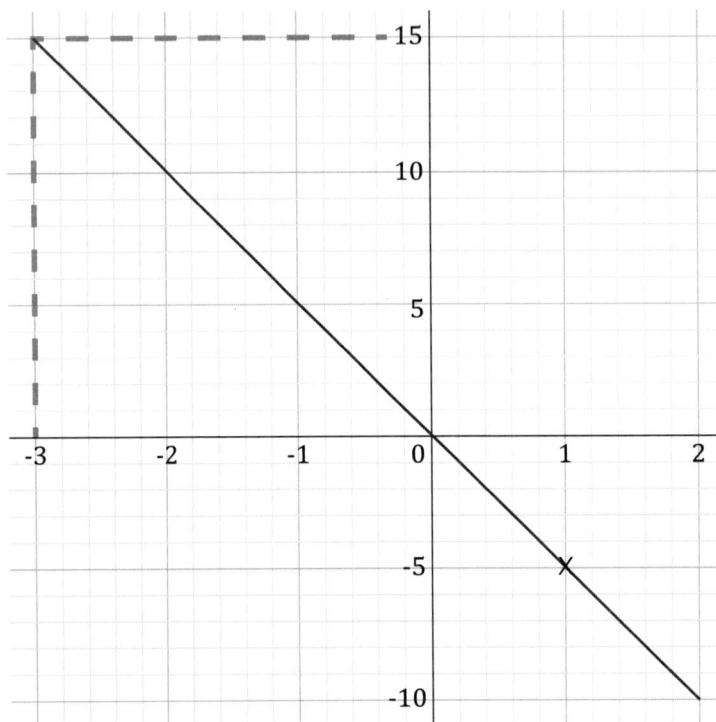

The line plotted is now -5, using (0, 0) and (1, -5). Reading off from a horizontal value of -3 gives a value of 15, which leads to the conclusion that -5 × -3 = 15.

The idea of two negatives multiplying to make a positive is generally one of the hardest ideas for pupils to conceptualise. Very little of what we understand about multiplication seems to allow us to arrive at this conclusion naturally. We cannot use the idea of repeated addition as, whilst we can repeatedly add -3 to itself 5 times, we cannot add -3 to itself -5 times – this simply doesn't make sense. The change of counting unit doesn't help either – we can no more count something -5 times than we can repeat something -5 times. And we have already seen that the idea of change of dimension will not allow for even one negative value, let alone two.

There are two further ways that we can consider the multiplication of two negative values, both of which have their difficulties. There is a proper algebraic proof that the product of two negative values is the same as the product of the additive **inverses**. Although few pupils would be able to follow this at the point when we would wish to introduce negative multiplication (somewhere between the age of 11 and 14 according to the English national curriculum), this could serve as an effective revisit for upper Key Stage 4 pupils, and so I include it here for this reason as well as to put our negative multiplication on a somewhat firmer footing:

Let $a$ and $b$ be two real numbers > 0. Define the value $x$ as:

$$x = ab + (-a)(b) + (-a)(-b)$$

Then: $\quad x = ab + (-a)[(b) + (-b)]$

$$x = ab + (-a)[0]$$

So: $\quad x = ab$

Also: $\quad x = (b)[a + (-a)] + (-a)(-b)$

$$x = (b)(0) + (-a)(-b)$$

So: $\quad x = (-a)(-b)$

We have: $\quad x = ab$ and $x = (-a)(-b)$ and so $ab = (-a)(-b)$

This is a really nice logical proof as to why two negative numbers (note, not only integers) give the same product as two positive numbers of the same magnitude.

The other approach that might provide some justification for two negatives multiplying to make a positive is vector representation. This can be applied to the problem of negative multiplication in two ways:

1   Treat -5 × -3 as the negative of 5 × -3.

2   Treat -5 × -3 as 0 – 5 × -3.

The diagrams for both of these are below:

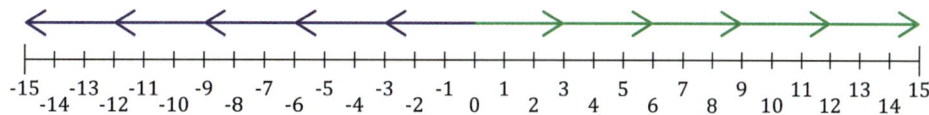

The blue arrows in the diagram above show 5 × -3. The negative of a vector is that vector rotated by 180° about 0. The green arrows show the result of this rotation, giving -5 × -3 = 15.

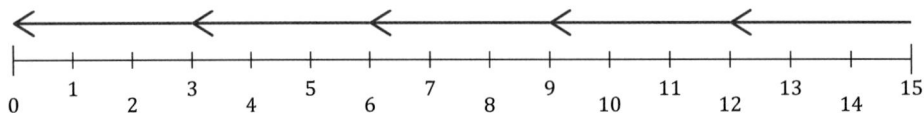

In this second diagram we have the subtraction of 5 × -3 from 0 using the classic vector subtraction of joining the head rather than the tail to 0. This shows that 0 – 5 × -3 = 15 and therefore -5 × -3 = 15.

This is probably the closest we can get to representing why two negatives multiply to give a positive, but ultimately we may have to accept that this is too abstract a concept to properly represent using any of our models.

We finish this chapter by examining division applied to negative integers. This time we need to examine three possibilities:

1    A negative integer divided by a positive integer: -15 ÷ 3.

2    A positive integer divided by a negative integer: 15 ÷ -3.

3    A negative integer divided by a negative integer: -15 ÷ -3.

Interestingly, the first and third calculations actually fit most closely with our pre-established ideas of division. Both can be modelled using either the grouping or sharing of -15:

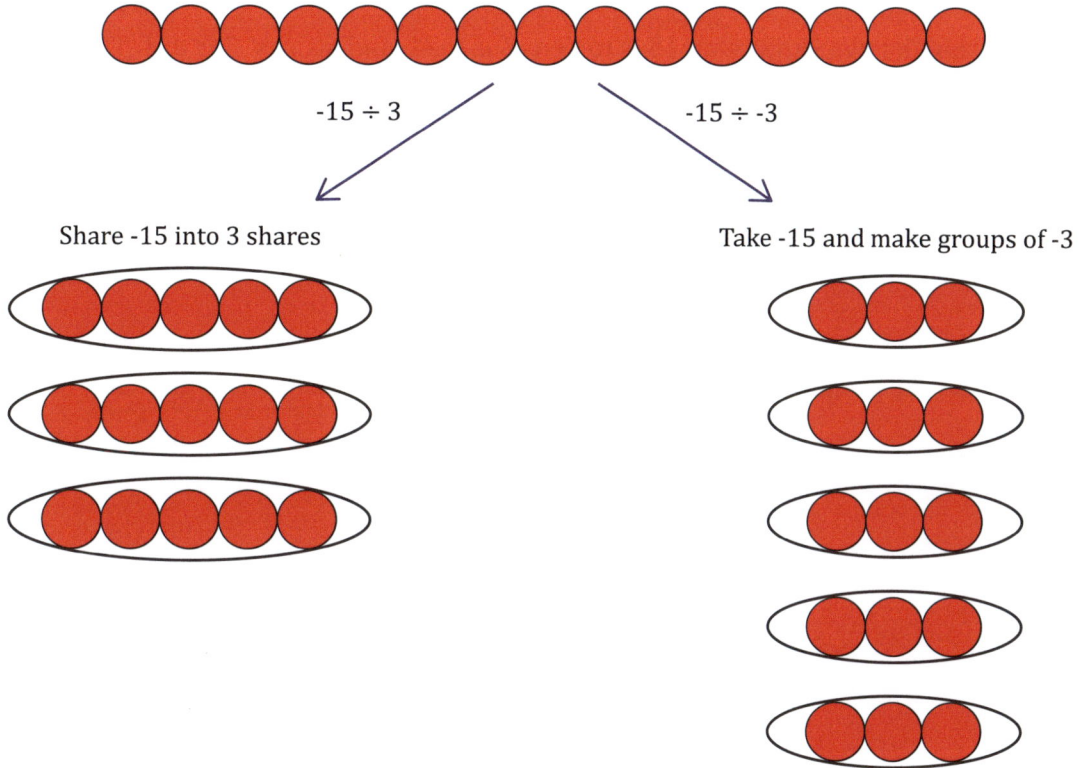

-15 ÷ 3                    -15 ÷ -3

Share -15 into 3 shares                    Take -15 and make groups of -3

Each share contains -5, so -15 ÷ 3 = -5                    There are 5 groups, so -15 ÷ -3 = 5

We have already seen when exploring multiplication that area models are not suited to working with negative values. However, a number line can allow us to access the second calculation, 15 ÷ -3.

Here we have the vectors for 15 and -3:

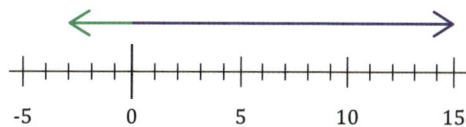

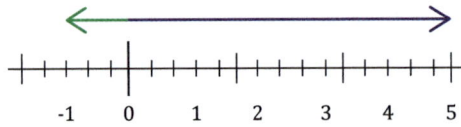

Comparing the two shows that 15 is to -3 as 5 is to -1, and also as -5 is to 1. Therefore 15 ÷ -3 = -5.

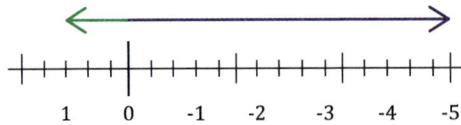

Of course, the representations that can capture all three of these are the ordered-pair graph and the proportion diagram – both of these representations appear below.

-15 ÷ 3 = -5

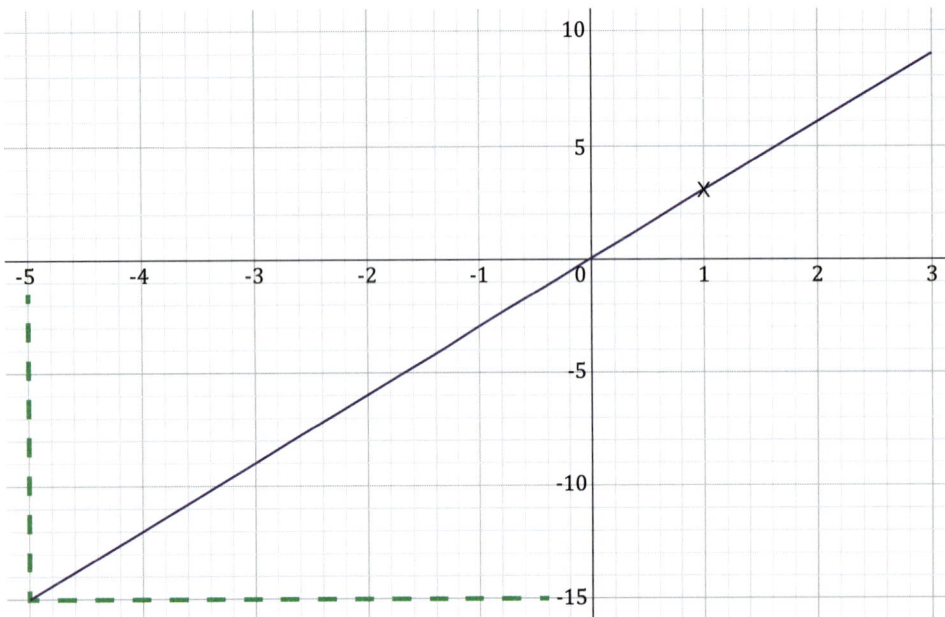

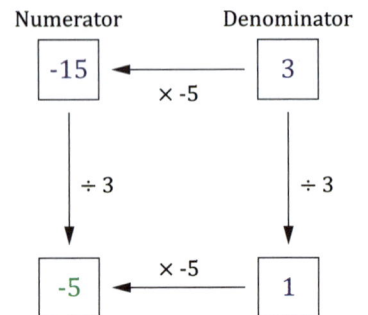

15 ÷ -3 = -5

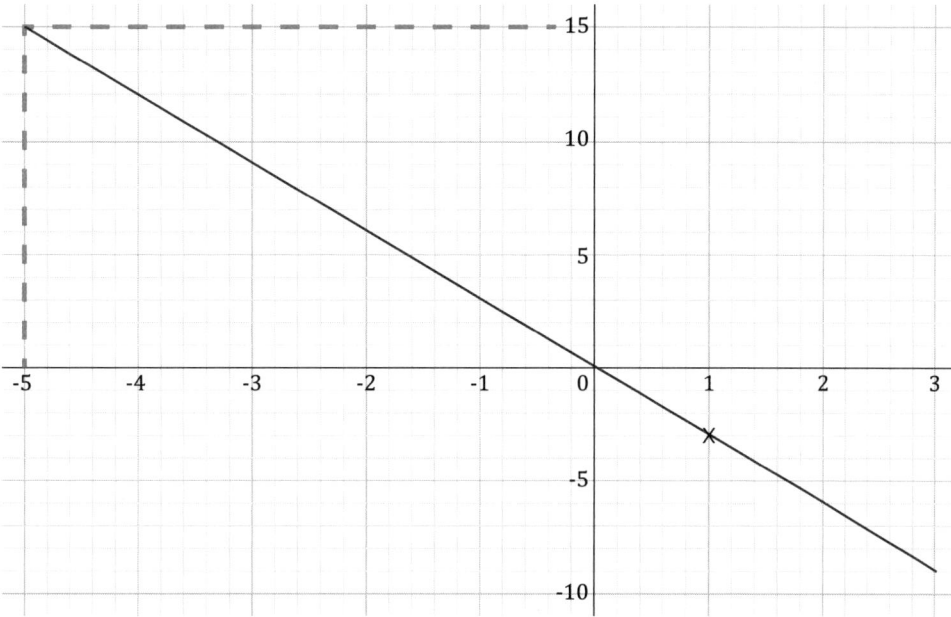

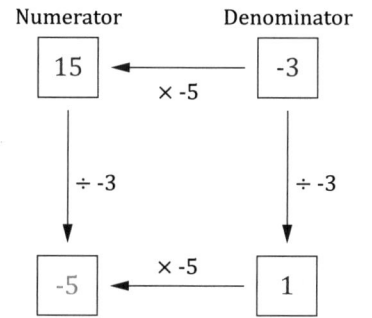

-15 ÷ -3 = 5

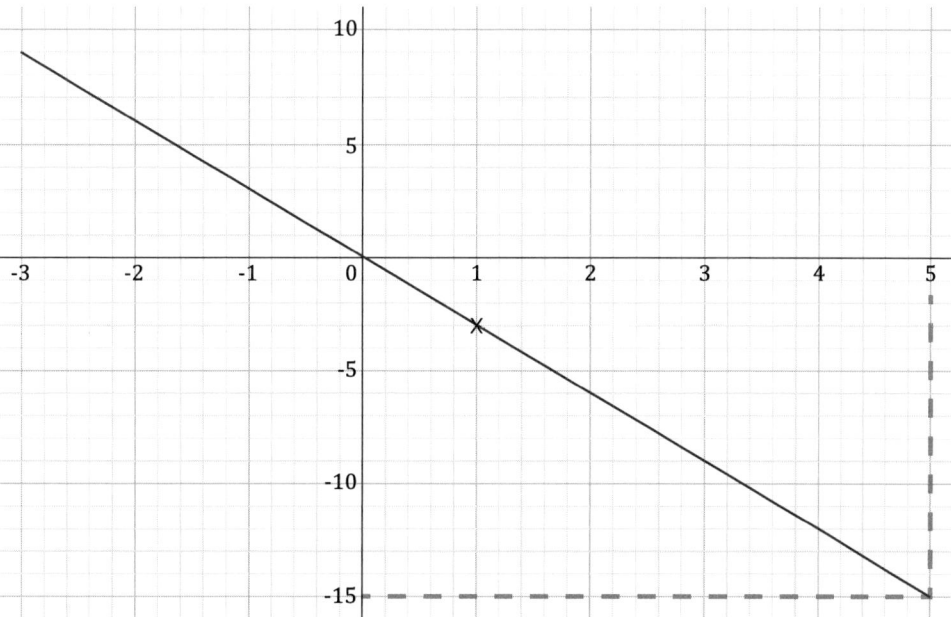

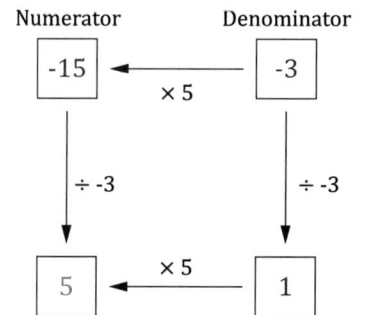

Having used our representations to explore addition, subtraction, multiplication and division with integers, and developed a deep understanding of these operations with our pupils, we have two operations left to examine – powers and roots.

# Chapter 5

# Powers and roots

There is a strong link between multiplication and **indices**, and so there will be some similarity in their representation and structure (as there was between addition and multiplication). There will also be some development, as powers are the next stage up on multiplication (in the same way that multiplication was on addition). Indeed, the first and most common interpretation of powers are as repeated multiplication:

$$3^5 = 3 \times 3 \times 3 \times 3 \times 3$$

The question, of course, is which (if any) of our interpretations of multiplication allow us to develop this idea? One representation that can help us to begin is the interpretation of increased dimension, particularly for smaller powers. Both of these are familiar representations of a single multiplication. The right-hand diagram will be an important representation of squaring when it comes to the development of algebra:

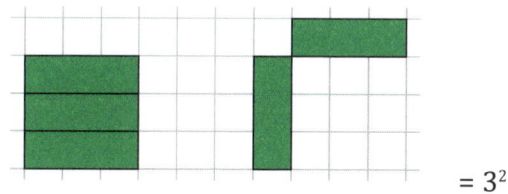

$$= 3^2$$

The next two representations take the dimension increase to the next stage – moving from two to three dimensions:

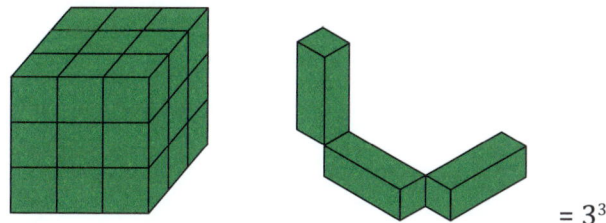

$$= 3^3$$

Obviously, the idea of increasing dimension becomes impossible to model at this point – we cannot visualise more than three spatial dimensions. Whilst these dimensions do exist in the realms of higher mathematics and physics (the Bosonic string theory of the universe suggests there are as many as 26 space-time dimensions[*]), our everyday experience of three dimensions limits our thinking. This is probably why this sort of work with powers is left until secondary school.

Interestingly, attempts have been made to create models of the fourth spatial dimension; in a similar way to our ability to draw three-dimensional effect diagrams on a two-dimensional (flat) surface, we can also create three-dimensional diagrams that aim to give a four-dimensional perspective. The most common image is that of a hypercube:

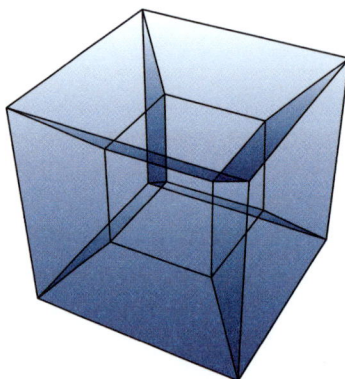

The hypercube represents the extension of a cube into the fourth dimension, in the same way that a cube can be seen as the extension of the square into three dimensions. The hypercube has even found its way into popular culture in the Marvel comics and films, where the alternative name for the hypercube, the Tesseract, is used for the Space Stone (one of six Infinity Stones that populate the Marvel universe).

I am not suggesting that we induct our pupils into the formal concepts of the mathematics of higher dimensions, but it may be useful to introduce pupils early on to the increasing dimension property of multiplication to give them a grounding in the geometric properties of powers. At the very least, this will give them a good foundation for why the power of 2 is referred to as 'squaring' and the power of 3 as 'cubing'.

An alternative approach for larger powers can be to complete the multiplication in stages. For example, $3^5$ can be performed as follows:

* D. Mason, The Physics of Everything: Understanding Superstring Theory, *Futurism* (10 September 2015). Available at: https://futurism.com/brane-science-complex-notions-of-superstring-theory/.

$3^2 =$  = 9    $3^3 =$  = 27

$3^4 =$  = 81

$3^5 =$  = 243

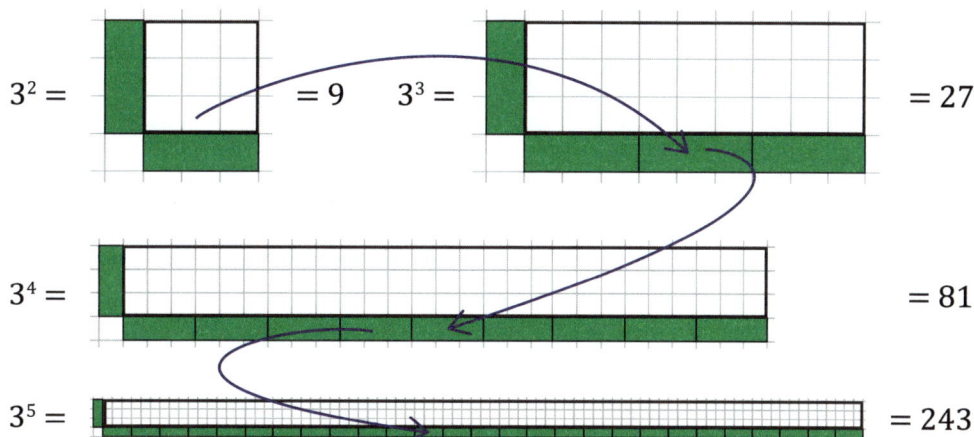

Whilst it seems a bit indirect to work these out in stages, it can be extremely valuable for pupils to understand how an area can be replaced with a length of corresponding value. They should be encouraged to see this process as a natural part of a repeated multiplication process. This sort of fluency supports the development of higher powers in algebra when increasing dimension cannot be visualised.

As well as the area interpretation of multiplication, it is also possible (at least to a point) to extend the idea of repeated addition to encompass small integer powers. The diagram below shows the first four powers of 3:

This form of geometric growth is a useful representation of powers. It links well to pupils' eventual work on geometric sequences as well as providing a link to the graph of an exponential function.

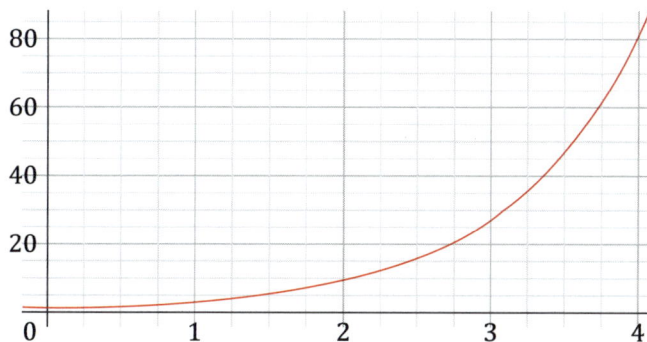

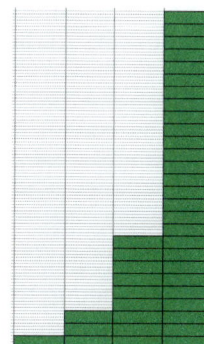

Unfortunately, these interpretations only apply with positive integer powers – we cannot multiply a number by itself anything other than a positive whole number of times. If we start to consider negative integer powers, for example $3^{-5}$, then we do not have a way of representing what is happening to 3 in this situation. We can, however, draw similarities to a representation that we are already familiar with for dealing with negative powers – place value counters.

We have already established that place value counters work with the different powers of 10:

Although there is nothing in the representation itself that would allow us to see that these are different powers of 10, the counters do at least give us a way of understanding these powers once we do know. For example, if we accept that these values are equivalent to:

Then it becomes relatively straightforward to see why $0.03 = 3 \times 10^{-2}$:

Standard index form uses this idea of multiplication as a change in counting unit (as we saw in Chapter 4), with the counting units being given in the largest power of 10.

However, there is no reason why we should limit this idea to powers of 10. We can use these counters to denote any powers sequence:

This begins to give substance to the idea of calculations in different bases, with binary arithmetic being the most commonly known beyond our own base 10 number system.

This doesn't mean that we cannot explain to pupils where negative powers come from, simply that we will struggle to model them using either concrete or pictorial approaches. The pattern below is a classic approach to justifying the link between fractions and negative integer powers:

$a^5 = a \times a \times a \times a \times a$
$a^4 = a \times a \times a \times a$
$a^3 = a \times a \times a$
$a^2 = a \times a$
$a^1 = a$
$a^0 = 1$
$a^{-1} = \frac{1}{a}$
$a^{-2} = \frac{1}{a^2}$

$\div a$ (repeated alongside each step)

In addition to negative integer powers, we also need to consider fractional powers. Again, there is no effective way to model these pictorially. For example, we know that $4^{\frac{1}{2}} = \sqrt{4}$, but there is nothing in our representations of powers that would make this clear. We can also prove that fractional powers are equivalent to roots – for example:

$$(a^{\frac{1}{2}})^2 = a^1 = a, \text{ but } (\sqrt{a})^2 = a, \text{ so } a^{\frac{1}{2}} = \sqrt{a}$$
$$(a^{\frac{1}{3}})^3 = a^1 = a, \text{ but } (\sqrt[3]{a})^3 = a \text{ so } a^{\frac{1}{3}} = \sqrt[3]{a} \text{ and so on.}$$

But this doesn't explain why the two should be equivalent. We can, however, bring some of our understanding of powers to bear on their inverse – roots.

A classic pupil misconception regarding square roots is that a number should be divided by itself. Ignoring for a moment the lack of understanding this shows about division (it is normally said in haste and easily corrected), we should sympathise with this misconception. Pupils often see the square as 'times a number by itself', so why wouldn't the opposite of this be 'divide a number by itself'? The key issue here is a poor grasp of the repeated multiplication aspect of powers.

One interpretation of multiplication is the repeated addition away from a start point of 0 (particularly in a vector representation). In a similar way, we can see powers as the repeated multiplication away from a start point. However, with powers the start point is not the additive identity of 0 but the multiplicative identity of 1. This start point of 1 is important in pupils' understanding of powers, in particular for roots, because if powers are repeated multiplication away from 1, then roots can be seen as the repeated division of a number back to 1.

This idea is strongly related to division as the repeated subtraction back to 0, also known as chunking. We can write this sort of calculation as follows, where it is important for each block to be completed with the same number:

$$\sqrt[5]{243} = 243 \div \square \div \square \div \square \div \square \div \square = 1$$

Whilst this interpretation of roots may be helpful for tying it to powers – or to circumvent the misconception about a number being divided by itself – it doesn't particularly help with calculation. The 'fill in the box' method encourages an approach by trial and improvement to finding the actual value of roots. Fortunately, there is a geometric interpretation of the square root and cube root – the inverse of the square and cube.

Consider the calculation $\sqrt{25}$. Using bars or similar this becomes, 'What is the length of a square containing 25 unit squares?' Pupils who don't know that $5^2 = 25$ may need to experiment with the bars before they hit on the correct answer, but the benefit here is they are able to investigate in a concrete rather than a purely abstract way. Eventually, the model the pupils form will perhaps look like the one below:

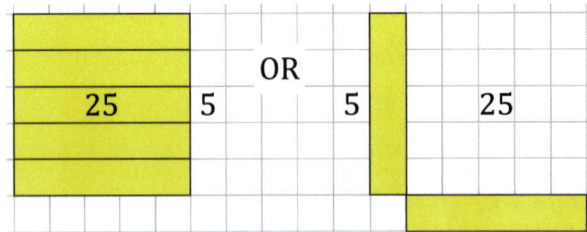

The calculation $\sqrt[3]{27}$ can be seen as, 'What is the length of a cube containing 27 unit cubes?' which eventually would produce a model like this:

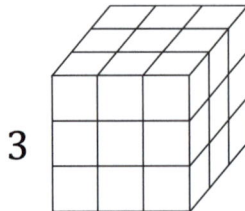

This is as far as an exploration of operations can go in terms of calculations applied to integers; to continue our exploration of the operations outlined in the previous three chapters, we will now consider the application of these representations to rational numbers.

# Chapter 6

# Operations with fractions and decimals

Pupils often find it difficult to understand and become fluent with calculations involving fractions and decimals, so focusing our teaching on representations and structures with which pupils are already comfortable and confident can be a useful strategy in bridging the gap to these calculations. This will begin around Year 4 and then develop throughout primary and secondary school.

An obvious extension to the addition and subtraction of decimals is the use of base ten blocks, with the larger cube standing for one whole:

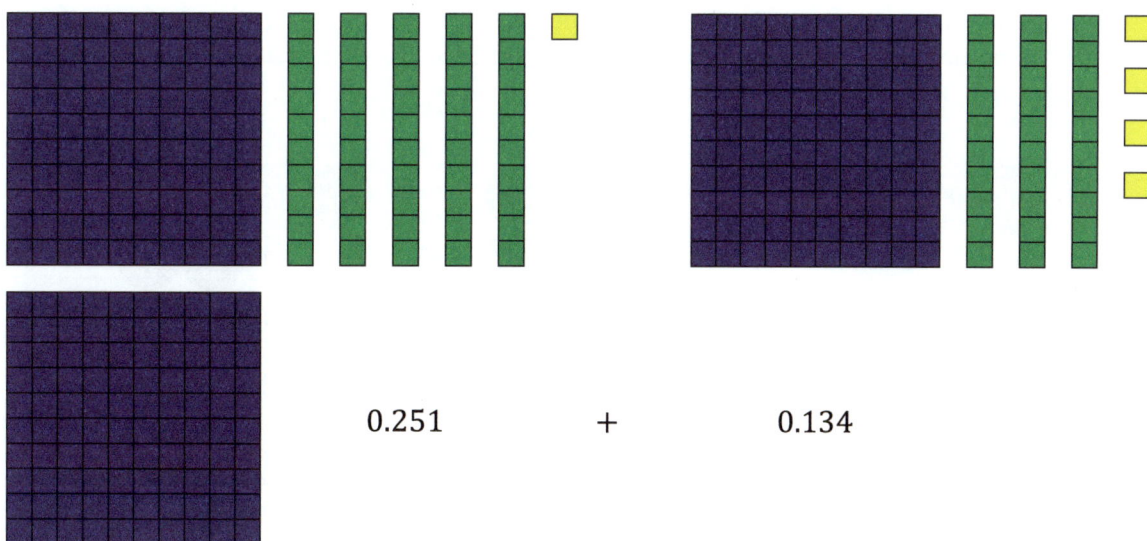

0.251          +          0.134

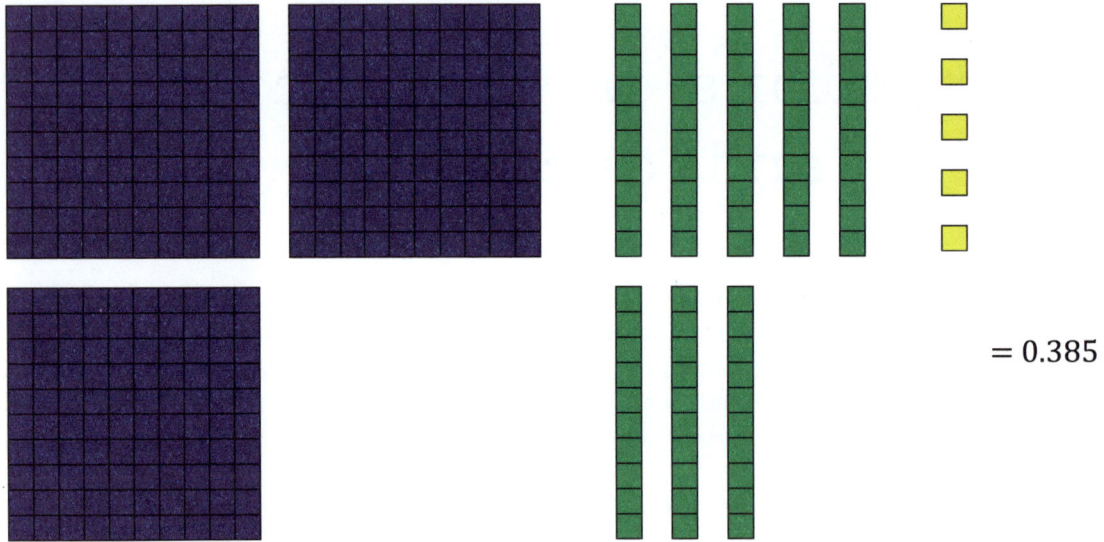

= 0.385

A similar approach can be applied using place value counters, which can be more flexible in allowing more places to be represented (provided pupils are secure with the concept of exchange – see Chapter 2):

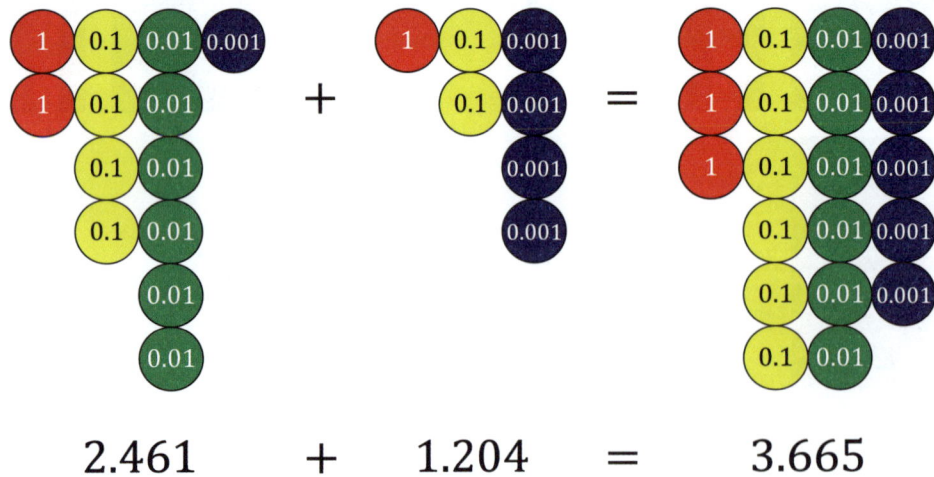

2.461    +    1.204    =    3.665

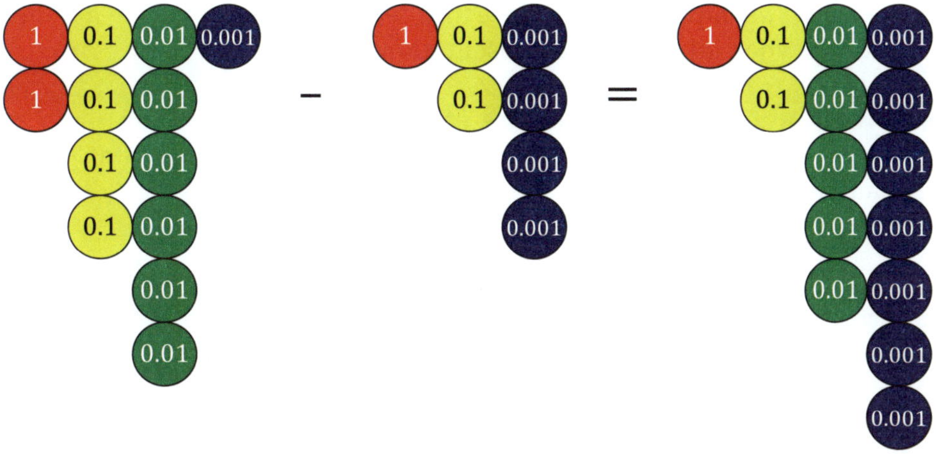

$$2.461 \quad - \quad 1.204 \quad = \quad 1.257$$

Likewise for the addition and subtraction of fractions, by assigning counters with suitable values:

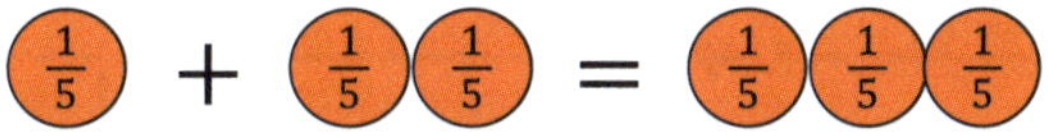

$$\frac{1}{5} \quad + \quad \frac{2}{5} \quad = \quad \frac{3}{5}$$

However, in order to extend this idea further to fractions with different denominators, pupils need to be comfortable with the idea of equivalent fractions and using exchange to secure 'like objects':

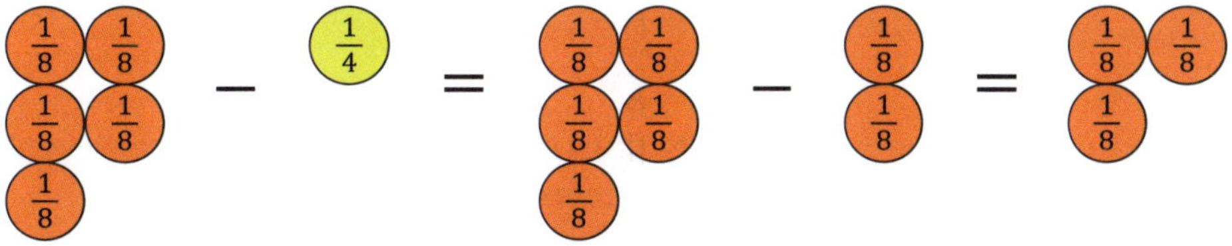

$$\frac{5}{8} \quad - \quad \frac{1}{4} \quad = \quad \frac{5}{8} \quad - \quad \frac{2}{8} \quad = \quad \frac{3}{8}$$

It is crucial that pupils understand that eighths and quarters are not 'like objects' and so an exchange is required, and that $\frac{1}{4}$ is equivalent and therefore exchangeable with

$\frac{2}{8}$. This is why it is so important to explore the idea of equivalence using number lines and bar models when introducing representations for fractions.

For those who prefer to reserve the use of counters for place value, or to see the exchange more naturally, the same calculation can be accomplished using bar models or Cuisenaire rods:

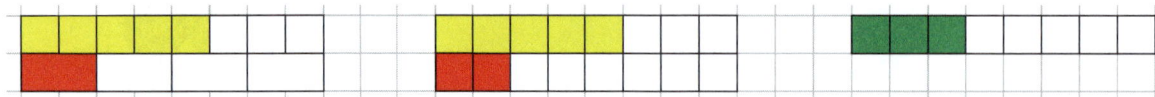

This is, of course, the difference interpretation of subtraction – the difference between $\frac{5}{8}$ and $\frac{1}{4}$ is $\frac{3}{8}$.

We can also use a similar idea with a number line, although this would mean either counting on for addition or counting back for subtraction:

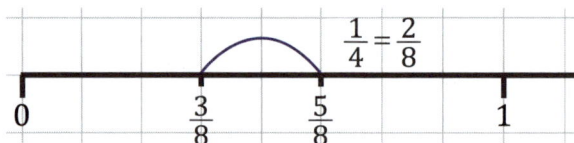

This shows either $\frac{3}{8} + \frac{1}{4} = \frac{5}{8}$ or $\frac{5}{8} - \frac{1}{4} = \frac{3}{8}$.

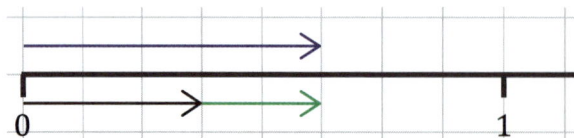

In the diagram above the same idea is illustrated using the vector representation, with the subtraction completed with the vectors head to head.

It is also possible to apply addition/subtraction as defined for the ordered-pair graph:

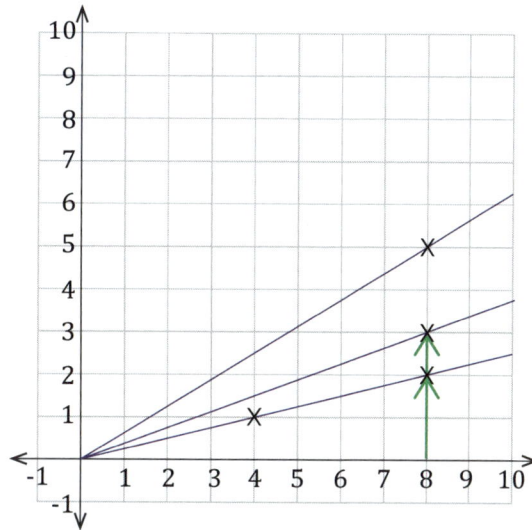

In this diagram $\frac{3}{8} + \frac{1}{4}$ is completed by drawing the line for $\frac{3}{8}$ and $\frac{1}{4}$ and combining their vertical distances at a point where their horizontal distance is the same. This is easiest to do where the horizontal distance is 8, as the vertical distances are both whole numbers (3 and 2 respectively). This gives the fraction $\frac{5}{8}$.

When we consider multiplication, the idea of repeated addition begins to cause difficulties. Providing that one of the numbers in the multiplication is an integer, repeated addition can still be used as a valid interpretation of the multiplication. For example, if multiplying 0.1 × 7 this is shown as:

$$\boxed{0.1}\;\boxed{0.1}\;\boxed{0.1}\;\boxed{0.1}\;\boxed{0.1}\;\boxed{0.1}\;\boxed{0.1} = 0.7$$

This could also be seen as the change of counting unit. The same would apply if we were multiplying a fraction by a whole number – for example, $\frac{2}{5} \times 3 = \frac{6}{5}$.

$$\tfrac{1}{5}\;\tfrac{1}{5}\qquad\tfrac{1}{5}\;\tfrac{1}{5}\qquad\tfrac{1}{5}\;\tfrac{1}{5}$$

However, if neither value in a multiplication calculation is an integer then the repeated addition interpretation of multiplication breaks down – for example, in the calculation $\frac{2}{5} \times \frac{1}{3}$ we cannot repeat $\frac{2}{5}$ one-thirds times, or vice versa.

The idea of changing the counting unit is still a useful interpretation though – indeed, it is probably one of the simplest ways to appreciate the link between $\frac{2}{5} \times \frac{1}{3}$ and $\frac{2}{5}$ of $\frac{1}{3}$. In this case, we consider the counting unit to be $\frac{1}{3}$ and rather than having, say, 7 of them, we have $\frac{2}{5}$ of a single $\frac{1}{3}$. In simple cases we can represent this using a bar model:

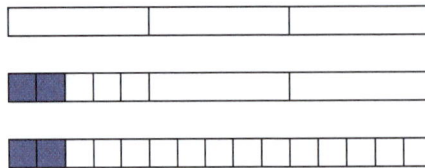

The first diagram shows the counting unit of thirds and the second shows having $\frac{2}{5}$ of $\frac{1}{3}$ (literally, $\frac{2}{5}$ of one of the thirds). However, because the pieces are different sizes, it is not possible in the second diagram to see precisely what fraction we have. For that we need to have the whole unit broken into equal sized parts. We do this in the third diagram and can see the result is $\frac{2}{15}$.

A number line can also be used to show a similar result, particularly using vector notation:

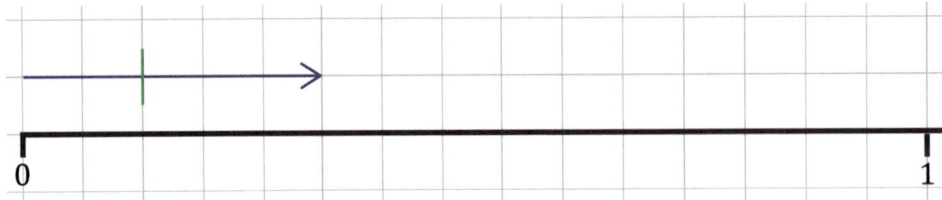

In this diagram the blue arrow can be seen as $\frac{1}{3}$ (which is our counting unit) and the green line shows $\frac{2}{5}$ of that $\frac{1}{3}$. Because of the carefully chosen number line, in particular the use of 15 squares for the distance from 0 to 1, it is possible to see that this represents the fraction $\frac{2}{15}$.

The obvious problem with this representation, and to a lesser extent with the previous bar models, is that it is too far removed from our experience of multiplication. The idea of breaking down a counting unit is not one that occurs naturally in our previous use of the interpretation. Indeed, when using the number line, it is possible to argue that we would need to know the answer to the multiplication before we started to represent it (how else would we know that 15 squares were required?). However, our interpretation of multiplication as an increased dimension (leading to the area model of multiplication) can allow a more natural view of this multiplication. Consider again the example of $\frac{2}{5} \times \frac{1}{3}$ seen as an increase in dimension:

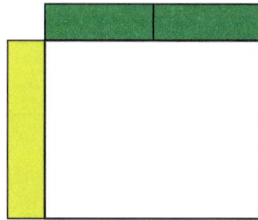

Pupils familiar with using Cuisenaire rods to represent different fractions (see Chapter 2) will know that in order to represent both $\frac{1}{3}$ and $\frac{1}{5}$ we need to consider a unit to be 15. This allows the yellow bar to represent $\frac{1}{3}$ and a green bar to represent $\frac{1}{5}$.

The big question, of course, is what value does this area represent? To answer this, we need to consider it as part of a whole unit area:

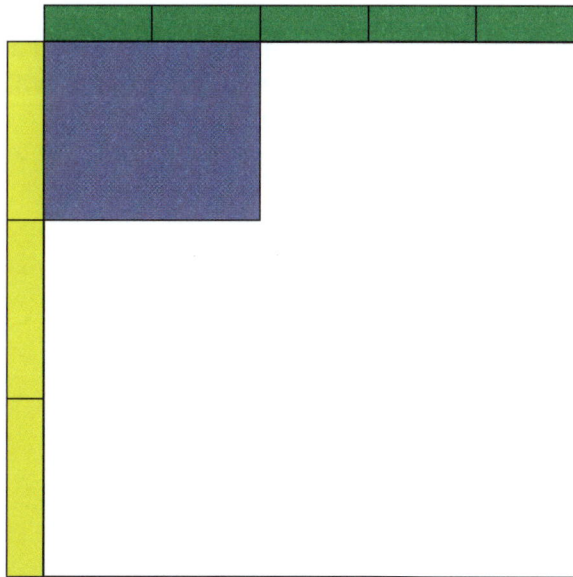

The diagram above shows the area (now shaded blue) we want as part of the larger unit area. This puts us in a position to start to ask what fraction the blue area represents, as we can compare it to one whole. In order to actually evaluate the fraction, however, we will need to break up this unit area into equal sized parts:

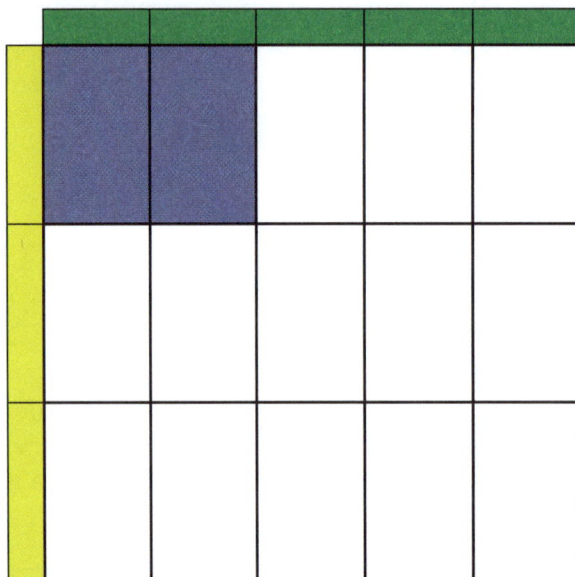

This second diagram allows us to see that the result of multiplying $\frac{2}{5} \times \frac{1}{3} = \frac{2}{15}$.

Some people may argue that this is no more natural than the bar model or number line discussed above, but I would disagree. I admit that pupils will probably not come to this representation instinctively, but I would maintain that a pupil who properly understands the idea of a fraction as part of a unit whole, and who properly understands the area model for multiplication, should be able to comprehend this as a logical extension of these ideas.

The other benefit of this model for multiplication is that it can be used for virtually any fractional multiplication:

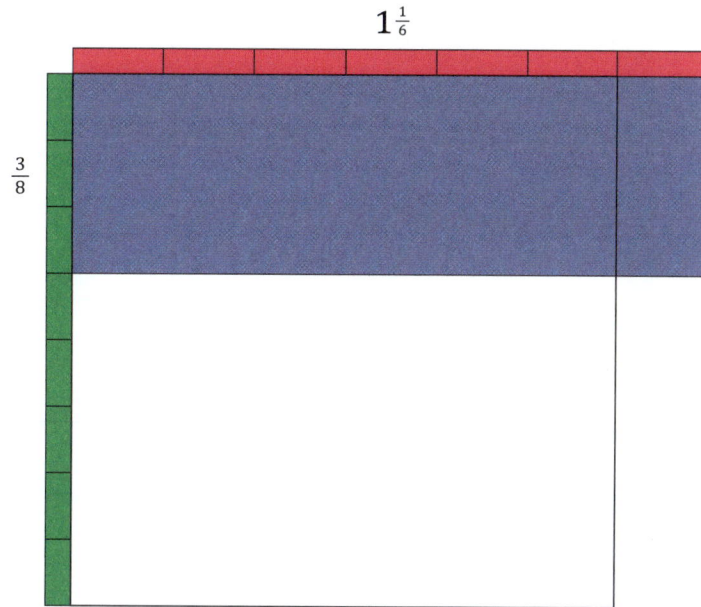

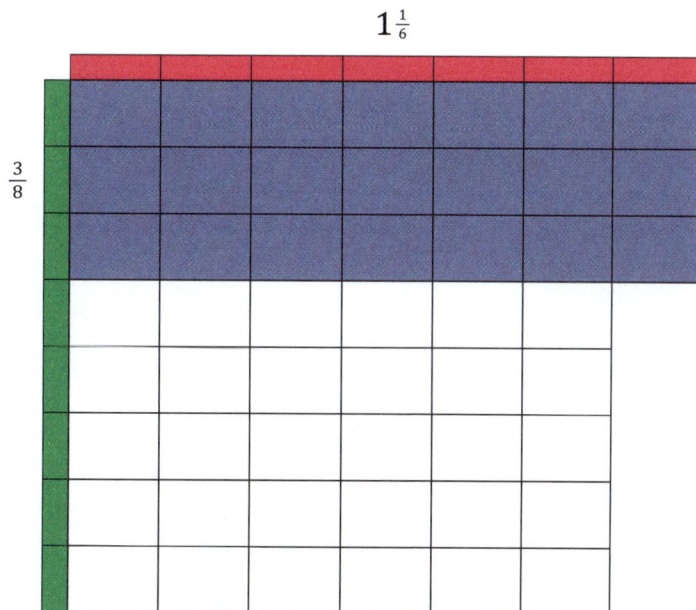

$$1\tfrac{1}{6}$$

$$\tfrac{3}{8}$$

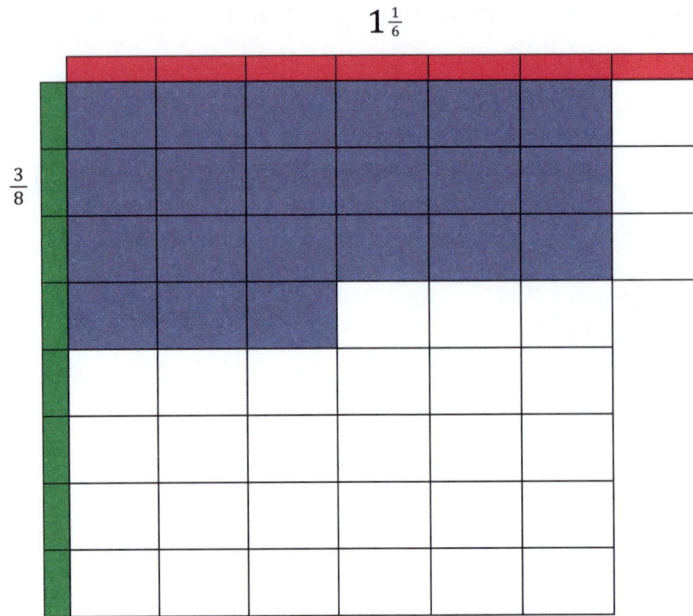

This diagram shows that $1\tfrac{1}{6} \times \tfrac{3}{8} = \tfrac{21}{48}$.

The same approach can be used to model the multiplication of two decimal values – for example, $0.4 \times 0.7 = 0.28$:

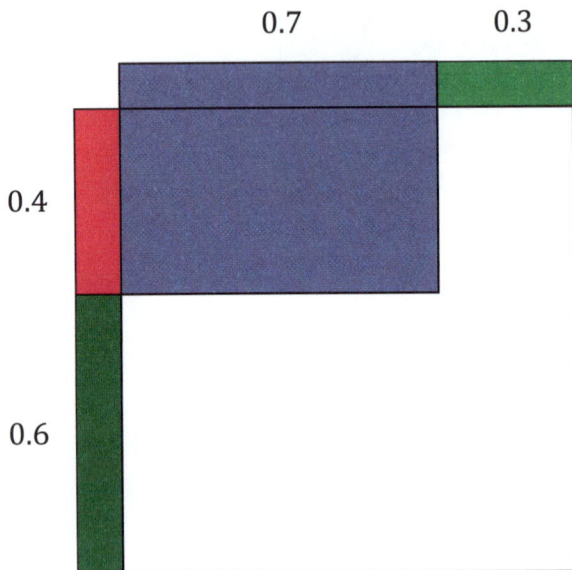

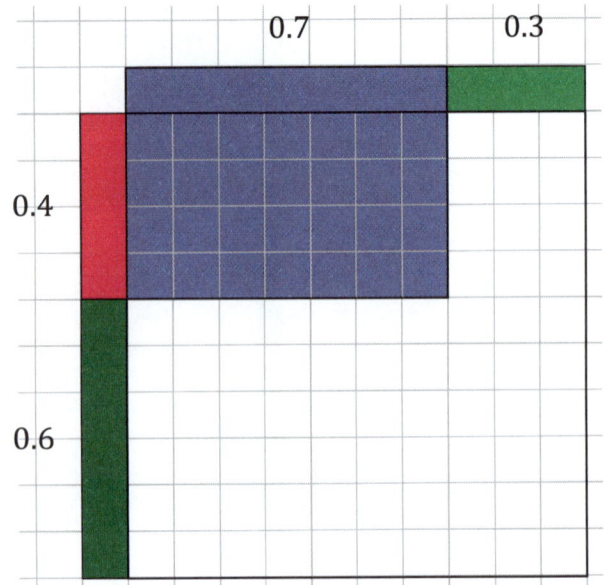

A similar thing happens when we come to division. If the divisor is a whole number, then sharing can still be considered as a valid interpretation of division – often with an exchange required. For example, this diagram shows the calculation $0.28 \div 7 = 0.04$:

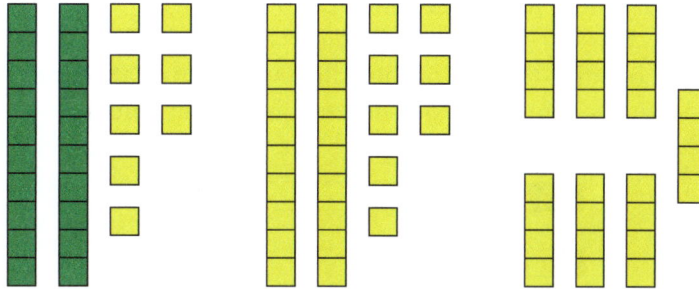

Alternatively, this is how the same calculation looks using place value counters:

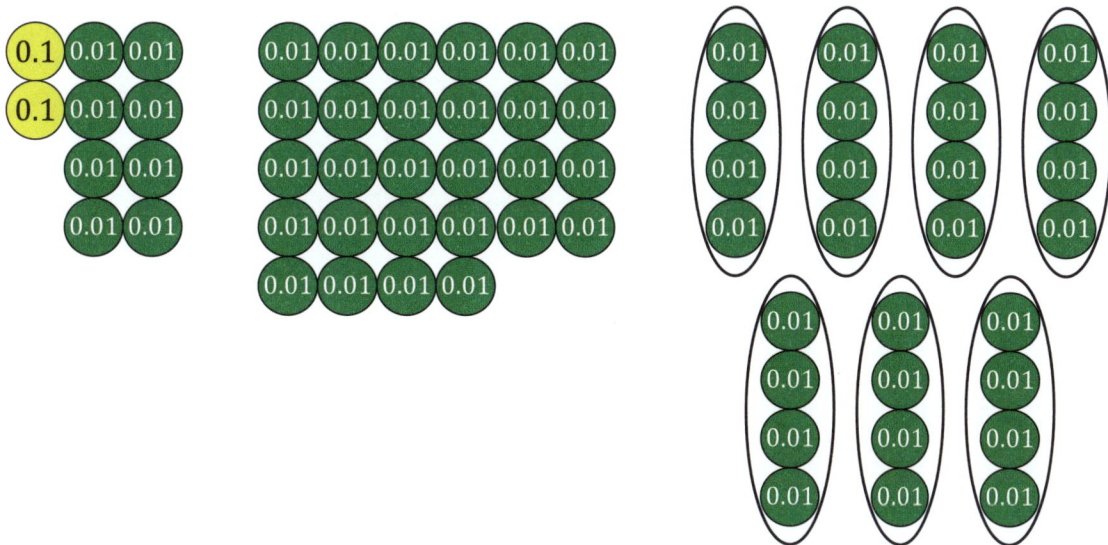

A similar approach can be taken to dividing a fraction by a whole number – in the example below, we are calculating $\frac{6}{7} \div 3$:

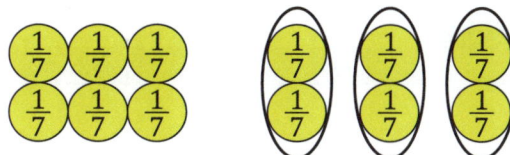

This works, at least in part, because 6 will divide by 3, so any fractional dividend with a numerator that is a multiple of the divisor will allow groupings like those shown at the foot of page 121. However, if we try to apply the same idea to $\frac{1}{8} \div 2$ it becomes more difficult. We can get around the problem by exchanging $\frac{1}{8}$ for $\frac{2}{16}$, but this seems to trivialise the division somewhat – and pupils who can make this leap for themselves hardly need a model for the division.

Instead, we might consider the use of the splitting interpretation of division for continuous number models, which can be shown using a bar model:

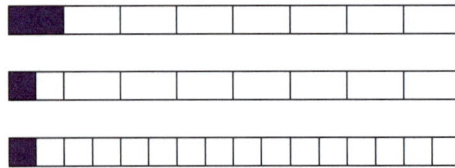

In the first diagram we see $\frac{1}{8}$, and in the second diagram we see this split into two pieces, $\frac{1}{8} \div 2$. Just as in the fraction multiplication (which provides a strong indication that division and fraction multiplication are the same), in order to properly evaluate the fraction we need all the pieces to be the same size, so we split each of the others to show that the fraction is $\frac{1}{16}$.

The same idea appears in the number line below:

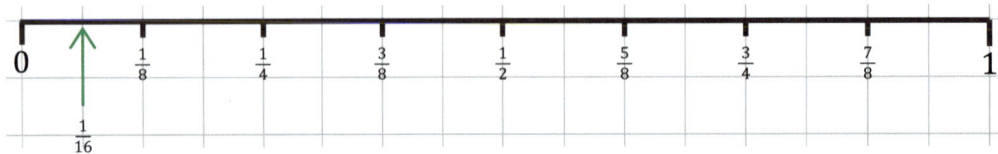

Earlier we saw that $\frac{6}{7}$ into three shares gives $\frac{2}{7}$ per share. Switch this around, though, and the idea of sharing breaks down: we cannot have $\frac{6}{7}$ of a share. The idea of splitting also becomes more difficult to model. Instead, the best way to interpret $3 \div \frac{6}{7}$ is to use a multiplicative comparison, which we can see below using a bar model or Cuisenaire rods:

We have used the '7' bar to represent one whole and the green bar to represent the fraction $\frac{6}{7}$. What we can see by looking at the grid is that $\frac{6}{7}$ is to 3 as 6 is to 21, which is as 2 is to 7, which is as 1 is to $3\frac{1}{2}$. The full progression can be seen below:

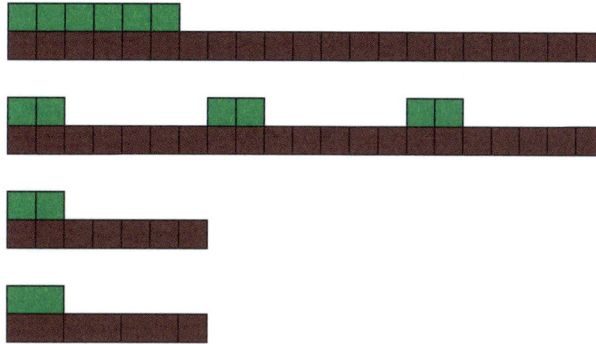

This sort of comparison can be used for purely fractional division – for example, $\frac{1}{3} \div \frac{2}{5}$:

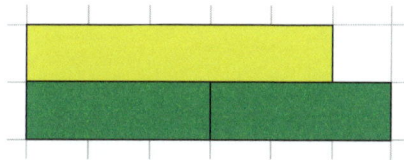

In this diagram the yellow bar represents $\frac{1}{3}$ and the green bar represents $\frac{1}{5}$. This shows that $\frac{2}{5}$ is to $\frac{1}{3}$ as 6 is to 5, or as 1 is to $\frac{5}{6}$.

An excellent representation to capture this sort of manipulation of comparison is the proportion diagram. Here is the same calculation of $\frac{1}{3} \div \frac{2}{5}$:

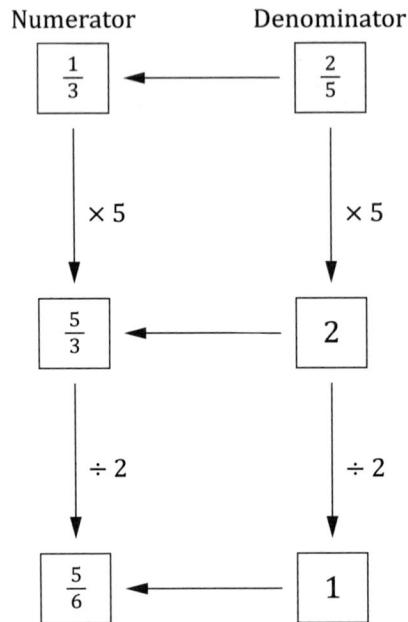

This reasoning here is slightly different to that used above, but the underlying idea of multiplicative comparison remains the same. In this case, the comparison is that $\frac{2}{5}$ is to $\frac{1}{3}$ as 2 is to $\frac{5}{3}$, or as $\frac{5}{6}$ is to 1.

One bonus of this representation is that it leads quite nicely into the idea of multiplication by a reciprocal. We can see on the left of the diagram above that the elements of the reciprocal of $\frac{2}{5}$ are present (i.e. the multiplication by 5 and the division by 2). It is then a short step to the diagram below:

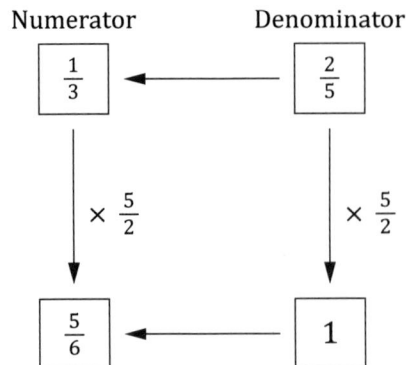

The use of a decimal divisor can be handled in a very similar way – for example, $1.5 \div 0.8$:

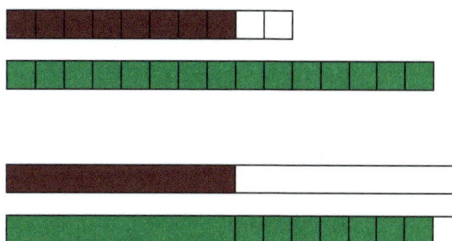

In this diagram 0.8 compares to 1.5 as 8 compares to 15, and that 8 compares to 15 as 1 compares to $1\frac{7}{8}$.

Alternatively, we can use the proportion diagram to show the same comparison:

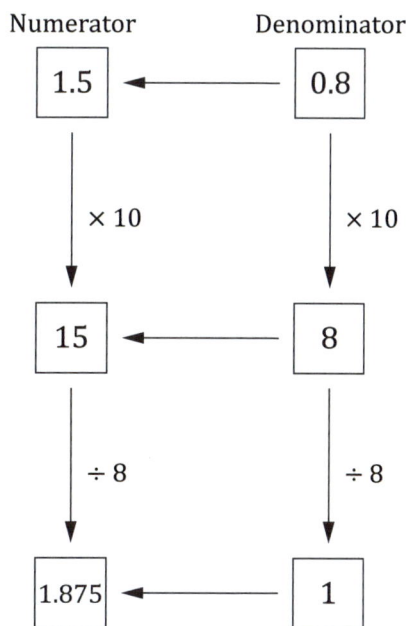

When it comes to powers and roots, you will recall that many of our representations struggled to accommodate higher powers and roots. The area model is the most successful, particularly with repeated applications for higher powers. The same is true for fractions, so if we are attempting to model $\left(\frac{3}{5}\right)^2$ we might have a diagram that looks a little like this:

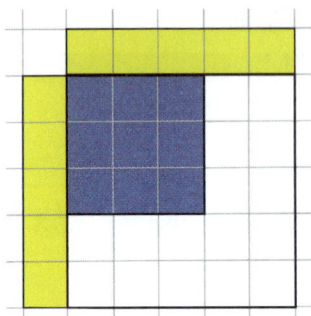

$$\left(\frac{3}{5}\right)^2 = \frac{9}{25}$$

If we want to go on to calculate higher powers – for example, $\left(\frac{3}{5}\right)^3$ – we would take this result of $\frac{9}{25}$ and multiply it again by $\frac{3}{5}$. This is probably preferable to a three-dimensional interpretation at this point, which might be difficult for pupils to understand (I include it below for the sake of completeness only).

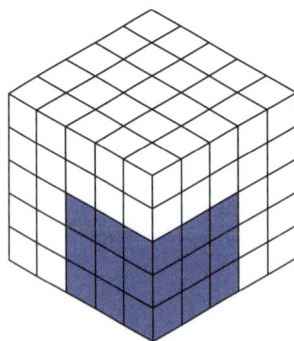

$$\left(\frac{3}{5}\right)^3 = \frac{27}{125}$$

We would hope that by the time our pupils have got to the point where they are apply-ing higher powers or roots to a fraction, then the work we have done in developing their understanding of powers and fractions means they will have moved beyond the need for modelling, although still understanding the repeated multiplication and geometrical interpretations.

Now that we have successfully modelled our operations across all rational numbers and have a good understanding of the concepts and interpretations underpinning integers, fractions, addition, subtraction, multiplication, division, powers and roots, we turn our attention to the laws that govern our arithmetic.

# Chapter 7
# Laws of arithmetic

The concepts of associativity, commutativity and distributivity are important in the study of mathematics and ones that pupils should understand when working with numbers, with a view to using them again when they move on to higher algebra. The representations for numbers and operations can be used to ensure that pupils understand why these laws are true and help them to recognise how and when these laws can be applied (as well as when they cannot).

We start by looking at associativity, which along with commutativity is introduced as early as Year 2 in the English national curriculum.

## Associativity

The associative law applies to addition and multiplication. In algebra, it is often written as A + (B + C) = (A + B) + C in the case of addition or A(BC) = (AB)C in the case of multiplication. The first of these can be depicted using many of our representations.

### Addition

We will first explore the associativity of addition with counters.

3 + (5 + 2) = (3 + 5) + 2

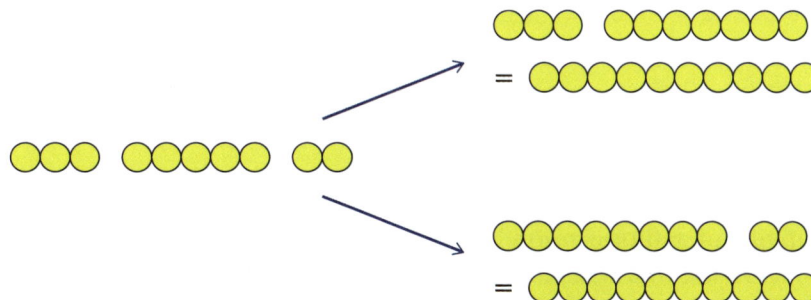

A similar approach can be used with bar models or Cuisenaire rods; the associativity emerges in the order in which they are combined in both this case and with counters.

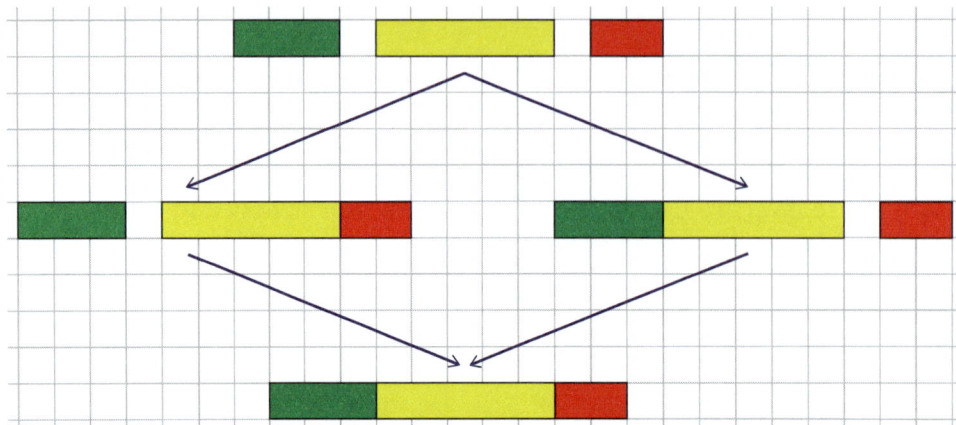

Associativity can be seen on a number line with either steps or vectors. In the diagrams below, the order of the calculation changes: the parts inside the bracket are completed first (in green), followed by the operation outside the brackets (in blue).

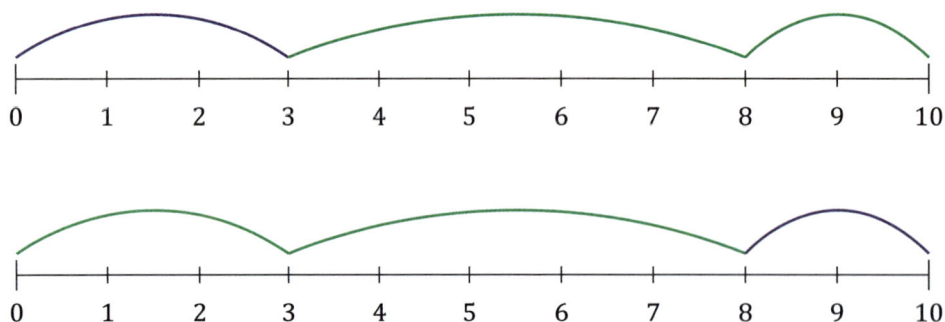

# Multiplication

The associativity of multiplication can be seen using the same representations. A good way of showing this with counters is to form an array and then use the idea of repeated addition of the arrays. However, it is important that pupils are comfortable with multiplication both as an array and as repeated addition.

$3 \times (5 \times 2) = (3 \times 5) \times 2$

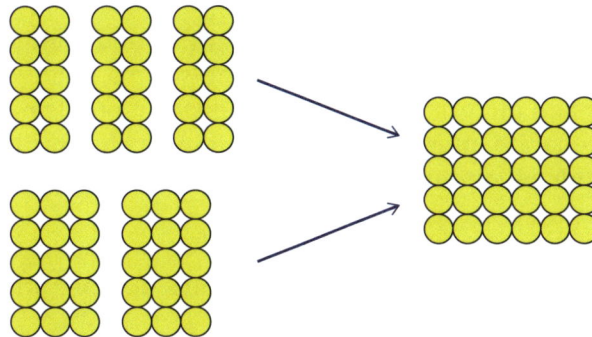

In the upper diagram we have a 5 × 2 array (or a 2 × 5 array, depending on how the arrays are visualised) repeated three times, combining to create a larger array of all 30 counters. In the lower diagram we have a 3 × 5 array (or 5 × 3 array) repeated twice, which results in the same array of 30 counters.

A similar approach can be taken with bar models/Cuisenaire rods, using a combination of area and repeat:

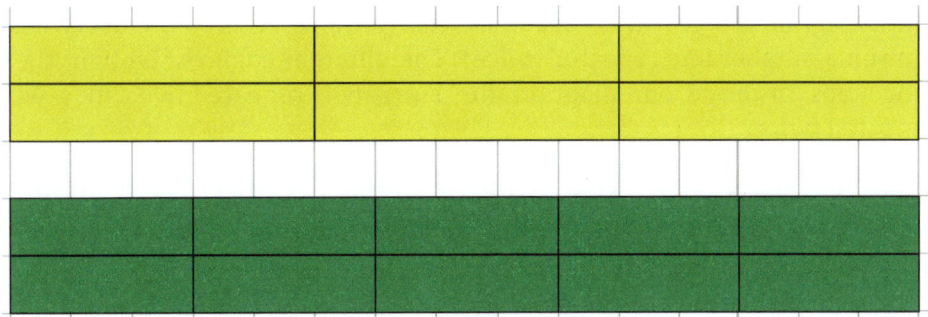

In the upper diagram there are two '5' bars combined to form an array which is repeated horizontally three times. In the lower diagram a '3' bar is repeated five times in a line, and two of these are combined to form an array. In both cases the area of the array is identical and shows the same result.

It is also possible to show this associativity using the idea of multiplication as repeated addition, although the lines of counters/bars tend to get prohibitively long. In order to show associativity using the idea of multiplication as increasing dimension, we would need to form a three-dimensional cuboid. This is not easy to show visually but it can be accomplished using Cuisenaire rods as a concrete representation or by stacking counters.

The combination of multiplication as repeated addition and multiplication as increasing dimension means that associativity can be shown in a relatively compact format using both concrete and pictorial approaches. However, pupils must be confident in juggling these two separate interpretations simultaneously. This needs to be built up slowly, allowing pupils plenty of opportunities to manipulate the bars and become comfortable with the concrete manipulation.

Associativity of multiplication can also be shown on a number line:

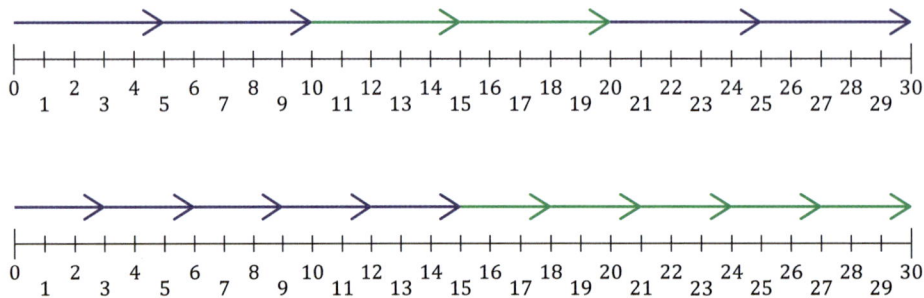

In the first diagram a '5' arrow is repeated twice (although this could just as easily be five steps on a number line repeated twice). The different colours highlight the three repeating steps. In the second diagram the '3' arrow is repeated five times, which is then repeated twice.

The other representations we have explored do not really add anything to this. It is possible to show similar images with base ten blocks, but it is impractical with ordered-pair graphs or proportion diagrams.

## Subtraction

When teaching pupils about the associativity of addition and multiplication, it is important for them to understand that subtraction and division are not associative. This is a common misconception which can occur when pupils begin to learn about associativity in Year 2 (or even prior to this). A suitable representation and structure can help to support pupils in securing this understanding.

$5 - (3 - 2) \neq (5 - 3) - 2$

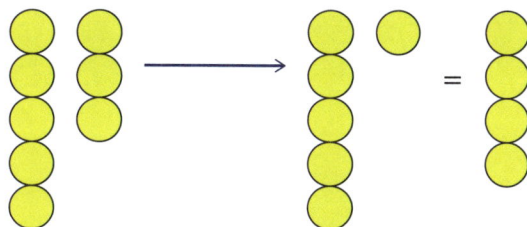

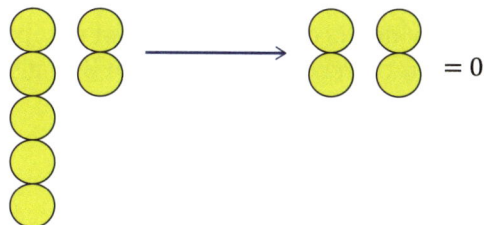

This approach relies on pupils using two separate interpretations of subtraction – namely, the physical act of taking away and a comparison of difference. In the first diagram above we have 5 compared to 3, and then we physically take away 2 from the 3, leaving the comparison between 5 and 1. This gives 4 as the result of the subtraction.

In the second diagram above we have 5 compared to 2, and then we physically take away 3 from the 5, leaving a comparison between 2 and 2, and therefore an answer of 0. This shows that the result is not the same, and so the subtraction is not associative. The same result can be seen using comparisons but only when presented in the correct order:

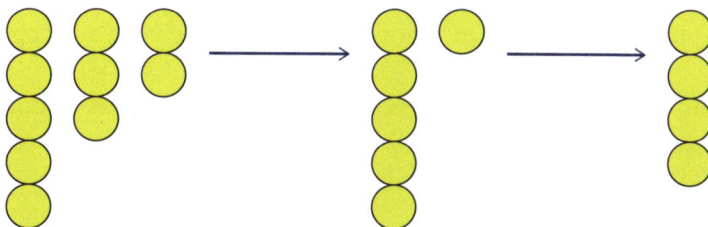

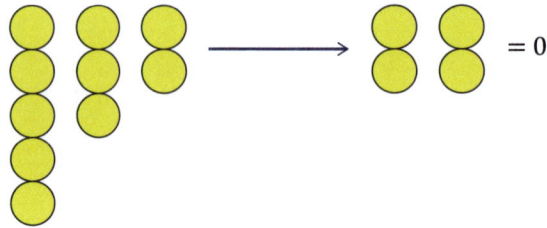

In the first diagram we see the comparison between 5, 3 and 2, with the comparison between 3 and 2 completed first and the difference being 1. This is then followed by the comparison between 5 and 1, giving the result of 4. In the second diagram we see the same starting comparison, which is completed by first comparing the 5 and the 3, resulting in a difference of 2, and then comparing 2 with 2 to give 0.

A similar approach can be used with bars or Cuisenaire rods, again examining the differences in the correct order:

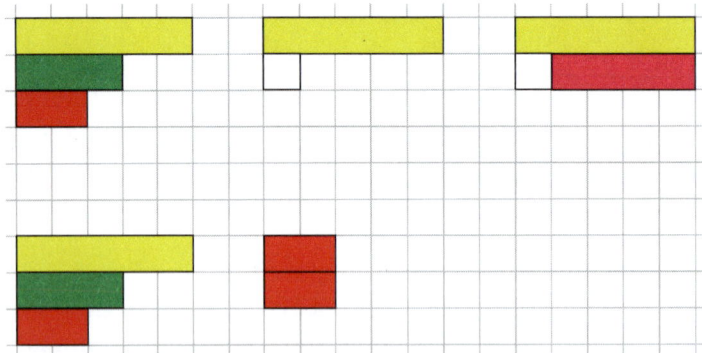

Here we see the '5' bar, '3' bar and '2' bar arranged to find the difference. In the upper diagram the difference between 3 and 2 is found first, which is 1. The difference between this '1' bar and the '5' bar is now found, with the result being 4.

In the lower diagram the difference between the '5' bar and the '3' bar is found first, which is 2. The difference between this '2' bar and the other '2' bar is then found, with the result being 0.

It is harder to use steps on a number line to show that subtraction is not associative in a single diagram, because the number line does not allow the order of steps in the subtraction to be specified. However, vector arrows on a number line work in a similar way to Cuisenaire rods:

In the diagrams below, 5, 3 and 2 are compared to each other. The first comparison completed is 3 and 2, which has a difference of 1. The difference can then be found between 5 and 1, with the result of 4.

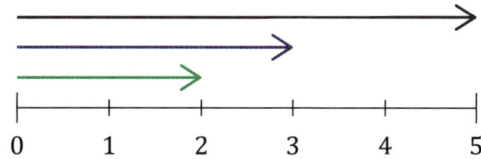

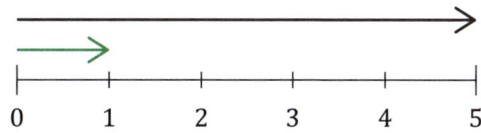

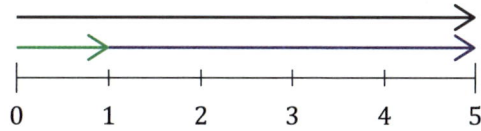

In the two diagrams that follow we can see the same starting comparison, but now the first comparison completed is 5 with 3, resulting in 2. The difference between the two is, of course, 0.

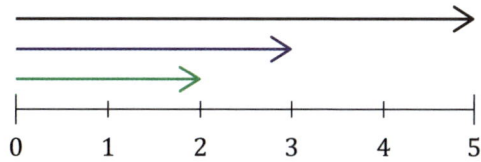

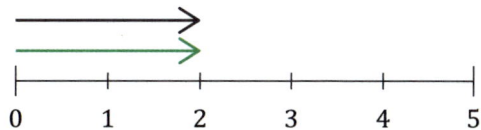

## Division

The fact that division is not associative is a bit trickier to represent, but it can be done using the same sort of multiplicative comparison that we saw earlier when exploring division.

$$12 \div (4 \div 2) \neq (12 \div 4) \div 2$$

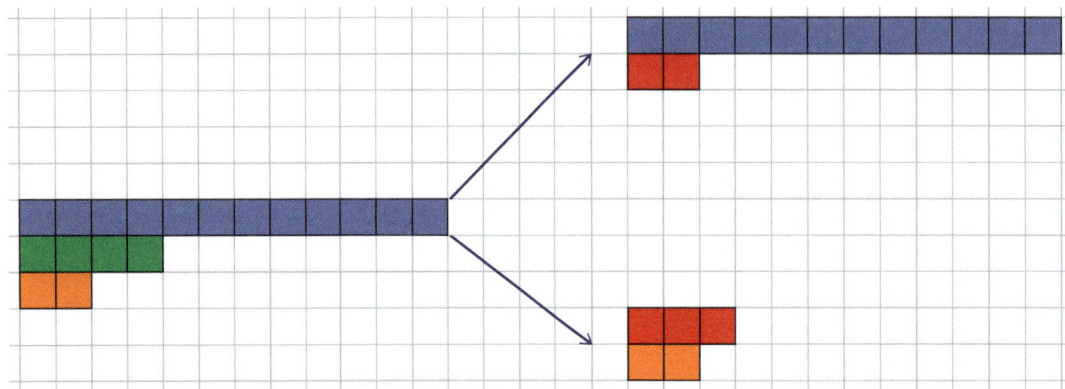

In this diagram we start with the comparison of 12, 4 and 2. By following the top arrow, the comparison of 4 and 2 is done first, resulting in 2. Then the comparison of 12 with 2 is completed, which results in 6. By following the bottom arrow, the comparison between 12 and 4 is done first, resulting in 3. Then the comparison can be completed between 3 and 2, which is $1\frac{1}{2}$. This shows clearly that the division is not associative.

The same comparison can be completed with vectors on a number line:

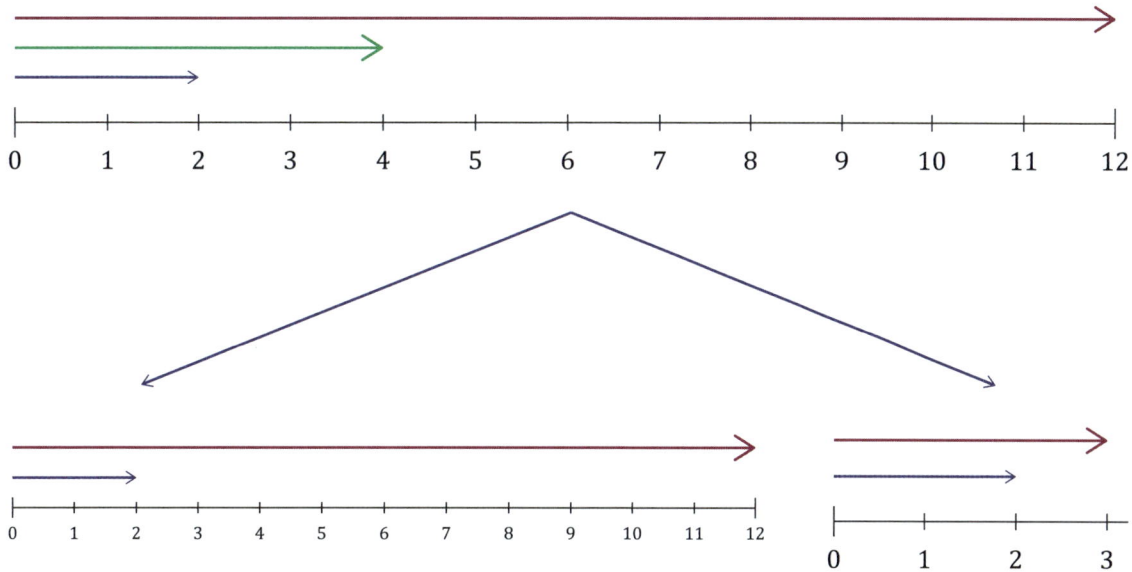

In the left-hand diagram the comparison has been completed first between 4 and 2, leaving 2. Then we can compare 12 and 2, which gives 6. In the right-hand diagram the comparison is between 12 and 4, resulting in 3. Then we compare 3 to 2, which is $1\frac{1}{2}$.

An interesting point to consider here is how to teach these laws in relation to the correct order of operations. Clearly, pupils will need an understanding of the role that brackets play in calculation, so it may be that you might make the decision to teach the order of operations before the laws of arithmetic. I would urge caution for two reasons:

1   Brackets are not in and of themselves an operation. Many diagrams or rules (such as BIDMAS) include brackets, but I believe this is a mistake. Brackets are used in calculations to clarify or change the natural order of the calculation, so keeping this separate from the operations themselves can be useful for pupil understanding.

2   The correct order of operations builds on the laws of arithmetic. As we will see later in this chapter, a grasp of associativity and commutativity can be crucial in developing a complete understanding of the correct order of operations, and why operations like multiplication and division are completed before addition and subtractions and why addition and subtraction can be done in either order.

For these reasons, I would advocate teaching the role of brackets separately to the correct order of operations. I would advise covering this topic before teaching the laws of arithmetic and leave the correct order of operations for later (perhaps even much later to allow for some spaced retrieval practice*). At the very least, pupils need to have an understanding of the role of brackets before they can understand associativity.

Now we have examined associativity, we will turn our attention to the next law of arithmetic: commutativity.

# Commutativity

In algebra, the commutative law is often written as A + B = B + A for addition and AB = BA for multiplication. Many of the representations we have explored so far can be used to explain and exemplify commutativity or allow pupils to explore the concept. We begin with the commutativity of addition.

## Addition

3 + 2 = 2 + 3

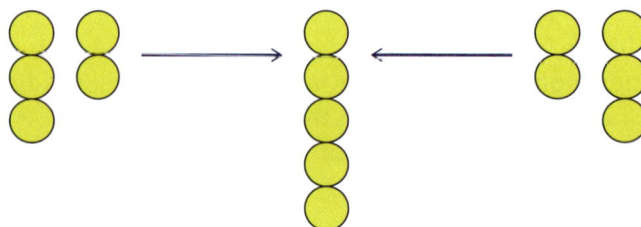

In this diagram the counters show that, regardless of the order, the result of the addition is the same. We could model this for our pupils or ask them to demonstrate this using counters.

Base ten blocks or base ten counters confirm that this remains true with larger numbers.

* Spaced retrieval practice is when practice of a process of skill, or recall of an idea, is spread out over time. It is linked to gains in long-term memory and learning. See Y. Weinstein and M. Smith, Learn How to Study Using … Spaced Practice, *Learning Scientists* [blog] (21 July 2016). Available at: http://www.learningscientists.org/blog/2016/7/21-1.

123 + 64 = 64 + 123

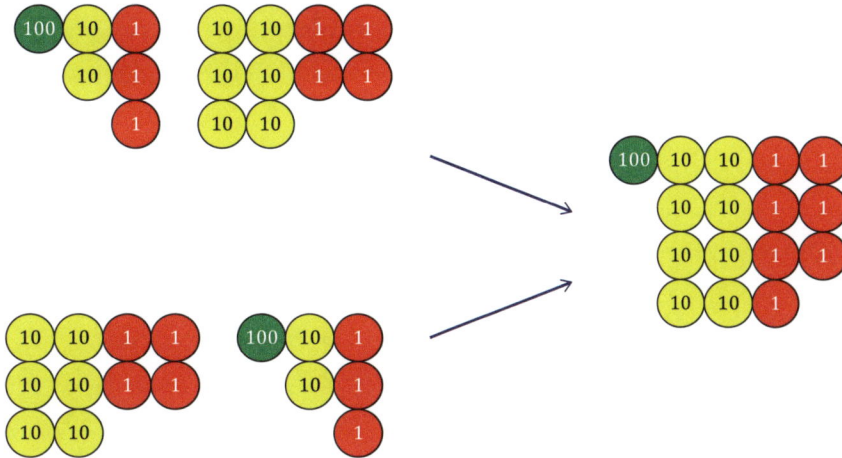

Commutativity of addition can be shown using a continuous representation of number. In the diagrams below this is shown using bar models and number lines.

3 + 2 = 2 + 3

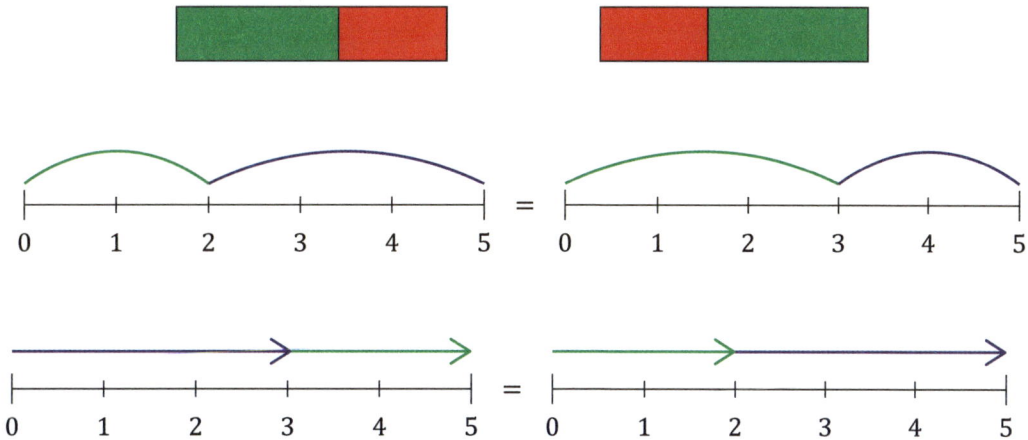

Commutativity of addition can also be demonstrated with tallies, although by this point we have firmly left tallies behind when it comes to operating on numbers.

It is, however, worth revisiting the ordered-pair graph and proportion diagrams:

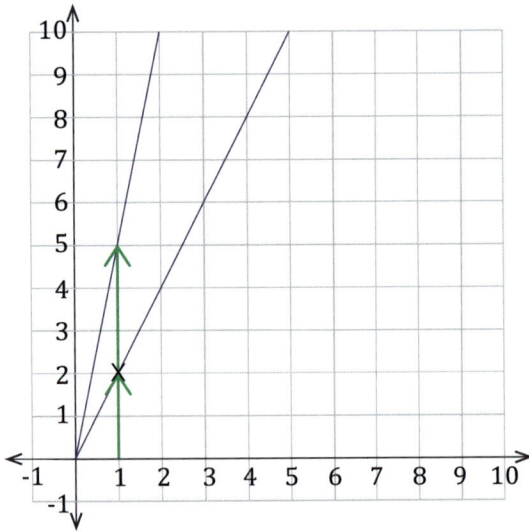

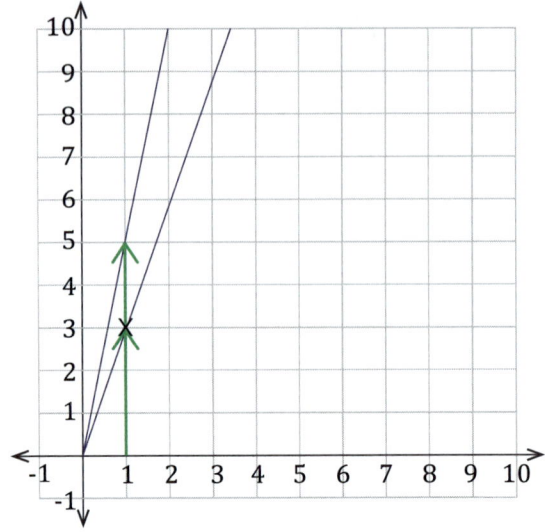

| Numerator | Denominator | | Numerator | Denominator |
|:---:|:---:|:---:|:---:|:---:|
| 3 | 1 | | 2 | 1 |
| + | | | + | |
| 2 | 1 | | 3 | 1 |
| = | | | = | |
| 5 | 1 | | 5 | 1 |

These don't really add anything to the concept (no pun intended!), but I find that it is always worth coming back to different representations where possible to reinforce how they work.

With the concept of commutativity of addition well established, we can look at the commutativity of multiplication.

## Multiplication

Multiple representations are available to explore or exemplify the concept:

3 × 4 = 4 × 3

This is often demonstrated using an array, as in the diagram above, with the commutativity shown by the fact that the array can be rotated:

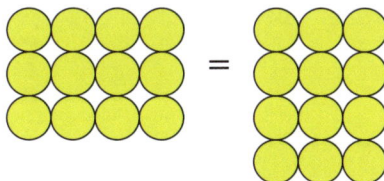

This, of course, leads to the full area model for multiplication (multiplication by increased dimension):

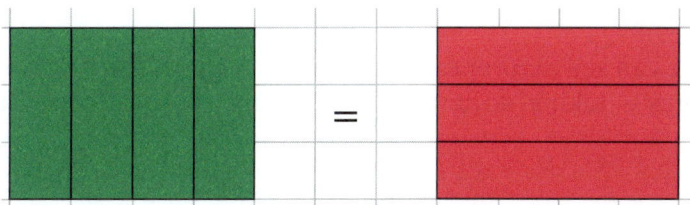

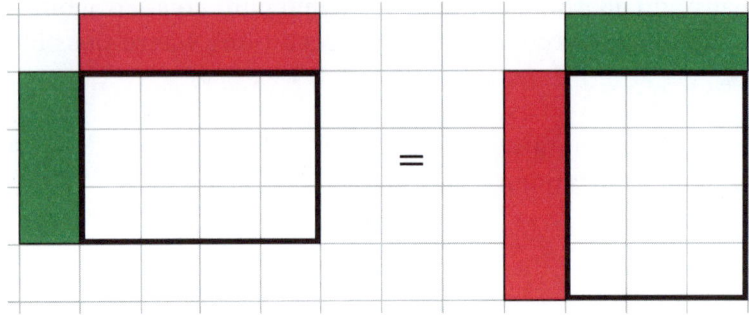

The commutativity of multiplication can also be shown on number lines:

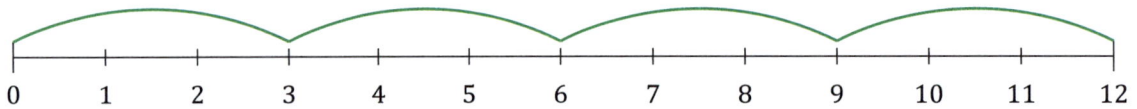

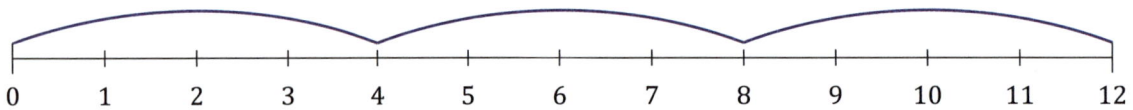

This includes vectors on number lines:

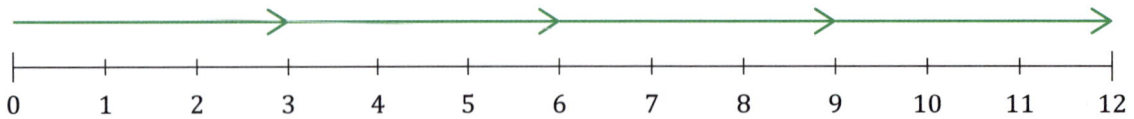

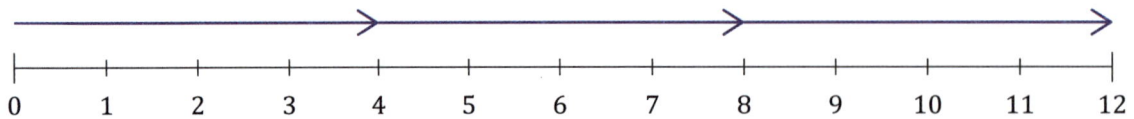

In both cases, we can see that repeating 3 four times gives the same result as repeating 4 three times – taking advantage of the repeated addition interpretation of multiplication.

We can also use the ordered-pair graph and proportion graph to demonstrate the commutativity of multiplication, provided pupils are familiar with how we represent multiplication in these representations:

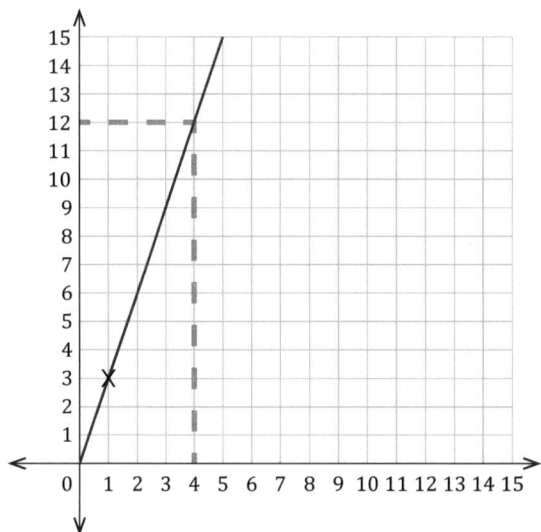

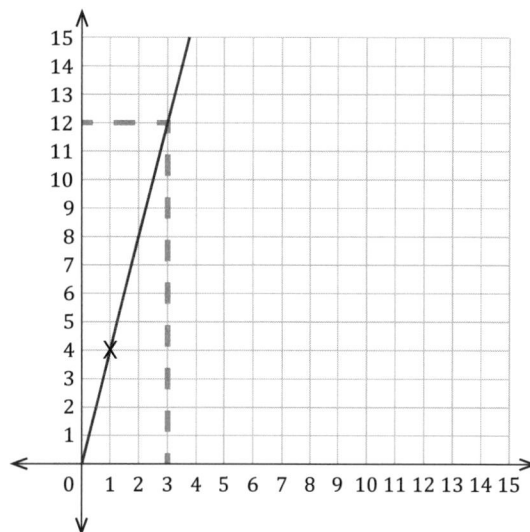

| Numerator | | Denominator | | Numerator | | Denominator |
|---|---|---|---|---|---|---|
| 3 | | 1 | | 4 | | 1 |
| ↓ × 4 | | ↓ × 1 | | ↓ × 3 | | ↓ × 1 |
| 12 | | 1 | | 12 | | 1 |

In both cases, the multiplication results in the same answer either way round. However, as when we first defined multiplication, there is nothing in these representations to suggest *why* this property is true, simply that it is. Given that the point of teaching pupils about the commutativity of multiplication is to allow them to see why multiplication has this property, these representations do not have the same power as the area model or arrays, for example.

It is important that pupils not only understand that commutativity applies to addition and multiplication, but also that the same law *doesn't* apply to subtraction or division. The same representations (for the most part) can be used to show this.

## Subtraction

The difference comparison approach can be tricky when it comes to showing that subtraction is not commutative. It is not always clear from this approach that there should be any difference between 5 – 2 and 2 – 5. For example, consider the bar model diagrams below:

5 – 2 ≠ 2 – 5

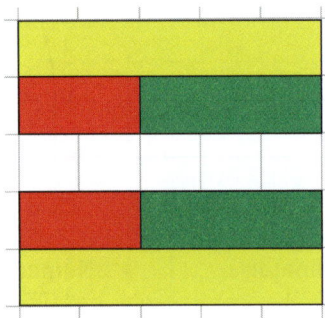

The upper diagram shows that the difference between 5 and 2 is 3. So far so good. The problem comes with the lower diagram. This would seem to show that the difference between 2 and 5 is also 3.

As we have already seen, bar models/Cuisenaire rods can pose problems when we are trying to simultaneously represent positive and negative values, and this is where the issue arises. This is not to say that this interpretation cannot be explained to pupils, just that it might be best not to lead with it when exploring why subtraction is not commutative – and even to be ready in case a pupil tries to make a case for subtraction being commutative by invoking such a diagram.

This problem can be solved, in part, by imposing the bars on a number line (as when we first introduced the representation):

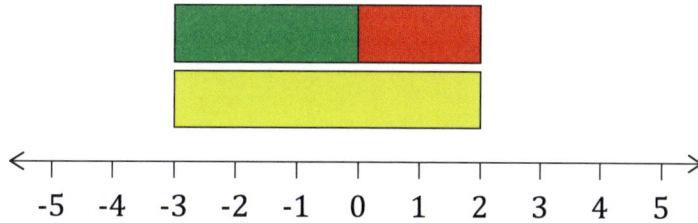

The eagle-eyed reader will spot that this is not the same diagram (irrespective of the number line), but more importantly, it is not the same interpretation of subtraction. Rather than the additive comparison or difference comparison, this diagram shows the view of subtraction that we termed 'counting back'. Indeed, counting back is typically a much better way of showing that subtraction is not associative, as in the above diagram or the ones below.

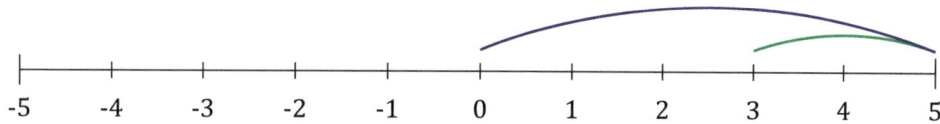

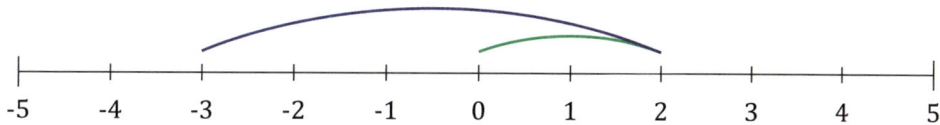

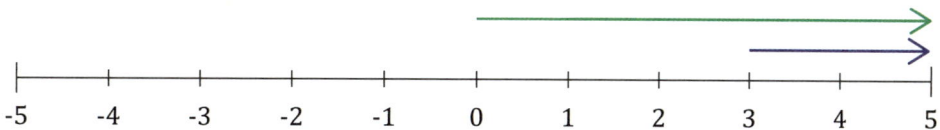

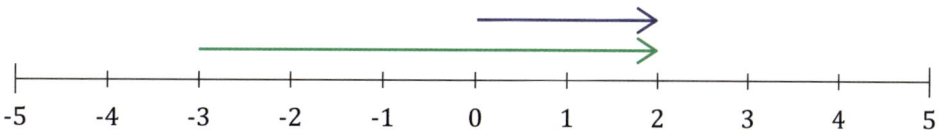

The first diagram above shows that 5 minus 2 is 5 and then count back 2, whilst the second diagram shows 2 count back 5. Clearly, the diagrams are different and therefore show that the subtraction is not commutative.

The physical act of taking away can also be used to demonstrate that subtraction is not commutative. This can be explored using counters (or base ten blocks/Cuisenaire rods):

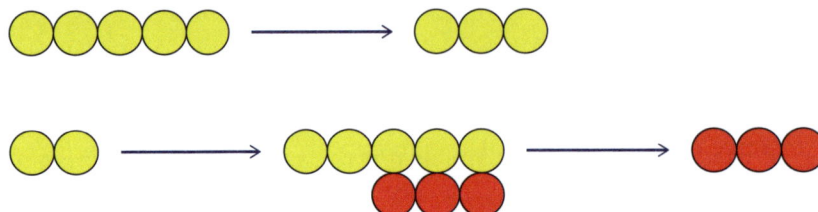

The first diagram here shows starting with 5 counters, and then removing 2 counters to leave 3. The second diagram shows starting with 2 counters, then adding 3 zero-pairs to enable the removal of 5 counters, leaving -3. Once again, the diagrams and results are different and show that the subtraction is not commutative.

The same result can be represented in an ordered-pair graph or proportion diagram. However, as with associativity, they add nothing to the concept beyond showing that the results are not the same.

## Division

We can use the same representations to show pupils why division is not commutative. This can be demonstrated in multiple ways, using both discrete and continuous representations.

$12 \div 4 \neq 4 \div 12$

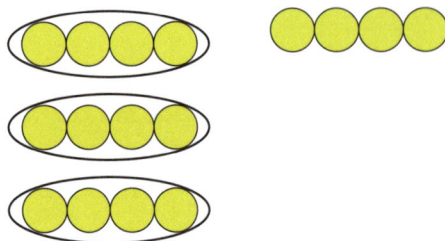

For the calculation $12 \div 4$, we can create groups of 4 from 12 quite straightforwardly (we could equally have created 4 shares). However, the alternative – trying to create groups of 12 (or 12 shares) from only 4 counters – is plainly impossible. Of course, this doesn't answer the question 'What is 4 ÷ 12?'; other representations will do that.

If pupils have already been introduced to fractions at this stage, then they should be familiar with the other representations. If not, then it will suffice to demonstrate that 12 ÷ 4 ≠ 4 ÷ 12 (which this clearly does), and the answer to the question of 4 ÷ 12 can be deferred to a later time. I would avoid telling pupils that we 'can't do' 4 ÷ 12; we should simply say that this representation doesn't allow us to see the answer, and that in time we will use other representations to explore what the answer is to the question of 4 ÷ 12.

Other representations not only have the power to show that 12 ÷ 4 ≠ 4 ÷ 12, but can also reveal the answer to 4 ÷ 12. One interesting example is the bar model, particularly Cuisenaire rods:

In this diagram we can see 12 ÷ 4 = 3. However, the same diagram also shows that 4 ÷ 12 is $\frac{1}{3}$. Using the idea of division as multiplicative comparison reveals that 4 is to 12 as 1 is to 3, which gives the result of $\frac{1}{3}$. Obviously care needs to be taken here: using the same diagram to demonstrate that two results are not equal (i.e. 12 ÷ 4 ≠ 4 ÷ 12) is a risky strategy, so we need to be sure that pupils have a very secure understanding of division as multiplicative comparison, built up using multiple representations, before we attempt to do so. In fact, I think it would be understandable if teachers choose to avoid it altogether.

The same approach can be taken with the proportion diagram. Here the distinction is a little clearer as the numerator and denominator clearly switch places; however, there is still enough similarity that we should progress with caution:

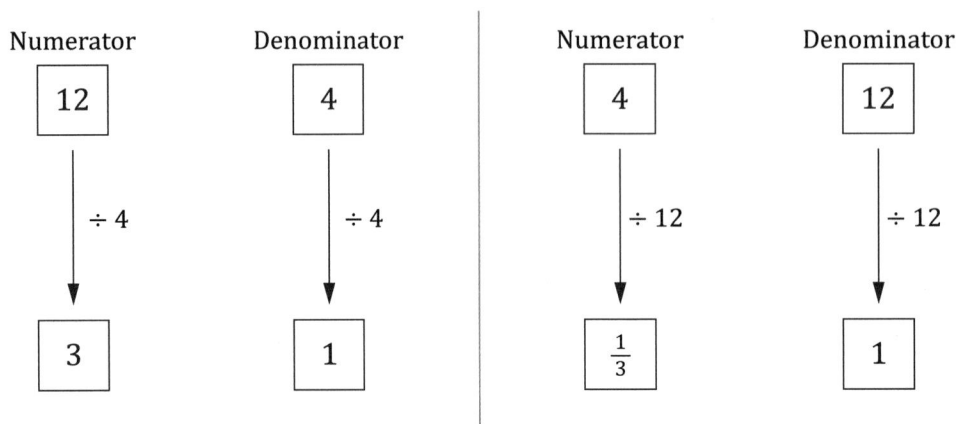

| Numerator | Denominator | | Numerator | Denominator |
|:---:|:---:|:---:|:---:|:---:|
| 12 | 4 | | 4 | 12 |
| ↓ ÷ 4 | ↓ ÷ 4 | | ↓ ÷ 12 | ↓ ÷ 12 |
| 3 | 1 | | $\frac{1}{3}$ | 1 |

The ordered-pair graph creates more of a distinction between the two, although the axes need to be scaled carefully if the representation is to show the correct answer to 4 ÷ 12. If we simply need to prove that it is not the same as 12 ÷ 4 then no such care is required.

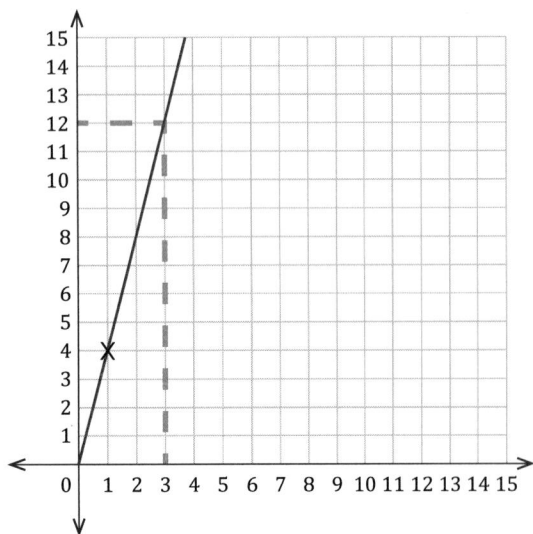

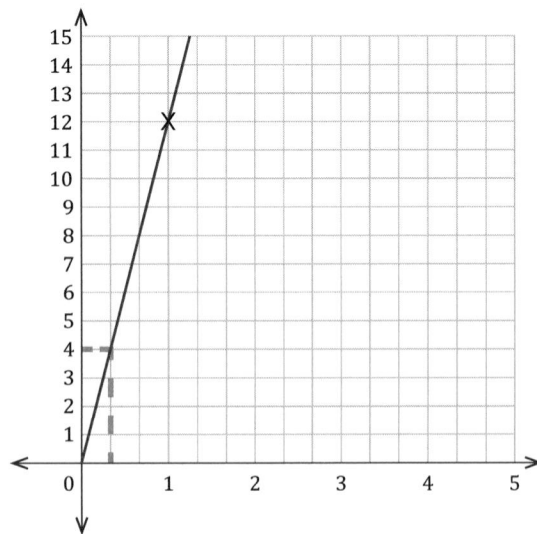

In these two diagrams, the horizontal axis has been scaled to allow us to see that the answer to 4 ÷ 12 = $\frac{1}{3}$, which is now clearly different to 12 ÷ 4 = 3.

# Distributivity

The final law of arithmetic that we will explore is the distributive law (normally first encountered by pupils in England in Year 4). A lot of caution needs to be taken when introducing distributivity to pupils, for two key reasons:

1    Distribution necessarily involves two operations, which makes it more likely to produce errors than either associativity or commutativity.

2    The distributive law can be applied with both subtraction and division, which is an obvious departure from the associative and commutative laws. This can lead to misconceptions around these laws if pupils do not understand this clearly – for example, believing that associativity or commutativity do apply to subtraction and division or believing that distributivity doesn't apply to subtraction and division.

Our representations can help to make it apparent why the distributive law applies with both subtraction and division. However, we will start by examining multiplication distributing over addition.

## Multiplication and addition

$3 \times (5 + 7) = 3 \times 5 + 3 \times 7$

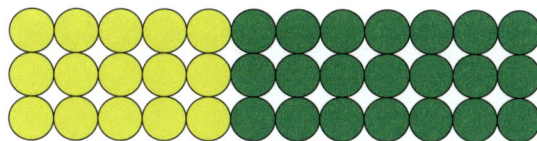

In this diagram we have 5 counters plus 7 counters in a line, with an array created by repeating this 3 times. However, within this array, there is also the array for $3 \times 5$ and the array for $3 \times 7$ (in yellow and green respectively).

A similar approach can be taken with bar models and Cuisenaire rods:

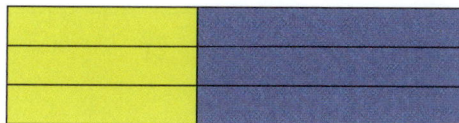

As with the array on page 147, the area model of multiplication using the '5' bar and the '7' bar shows the multiplication 3 × (5 + 7), but within that we can also see a 3 × 5 and a 3 × 7 area.

The same idea can be illustrated using the second version of the area model:

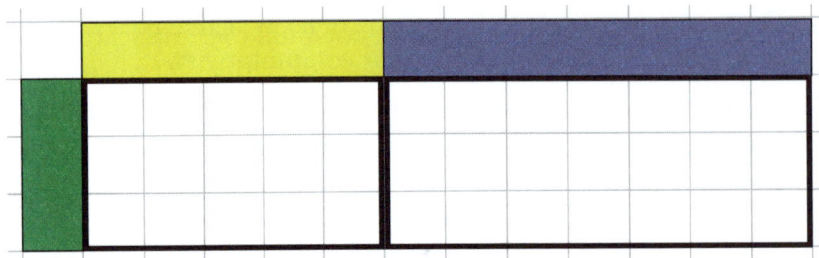

Again, we can recognise the area model as a precursor to the grid method of multiplication – indeed, many of our approaches to multiplication have the idea of distributing the multiplication over the addition at their heart. Whenever we use a grid to complete a calculation such as 7 × 23, by separating the 20 and the 3, we use distributivity. When we use a column method to multiply, we use the same distributivity, multiplying the 3 by the 7 separately and then the 20 by the 7.

An alternate use of counters can show the same idea using the interpretation of multiplication as a change of the counting unit – but this time in reverse:

In this representation we see 3 × 5 as a counting unit of 3 repeated 5 times, and then attached to this we see the same counting unit of 3 repeated 7 times to give 3 × 7. These can be combined to create 3 × (5 + 7).

As well as using practical apparatus such as counters and Cuisenaire rods to explore and exemplify distributivity, we can also show the same concept on a number line:

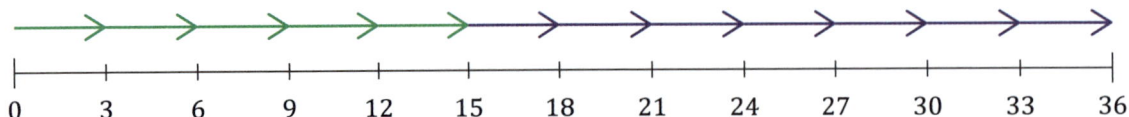

This diagram uses the same idea as the counters above – that is, 3 × 5 as 3 repeated 5 times, and then added to that 3 × 7 (so we have 3 × 5 + 3 × 7). However, the different coloured arrows aside, the same diagram can also be interpreted as 3 × 12 – that is, 3 × (5 + 7).

The ordered-pair graph and proportion diagram are not suitable representations to show the distributivity of multiplication over addition; whilst it is possible to do so, it adds nothing to the concept and has the real potential to complicate understanding that could otherwise be garnered from these representations. The ordered-pair graph is shown below for the sake of completeness only; it is definitely not recommended for use in this instance.

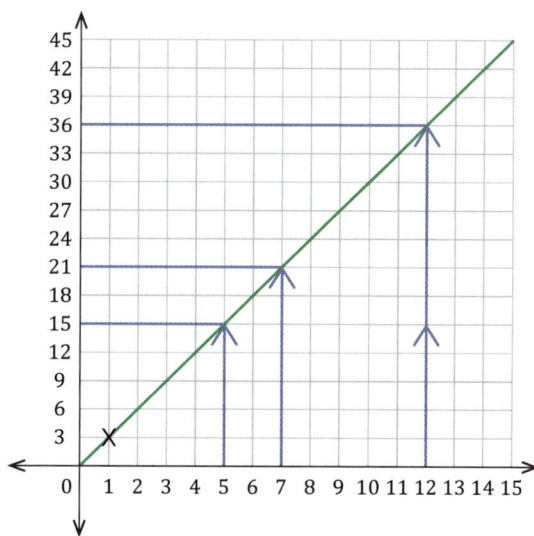

The number 3 is plotted, showing the separate multiplications by 5 and 7. The two arrows are then combined to demonstrate that 3 × 5 + 3 × 7 = 3 × (5 + 7).

## Multiplication and subtraction

Distributivity can also be applied to multiplication and subtraction. This can be shown in a similar way to the distributivity of multiplication over addition. However, not all representations of subtraction make the concept clear – in particular, the difference or counting back interpretations rather than the taking away.

3 × (7 – 5) = 3 × 7 – 3 × 5

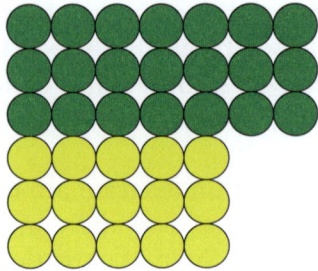

In the diagram above we see 3 × 7 as an array. This can be additively compared to 3 × 5 to determine the difference. The difference is a 3 × 2 array, or 3 × (7 − 5).

This idea can be simplified somewhat by changing the counting unit, so that each counter doesn't stand for 1 but instead represents a value of 3. A comparison shows that the difference between having seven 3s and five 3s is two 3s, or (7 − 5):

Notice that the alternative counting unit doesn't make the property nearly as clear. When considering the different counting units of 7 and 5, it isn't apparent that the difference is two 3s (or three 2s):

Bar models can also be used to show the distributive property of multiplication with subtraction, either using an array or a counting unit comparison:

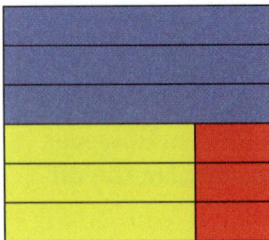

In the left-hand diagram we see an array of three 7s compared to an array of three 5s, with the difference being three 2s, or 3 lots of (7 – 5). In the right-hand diagram we see a counting unit of 3, with seven 3s compared to five 3s, which leaves a difference of two 3s.

In the area model we can compare the difference between the overlapping areas:

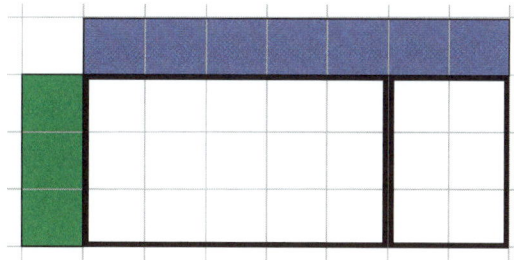

Here, starting with an initial area of 3 × 7 and then overlapping the area of 3 × 5, we can see a difference of 3 × 2, or 3 × (7 – 5).

The benefit of the bar model/Cuisenaire rods is that we can also use the difference method with the counting units of 7 and 5:

The benefit of this interpretation is that we can demonstrate directly that 3 × 7 – 3 × 5 = 3 × (7 – 5), without referencing directly the fact that 7 – 5 = 2. In the left-hand diagram we can see the difference between three 7s and five 3s. In the right-hand diagram this is transformed into 3 sets of the difference between 7 and 5 – that is, 3 × (7 – 5).

This could also be shown using the count back approach:

The equivalent number line would look like this:

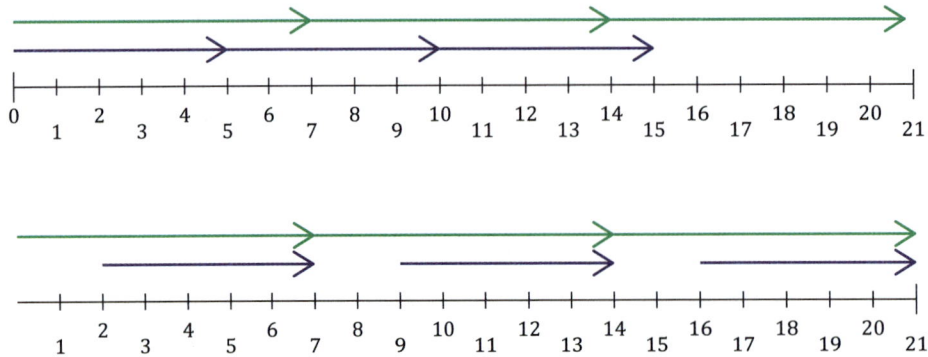

The importance of this representation is that it shows *why* the distributivity works, rather than just that it does work. The earlier diagrams demonstrated that the result of 3 × 7 – 3 × 5 is the same as the result of 3 × (7 – 5), without necessarily explaining what it is about the situation that makes this true. The number lines are powerful because they show clearly that the distributivity is a result of having 3 of each value (or whatever the multiplier is), and that this can be rearranged from a single comparison into 3 comparisons.

## Division and addition

Care needs to be taken with the distributivity of division over addition and subtraction, as some representations do not make this property of arithmetic obvious. Grouped counters can be an effective representation.

We can look at this sum by creating groups of 3 counters:

$$\frac{9 + 6}{3} = \frac{9}{3} + \frac{6}{3}$$

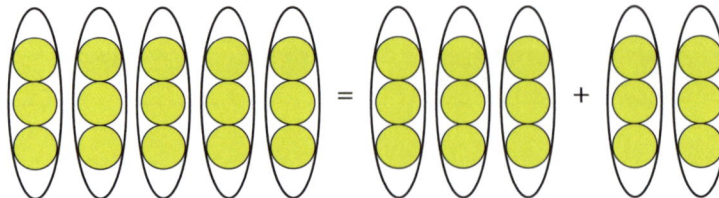

We can see that creating groups of 3 from 9 + 6 is the same as adding the groups of 3 from 9 to the groups of 3 from 6.

A similar approach with numbers that do not divide exactly can be used – with a bit of tweaking. We can again create groups of 3:

$$\frac{8 + 5}{3} = \frac{8}{3} + \frac{5}{3}$$

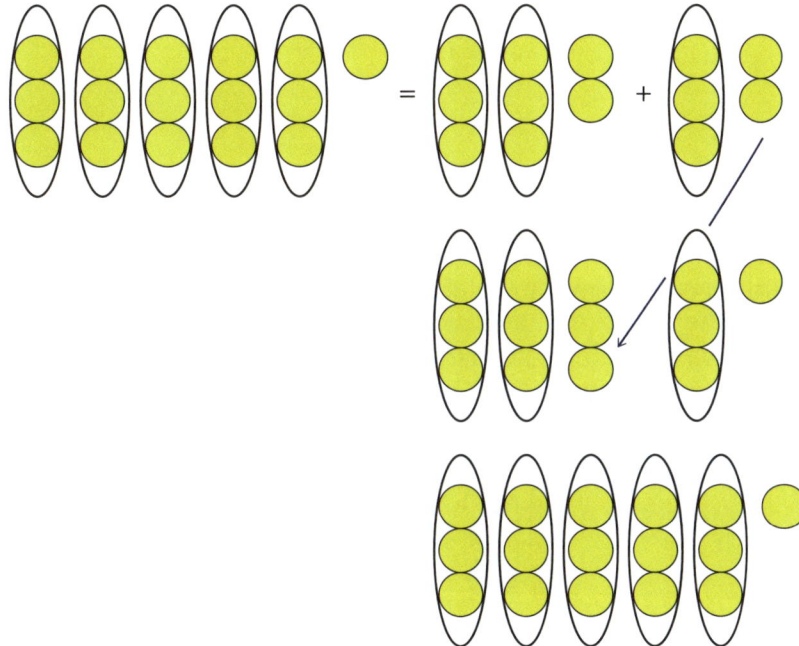

## Division and subtraction

The same strategy can be used to show the distributivity of division over subtraction by considering the subtraction as an additive comparison or difference between two values:

$$\frac{9 - 6}{3} = \frac{9}{3} - \frac{6}{3}$$

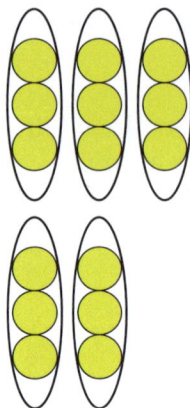

In the diagram above we see that the difference between 9 split into groups of 3 and 6 split into groups of 3 is a 3 split into a group of 3.

A similar additive comparison can be used with numbers that do not divide exactly:

$$\frac{8-5}{3} = \frac{8}{3} - \frac{5}{3}$$

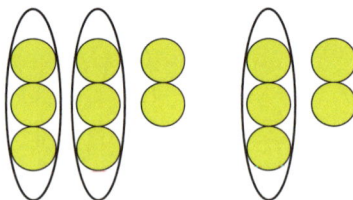

These diagrams show that the difference between 8 split into groups of 3 and 5 split into groups of 3 is a single group of 3 – that is, 8 – 5 = 3 split into a group of 3. In this case, the result divides nicely by 3.

The next example explores a calculation where the answer doesn't divide exactly by 3:

$$\frac{10-5}{3} = \frac{10}{3} - \frac{5}{3}$$

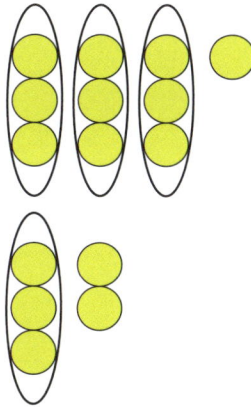

The comparison here is a little harder to interpret. There is an extra group of 3 in the upper diagram when compared to the lower one. Some pupils might think there is a difference of a second group of 3, but if we look carefully we can see that this would leave one too many counters in the second diagram. In fact, we only need 2 more counters following the single group of 3. So, the difference is a group of 3 and 2 counters, which is the result of 10 − 5 = 5 ÷ 3.

The area model for division shows the distributive law in a similar way.

$$\frac{9 + 6}{3} = \frac{9}{3} + \frac{6}{3}$$

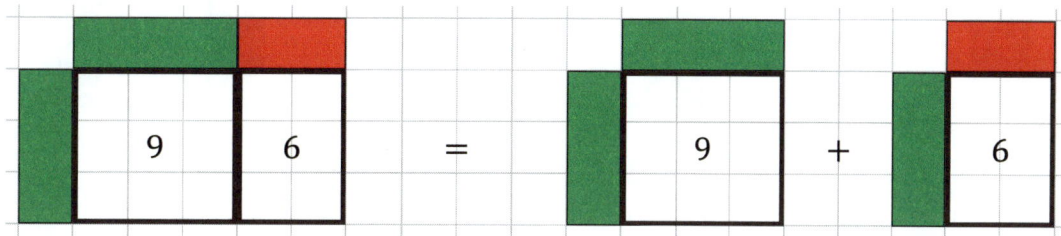

The benefit of this approach mirrors the benefit when showing the distributivity of multiplication, in that we don't actually have to evaluate what 9 + 6 is in order to demonstrate the distributivity. In the left-hand diagram we have the areas of 9 and 6 added together, with the combined area shared into 3 shares. This results in the same two bars (shown in green and red) sharing the areas separately into 3 shares.

It is slightly harder to show the same property when the values do not divide exactly; however, a few tweaks can demonstrate the same property.

$$\frac{8+5}{3} = \frac{8}{3} + \frac{5}{3}$$

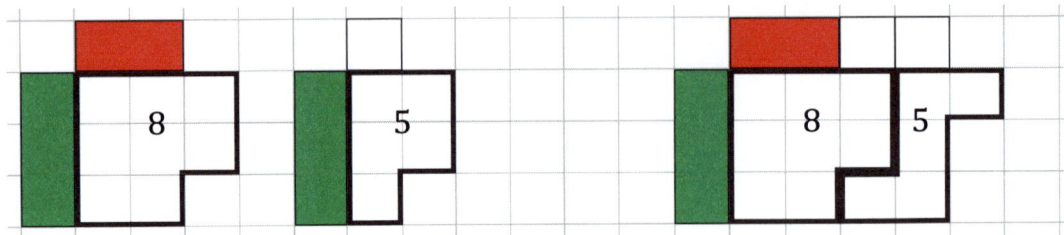

In a similar way to moving the counter, by moving the square we can take the result of $8 \div 3$ and $5 \div 3$ and combine them to produce the same result as $(8 + 5) \div 3$.

We can also use the overlapping areas to examine the difference and show that the division distributes over the subtraction:

$$\frac{9-6}{3} = \frac{9}{3} - \frac{6}{3}$$

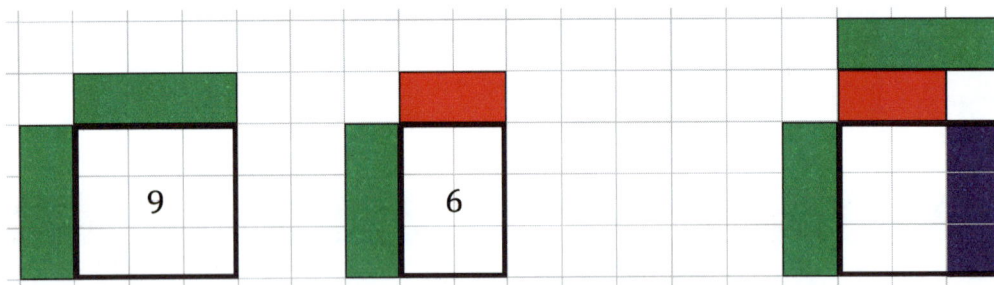

The diagrams above show that the difference between the area of 9 and the area of 6 is a single column of 3, leading to a result of 1. In the diagram on the right, the difference between the areas of 9 and 6 is shown as the column of 3, which is then shared into 3 shares, resulting in 1.

The same approach can be used with divisions that are not exact.

$$\frac{8-5}{3} = \frac{8}{3} - \frac{5}{3}$$

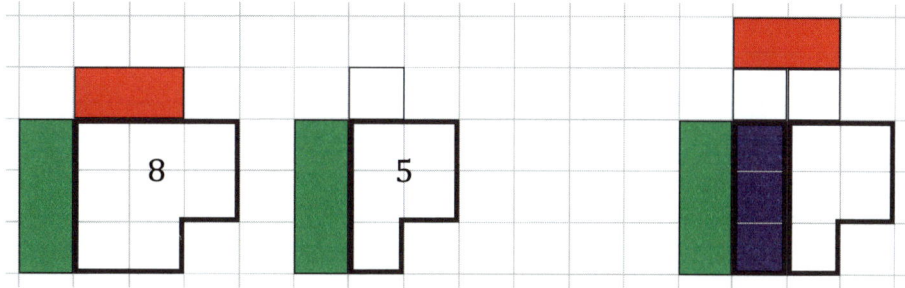

As in the diagrams for 9 and 6 on page 156, the difference between the area of 8 and the area of 5 is a single line of 3, which when shared into 3 shares gives 1.

When the final division is not exact the representation still suggests the distributivity.

$$\frac{10-5}{3} = \frac{10}{3} - \frac{5}{3}$$

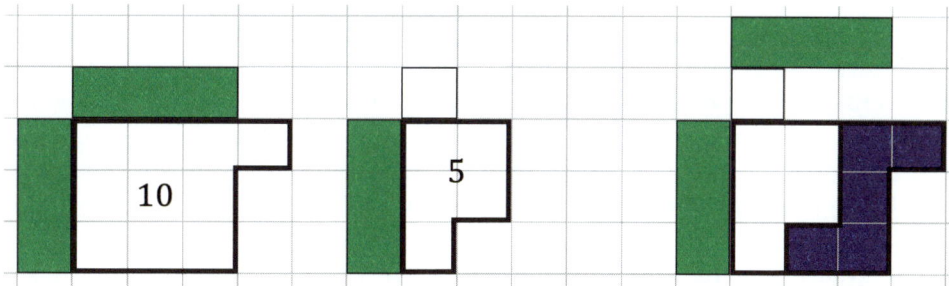

In these diagrams we see the difference between an area of 10 shared into 3 shares, leaving the $3\frac{1}{3}$, and 5 shared into 3 shares, giving $1\frac{2}{3}$. When the difference in the areas is examined, and then shared into the 3 shares, there is 1 square in each share along with 2 squares left, leading to the $1\frac{2}{3}$.

A powerful representation for showing distributivity of division is the number line, particularly when combined with vectors in a single dimension. Due to the effectiveness of the number line in showing addition and subtraction, and the ease with which it demonstrates the division, the concept becomes almost self-evident.

$$\frac{9+6}{3} = \frac{9}{3} + \frac{6}{3}$$

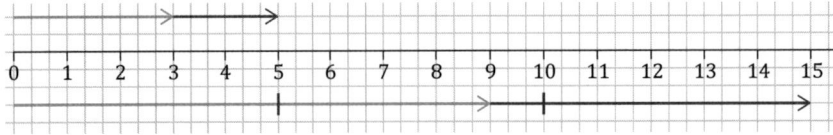

The upper diagram shows the sum of 9 thirds and 6 thirds. The lower diagram shows the sum of 9 and 6 divided into 3 equal shares. Of course, each share is the same size as in the upper diagram, revealing that the two are equal.

What is particularly valuable about this representation is that the change to numbers where the division is exact is no more complicated:

$$\frac{8+5}{3} = \frac{8}{3} + \frac{5}{3}$$

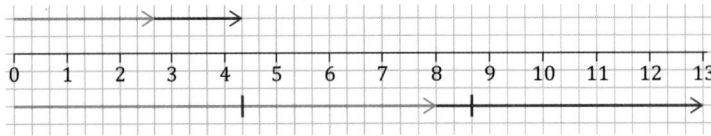

In this example, the upper diagram shows the sum of 8 thirds and 5 thirds, whilst the lower shows the sum of 8 and 5 divided into 3 equal shares. Again, we see that a single share in the bottom part of the diagram is the same length as the sum in the upper part of the diagram, indicating the equality.

The distributivity of subtraction over division can be represented in a very similar way, although it is beneficial to use the counting back approach for subtraction. Whilst the difference interpretation will yield the same result, counting back allows for a more direct demonstration of the equality.

$$\frac{9-6}{3} = \frac{9}{3} - \frac{6}{3}$$

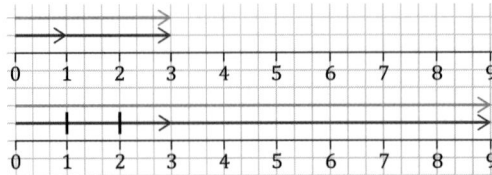

In the upper diagram we see the result of starting with 9 thirds and counting back 6 thirds. In the lower diagram we see 9 count back 6, with the result divided into 3 equal shares. Once again, the length of the resultant in the first diagram is the same length as a single share in the second, demonstrating the equal nature.

If we now examine the same representations when the divisions are not exact, the result is equivalent.

$$\frac{8-5}{3} = \frac{8}{3} - \frac{5}{3}$$

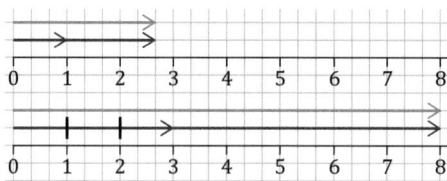

As in the previous example, we see the result of 8 thirds count back 5 thirds in the upper diagram, and 8 count back 5 divided into 3 equal shares in the lower diagram. The equivalence is once again clear from the equal length.

A real benefit here is that even when the division/subtraction doesn't result in an exact answer, the representation behaves in an indistinguishable manner from the previous two examples:

$$\frac{10-5}{3} = \frac{10}{3} - \frac{5}{3}$$

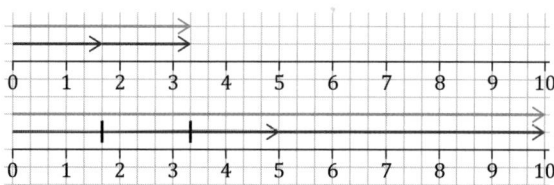

Now the upper diagram shows the result of 10 thirds count back 5 thirds, and the lower diagram shows the result of dividing 10 count back 5 into 3 equal shares. Like the first two examples, the length of the result in the upper diagram is equal to the length of a single share in the lower one.

The same approach can be taken with bar models, although this comes with both advantages and drawbacks.

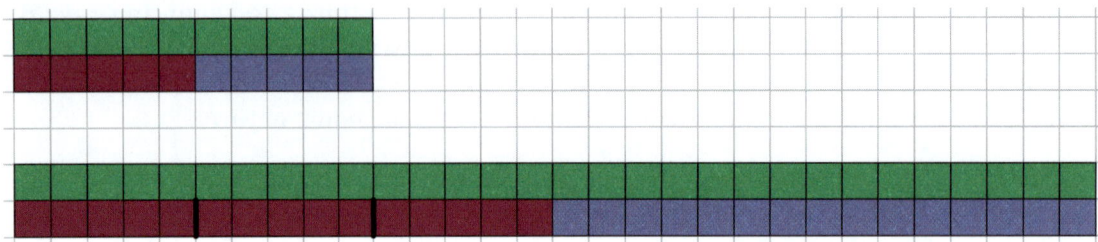

This pair of diagrams above shows an identical example to the one previous, with 10 thirds subtract 5 thirds in the upper diagram, and 10 subtract 5 shared into 3 parts in the lower one. The advantage of this representation is that it begins to hint at the generalisation of the idea – that 10 thirds could just as easily be considered as 10 quarters, 10 fifths or 10 of anything. Whilst the lower part of the diagram would have to change to accommodate whichever division had occurred (e.g. if we switched to 10 quarters then the lower green bar would have to become 40 units long, with each of the blue and purple units representing 20 and the purple bar being split into 4), this should not be a huge step for pupils take.

# Powers

So far, we have ignored the laws of arithmetic as they apply to indices. We conclude this chapter with a brief look at how and when the laws of arithmetic apply to powers.

Does $a^{(b^c)^d} = a^{b^{(c^d)}}$? This would be the natural extension of the associative law if it applied to powers. But a quick numerical check would suggest that this law does *not* apply to indices:

$$a^{(2^3)^4} = a^{8^4} = a^{4096}$$
$$a^{2^{(3^4)}} = a^{2^{81}}$$

$2^{81}$ is an incredibly large number of the order of $10^{24}$, which is clearly significantly larger than 4096. However, exploring this through representation is challenging to the point of not being worthwhile. We have previously seen that representing powers of higher than 2 or 3 is difficult – it requires continuing evaluation of each multiplication in order to create the geometric series. Evaluating 4096 separate multiplications is undesirable, and evaluating $2^{81}$ multiplications would take more than a lifetime to achieve if we attempted one at a time. We will each need to judge for ourselves if, and when, to introduce this idea to our pupils as a purely abstract or symbolic exercise.

Does $a^{b^c} = a^{c^b}$? This would be a natural extension of the commutative law if it applied to powers. A similar numerical check would suggest that this law does *not* apply to indices:

$a^{2^3} = a^8$

$a^{3^2} = a^9$

Once again, these higher powers make representation somewhat tricky (although clearly not as tricky as the significantly larger powers involved in applying the associative law). This is probably best left to the point where pupils can appreciate this simply as a numerical exercise, which will again come down to teacher judgement.

Distributivity of powers is probably the most interesting operation to explore as there are four operations that powers can distribute over – namely, addition, subtraction, multiplication and division. If we limit the power to squaring, then it is possible to represent these operations effectively using the representations we have examined.

We will start by examining powers in relation to addition and subtraction.

## Addition and subtraction

$(5 + 2)^2 \neq 5^2 + 2^2$

The area model of multiplication can make clear that powers do not distribute over addition. If we use bar models/Cuisenaire rods to show $(5 + 2)^2$, we get a diagram that looks like this:

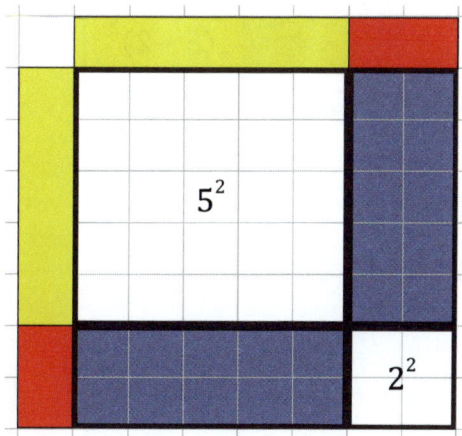

Within this diagram of $(5 + 2)^2$ we have $5^2$ and $2^2$. However, importantly we can also see that $5^2$ and $2^2$ do not take up all of the space. The difference is represented by the blue shaded areas. This clearly indicates that $5^2 + 2^2 \neq (5+2)^2$.

A similar approach can be taken to show that $(5 - 2)^2 \neq 5^2 - 2^2$:

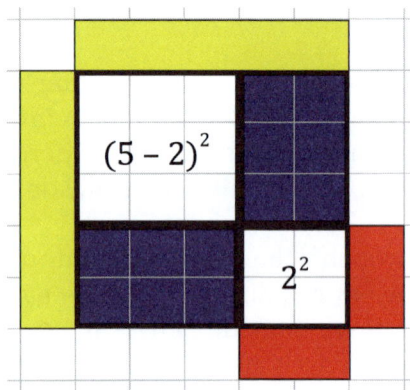

In the diagram above we can observe the difference between $5^2$ and $2^2$ – that is, $5^2 - 2^2$. We can also see $(5 - 2)^2$; the subtraction is completed by counting back. As before, the two areas are not the same: the blue shaded area indicates that $(5 - 2)^2 \neq 5^2 - 2^2$. An alternative diagram might look something like this:

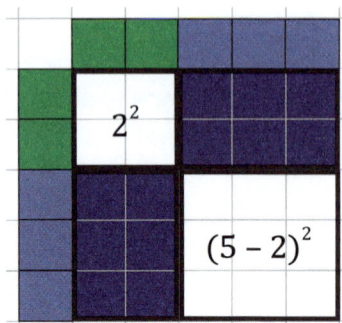

# Multiplication and division

Representing distributing powers over multiplication and division is more challenging. In part, this is because powers can be considered as repeated multiplication, so we are trying to impose one multiplication onto another. Using small numbers and limiting the power to 2 in our representations can help, but importantly there is a need to be able to hold two different views of multiplication simultaneously – namely, repeated addition and area.

$(3 \times 4)^2 = 3^2 \times 4^2$

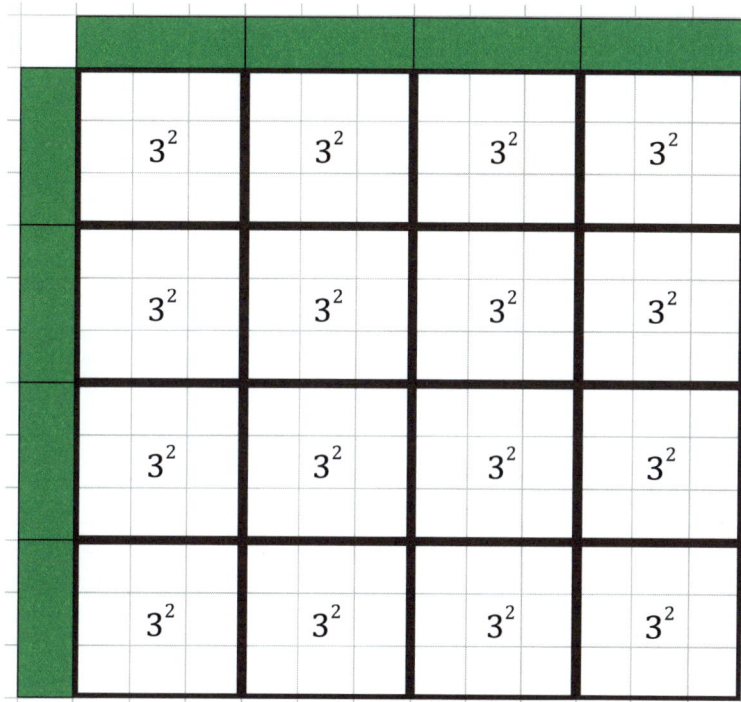

The green bars show 3 repeated 4 times, which has then been squared using the area model. Within this is an area created from $4^2$ lots of tiles that are $3^2$ in size – that is, $3^2 \times 4^2$. The fact that the two areas are identical suggests the equality – that $(3 \times 4)^2$ does indeed equal $3^2 \times 4^2$.

An alternative diagram using a length of 4 repeated 3 times and then squared would appear like this:

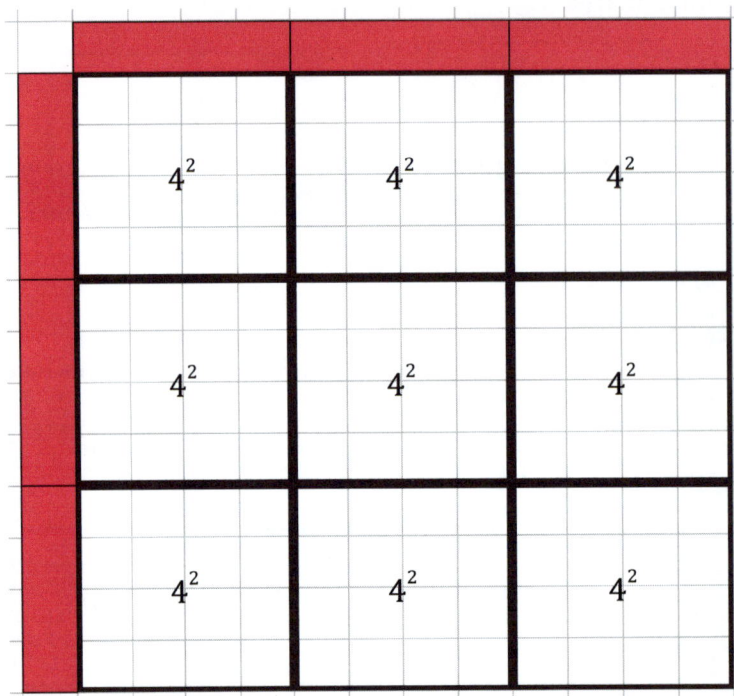

In this diagram we see the '4' bar repeated 3 times and then squared. This leads to a $3 \times 3$ square made up of tiles that are $4 \times 4$ in size – that is, $3^2 \times 4^2$. So again $(3 \times 4)^2 = 3^2 \times 4^2$. It is also worth noting that the two diagrams contain precisely the same area overall, which is another confirmation of the commutative law as it applies to multiplication ($3^2 \times 4^2 = 4^2 \times 3^2$).

We can use similar approaches when we consider division and the distributivity of powers over division.

$$\left(\frac{3}{4}\right)^2 = \frac{3^2}{4^2}$$

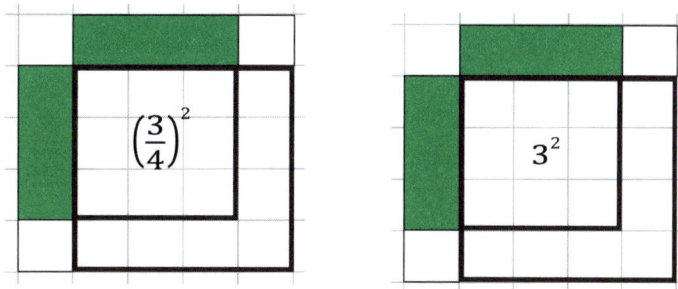

In the left-hand diagram we are considering 4 squares to be a single unit, so the '3' bar represents $\frac{3}{4}$ and therefore the area represents $\left(\frac{3}{4}\right)^2$. In the right-hand diagram we are treating a single square as 1, so the area is $3^2$, and this is shown as a proportion of the larger $4^2$. Of course, the obvious point here is the same diagram has actually been used both times, and so the obvious conclusion is that the two values are identical as well.

Now that we have established a clear idea of the laws of arithmetic and how they apply to our operations, it is time to consider what this implies for calculations that use multiple operations and the correct order for these calculations to happen.

# Chapter 8

# Order of operations

Many teachers treat the order of operations as what Dr Dave Hewitt calls 'arbitrary knowledge' – that, by convention, multiplication has to be done before addition, but had we defined it differently it could equally work the other way around.[*] However, exploring these operations using our understanding of the laws of arithmetic, along with suitable representations, can make it clear that this is not arbitrary knowledge but necessary knowledge – that is, it *must* work in this way or inconsistencies appear elsewhere. As order of operations is not taught until Year 6, at least according to the English national curriculum, this would mean that well-taught pupils will have developed the required understanding of the laws of arithmetic to approach the order of operations in this way.

Another common approach in schools is to immediately approach operations from the point of view of order. However, I have found it much more beneficial to start by exploring and explaining why the order *doesn't* affect the outcome with certain operations.

## Calculations where order isn't important

$3 + 5 - 2 = 3 - 2 + 5$

There are multiple representations that can show this is true. Counters, number lines and bar models/Cuisenaire rods can all be effective in demonstrating the truth of this equality:

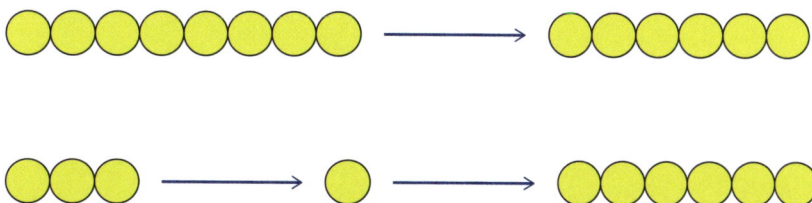

---

[*] Dave Hewitt, Arbitrary and Necessary: Part 1, A Way of Viewing the Mathematics Curriculum, *For the Learning of Mathematics: An International Journal of Mathematics Education*, 19(3) (1999): 2–9.

The first diagram on page 167 shows the sum of 3 and 5, and then the physical taking away of 2 counters, leaving 6. In the second diagram we start with 3 counters, from which 2 counters are removed and 5 added, which results in the same 6 counters.

A number line/vector representation can illustrate this all in one diagram, using the counting back approach to subtraction:

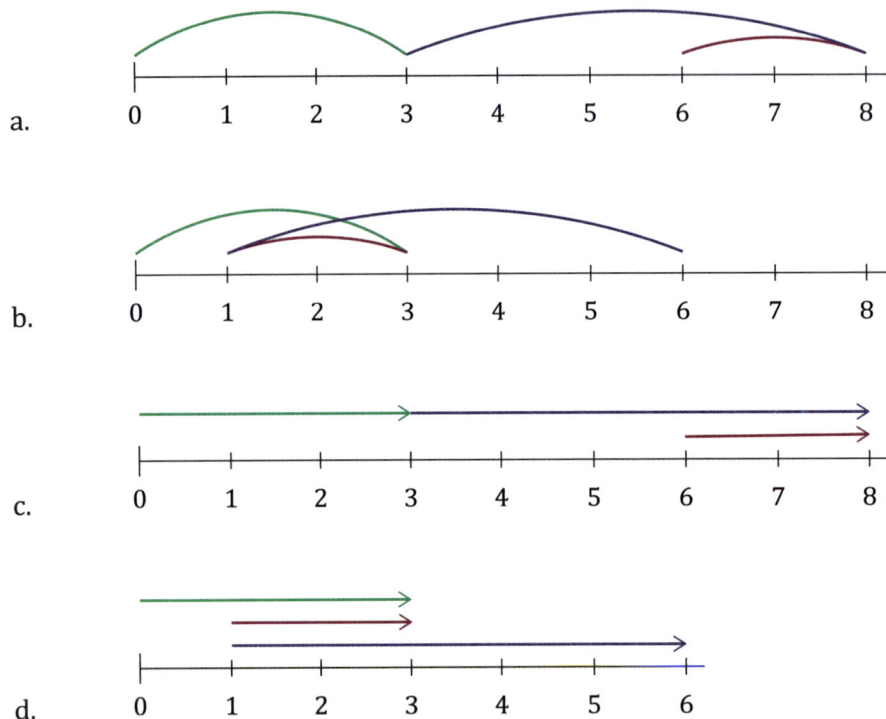

a.

b.

c.

d.

In diagrams a and c we see 3 + 5 and then count back 2, leading to the result of 6. Diagrams b and d show 3 count back 2, and then the 5 added afterwards. This leads to the same result of 6.

A very similar approach can be taken with bars/Cuisenaire rods:

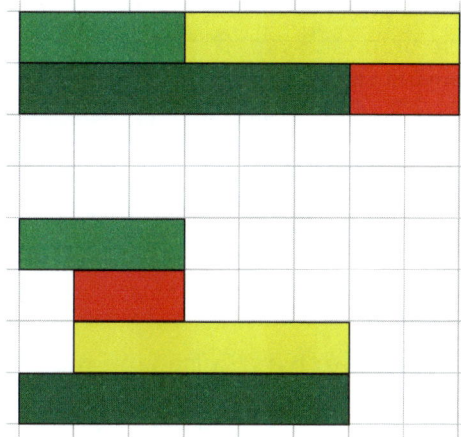

In the upper diagram we see a '5' bar added to a '3' bar, and then a '2' bar counting back, leaving a space of 6 (shown using the '6' bar). In the lower diagram we see a '3' bar and then a '2' bar counting back, followed by the addition of a '5' bar, giving a total distance of 6 (again shown by the '6' bar).

Ultimately, the properties of addition and subtraction can be understood as a requirement of the commutative law as applied to addition. If we think about 3 + 5 – 2 as 3 + 5 + (-2), then we can clearly apply the commutative law to the second sum and switch the order to 3 + (-2) + 5. This has to lead to the conclusion that 3 + 5 – 2 = 3 – 2 + 5.

As well as order being unimportant when applied to addition and subtraction, we can also show that order doesn't affect the result when combining multiplication with division.

5 × 6 ÷ 2 = 6 ÷ 2 × 5

A number line is extremely powerful in showing the truth of this relationship:

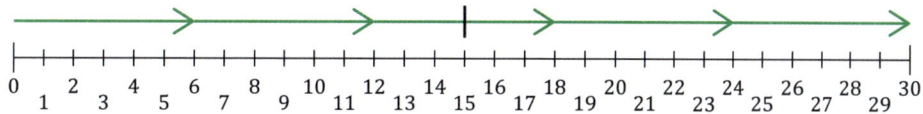

In this diagram we see 6 repeated 5 times, and then divided into 2 equal splits/shares.

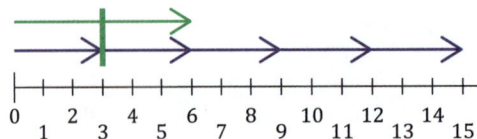

In this second diagram we see 6 split into 2 equal shares, and then a single share repeated 5 times. Both of these approaches lead to the same value, indicating the equality.

A similar approach can be used with bars/Cuisenaire rods:

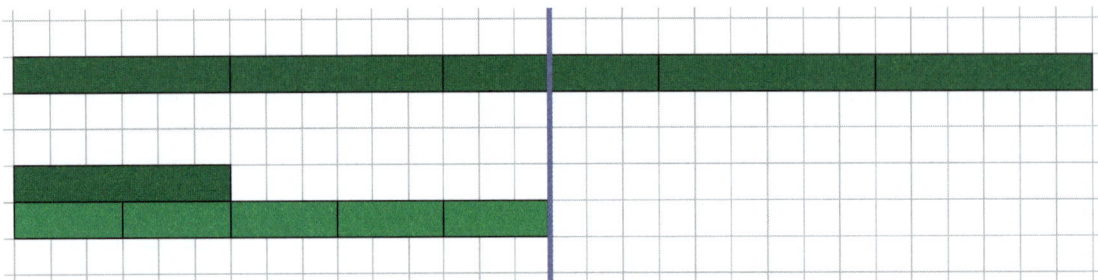

In the above, the upper diagram shows 6 repeated 5 times and divided into 2, whilst the lower diagram shows 6 split into 2 equal parts, with a single part repeated 5 times. These two approaches end in the same place, indicating their equality.

The area model for multiplication can also be used to demonstrate the equality:

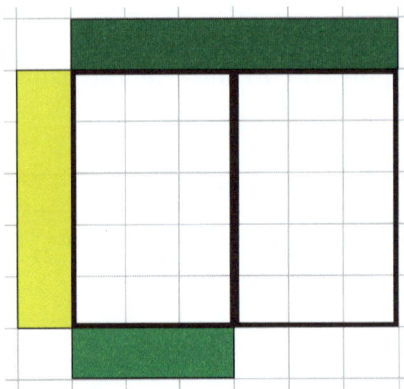

One benefit of this representation is that the two views can be captured within a single diagram: the 5 by 6 rectangle creates the larger area, which is then divided into two equal areas. Alternatively, we could see the 6 split in half (hence the '3' bar at the bottom of the diagram), and then an area created by multiplying 3 by 5.

Like addition and subtraction, the idea of multiplication and division giving the same result, irrespective of order, can be seen as a consequence of the commutative law as applied to multiplication. If we treat the calculation $5 \times 6 \div 2$ as $5 \times 6 \times \frac{1}{2}$ then clearly we can apply the commutative law to the first multiplication and switch the 5 with the $(6 \times \frac{1}{2})$ to give $6 \times \frac{1}{2} \times 5$, which can then be considered as $6 \div 2 \times 5$.

Whilst it is possible to demonstrate that powers and roots can be done in either order – i.e. that $\sqrt[3]{8^2} = (\sqrt[3]{8})^2$ – the problems with representing powers and roots come into effect and make the diagrams difficult to interpret. In a similar way to demonstrating that powers are not associative or commutative, this may well be better left and explored in a numerical exercise once we are sure that pupils are sufficiently confident with these concepts.

Now that we understand those operations which can be performed without considering order, we will attend to those calculations where order *is* important, and demonstrate why this is the case. We will start by mixing addition and subtraction with multiplication.

## Calculations where order is important

$4 \times 3 + 5 \neq 5 + 4 \times 3$ (when read from left to right)

There are many representations that can demonstrate the truth of this statement. Simple counters can show the inequality:

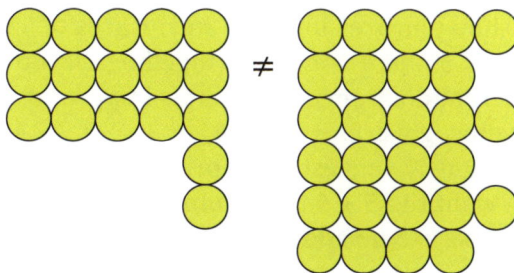

Cuisenaire rods/bar models can also illustrate the same idea:

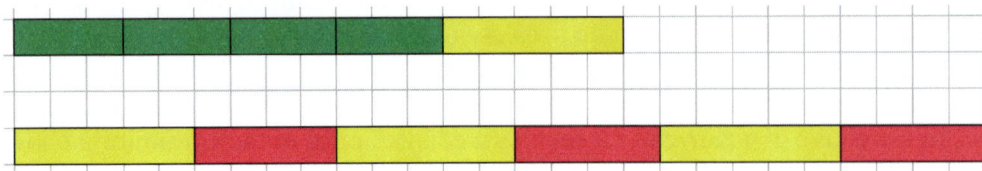

In the upper diagram the '3' bar is repeated 4 times (we could equally have used a '4' bar repeated 3 times) and then this is added to a '5' bar. In the lower diagram the '5' bar is added to a '4' bar and then this is repeated 3 times. The results are clearly not equal.

Whilst proper use of these representations can help to show the importance of order, they do not give us an indication as to which is the correct interpretation. They do indicate a problem because this representation would seem to violate the commutativity of addition – that is, 4 × 3 + 5 should be equal to 5 + 4 × 3 as the order of the sum of 5 and 4 × 3 shouldn't matter.

The representation that brings clarity to this situation is the area model for multiplication. The diagrams below make it clear why 5 + 4 × 3 cannot be read from left to right and the change that needs to be made in order to correct this error:

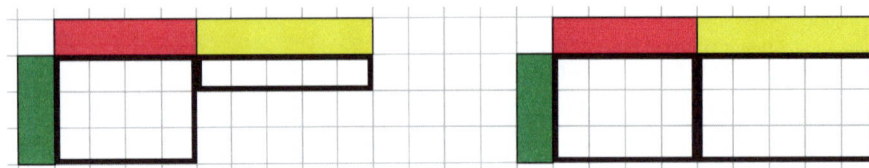

The left-hand diagram shows an area for 4 × 3 and an area of 5 (shown as 1 by 5). The right-hand diagram shows 5 and 4 combined together, with the result multiplied by 3. Clearly, these are different diagrams, but what is important here is that the second diagram shows what we recognise as 3 × (5 + 4) or 3 × 5 + 3 × 4 from our examination of distributivity. This obviously suggests that brackets should be included in the calculation 5 + 4 × 3 if we want the 5 + 4 to be completed first, or without the brackets if we don't want the numbers to be added prior to the multiplication.

It is worth noting that the commutativity of multiplication suggests that this would be true – that is, 5 + 4 × 3 should be equal to 5 + 3 × 4. However, this is only true if the multiplication is happening independently of the addition rather than following it. In addition, if the 5 + 4 is to be carried out before the × 3, then it should be true that 5 + 4 × 3 is equal to 3 × 5 + 4 (i.e. the two parts either side of the multiplication sign can be swapped). But this is only the case if we apply the commutative and distributive laws: 3 × (5 + 4) = (5 + 4) × 3.

All of this suggests that in the case of a calculation such as 5 + 4 × 3, we should consider the 4 × 3 separately to the 5 +, *unless* brackets are used to indicate that the sum should be evaluated before the product.

We can use similar logic and representation to show why 4 ÷ 2 + 5 ≠ 5 + 4 ÷ 2 (when read left to right) – again, seemingly in violation of the commutative law of addition. However, this is hardly necessary. For a start, when written using a vinculum (or horizontal bar) the expressions look different:

$$\frac{4}{2} + 5 \neq \frac{5 + 4}{2}$$

They can only be brought back into balance by considering the division as applying only to the 4:

$$\frac{4}{2} + 5 = 5 + \frac{4}{2}$$

We can also consider the idea of distributivity as applied to division – that if the 5 + 4 was to be completed before the division then this would equate it to (5 + 4) ÷ 2, which is equivalent to 5 ÷ 2 + 4 ÷ 2. Clearly, 5 ÷ 2 + 4 ÷ 2 cannot be equal to 4 ÷ 2 + 5, as the 5 is being divided by 2 in the first calculation but not in the second. For pupils who may struggle to follow this logic, we can demonstrate it directly using a bar model:

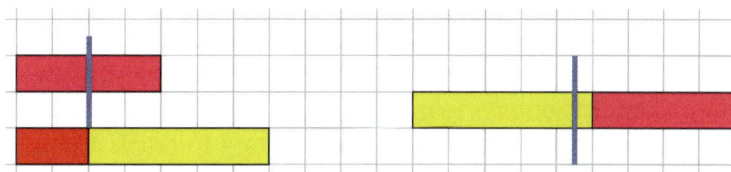

In the left-hand diagram we see 4 split into 2 equal shares, with 5 then added to a single share. In the right-hand diagram we see the 5 + 4 completed and then the result split into 2 equal shares. The final length on the left is not equal to the final length on the right, and therefore they are unequal. We can regain the equality by only considering the division as applied to the 4; this produces the diagram below:

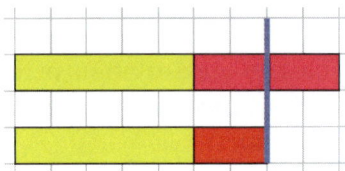

We can now see the result of completing the calculation $5 + 4 \div 2$ as 5 plus the result of 4 divided by 2, and we have now restored the equality with the calculation $4 \div 2 + 5$.

In this way, we can help our pupils to start to see how the correct order of operations is not an arbitrary set of rules imposed by wiser mathematicians; rather they are a consequence of needing to maintain the laws of arithmetic (particularly the commutative and distributive laws). The correct order of operations is not then arbitrary knowledge, but necessary knowledge – that is, it is a consequence of other knowledge.

This has an impact on how we teach the order of operations – if we are to believe the writings of Dr Dave Hewitt (among others). He suggests that if we teach the order of operations as arbitrary knowledge, then we are basically asking pupils to believe us that they work in this way – and the pupils will then either remember or forget to do so. However, if we support pupils to connect the laws of arithmetic with their impact on the correct order of operations, then this knowledge stops existing in the 'realm of memory' and enters the 'realm of awareness'.[*] Instead of pupils having to remember that operations are done in a certain order, they become aware of the need for calculations to obey the commutative and distributive laws. It is for this reason that I advocate not teaching the order of operations before teaching the laws of arithmetic. The correct order of operations is clearly a consequence of the laws of arithmetic, so to teach them in reverse order would be akin to trying to teach a child to run before they have ever walked (if you will forgive the cliché).

We can produce similar diagrams to represent the result of mixing subtraction with multiplication and/or division but, as before, they are hardly required. Simply by treating the idea of subtracting 5 as being the same as adding (-5), it is clear that anything that is true for addition will be equally true for subtraction (and the equivalent interplay with multiplication and division). Indeed, the argument can be made (and I frequently make it with pupils) that we only really need to consider addition,

---

*   Hewitt, Arbitrary and Necessary: Part 1, 2, 4.

multiplication and powers when thinking about distributivity and the order of operations, because subtraction is just a form of addition (the addition of negative values), division is just a form of multiplication (the multiplication of fractions) and roots are just a form of powers (taking a number to a fractional power). If we consider a hierarchy of addition leading to multiplication and multiplication leading to powers, then distributivity only applies to the two operations next to each other in the hierarchy. This can help to support pupils in remembering when distributivity can be applied and the correct order of operations.

I will admit that it seems strange to refer to 'remembering' the correct order of operations, given that I have just described understanding them as a consequence of the laws of arithmetic. However, I feel justified in this as it is evident that understanding, whilst being a desirable attribute for memory (and perhaps in most cases a necessary attribute for memory), is not a sufficient one. We simply do not remember everything we come to understand – the cues to that understanding fade over time if they are not strengthened and the material is not revisited and practised. My admired friend and colleague, Kris Boulton, has written about this on his blog,[*] and as this book is not primarily concerned with the workings of memory I will leave this for now. I see nothing wrong with the use of memory aids such as summaries, mnemonics and so on to support a previously developed understanding. It is when these take the place of understanding – when teachers rely on the tricks and not the substance, or when they try to turn necessary knowledge into arbitrary knowledge, as Dave Hewitt would say – that I have reservations.

# Powers

In the remaining part of this chapter, we will explore how it can be shown that powers must be completed before addition and/or multiplication. I will again limit the power to 2 so that it may be more easily represented.

$4^2 + 3 \neq 3 + 4^2$ (when read from left to right)

To be fair, this example hardly needs representing as it is identical to the multiplication examples we saw earlier: $3 + 4^2$ can be seen as $3 + 4 \times 4$, and we have already explored how this cannot be seen as $(3 + 4) \times 4$ without violating the commutative and distributive laws as they apply to multiplication and addition. However, just to ensure that pupils understand this we will briefly consider the appropriate representations.

---

[*]    Kris Boulton, Why Is It That Students Always Seem to Understand, But Then Never Remember? ... *To the Real* [blog] (6 May 2013). Available at: https://tothereal.wordpress.com/2013/05/06/why-is-it-that-students-always-seem-to-understand-but-then-never-remember/.

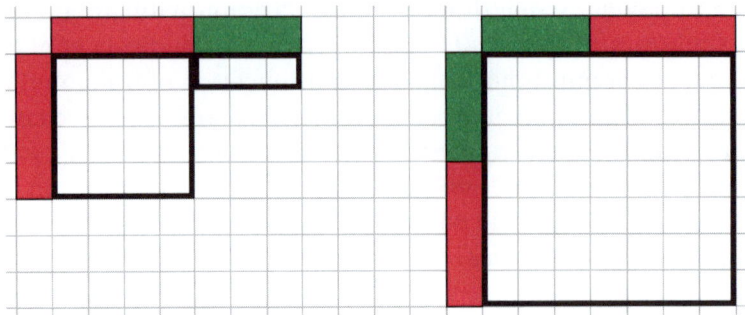

It is evident in the two bar models above that taking $4^2$ and adding 3 doesn't give the same result as $3 + 4^2$ when read from left to right. The right-hand diagram is identical to the one produced when considering $(3 + 4)^2$ (we did something similar when investigating why powers do not distribute over addition), which makes clear that the bracket needs to be included if we want to treat $3 + 4^2$ as the square of $3 + 4$, rather than 3 added to the square of 4.

We can now consider the interplay between multiplication and division with powers.

$4^2 \times 3 \neq 3 \times 4^2$ (when read from left to right)

Once again, the area model of multiplication is the most appropriate representation for showing the square. However, the multiplication by 3 needs a different interpretation to be used simultaneously – namely, the idea of repeated addition:

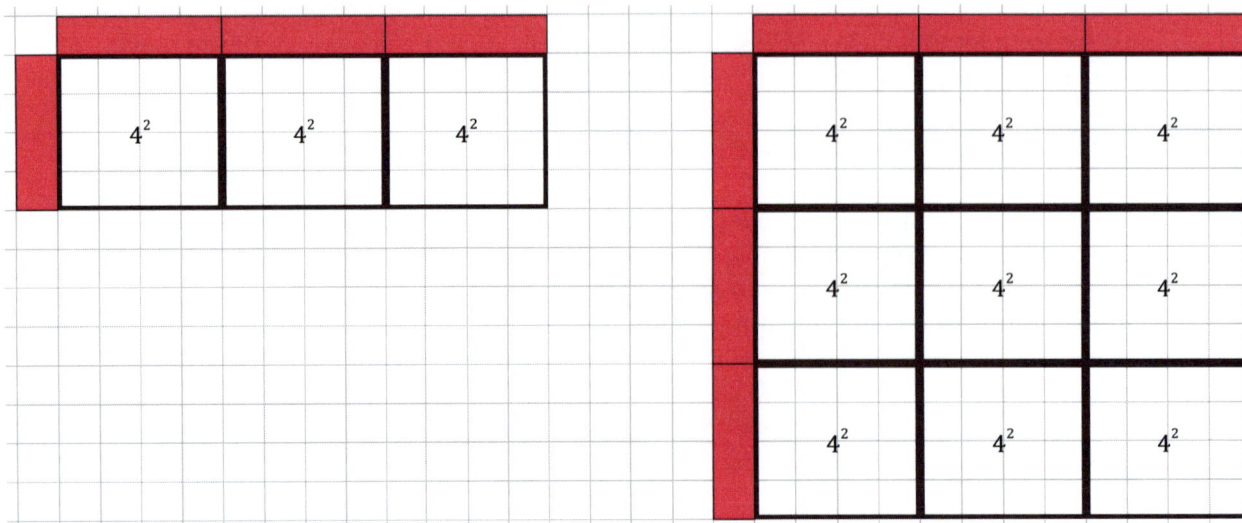

The left-hand diagram shows $4^2$ repeated 3 times (multiplied by 3). The right-hand diagram shows 3 × 4 as 4 repeated 3 times, which is then squared. Clearly the two diagrams do not produce the same result, which is again in conflict with the commutative law as applied to multiplication (which states that $3 × 4^2$ should give the same result as $4^2 × 3$). However, we notice that the right-hand diagram is identical to the diagram we generated when evaluating $(3 × 4)^2$ when applying the distributive law to multiplication (see page 164). Indeed, this representation makes it clear that the two cannot be equal as we have already established that $(3 × 4)^2 = 3^2 × 4^2$, and this cannot possibly be equal to $4^2 × 3$. This implies that we need a bracket if we wish to consider the square of 3 × 4, and that the calculation $3 × 4^2$ must be viewed as 3 lots of the square of 4 if it is going to obey the laws of arithmetic.

We now consider a similar process applied to division. Note in this case that it is pointless to examine the inequality of $4^2 ÷ 3 ≠ 3 ÷ 4^2$. We have no reason to suspect that they are equal – we already know that the commutative law does not apply to division. The aim here is not to demonstrate that these are not equal, but rather to establish that $3 ÷ 4^2$ should not be read as '3 divided by 4 and then squared'. Instead, we seek to prove that $3 ÷ 4^2$ should be read as '3 divided by the square of 4'.

We might suspect at this point that representations are not required. If our pupils understand the distribution of powers over division then it is clear that $3 ÷ 4^2$ cannot be equal to $(\frac{3}{4})^2$, as we have already seen that $(\frac{3}{4})^2 = \frac{3^2}{4^2}$ cannot possibly equal $\frac{3}{4}$. Indeed, if our pupils are secure in following such an argument, we could argue that no more is required. However, it may be helpful for some pupils to see the difference between the two representations, which are explored below.

$4^2 ÷ 3 ≠ 3 ÷ 4^2$

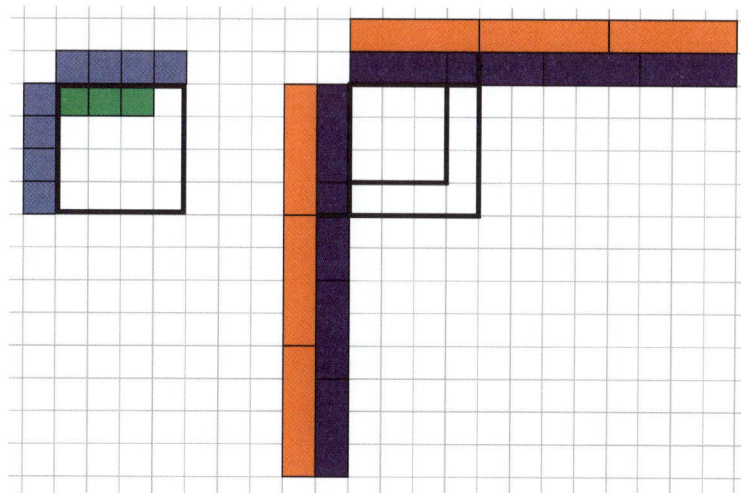

The left-hand diagram shows the relationship between 3 and $4^2$ as a multiplicative comparison (i.e. that 3 is $\frac{3}{16}$ of $4^2$). The right-hand diagram shows 3 broken into 4 pieces – each orange bar is worth 1, so a set of 3 orange bars is worth 3, which the purple bars split into 4 equal pieces. A purple bar is then squared, giving the 3-by-3 square, which when compared to the unit square (shown by the 4-by-4 square or the square of the orange bar) shows the value of $\frac{9}{16}$. The results are obviously not the same; however, the squares in the second diagram are identical to the squares shown when we considered $\left(\frac{3}{4}\right)^2$ (as we would expect), which we have already proven is the same as $\frac{3^2}{4^2}$. Of course, this doesn't fully demonstrate that $3 \div 4^2$ shouldn't be considered as 3 divided by 4 and then squared, only that if it is then this is the same as $3^2 \div 4^2$. The natural question is, then, if $3 \div 4^2$ is the same as $3^2 \div 4^2$, why would we bother with the distinction?

We have now nearly completed defining the different ways we view numbers, how the different operations interact with these numbers, and the laws of arithmetic that these operations obey. We have yet to explore irrational numbers, which we will get to in Chapter 10, but in the next chapter we are going to step into the world of accuracy and explore how our representations can shed light on the idea of rounding numbers.

# Chapter 9
# Accuracy and numerical representations

The ideas of accuracy and rounding have been transformed over recent years. In the past, rounding and accuracy were mainly used in the realms of estimation and measurement. Quantities measured to a certain value had an inherent inaccuracy due to the tools and conditions in which they were measured, and this inaccuracy was captured by rounding the value and giving the accuracy of the rounded value. Alternatively, estimated values were used to give an indication as to size without the need for complex calculation – for example, we might estimate a shopping bill by calculating using approximate values, as this is much more straightforward than calculating with the exact prices of everything in our shopping basket.

The major point about rounded and estimated values is that they are always positive – you are never going to pay a negative amount of money or measure a negative quantity. Indeed, it is still rare today for the rounding of negative values to be discussed in any great detail in a mathematics classroom. However, the advent of computers and their use with complex calculations has changed the face of rounding; the way computers calculate requires a different approach to rounding, which we will explore later in the chapter.

The links between rounding and measurement mean that the most effective representations for rounding tend to be continuous number representations, particularly the vector representation of number. This is not to say that discrete views will not be useful, particularly to resolve one key issue.

## Positive rounding

We will start by looking at rounding to different positive integer powers of 10.

2532 rounded to the nearest 1000, 100 and 10

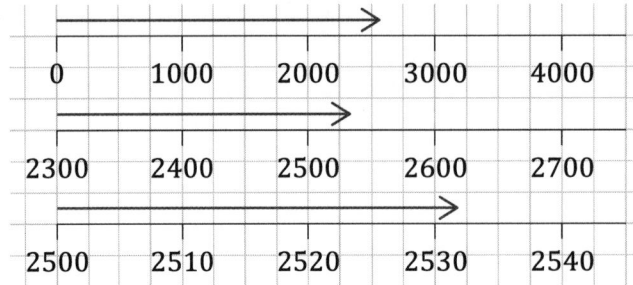

The three number lines above are graduated in 1000s, 100s and 10s respectively, reflecting the accuracy required at each stage. On each number line the value of 2532 has been (approximately) represented. The concept of rounding then can be summarised as, 'Which graduation on the number line is the value closest to?' In the case of the nearest 1000, the number 2532 is slightly closer to 3000 than 2000, indicating that 2532 would round to 3000. However, in the case of the number line graduated in 100s the number 2532 is closer to 2500 than 2600, indicating that 2532 would round to 2500. Finally, when graduated in 10s the value of 2532 is closer to 2530 than 2540, showing that 2532 rounds to 2530.

This idea can then be extended into non-positive integer powers of 10.

2532.6342 rounded to the nearest whole number, 1 decimal place and 2 decimal places

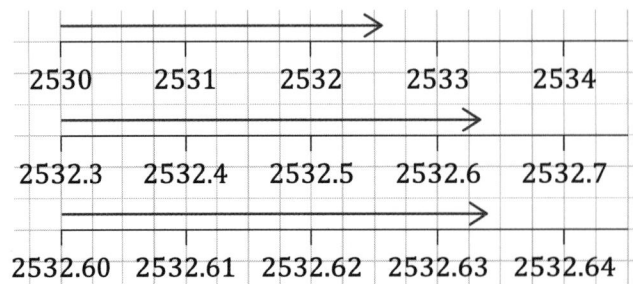

As before, we have number lines graduated in whole numbers, 10s (the first decimal place) and 100s (the second decimal place). Again, the number 2532.6342 is shown (at least approximately): on the first number line the value is closer to 2533, on the second to 2532.6, and on the third to 2532.63.

Of course, we not only consider rounding to the nearest power of 10 but also to significant figures (once pupils are in secondary school). This is particularly useful when we have lots of values of varying sizes. Consider the following:

- 2532.6342 rounded to the nearest 1000
- 532.6342 rounded to the nearest 100
- 32.6342 rounded to the nearest 10
- 2.6342 rounded to the nearest whole number
- 0.6342 rounded to 1 decimal place
- 0.0342 rounded to 2 decimal places
- 0.0042 rounded to 3 decimal places

All of these questions require differing levels of accuracy; however, they all can be replaced with the following:

Round these numbers to 1 significant figure:
- 2532.6342
- 532.6342
- 32.6342
- 2.6342
- 0.6342
- 0.0342
- 0.0042

Many teachers will teach how to identify significant figures based on rules such as, 'The first non-zero digit is the first significant figure'. Rarely do teachers explain why these rules work and why certain digits are considered significant. Our number line representation can do little to aid us here; however, counters (or base ten blocks) can help to make clear why certain digits are significant. Consider the number 2500 represented using place value counters:

What is apparent here is that we only need to represent the thousands and the hundreds value to represent the whole value of the number. This suggests that there are only two significant figures in the number. The only columns that give the 2500 its value are the thousands and the hundreds columns, with most of the responsibility lying with the thousands column. The other columns simply 'hold' the place because we insist on counting in 1s – when we write 2500 we are saying that we have 2500 1s as much as we are saying we have two 1000s and five 100s.

This concept has strong links to writing values in scientific notation or standard index form. If we write 2500 in standard form the result is $2.5 \times 10^3$, which can be seen as the following:

Again, the only values that are represented are the thousands and the hundreds. Notice that because we are counting thousands rather than ones ($2.5 \times 10^3$ can literally be read as 2.5 thousands), we no longer need the two 0s to hold the place.

Consider the number 0.0342. This can be represented using place value counters as follows:

This leads to the conclusion that only the hundredths, thousandths and ten-thousandths are significant in this number. This is again suggested by looking at the number in standard form, which gives $3.42 \times 10^{-2}$ – showing that the 3, 4 and 2 are the significant figures.

A slight tweak is needed when we consider the number 0.03042. Representing this using place value counters gives us:

This might give the appearance that only the 3, 4 and 2 are significant digits in this number. However, there is a gap between the hundredths column and the ten-thousandths column. Using a place value frame helps to make this clear:

| 1s | 0.1s | 0.01s | 0.001s | 0.0001s | 0.00001s |
|---|---|---|---|---|---|
| | | 0.01 | | 0.0001 | 0.00001 |
| | | 0.01 | | 0.0001 | 0.00001 |
| | | 0.01 | | 0.0001 | |
| | | | | 0.0001 | |

Now it is clear that we require $0 \times 10^{-3}$ to hold the place between the $10^{-2}$ column and the $10^{-4}$ column. However, this is a different type of place holding. When we had a number like 2500, the 0s were only necessary to hold the place because we were counting in 1s; once we started counting in 1000s (i.e. writing in standard form) these 0s were no longer necessary. The 0 in-between the 3 and the 4 in 0.03042 will be required no matter what counting unit we use – even if we write the number counting from the hundredths column we would write $3.042 \times 10^{-2}$ (notice that the 0s preceding the 3 are now no longer necessary). This type of place holding, therefore, does not simply correct the columns because we insist on writing numbers by their size in reference to the ones column. Instead, this type of place holding is a fundamental part of the number – without it the separate values of the columns are unclear. I usually refer to these two types of place holding as 'column correction' and 'digit separation', and hopefully this diagram demonstrates why the first of these is not significant whilst the second is.

In terms of rounding to a given number of significant figures (once pupils understand the concept of what makes a figure significant), it is typical just to translate a problem given in significant figures back into a problem regarding rounding to a specific place value column. For example, if asked to round 0.03042 to one significant figure, we would identify the first significant figure as the 3, that 3 is in the hundredths column (or the second decimal place) and then round to that place.

A useful role that counters play in understanding why numbers round in the way they do is to solve the 'key issue' of the halfway point. Consider rounding 2.5 to the nearest whole number. When viewed on a number line, 2.5 appears like this:

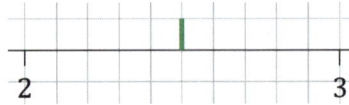

The issue here is that, when viewed continuously, 2.5 lies precisely halfway between 2 and 3 – it is neither closer to 2 nor 3. This means that there is no clear indication as to whether 2.5 should round to 2 or 3. In mathematics, though, the concept of half is different for discrete and continuous values. When viewed continuously, half of 10 is 5, but if you split a group of 10 objects in half then the halfway point is between the fifth and sixth object. This second approach is useful in helping us to see where half-way points should round to.

The place value frame can help us to represent the possible tenths between 2 and 3:

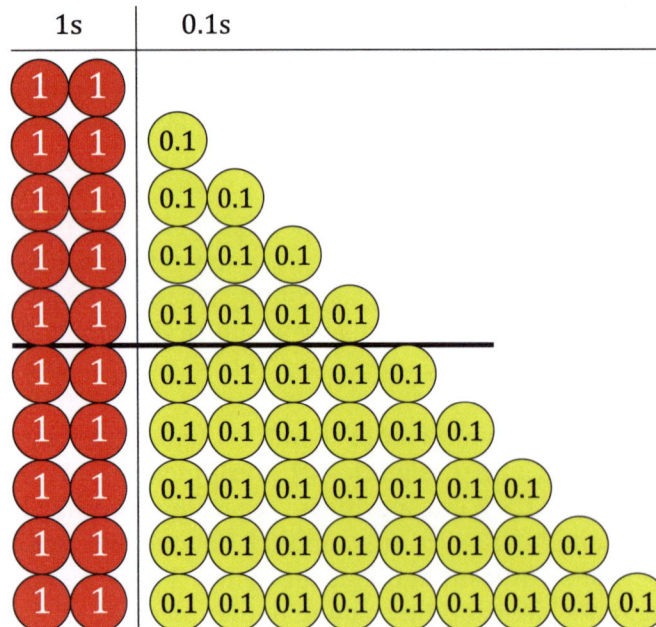

We can see that the number 2 can be followed by 10 possible combinations of '0.1' counters – namely, the 10 digits of 0 through to 9. The thicker black line (between the fifth and sixth counters) shows the halfway point of these possibilities. This leads to the conclusion that 2.5 should round up as it is in the same group as 2.6, 2.7, 2.8 and 2.9.

This idea will clearly generalise to other place value columns, and so combined with the number line view it can account for the rounding of all positive numbers. In the next part of this chapter we will turn our attention to negative rounding.

# Negative rounding

The rounding of negative values opens up some interesting interpretations. Most values work identically to the rounding of positive values. For example, take the value of -3.2 rounded to the nearest whole number:

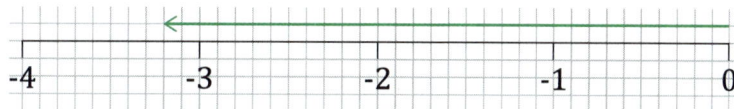

The end of the vector is closer to -3 than any other whole number, so the result is -3. However, this becomes a little less clear when considering -3.5:

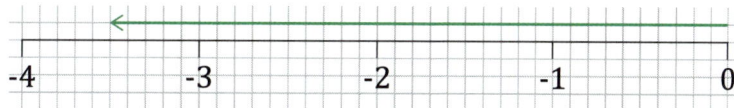

Using the same argument as we did for positive numbers on a number line, we can make a case for the rounded value being -4. This is what is termed 'symmetrical rounding' because the rounding is symmetrical around 0:

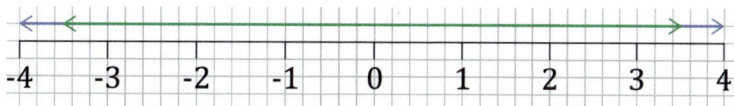

This is generally the approach favoured by mathematicians, and tends to be what is taught by teachers who explore negative rounding in the mathematics classroom.

A different interpretation results from the idea that halfway values always round up. This creates an asymmetrical rounding model as 'up' is generally considered to be in the direction of positive infinity:

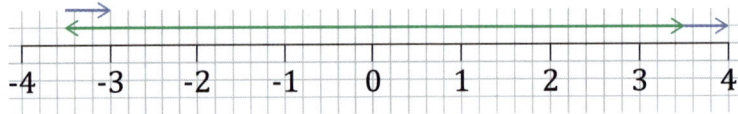

When it comes to computing, both of these rounding models present problems: with symmetrical rounding halfway values always increase in magnitude, and with rounding up the values always increase in size. Because of the floating-point arithmetic operated by most software, computers are often forced to do something that teachers try hard to ensure pupils never do – use rounded values in further calculations. Unfortunately, this is unavoidable because a number can only use a finite number of digits in a computer's memory. The problem arises when a lot of half values arise from the data; if they were all rounded in the same direction, then errors would be propagated with each further calculation. Half values occur frequently in the finance sector, so financial models use a different version of rounding called 'round half to even'.

Rounding half to even works in precisely the same way as ordinary rounding does, but with the exception that halfway values are always rounded to even values. So, in the examples above, 3.5 would round to 4 and -3.5 would round to -4. Importantly, however, 4.5 would also round to 4 and -4.5 would also round to -4. Given that in a large enough data set the number of half values will be equally distributed between how many round up to an even number and how many round down, this will generally lead to many of the rounding errors being cancelled rather than propagated, and so produce a much closer final value than would be obtained from ordinary rounding.

Round half to even is a symmetrical rounding system.

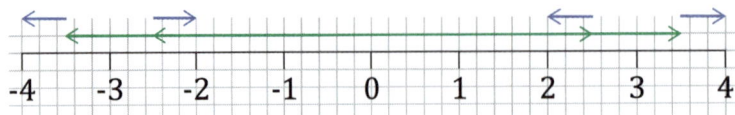

The number line (with or without vectors) is the most powerful way of representing what is happening when we round numbers; none of the other representations can really capture this (although place value counters and base ten blocks can support certain aspects).

However, there is another aspect of accuracy which we have not yet explored – the idea of bounds on rounded numbers. Number lines are again the most useful representation to capture the concept of bounds, and can be used to open up an understanding of bounds to many more pupils than might currently work with them – normally the province of only the more able Key Stage 4 pupils.

The idea of bounds arises from the inaccuracy of measurement. If we have measured a value and due to the conditions or measuring tool used we have only been able to reach a certain level of accuracy, bounds are a way of communicating that inaccuracy. For example, we could measure a length as 2.4 cm ± 0.05 cm. But why ± 0.05 cm? Well, for the answer to this question we return to our number line representation:

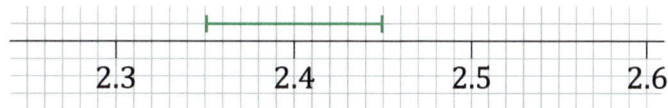

The diagram above shows the value of 2.4 and marks the space where values will round to 2.4 (rather than 2.3 or 2.5.) What we can see here is that the boundary values (bounds) are at 2.35 and 2.45 cm – that is, ± 0.05 cm away from 2.4 cm.

An alternative way of stating this is that the length ($l$) must obey the inequality $2.35 \leq l < 2.45$.

An interesting application of bounds is to analyse how errors propagate in calculations using measured values. For now, we will limit this to considering the four basic operations applied to bounded values.

$(2.4 \pm 0.05) + (1.1 \pm 0.05)$

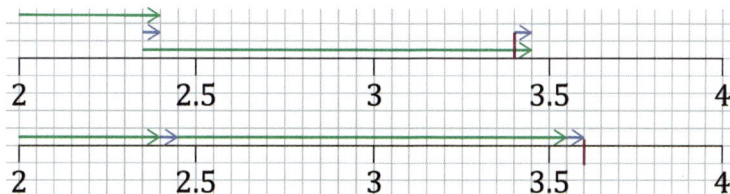

The upper part of the diagram shows the lower bound calculation. We start with the vector for 2.4 (the space between 0 and 2 has been omitted), then subtract 0.05 using the standard head-to-head subtraction for vectors, followed by a sum of 1.1, and then finally another subtraction of 0.05. This results in a lower bound value of 3.4.

The lower part of the diagram shows the upper bound calculation. We can again see the vector for 2.4, but then the 0.05 is added. This is followed by the addition of 1.1, along with the second 0.05. This results in an upper bound value of 3.6. This gives the final bounds on the result of the calculation as $3.4 \leq l < 3.6$. An important detail to notice here is that the size of the possible error has doubled (from 0.05 to 0.1). If we generalise this idea to adding multiple values, it would suggest that the maximum error propagates through multiplication.

$(2.4 \pm 0.05) - (1.1 \pm 0.05)$

Before tackling this example, we must remind ourselves that we are aiming to create the smallest and largest space between the two possible answers. Teachers who regularly teach calculations with bounds will recognise the classic misconception of pupils calculating 2.45 – 1.15 for the upper bound and 2.35 – 1.05 for the lower bound. Our number line representations can show us, respectively, that this does not create the largest or smallest possible space. The diagrams below show this mistaken approach:

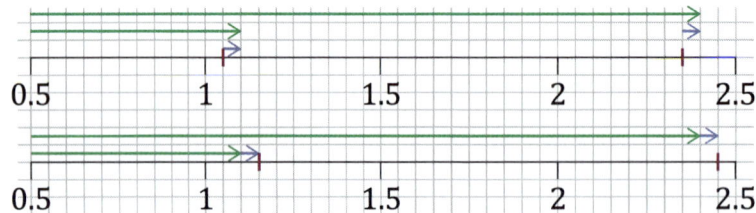

In the upper diagram we see 2.4 – 0.05 using standard head-to-head vector subtraction. On the same number line, we can also see 1.1 – 0.05 using the same approach. The subtraction between the two values is then completed by comparing the differences, with the difference between the two values marked on the number line. In the lower diagram the same idea is used, but with 2.4 + 0.05 and 1.1 + 0.05. The subtraction is again performed as a comparison. What becomes clear is that in both cases the difference is the same. This could indicate that the error has disappeared but, of course, this is impossible. As we know, the reason for this is the mistaken logic in finding the largest and smallest values. The diagrams below show the correct approach:

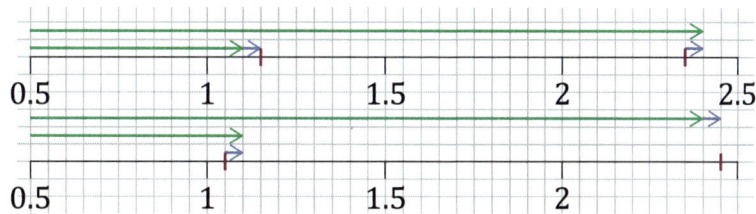

The subtractions here have been completed in the same way, using the comparison between the numbers but head-to-head subtraction for the subtraction within the bounds. This time we see in the upper diagram that the lower bound is the difference between 1.15 and 2.35 (i.e. 1.2), and in the lower diagram that the upper bound is the difference between 1.05 and 2.45 (i.e. 1.4). Now the result is within the bounds $1.2 \leq l < 1.4$. Pupils comfortable with this representation should be more than capable of reasoning this for themselves given the correct task set-up – something along the lines of, 'You have a 2.4 vector and a 1.1 vector and you either add or subtract a 0.05 vector from either one. What is the smallest and largest difference you can find between your two values?' works well. Again, we notice that the bounds have doubled in size, suggesting that – like addition – subtraction of inaccurate values also propagates the error in a multiplicative way.

When it comes to multiplication and division, it is possible to represent the situation using an area model. However, it is my belief that the representation becomes so cumbersome that it is increasingly difficult to illuminate the concept; instead, the representations are more likely to obscure it (or, at worse, just mirror a process without bringing a deeper understanding).

Ultimately, multiplying a decimal number with three digits by another decimal number with three digits is hard work in any representation, so we might be better off using simpler cases of multiplication before tackling multiplications with more digits. I will include just one relatively simple example to illustrate.

$3 \pm 0.5 \times 2 \pm 0.5$

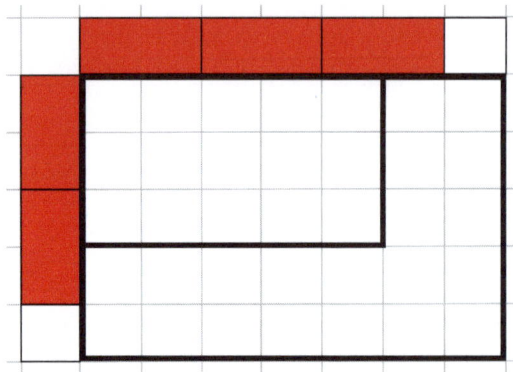

In this representation a '2' bar is being used to stand for 1, so the '1' bar is 0.5. This makes each small square a $0.5^2$ area, which is 0.25. The area of 3.5 × 2.5 is shown compared to the area of 2.5 × 1.5. The difference in areas is a total of 5 units (20 × 0.25), suggesting an answer of 6 ± 2.5 for the area. Given that 25 is the square of 5, this suggests that the error propagates through a process like squaring.

Whilst this illustration is fairly straightforward to follow, an example with a whole number and 2 decimal places (i.e. 2.4 ± 0.05) would require a '20' bar to represent 1 in order to ensure that the number of smaller squares was an easily countable whole number. This would mean that even for a calculation such as 2.4 ± 0.05 × 1.1 ± 0.05, the rectangle would have to be 49 squares long by 23 squares wide. The number of squares could be limited somewhat by using 24.5 squares by 11.5 squares (i.e. using a '10' bar as 1), but even then the number of half squares would make it difficult to see clearly the difference between the two areas. This problem is exacerbated when considering division, where we need to create an area of 2.45 squares using a rectangle with a length of 1.05. For these reasons, I suspect that it is best to simply secure the concept of bounds calculations using addition and subtraction, using representations where necessary, before moving on to look at multiplication and division purely as a calculation exercise.

We are nearly ready to begin the generalisation of the approaches and representations we have developed to the manipulation of algebra. However, before we do, we have one aspect of number left to explore – irrational numbers.

# Chapter 10

# Representing irrational numbers

Irrational numbers are a strange group of numbers – they can't be expressed as fractions, and when written as decimals their expansion becomes a bewildering array of digits without any discernible pattern. With the exception of π, which is used at Key Stage 3 for circle calculations, most work with irrational numbers is left to pupils working towards higher tier GCSE. Despite this, our representations can provide support in both defining and manipulating irrational expressions.

Back in Chapter 2, we met the story of Hippasus and his tribulations with √2. Hippasus was able to show that √2 is irrational, and was ultimately drowned for his efforts. But what had caused Hippasus to begin considering the square root of 2 in the first place? Well, the square root of 2 had been known to Hippasus and his peers for some time as a consequence of perhaps the most well-known Greek mathematical legacy – Pythagoras' theorem.

Consider the triangle below:

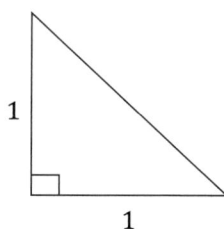

Pythagoras' theorem tells us that the square of the length of the **hypotenuse** in this triangle can be found by squaring each shorter side and adding the results together. This gives:

$1^2 + 1^2 = hypotenuse^2$

$1 + 1 = hypotenuse^2$

$2 = hypotenuse^2$

$\sqrt{2} = hypotenuse$

This implies that there is a length that is equal to √2. The proof that this is irrational is a separate matter (which I will leave to the interested reader to seek out). Given that we accept for now that this is irrational, then that means this length can be shown on a number line:

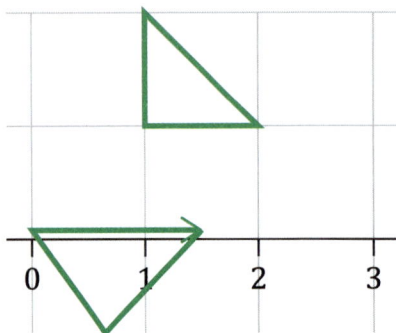

This is actually more important than it looks. We cannot approach the representation of the square root of 2 on a number line as we might do a fraction or terminating decimal. The fact that the decimal expansion of √2 has no discernible pattern means that, no matter how many squares we use to define the space between 0 and 1, we will always end up with our arrow part way along a square. This is in part what makes irrational numbers difficult to understand – where are they? If we can always find a fraction between two other fractions, then surely every point on the number line must be a fraction. What place then does this leave for irrational numbers? Well, as we can see, if irrational length exists, then irrational numbers must exist within the number line. This argument was first made by the Greek astronomer Eudoxus of Cnidus in about 370 BC – and is all the more impressive because the Greeks didn't have the concept of a number line in the same way we do today.

Of course, if we can represent irrational numbers as lengths on a number line, then we must be able to manipulate them as we do other numbers. We will now turn our attention to manipulating irrational numbers.

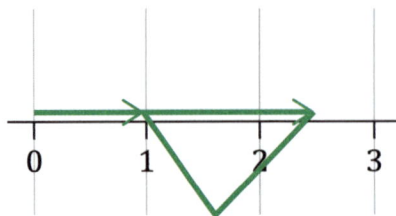

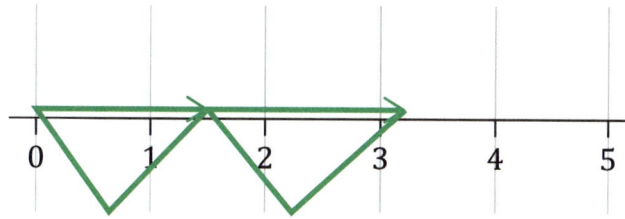

In the first number line the vector for √2 has been translated by one unit to the right, in effect adding 1 to the number. This shows the value of 1 + √2. What is more, given that √2 cannot be expressed more simply, it is also the case that this sum cannot be expressed any more simply.

The second number line shows √2 added to √3 (the shorter lengths on the right triangle are 1 and √2), which again cannot be simplified further and results simply in √2 + √3.

This can also be seen using counters:

We recall from our work with fractions that two differently valued counters can only be added if an exchange can be accomplished that makes the counters the same (i.e. when a $\frac{1}{4}$ counter can be exchanged for two counters of the value $\frac{1}{8}$), so they are like objects for collecting. Clearly, because √2 and √3 are irrational, no such exchange is possible. The implication is therefore that these sums cannot be simplified, and results in 1 + √2 and √2 + √3 respectively.

However, if we look at the same idea when the vectors/counters are all √2, then there are alternative ways to interpret the result:

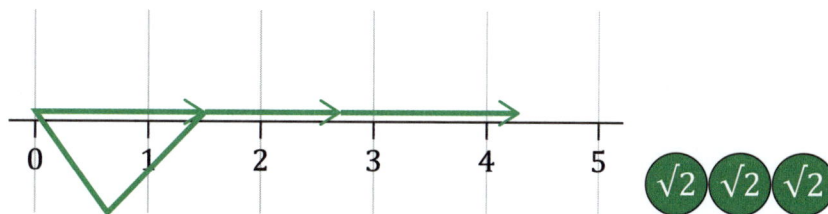

193

In both cases, these representations result in the sort of diagrams we see when multiplying a value by 3. This means that our sum of √2 + √2 + √2 can be written as the multiplication 3 × √2, or simply 3√2. Of course, all of this is a consequence of the distributive law of multiplication as applied to addition: if we have √2 + √2 + √2 then this can be written as √2(1 + 1 + 1) = √2 × 3.

We have seen how the addition of irrational numbers can give rise to the multiplication of an irrational number by a rational number, so the obvious question is, 'What happens when we multiply two irrational numbers?' For now, we will focus on a particular type of number – the square roots of non-square integers (typically called **surds**).

## Surds

A point to note here is that surds can again be dealt with using the distributive law of powers over multiplication. We know that roots are equivalent to power $\frac{1}{2}$, so the idea of multiplying surds can be thought of as akin to multiplying powers. This means that a calculation like √2 × √3 can be considered equivalent to $2^{\frac{1}{2}} \times 3^{\frac{1}{2}}$. This is simply the result of applying the power of $\frac{1}{2}$ to a product – that is, $(2 \times 3)^{\frac{1}{2}}$ or $6^{\frac{1}{2}}$. This makes √2 × √3 equal to √6.

If we apply the area model to √2 × √3, the result might look something like this:

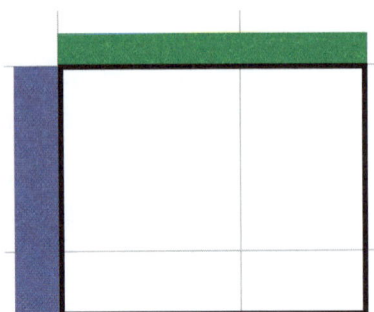

The green bar represents √3 and the blue √2. The area then represents the product of √2 × √3. The difficulty here is that there is no real way to show that this area has a value equal to √6. We can try a comparison to a 1 × √6 area (as shown in the right-hand diagram that follows), but whilst the two may look like they could be equal, there is no obvious way to determine from the diagram that they are precisely equal. This is due to the inherent inaccuracy in producing the lengths and the fact that these inaccuracies will propagate through the area calculation (you can see now why we

explored accuracy before looking at irrational numbers), producing physically different areas in the diagrams that should actually be the same.

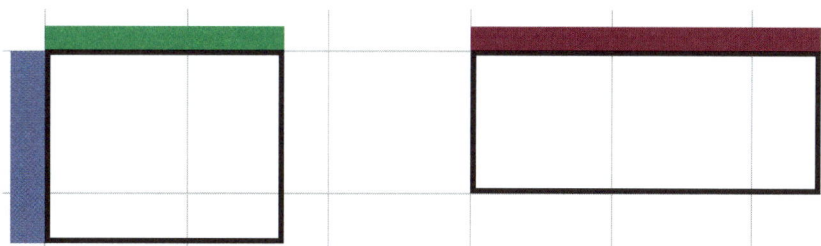

For the same reasons, the multiplication of, or by, compound surd values are equally
difficult to represent, to the point that it is better simply to explore these concepts as
numerical exercises (such as how we showed $\sqrt{2} \times \sqrt{3} = \sqrt{6}$). For example, some
teachers may be tempted to explore the multiplication of compound values using the
area model, such as the diagram below which shows $(1 + \sqrt{3})(2 + \sqrt{2})$:

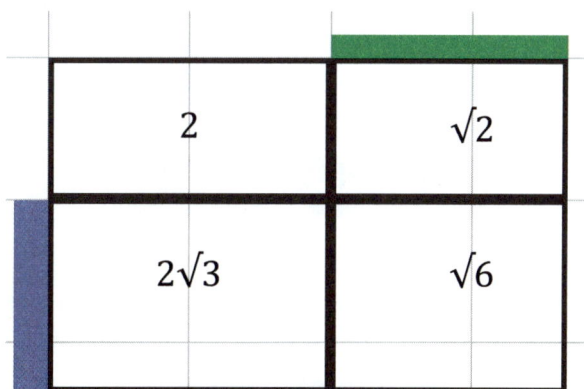

However, if pupils have properly understood our teaching of multiplication and of
surds then this should be something that they already appreciate. Pupils who make
mistakes, such as writing $(1 + \sqrt{3})(2 + \sqrt{2}) = 2 + \sqrt{6}$, are showing one of two things:
either they are just being a bit sloppy and forgetful in their work or they don't understand multiplication properly. If the former, then pupils probably don't need this to be
re-explained – simply drawing their attention to the mistake should be enough to
allow them to self-correct. If the latter, the pupils probably need more support on
multiplication generally, which may require going back to earlier examples of multiplication. This diagram could be part of that re-exploration of multiplication and its

links to area, but it is unlikely to solve the problem on its own (particularly as at least one of the areas is not clearly identifiable from its components).

This is not to say that a grid method is not suitable for the multiplication of surds (it is the method I use in order to create links for pupils between multiplying integers, surds and algebraic expressions, which we will come to later), but an actual scale area model is unlikely to add anything extra to the development of the concept.

For similar reasons, it is not particularly useful to use representations to explore the concept of division with surds. Whilst it is possible to create a rectangle with a length of $\sqrt{3}$, for example, it is virtually impossible to confirm that the area of the rectangle has, say, 12 squares. So, whilst we can consider $12 \div \sqrt{3}$ as a rectangle with an area of 12 and one side of $\sqrt{3}$, it doesn't really develop the concept. If pupils are already comfortable with the link between division and area/length, then this will not improve by trying to represent this particular division, and it certainly will do nothing to help solve the division itself.

One aspect of surds that we do explore in the secondary classroom is the equivalence of two surds – for example, $\sqrt{12} = 2\sqrt{3}$. Clearly, this has implications for the addition and subtraction of surds. Consider the calculation $\sqrt{12} + 5\sqrt{3}$. At first glance this may appear to be a calculation that cannot be simplified. This supposition would seem to be confirmed if we view it as the collection of objects using counters:

However, if we know that $\sqrt{12}$ can be exchanged for $2\sqrt{3}$ then the picture changes:

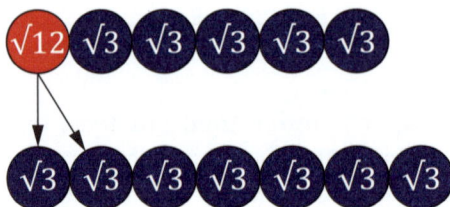

So, the result is that $\sqrt{12} + 5\sqrt{3} = 7\sqrt{3}$.

Some understandable questions to ask are: 'Can we see why this exchange is happening?', 'Why do $\sqrt{12}$ and $2\sqrt{3}$ end up with the same value?' and 'Can we represent this in a way to reveal the structure that makes this true?' Well, if we return to the beginning of the chapter, it was Pythagoras' theorem that allowed us to define irrational numbers as a length on the number line, and it can also show us if two surds are of equal length.

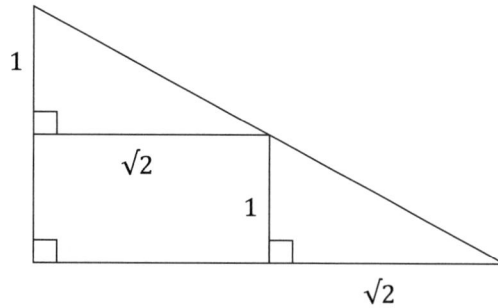

If we first apply Pythagoras' theorem to the two smaller right-angled triangles, the calculations appear as follows:

$1^2 + (\sqrt{2})^2 = hypotenuse^2$

$1 + 2 = hypotenuse^2$

$3 = hypotenuse^2$

$\sqrt{3} = hypotenuse$

If we apply the same logic to the larger right-angled triangle, we get the following:

$2^2 + (2\sqrt{2})^2 = hypotenuse^2$

$4 + 2^2(\sqrt{2})^2 = hypotenuse^2$

$4 + 4 \times 2 = hypotenuse^2$

$4 + 8 = hypotenuse^2$

$12 = hypotenuse^2$

$\sqrt{12} = hypotenuse$

This shows that the length of √12 is equal to 2 × √3:

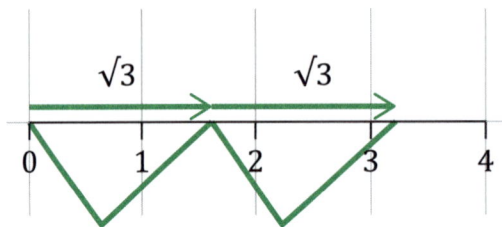

Whilst this allows us to demonstrate that two apparently different surd expressions are related, it doesn't actually provide an efficient approach for simplifying a surd expression. In the above example we can demonstrate that √12 and 2√3 are equal, but if we didn't know that they were equal this wouldn't necessarily help us to decide whether √12 simplified or not. Of course, as a numerical exercise using our understanding of roots distributing over multiplication, this is a relatively straightforward proposition:

$$\sqrt{12} = \sqrt{4 \times 3}$$
$$= \sqrt{4} \times \sqrt{3} \text{ (by the distributive law)}$$
$$= 2 \times \sqrt{3}$$
$$= 2\sqrt{3}$$

This process is not very compatible with representation – creating a square of area 12 and then showing that the length of the square is 2√3 is so difficult as to be almost meaningless, particularly when demonstrated to pupils. The strong suggestion is that Pythagoras' theorem can be used to demonstrate that there are surd expressions that are equivalent. Once pupils are comfortable with this idea, then the numerical approach to simplifying surds can be explored with them, modelling the process and allowing them time to practise and become fluent.

We have now explored all of the aspects of number that we are going to cover in this book. Whilst it is worth noting that representing complex numbers in an Argand diagram is a natural extension of the vector notation on a number line that we have explored here, it is not my intention to stray into the realms of mathematics taught exclusively at A level (it would need a much longer book!). This means that we are now ready to look at generalising what we have seen in number to the world of algebra.

# Chapter 11

# Introducing algebra

An interesting aspect of all our representations to date is the way we have defined value. In all cases, the value of the key part of the representation has been externally defined. Take the simple counter:

At first there was an implicit suggestion that this counter stood for 1. However, the same counter can be assigned other integer values, fractional and decimal values, and even surd values. Similarly, we started with number lines graduated in 1s, but we have also seen them graduated in 5s, 10s, 100s, 1000s, as well as fractional and decimal values. Vectors must be imposed on a number line in order to have a value, therefore a vector without a corresponding number line (such as the one below) has a completely unknown value.

Even bars or Cuisenaire rods can have different values attached to them. Although Cuisenaire rods very naturally assume the values from 1 to 10, we have also defined them to show different fractional and decimal values. Their value is unknown unless they have been properly classified. Consider the bar below:

Is this a '10' bar? Is it a bar from a base ten block set? In fact, if we set it on a grid to define its length, we can see that it has a length of 12 squares:

But to be certain that it does actually have a length of 12, we need to be sure that each square is worth 1. What if each square represents 2? Or $\frac{1}{2}$? Or what if each square is itself an unknown length? All we can say for sure is that the orange bar is 12 times longer (or 11 squares longer) than a single square.

This is the beginning of algebra. If we see algebra as a generalisation of the relationships we observe in number, then this representation exemplifies the emergence of that generalisation – the idea that, regardless of value, the relationship between a single square and the orange bar remains the same.

Other important aspects of algebra also begin to emerge, such as the value of a counter or the length of a square, vector or bar being variable – we can choose them to suit our requirements. Of course, these needs might be externally imposed (they might have to adhere to certain values in order for a statement of equality, or inequality, to be true) or we might be free to explore the relationships (we might set the length equal to 1, 2, 3, etc. in order to analyse and graph the changes in a related variable). These concepts are first introduced in England during upper primary school (when pupils are around 9 or 10) and are developed all the way through to when pupils stop compulsory maths study at age 16.

In this chapter, we will focus on using manipulatives that support the introduction of this symbolic representation, as well as the different types of algebra we see during our work with pupils in the classroom, starting with the formation of basic expressions.

Most of the representations we have explored can support the introduction of algebraic expressions, including simple counters:

Here we see the variable value of the counter assigned a symbol, typically $x$. I am sure many teachers will have been faced with the question, 'What is $x$?' This is the time to remind pupils about all the different values we have assigned to individual counters in the past, and that the point of this is not so much the value of $x$ as it is to explore the relationship between $x$ and other sets of counters. We can then begin to relate this to other sets of counters, starting simply with an example like this:

Pupils familiar with this sort of representation should have little trouble in seeing these diagrams as something akin to 'two more than $x$', which we can represent symbolically as $x + 2$.

We can create other sets of counters, such as:

which give expressions equivalent to $x - 2$ and $2x$, respectively. The important point to stress to pupils is that we are representing the relationship between the variable value of $x$ as the single counter and the set of counters we end up with. No matter what the value of $x$, the first and second set of counters represent something that is 2 less than $x$, whereas the third set represents something that is twice the value of a single $x$.

The same approach can be taken by 'freeing' a vector from the number line. These free vectors can be combined with vectors of defined lengths to produce similar expressions:

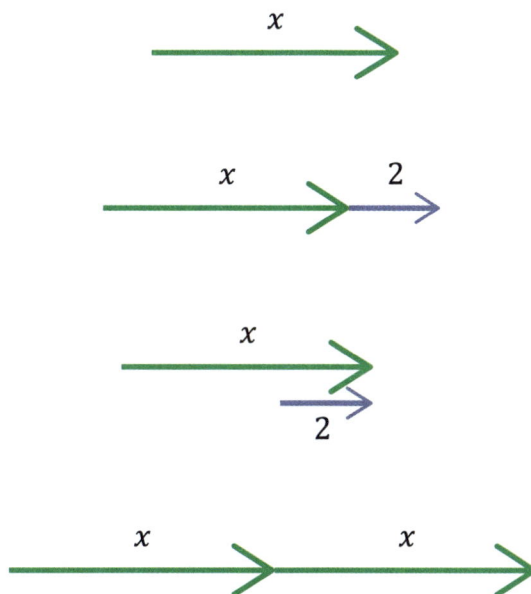

Here we see the free vector defined as $x$, and then other expressions defined in relation to it, namely $x + 2$, $x - 2$, and $2x$ respectively.

If pupils are familiar with these representations then they should have little trouble seeing these as general expressions of relationships with which they are already comfortable. However, if pupils are not familiar with these representations then they won't recognise either the form of the relationship or the general expressions. This speaks to the point I made in the very first chapter: it is counterproductive to wait until the point of use to introduce a representation. If the first time pupils see a vector representation is when it is being used to outline the ideas of algebra, then it is going to fail. Conversely, if pupils understand that these representations show relationships between numbers then they will develop the understanding of these relationships generalised.

One advantage of vectors over counters in this context is that they are better at illustrating the division of the variable. For example, in order to show $x$ divided by 2 using counters, we really need to define 2 counters to be $x$. Whilst this may well prove useful later when manipulating expressions, it is perhaps not the best way to begin early generalisations of the concept. With vector representations, however, the division can be represented in the same way as division was shown for known vector values – namely by splitting:

The blue arrows here are half the size of the green arrow, which is defined as $x$, and so each of the blue arrows is related to $x$ as they are $\frac{1}{2}x$ or $\frac{x}{2}$.

Unfortunately, even with vectors it can be difficult to capture three particular types of expression – squaring, division by the variable, and multiplication of two variables. Multiplication with vectors typically appears as repeated addition, but it is not possible to repeat a vector an unknown number of times. Division is shown by splitting the vector, but you cannot split the vector into an unknown number of pieces. We will now explore these three expressions in more detail.

# Squaring

Squaring can be solved by employing and adapting a representation that can cope with different views of multiplication – bars, or their related representation, algebra tiles.

The application of bar modelling to algebra, or algebra tiles, has grown in popularity in the UK and US in recent years, although their use can be traced back to the mid-1980s. The popularity of algebra tiles stems from their utility in allowing the concrete manipulation of algebraic expressions. The same basic expressions we have explored so far in this chapter can be seen below using algebra tiles:

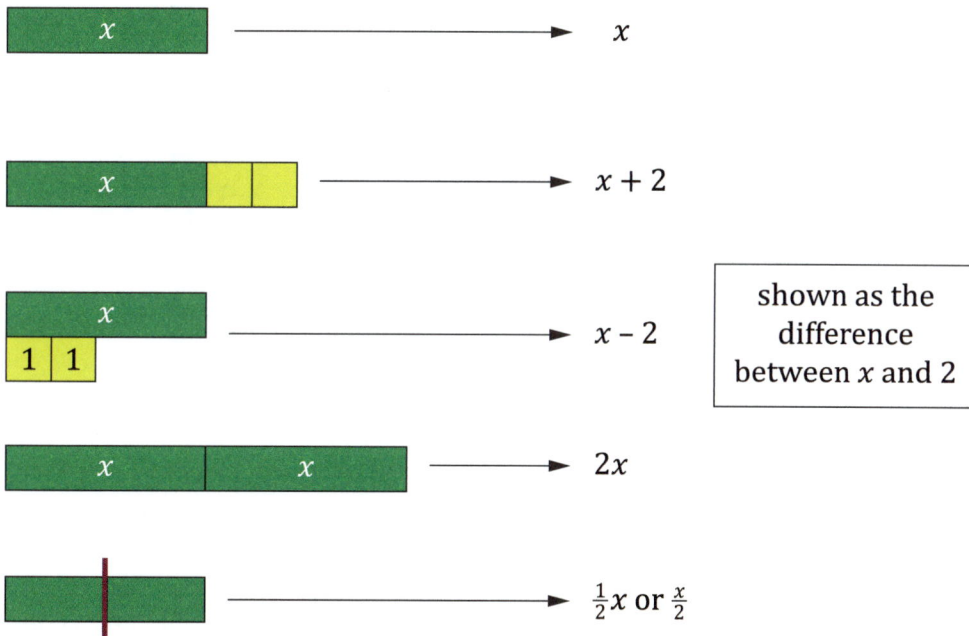

The real benefit of algebra tiles, however, is that they can be used to represent multiplication using the area model. This versatility enables much greater manipulation of expressions, including the introduction of squaring.

Back in Chapter 5, when powers were introduced, we touched on the importance of the change of dimension in supporting the development of algebra.

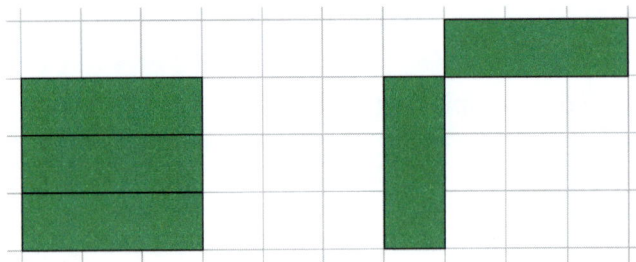

The pair of diagrams above introduces the idea of squaring by showing the square of 3 in two forms. The left-hand diagram is the typical array approach – 3 stacks of the '3' bar to create a square with a value of 9. Clearly, this approach cannot be used to define $x^2$ as we are unable to create a stack of unknown height. However, the approach in the right-hand diagram can be used with algebra tiles to create an $x$ square – a square with an '$x$' bar on the side and an '$x$' bar along the top.

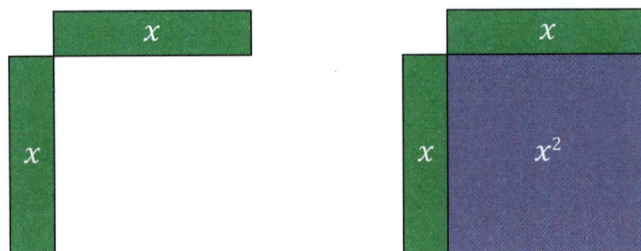

In the above, the left-hand diagram shows the '$x$' bars arranged to form an '$x$' square. The right-hand diagram shows the same, but with a tile unique to the algebra tiles created to specifically represent $x^2$. It is the $x$ and $x^2$ tiles, along with the yellow '1' tiles, that typically make up a set of algebra tiles. These three tiles together enable the manipulation of algebra in a concrete fashion and can really support pupils' understanding of the underlying structure inherent in algebraic relationships.

For the second time now, I suspect you might be thinking that I have broken my own cardinal rule which I mentioned again at the start of this chapter – that representations should not wait to be introduced until the point of utility. I justify this here because I strongly believe that pupils need to see algebra tiles not as a separate representation but as a generalisation of bar modelling. Everything we have seen (and we will see) around the use of algebra tiles will mirror precisely how we have used bars to work with numbers and operations. Algebra tiles are not a new representation; they are simply a bar model where the length of the bar is variable. Algebra tiles will prove to be a key representation as we continue to explore algebra, particularly when multiplying algebraic terms.

# Division by the variable

The next type of expression we need to consider is division by a variable – for example, $\frac{2}{x}$. This is the most difficult type of expression to represent, as we cannot adequately represent a known length divided into an unknown number of pieces unless the final number of pieces is known. Take $\frac{6x}{x}$, which is shown below using counters:

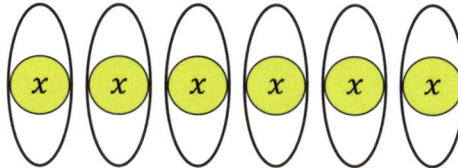

The division here is represented as creating groups of size $x$, with the result being 6 groups. This shows that $\frac{6x}{x} = 6$. Of course, this only works because the variable also appears in the numerator and to the same power as the denominator. The same idea can be represented in vector or bar form:

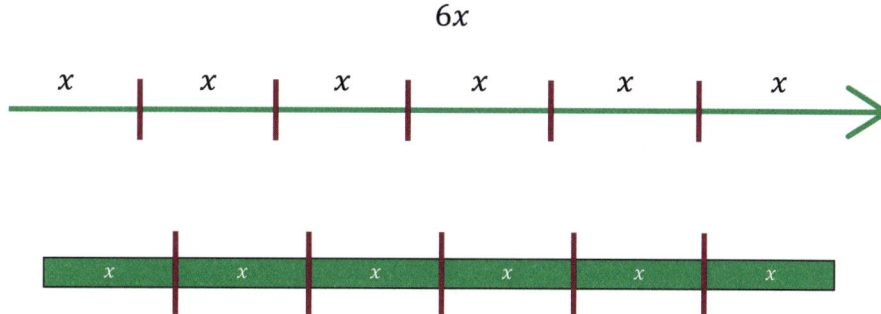

The division here is represented as creating groups of size $x$, with the result being 6 groups. This shows that $\frac{6x}{x} = 6$. Of course, this only works because the variable also appears in the numerator and to the same power as the denominator. The same idea can be represented in vector or bar form:

In both cases the $6x$ is split into groups of size $x$, giving 6 groups. Alternatively, this can be interpreted as $6x$ split into 6 shares, with the size of each share giving 6. This shows us that the result $\frac{6x}{x} = 6$ also implies that $\frac{6x}{6} = x$, which is an implication we are familiar with from ordinary division.

Returning to $\frac{2}{x}$, we cannot use the same idea. Each of the three representations that follow show 2, but it is hard to see how we could create either groups of size $x$ or split them into $x$ pieces without choosing the value of $x$.

We can get closer to seeing how this division works by revisiting the area model and using it with division:

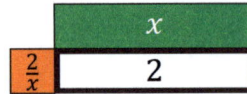

This at least shows us an interpretation of $\frac{2}{x}$, although it doesn't really add any value to the concept, beyond perhaps allowing us to recognise that there is a length that exists that can represent $\frac{2}{x}$.

My view is that this type of expression is another one that is best left to symbolic representation. I will leave it to the informed teacher to decide whether this means we postpone the introduction of expressions like this to a point after the ones we have considered above or explore them all at the same time.

A final alternative representation for $\frac{2}{x}$ is the ordered-pair graph, with one axis scaled in numbers and the other scaled in $x$.

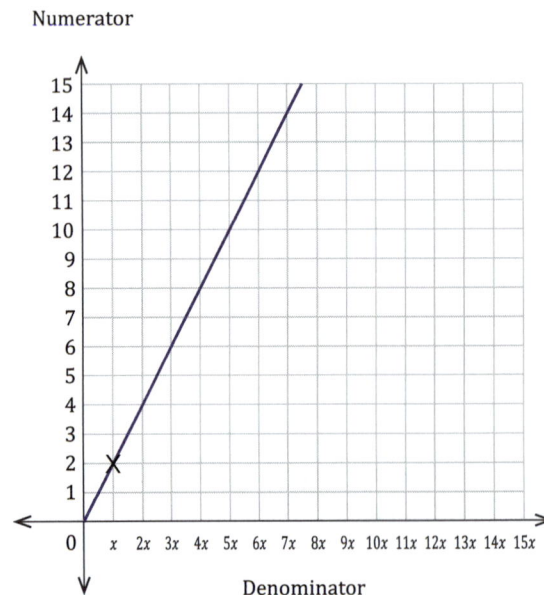

Again, I'm not convinced that this adds much to the idea of what $\frac{2}{x}$ means. What it does make clear is that $\frac{2}{x}$ is equal to $\frac{4}{2x}$, $\frac{6}{3x}$, $\frac{8}{4x}$ and so on. It really does seem that whilst we can talk about $\frac{2}{x}$ being 2 split into $x$ shares (or groups of size $x$), representing this in a meaningful way seems to be beyond the representations we have explored (and is possibly beyond any meaningful representation).

# Multiplication of two variables

The final type of expression we will consider is the multiplication of separate variables – for example, $xy$. Standard algebra tile sets cannot represent these in a concrete fashion as they only include single variable bars (i.e. you can use them to represent either $x$ or $y$ but not both simultaneously). However, it is possible to accomplish this visually using an area model:

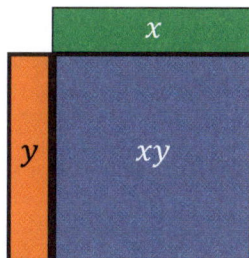

We will find that this sort of visualisation will be useful when **expanding** and **factorising** expressions (see Chapter 14), as well as illustrating why certain expressions will and won't simplify. It is therefore valuable to consider it here before we move on to manipulating expressions.

Expressions are only one form of algebraic construct that we use with pupils. It is now time to explore the other algebraic relationships that we study in the classroom – equations, formulae and identities.

# Equations

In Chapter 15, we will look at solving equations and how different representations can support pupils in seeing the underlying logic behind this process, so for now we will consider only how equations appear and their similarity and difference to formulae as well as to identities.

In the early part of this chapter we examined the idea of whether conditions on the variable or unknown value can be imposed externally. This includes where the relationship has to satisfy a given equality. For example, consider the simple equation $x + 4 = 9$. We have seen different ways of representing the expression $x + 4$, so for the time being we need to focus on the equality:

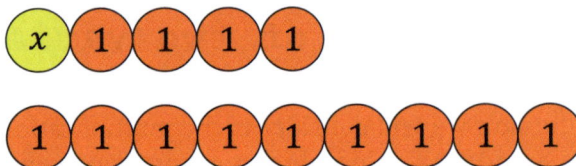

When represented using counters (although we could represent the 4 and the 9 as single counters with their own value) we find that we would have to exchange the 4 and 9 counters for single counters in order to solve the equation later. The important point for now is that pupils recognise that the equation implies that the two sets of counters must be worth the same, and so this limits the possible values that $x$ could take.

The same equation can be shown using vectors:

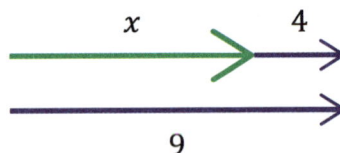

Here the equality is represented by the fact that the vectors are the same length.

Bars/algebra tiles perform in an identical way to the vectors for this equation:

Again, we see the equal length showing the equality between the two expressions.

# Formulae

Formulae appear almost identical to equations in the following representations:

$y = x + 4$

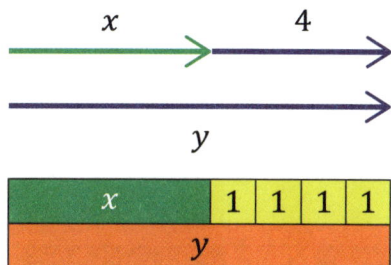

The obvious difference here is that $x + 4$ is no longer constrained by the fact that it must total 9. Instead, we have a relationship between the two variables, so we are free to choose either $x$ or $y$, but once chosen the other becomes fixed. I have only included the vector and algebra tile models here because it is harder to make the equality work with counters.

A benefit of these representations for formulae is that they can make manipulation quite straightforward. For example, we are used to seeing the sorts of arrangements in the **formula** above as both sums and subtractions. We may have represented $y = x + 4$, but it could equally represent $y - 4 = x$ or even $y - x = 4$ using the count back or difference interpretations of subtraction, respectively. We can apply the same strategies to more complicated formulae:

$$F = \frac{5C - 160}{9}$$

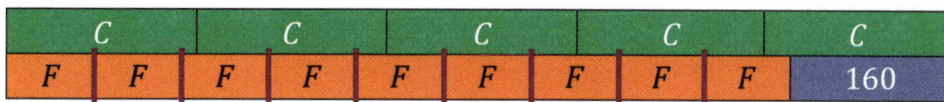

Whilst this formula was originally written as $F = \frac{5C - 160}{9}$, it could just as easily be considered as any of the following:

$5C - 160 = 9F$

$9F + 160 = 5C$

$$C = \frac{9F + 160}{5}$$

A vector form can show the same formula, but counters make it difficult to capture the essence of the formula and the equality in the same way.

Finally we will look at identities.

## Identities

Consider $x + 2 + x + 3 \equiv 2x + 5$:

Admittedly, pupils would need simplifying skills to fully appreciate this diagram (which we will cover in the next chapter), but they should be able to see that what makes this an identity is that the top line can be rearranged to be identical to the bottom line. In general, most algebraic manipulations can be rewritten to produce identities – for example, we can ask pupils to factorise $x^2 + 5x + 6$ or we can ask them to show that $x^2 + 5x + 6 \equiv (x + 2)(x + 3)$. We will explore how algebra tiles can be used to support an understanding of this process in Chapter 14.

Now that we have developed an understanding of how algebra serves to generalise the relationships we see in numbers, how representations can support with this generalisation, and the different forms of algebra that we might ask pupils to work with, we can explore the manipulation of different algebraic relationships. We start with manipulating expressions.

# Chapter 12

# Simplifying algebraic expressions

Simplification is often taught as a process, commonly called something like 'collecting like terms'. Teachers will model for pupils the idea that variables represented by the same symbol can be collected together, but that variables represented by different symbols cannot be collected together. For example, with an expression like $3x + 2y + 4x + 5y$, the $x$ terms will be added to give $7x$ and then the $y$ terms collected to give $7y$, so the expression is simplified to give $7x + 7y$. What teachers often skip is one of the most important aspects of this process – *why* we collect together like terms.

In the previous chapter, we looked at the idea that the purpose of algebra is to generalise the relationships we see in number. Here are some examples of these sorts of relationships:

1   Adding 4 to a number and then adding 5 to a number gives the same result as adding 9 to the number.

2   Starting with a number, adding 4, then adding the same starting number and then adding 5 gives the same result as doubling the starting number and then adding 9.

3   Starting with a number, doubling it and then adding 10 is the same as starting with the same number, adding 5 and then doubling the number.

4   Starting with a number, squaring it and then adding the starting number is the same as taking the starting number and multiplying it by 1 more than the starting number.

Some of these processes result in fewer calculation steps than the alternatives (e.g. 1 and 2) – that is, the calculation becomes *simpler* than it might otherwise have been. This illustrates the point of simplification: it takes complex calculations and reduces the number of calculation steps required to compute the result. Indeed, the use of the word 'compute' is deliberate here – in the early days of computers, when memory space was at a premium, it was important to ensure that calculations did not include any more steps than necessary, as every step in the calculation required memory space. Today, with random access memory (or RAM) so abundant in most computers, the need is less pressing, but it is still considered good practice to ensure that computers spend no more than the minimum amount of memory space and processing time in carrying out necessary functions. So, it is important that pupils don't just understand the process of simplification but also the concept – what it is aiming to achieve in terms of reducing calculation steps. The English national curriculum suggests that simplification (as well as the material covered in Chapters 13–16) should be taught when pupils start secondary school, with some of it waiting until pupils are at least 14 years old.

An understanding of simplification, as well as procedural fluency, can be supported by using suitable representations to allow a visualisation of the manipulation. One of the simplest ways to do this is with counters:

$2x + 4 + x + 5$

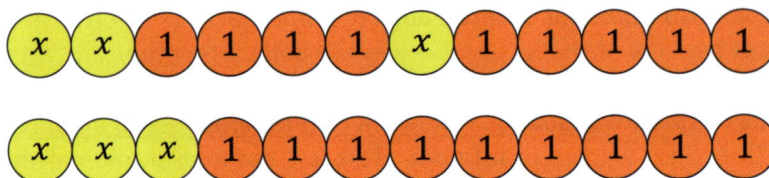

If the idea of simplification is to make the groups as simple as possible, what could be more straightforward than putting all of the $x$ counters next to each other and then putting all of the '1' counters next to each other? The benefit of using the '1' counters here, rather than separate '4' and '5' counters, is that the two strings of counters end up being the same length, reinforcing the fact that the two expressions are equal.

There are two key points here that we want to keep in mind:

1   The point of this simplification is the reduction in calculation steps. Pupils should be aware that this process is literally saying, 'If we take any number, double it, add 4, add the starting number again and then add 5, then we can shorten the process by simply taking the same starting number, multiplying by 3 and adding 9.' If we are going to avoid pupils losing sight of the purpose and just becoming bogged down in the process of simplifying, then it will be important to keep revisiting this idea.

2   The steps in this simplification are nothing more than a consequence of the laws of arithmetic. The switching of $2x + 4 + x + 5$ to $2x + x + 4 + 5$ is due to the commutative law of addition: $2x$ and $x$ come together and $2x + x$ becomes $(2 + 1)x$ or $3x$. The fact that $3x + 4 + 5$ becomes $3x + 9$ is due to the associative law, allowing us to sum the 4 and 5 before adding the $3x$. This can be a useful way of reinforcing that pupils' work with algebra is about the generalisation of the relationships between numbers – providing they have the proper depth of

understanding of the laws of arithmetic as developed using the approaches outlined in Chapter 7.

The same simplification can be shown using vectors:

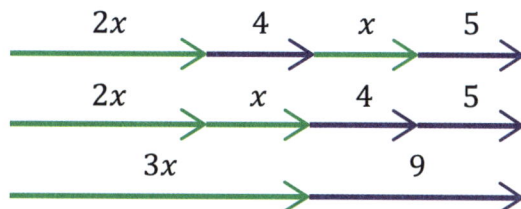

It can also be illustrated using bars/algebra tiles:

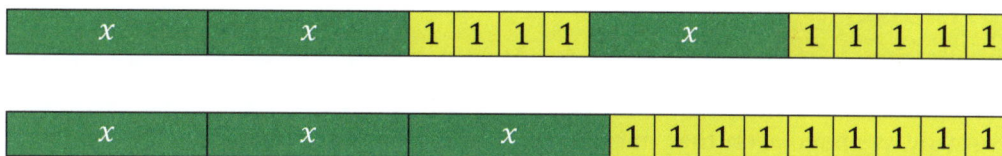

We can explore expressions involving subtraction in a similar way, including those that result in negative results:

$2x + 4 - x - 5$

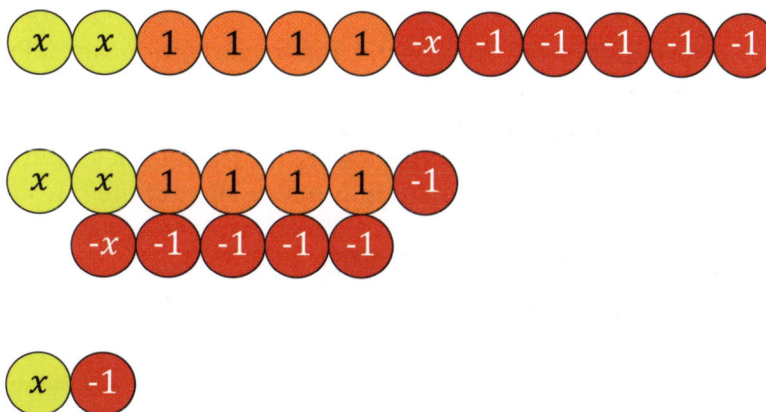

In this diagram we see the concept of zero-pairs applied to both numbers and algebra. The '-$x$' counter forms a zero-pair with one of the '$x$' counters, leaving one '$x$' counter remaining. The four '1' counters form zero-pairs with four of the '-1' counters, result-ing in a single '-1' counter remaining. This leaves the result as $x - 1$. Once again, this should reinforce the idea that algebra behaves in the same way as numbers, and that the relationships which hold true for numbers are generalised into algebra.

A virtually identical diagram emerges when we use bars/algebra tiles:

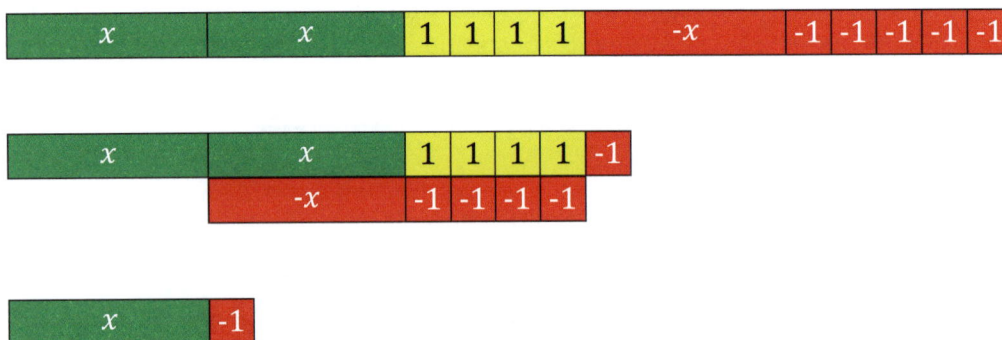

Previously, we have seen that bars do not handle negative values well. Algebra tiles seek to circumvent this by combining bars with the idea of zero-pairs, typically asso-ciated with counters. In concrete sets of algebra tiles, one side of the tile usually indicates the positive values of $x$, $x^2$ and 1, whilst the reverse depicts the negative version of each tile, so $-x$, $-x^2$ and $-1$. This enables algebra tiles to work with expres-sions where part, or all, of the expression turns out to have negative coefficients.

Strictly speaking, we don't need the negative tiles in this case; however, we can just complete the subtractions as comparisons, like we do with ordinary bars:

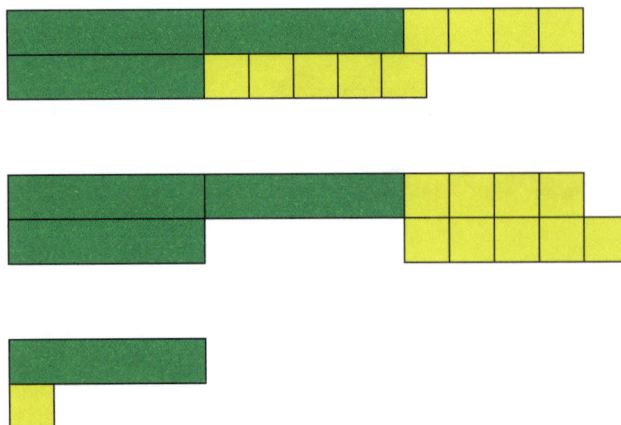

The logic here is that having started with $2x + 4$, we subtract $x$ and 5; technically, this is reimagining the expression as $2x + 4 - (x + 5)$ using the difference interpretation of subtraction. The comparisons are then completed separately in the second line, with $2x$ compared to $x$ and 4 to 5. This leaves a single $x$ as the difference in the '$x$' bars, and a 5 underneath as the difference between 4 and 5. The result is the difference between $x$ and 1, or $x - 1$.

The vector representation can also be used to simplify this expression (and others like it) with a couple of interesting interpretations:

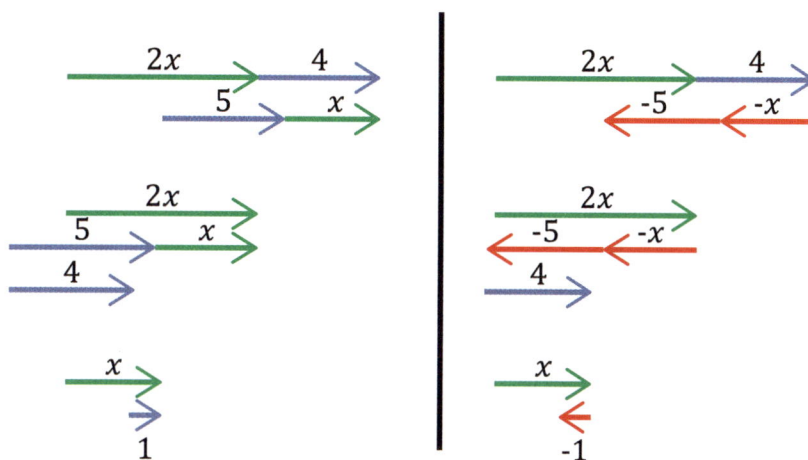

In the left-hand diagram we see the $2x$ and 4 added together, and then an $x$ and a 5 both subtracted. This is then rearranged to pair the $2x$ with the subtracted $x$, then the subtracted 5 and the 4 (shown as the difference between 5 and 4). This leaves a single $x$, with the remaining 1 subtracted.

In the right-hand diagram, we still see the $2x$ and 4 added, but now the -$x$ and -5 are interpreted as negative vectors rather than vectors subtracted – in effect, the expression is reimagined as $2x + 4 + (-x) + (-5)$. Again, the vectors are rearranged to pair the $2x$ with the -$x$, followed by the -5 which then has 4 added to it. The result once again is a single $x$, but now with a resultant from the numerical values of -1.

There are benefits and drawbacks to the vector approaches set out above, and these are similar to those effecting the two approaches using bars/algebra tiles. One of the major benefits is the reinforcing of the idea that subtraction and addition are two sides of the same coin – that subtraction can be considered as a form of addition. On the downside, it is difficult to draw the vectors to accurately capture the relationships – for example, drawing $x$ as precisely half of $2x$. Another problem is the introduction of further bars or vectors to represent the negative values where they are not strictly necessary. However, it is worth noting that these negative bars will be extremely useful later on (when we consider factorisation) to avoid the need for overlapping areas.

Most expressions that can be simplified can be manipulated using counters, tiles or vectors. A few of these are worth exploring in order to remind us of some of the important considerations we touched on in earlier chapters or that can give rise to pupil misconceptions.

$2x + 4 - 3x - 5$

Counters, using zero-pairs, can support the understanding of this simplification quite well:

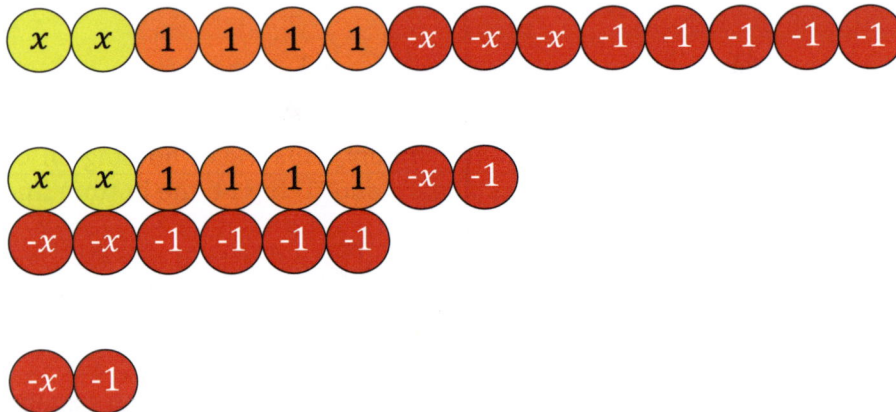

This time the zero-pairs formed leave only a -x and a -1, showing that the expression simplifies to -x – 1.

There is the possibility for misunderstanding to creep in with algebra tiles, particularly if we choose to use the difference interpretation of subtraction rather than negative tiles:

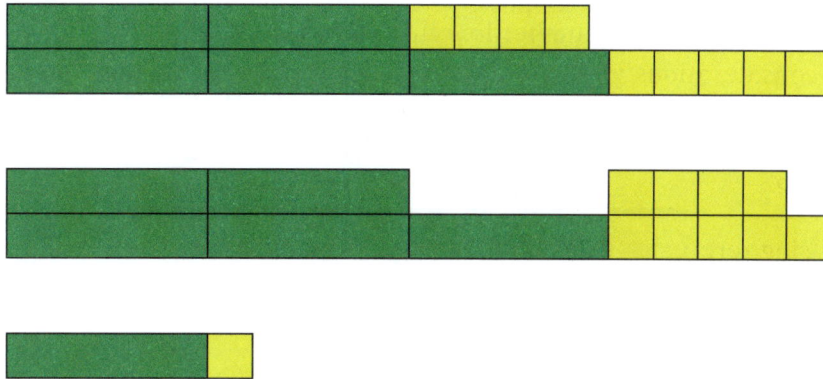

The sequence above starts with the comparison between $2x + 4$ and $3x + 5$, with the comparisons then separated in the second diagram. This leaves nothing on the top line in the third diagram, compared to a single $x$ and '1' bar on the bottom line. The obvious misconception is that this results in $x + 1$, rather than $-(x + 1)$ (or $-x - 1$). In order to correctly interpret this, pupils would need to understand that the third diagram actually shows $0 - (x + 1)$, leading to $-x - 1$. Whilst some pupils may be able to follow this idea, for others it may add a layer of confusion.

This misconception can be avoided by using negative tiles to support the visualisation of the simplification:

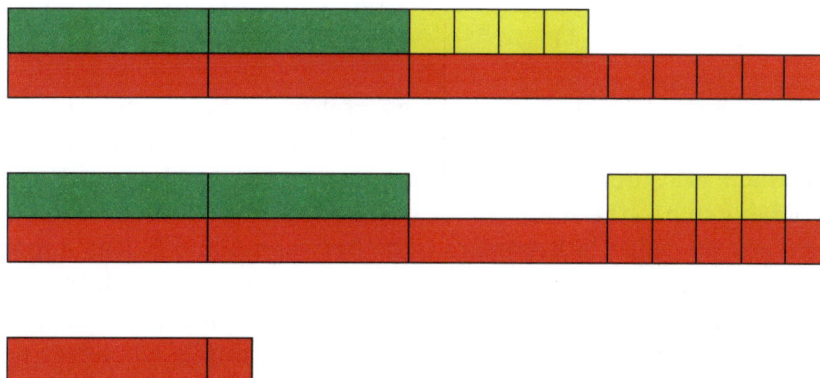

In this second sequence we have the $2x$ and 4 with the $-3x$ and -5. Zero-pairs are then formed, leaving a single $-x$ and a single -1.

The vector representation works in much the same way. However, it is possible to avoid the misconception we encountered earlier by imposing the vectors on an unscaled number line (i.e. a number line that shows 0 but no other values):

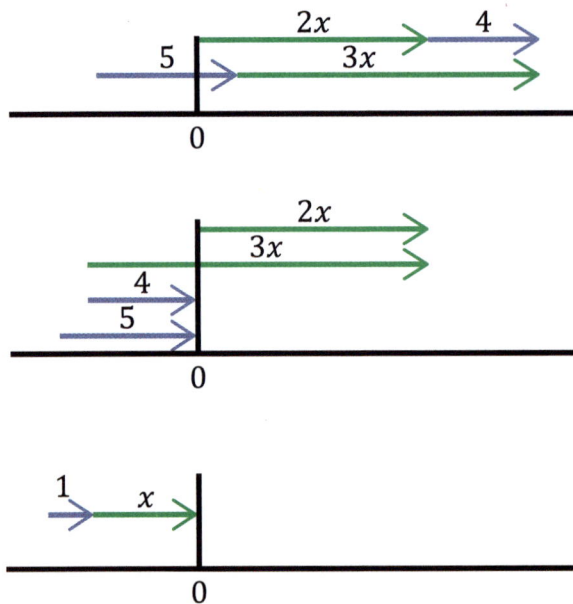

The sequence above shows the $2x + 4$ and then the $3x$ and 5 subtracted. This is then reconfigured to bring together the $2x$ subtract $3x$, which then has 4 added and 5 subtracted. The result of this is an $x$ subtracted from 0, followed by a further subtraction of 1 – or, technically, the $-(x + 1)$.

The obvious problem with this vector representation is that it gives a false sense of the relationship between $x$ and the numbers. A casual glance at the second number line suggests that $x$ is a similar size to 4, which may or may not be true. Unfortunately, this is unavoidable due to the static nature of the representations. You will notice that with algebra tiles the value of $x$ appears to be between 4 and 5. It is important that pupils understand that this is just a representation and is not necessarily considered to be an accurate reflection of the relative size of the numbers. We can explain this when we first use free vectors with algebra, reminding pupils whenever we use this representation that just because vectors may look the same size, they will not necessarily have the same value.

We can dispense with the number line and the 0 if we use negative vectors to represent the negative quantities (rather than using the standard vector subtractions):

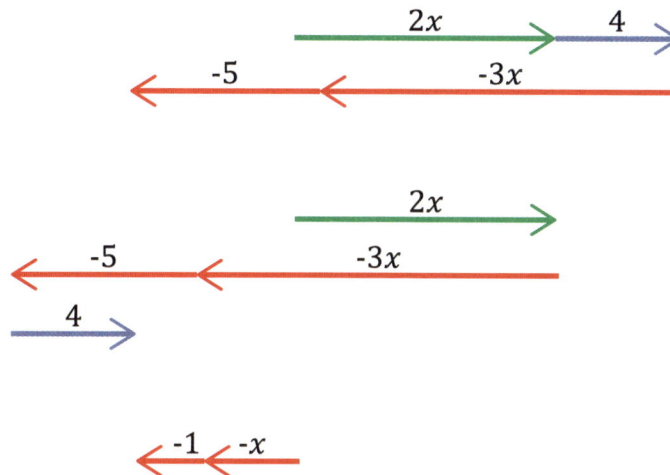

As well as examples that result in expressions where the terms all have negative coefficients, we also need to consider expressions that are the result of algebraic products – for example, $x^2$ or $xy$. We saw in the previous chapter that expressions like these require area to visualise them, and so an obvious place to start is to consider these expressions using algebra tiles and represented as areas:

$x^2 + x + 2x^2 - 3x$

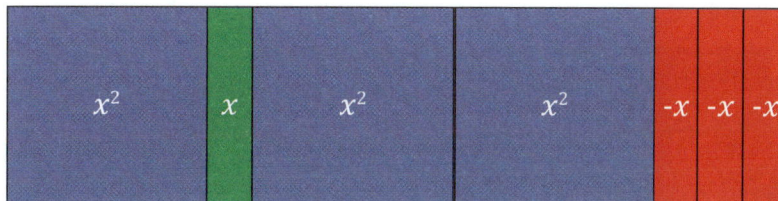

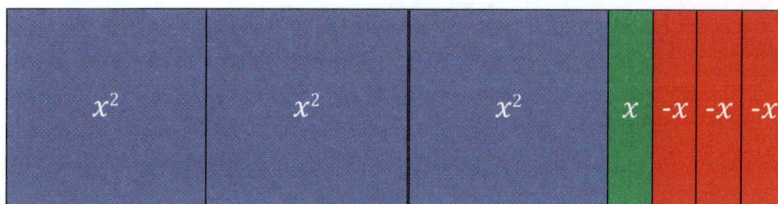

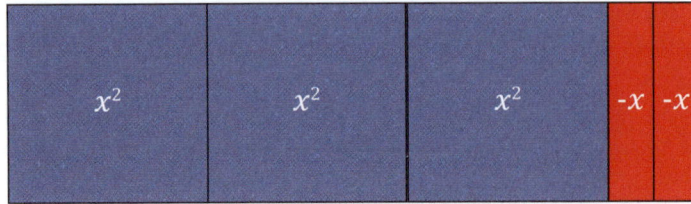

The areas depicted here show a single $x^2$ followed by the single $x$, then $2x^2$ and then three $-x$. Like other simplifications, the pieces are then rearranged so that the '$x^2$' tiles come together, with the '$x$' and the '$-x$' tiles following. This creates a zero-pair between the $x$ and one of the '$-x$' tiles, so these are removed and the result is $3x^2 - 2x$.

A similar approach can be used for expressions using products other than squares:

$2xy + 3x + 2y + xy$

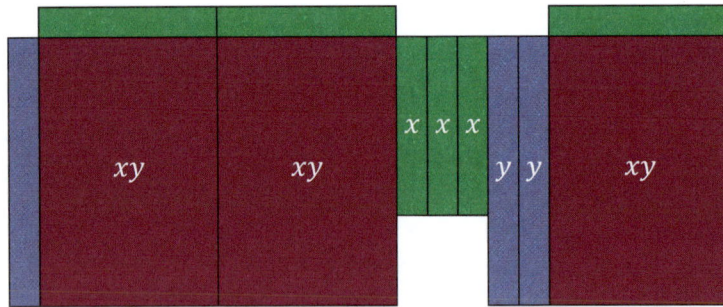

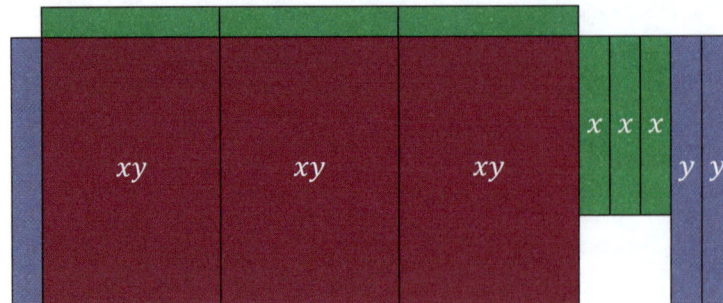

Care needs to be taken here to ensure pupils understand that the blue bar on the left and the green bars at the top are not part of the expression – they are being asked to define the area $xy$. Pupils who have used Cuisenaire rods for multiplication using the area model should be familiar with this idea, but it is worth reminding them. The result is the expression $3xy + 3x + 2y$. A benefit of this representation is that it shows that the '$x$' bars and '$y$' bars won't simplify and have to be left as they are.

However, there is an alternative approach that avoids the need to use extra bars to define the area. Recall from Chapter 5 that an approach to powers is to repeatedly multiply, turning the area into a length for each successive multiplication. For example, we can examine $4^3$ in two stages as follows:

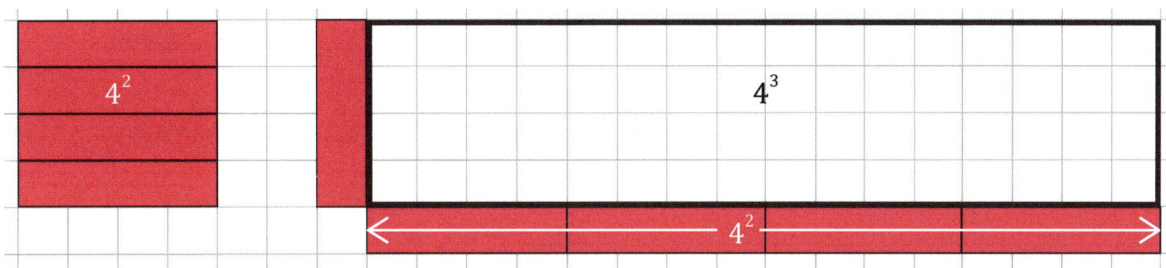

The important point here is that the area of $4^2$ becomes a length in the following calculation – or, alternatively, the square area changes to a rectangular area with a width of 1. This means that the area of $x^2$ can also become a length. We cannot represent this with bars/algebra tiles (although we can repeat the '4' bar four times, we cannot repeat the '$x$' bar $x$ times), but we can represent it using a vector length:

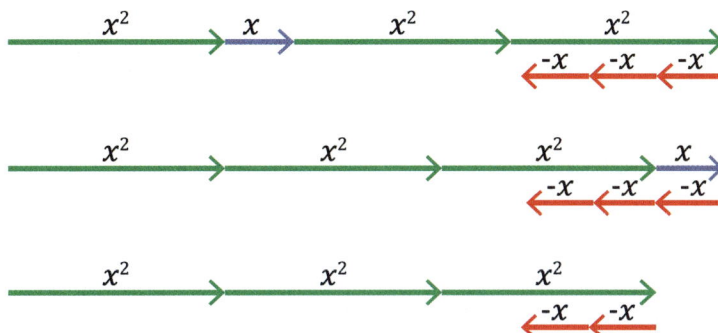

In the above we see the same example of $x^2 + x + 2x^2 - 3x$ that we saw earlier with algebra tiles. Now that we are comfortable with the idea that vectors are not scaled in relation to each other, and also that an area of $x^2$ indicates a separate unknown value that can therefore be represented as a separate length to that of $x$, we can apply the vector representation even in the case of expressions that require the product of two algebraic terms. The example of $2xy + 3x + 2y + xy$ is shown below:

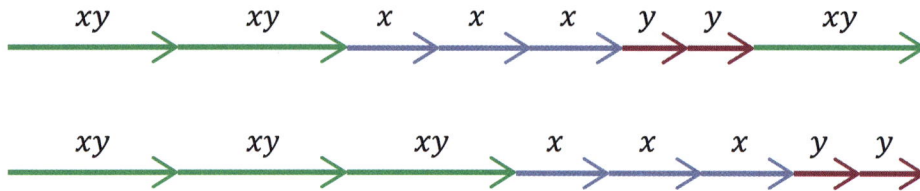

Given the same understanding, we can also use counters for the same expressions:

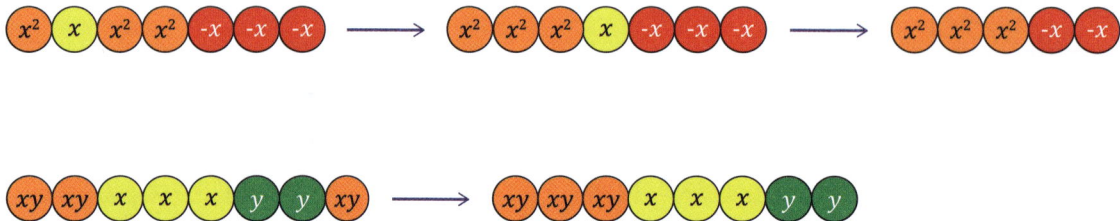

To correctly interpret this representation, pupils will need to understand that variables such as $x$, $y$, $x^2$ and $xy$ can have different values (unless $x = y = 1$ (or 0)), and so without further information about how they relate to each other, there is no way to exchange between them, and hence simplify.

As important as it is for pupils to recognise when expressions will simplify, and to process that simplification, it is equally important that they recognise when expressions won't simplify. Indeed, much has been made recently in mathematics education about the use of examples and non-examples to illustrate concepts. The idea goes that in order to form a deep understanding of a concept, learners must be exposed to many examples of what the concept is, but crucially also what the concept is not. This is known as 'conceptual variation'.

For instance, young children begin to recognise what a cat is by seeing examples of different cats, but their understanding is deepened further by seeing a dog and being told that it is a dog, not a cat. Conceptual variation in mathematics seeks to work in the same way: teachers show pupils examples of both when angles form a straight line, say, but also examples of where they do not. In the best practice, these non-examples vary from cases that look very similar to the concept to those that are very far removed. The diagram below provides some examples and non-examples of angles that form a straight line:

Angles at a point on a straight line     Not-angles at a point on a straight line

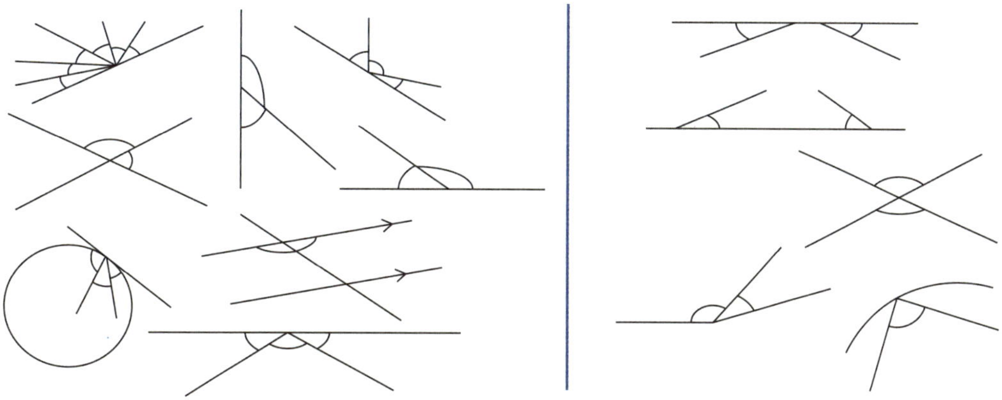

Whilst the act of simplifying is definitely a process, whether or not an expression will simplify is a separate concept that needs to be illustrated in its own right. Showing pupils examples of expressions that will simplify, but also expressions that won't, and asking pupils to identify whether they will simplify or not (even without actually performing the simplification) is a great way of securing pupils' understanding of the concept.

We conclude this chapter with some of the classic misconceptions that pupils have when they are first beginning to simplify expressions, and how our representations can support them in seeing the gaps in their understanding. We could choose to do this as an explicit teaching point – that is, presenting pupils with the diagrams and explaining what they show – or alternatively we could provide pupils with concrete materials and ask them to demonstrate for themselves (e.g. 'Show me why $x + 1 \neq 2x$'). This will depend greatly on the pupils we are working with as well as our preferred pedagogy and approaches in the classroom.

$x + 1 \neq 2x$

The algebra bars should be sufficient to make this clear – the two bars are not equal in length. The only exception is when $x = 1$, in which case the diagram looks like this:

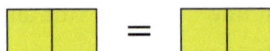

When each of the green '$x$' bars are replaced with '1' bars, the two lengths are the same, showing a special case of when $x + 1 = 2x$ (or alternatively, the solution to the equation $x + 1 = 2x$ is that $x = 1$).

$x^2 \neq 2x$

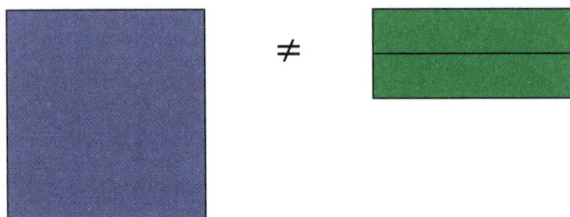

Again, the algebra tiles demonstrate the truth of this statement comfortably. This time the areas represent the values which are not equal sized. An exception is if $x = 2$, which is also true of the misconception below.

$x + y \neq xy$

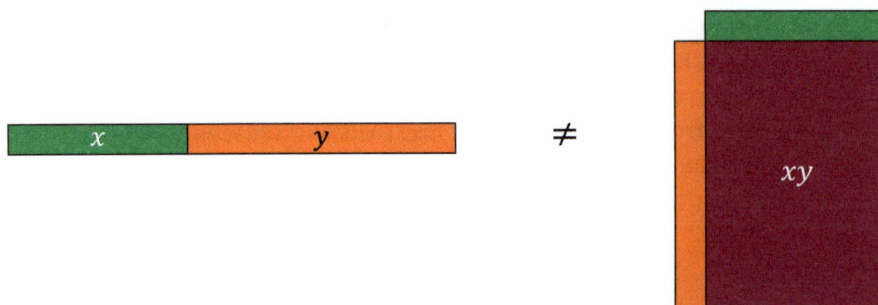

The area of the strip compared to the purple shaded area illustrates that there is no equality between these two expressions – except, of course, when $x$ and $y$ are both 2.

In the case that $x = y = 2$, then both of the previous two examples become one of these two diagrams:

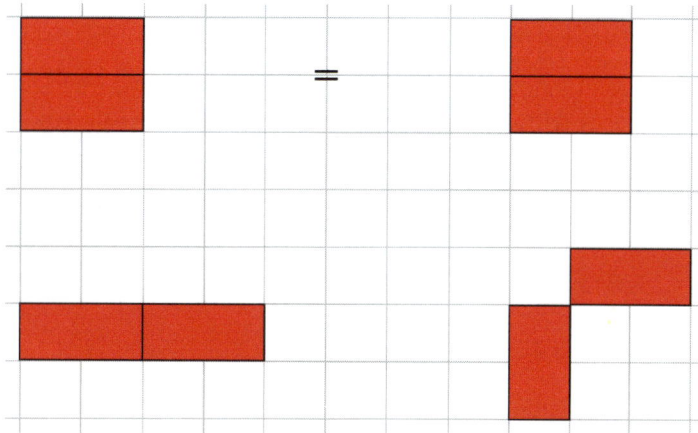

In the upper diagram we see the area of the square as being equal to the two bars stacked together. In the lower diagram the length of the bar is of equal value to the area of the square created by the two bars.

The other exception to the last two examples is when $x = 0$. In this case, the result is trivially true and it is not necessary to represent the idea that nothing = nothing.

$2x - x = 2$

In the diagram above we see $2x - x$, with the expression evaluated using the zero-pair, leaving the single $x$. The length of this $x$ compared to 2 clearly shows that the expressions are not equal. Once again, the exception is when $x = 2$, which changes the diagram to this:

When we replace each green '$x$' bar with 2 unit bars, as well as the '$-x$' bar with 2 negative unit bars, we do get a value equal to 2.

So far, we have concentrated on the simplification of terms that have been added and subtracted, even when some of those terms are the result of multiplication. Next, we look at simplification when terms are multiplied.

# Chapter 13
# Multiplying algebraic expressions

Before we examine simplifying algebraic expressions by multiplying terms, we shouldn't lose sight of the fact, as in the previous chapter, that the purpose of this simplification is to generalise those relationships we see in numbers and to show where calculations could be completed in a reduced number of steps.

From what we have seen thus far, we can probably infer that the area model is going to be an important representation for understanding the structure that allows these simplifications, and so we will start with this representation:

$3x \times 2 = 6x$

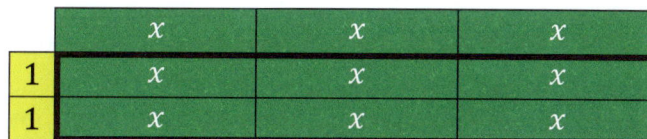

This area model diagram provides a clear indication as to why this result is true. We see the $3x$ as the length of the rectangle, which has a width of 2. The area contained within the thick black outline has a value equal to 6 of the '$x$' bars, showing the $6x$. What we are capturing here is the idea that if we multiply a number by 3 and then by 2, the result is the same as multiplying by 6. Alternatively, this can be seen as a proof of the idea that a value which is a multiple of both 2 and 3 is, by necessity, a multiple of 6.

The area model is not the only representation that can afford us a view of this structure at work. Algebra tiles can show the result using length as well as area:

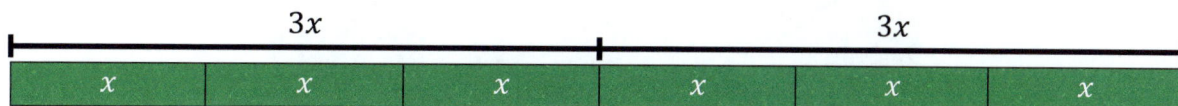

This diagram shows a collection of three '$x$' tiles, using the repeated addition interpretation of multiplication (in the same way as we formed the length of the rectangle above). The repeated addition then continues and the whole set of $3x$ is repeated again – in other words, multiplied by 2. The result is 6 of the '$x$' tiles, indicating a value of $6x$.

Precisely the same approach can be used with vector lengths:

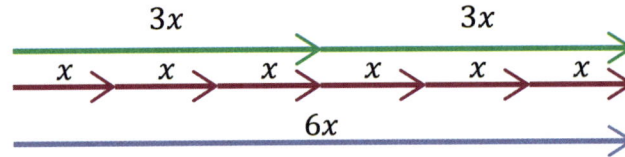

A similar approach can also be employed by repeating sets of counters:

Of course, these views are open to us because the second multiplication is only by a numerical value. This will change if we multiply two algebraic terms. Fortunately, the area model still allows us to represent these sorts of multiplications:

$3x \times 2x = 6x^2$

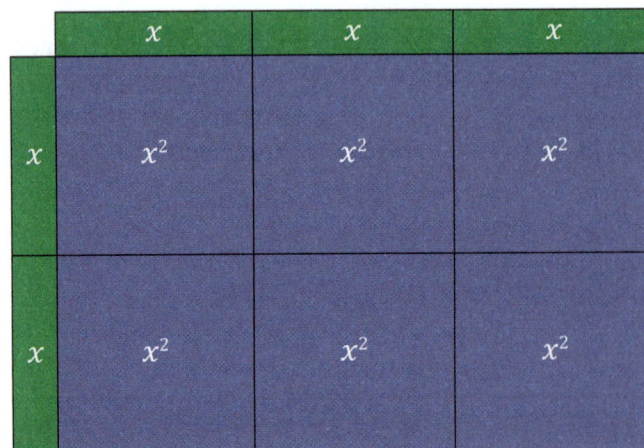

In this diagram we again see the repeated addition version of multiplication to generate the length and width of the rectangle ($3x$ and $2x$). The area of the rectangle can then be understood as being equivalent to 6 of the '$x^2$' tiles, or $6x^2$.

This point of this, of course, is to capture the relationship that if we take any number, multiply it separately by 3 and by 2, and then multiply the two results together, the result is the same as the result of the simpler process – which is to square the number and then multiply by 6.

It is worth noting at this point that these simplifications are purely the result of applications of the laws of arithmetic. If we take the first example of $3x \times 2$, this can be read as $3 \times x \times 2$. Application of the commutative law as it applies to multiplication allows us to switch the $x$ and the 2, leading to $3 \times 2 \times x$. The associative law allows us to multiply the 3 and the 2 first, giving $6 \times x$, which we typically write as $6x$.

The second example can be handled in a similar way. If we start with $3x \times 2x$, this can be written as $3 \times x \times 2 \times x$. An application of the commutative law to the first $x$ and the 2 allows us to rewrite the calculation as $3 \times 2 \times x \times x$. The associative law then allows us to complete the $3 \times 2$ first, giving $6 \times x \times x$, and a further application of the same associative law allows us to multiply the $x$ and $x$ together before considering the 6. This leads to $6 \times x^2 = 6x^2$.

Any pupil who recognises that $x \times x = x^2$ could probably use a vector or counter approach to the same multiplication, by exchanging the $x \times x$ with an $x^2$. Of course, any pupil who could handle that probably doesn't need the representation to start with – although the area approach may still give them an insight into the underlying structure of the calculation. For this reason, I would avoid using vector and counter approaches for the multiplication of algebraic terms.

The area model can also give us an insight into calculations that involve different variables, although a standard set of algebra tiles will not allow pupils to model this. However, some visual representations are still available to us:

$3x \times 2y = 6xy$

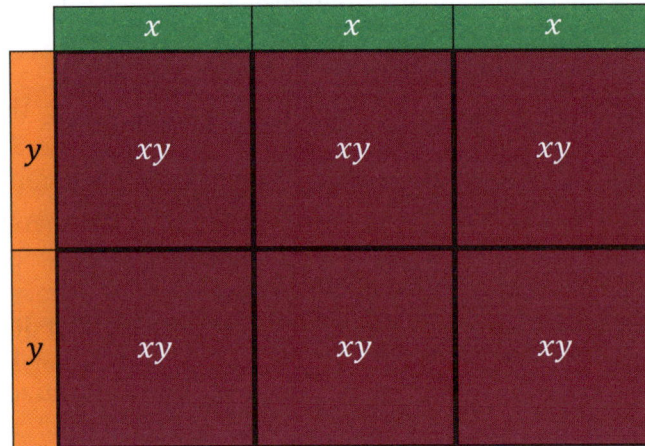

In the diagram above, the rectangle has a length of $3x$ and a width of $2y$. This leads to a total area for the rectangle that is equivalent to $6xy$.

The area model of multiplication does have its drawbacks, however, particularly when one of the terms is negative. Some negative multiplications can be handled fairly straightforwardly – for example, $-3x \times 2$. This can be dealt with using counters, vectors or algebra tiles.

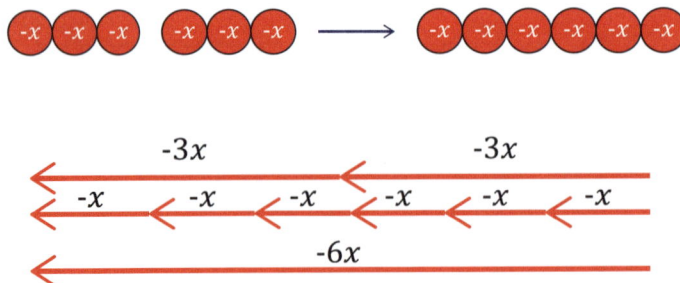

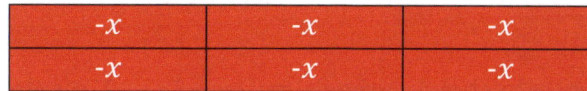

The algebra tiles view provides an indication of a more general approach that we might take to negative terms, as it begins to show how we can create 'negative' areas. This approach is not without its concerns – principally, that it is possibly unwise to suggest that an area can be negative. As we know, area is a scalar and not a vector quantity. Suggesting otherwise to our pupils runs the risk of introducing misconceptions into the concept of area, even as we are trying to shed light on the multiplication of algebra.

For now, though, we will put aside the risk of introducing area misconceptions and explore the other possibilities and difficulties of using negative tiles to support with the multiplication of algebraic terms with negative coefficients.

We will start by taking a closer look at the area we considered above, which was formed by rearranging the -6x length into an array:

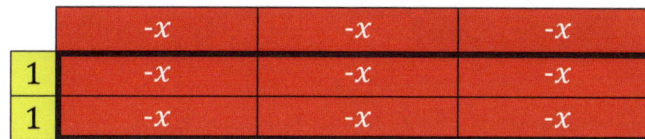

This diagram shows the calculation -3x × 2, giving -6x. However, there are a few issues with this representation. The first is that the area could equally be filled with positive x tiles rather than -x tiles:

Alternatively, different combinations could show the length and width of the area of -6x:

The first of these is correct, showing the calculation $3x \times -2$, resulting in $-6x$. However, the second shows a classic misconception – that $-3x \times -2 = -6x$. In fact, there is nothing within the representation that would stop us from setting the length and width in this way and concluding that $3x \times 2 = -6x$:

Of course, all of this is a consequence of the fact that area is not a vector quantity and so cannot take account of the signs. Any '$x$' or '$-x$' tile can stand in place of each other, as can any 1 or -1 or $x^2$ or $-x^2$. In fact, we could even start creating diagrams like this:

Believe it or not, this calculation does prove to be numerically accurate, as it can be interpreted as $0 \times x = 0$ (I will leave it to the reader to figure out how!), but clearly it is a nonsense in terms of representing the underlying structure of any calculation.

All of this assumes that our pupils are not bringing any understanding of directed number into their work – they are simply playing with the tiles to try to fit them together. By this point, of course, we would hope that they do have a strong under-standing of the interaction between positive and negative values (using the approaches outlined earlier in this book), and could bring this understanding to bear in their modelling of different algebraic multiplications. For example, here is -3$x$ × -2 represented as the length and width of a rectangle:

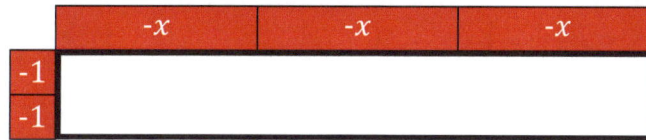

We would expect pupils to recognise that -1 × -$x$ = $x$ and so realise that this area needs to be tiled with positive $x$ tiles:

At this point, the argument could be made that any pupil who can bring this level of understanding to the situation may well not need concrete or visual representations. It makes perfect sense to me if teachers conclude that the best approach is to support pupil understanding of the multiplication of algebraic terms using wholly positive expressions up to the point where they can work purely symbolically. Subsequently, they can then combine this with a strong understanding of directed number calculation to work with the multiplication of terms with negative coefficients.

Should teachers choose to continue to use concrete and visual representations when working with negative multiplications (e.g. to support the identification of misconceptions around directed number calculation), then this can be extended to multiplying two algebraic terms where one or both have negative coefficients:

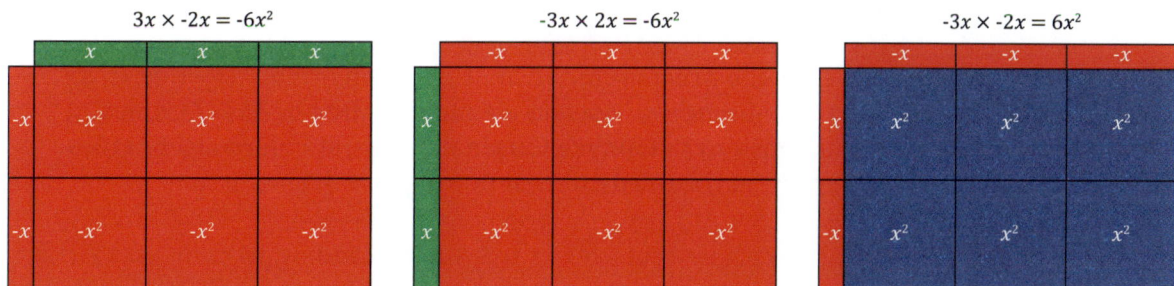

$3x × -2x = -6x^2$

$-3x × 2x = -6x^2$

$-3x × -2x = 6x^2$

$$3x \times -2y = -6xy$$

| | x | x | x |
|---|---|---|---|
| -y | -xy | -xy | -xy |
| -y | -xy | -xy | -xy |

$$-3x \times 2y = -6xy$$

| | -x | -x | -x |
|---|---|---|---|
| y | -xy | -xy | -xy |
| y | -xy | -xy | -xy |

$$-3x \times -2y = 6xy$$

| | -x | -x | -x |
|---|---|---|---|
| -y | xy | xy | xy |
| -y | xy | xy | xy |

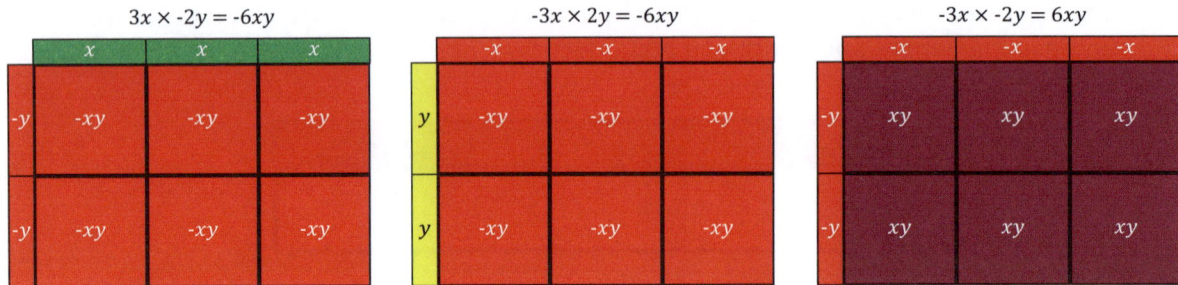

The other multiplications that we will struggle to represent are those resulting in higher powers of the variable. We saw in Chapter 5 the difficulties inherent in representing higher powers of numbers, with the only constructive approach being to evaluate in stages. The same problems result when trying to represent higher powers of algebraic terms:

$$3x \times 2x \times 5x$$

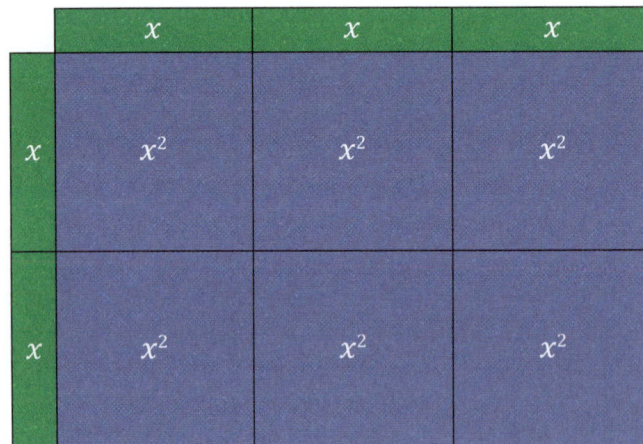

| | x | x | x |
|---|---|---|---|
| x | $x^2$ | $x^2$ | $x^2$ |
| x | $x^2$ | $x^2$ | $x^2$ |

In the diagram above we see the first part of the multiplication evaluated – that is, $3x \times 2x = 6x^2$. The question then becomes, 'How do we multiply this by $5x$?' Technically, we could go into three dimensions but, unlike Cuisenaire rods, standard algebra tiles are flat and so cannot represent the third dimension well.

The alternative is to apply a similar approach to the one we took in Chapter 5. Having multiplied the first two terms to get $6x^2$, we can represent the $6x^2$ as a length and use a new area model to represent $6x^2 \times 5x$:

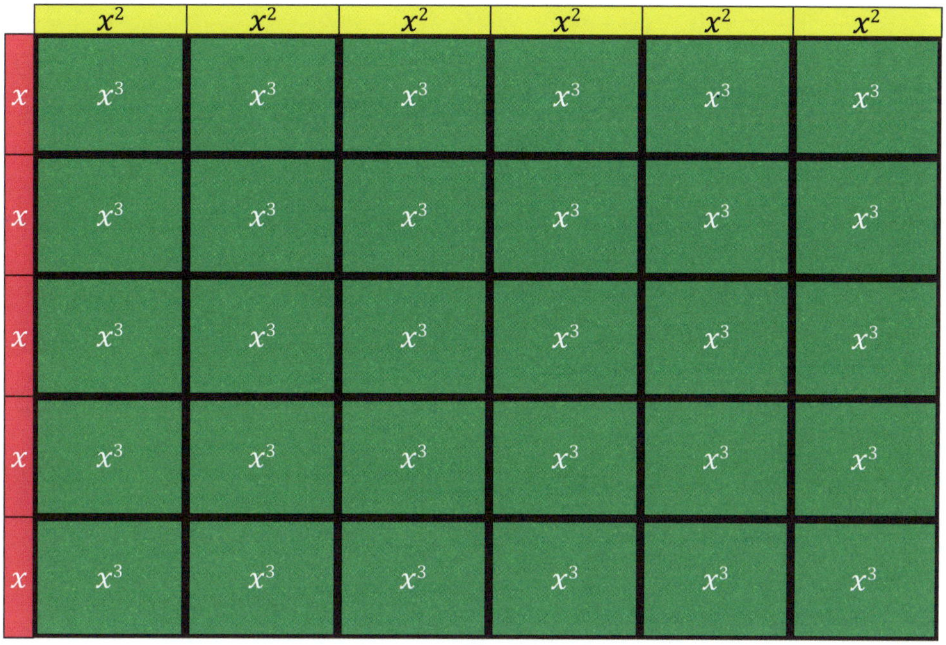

| | $x^2$ | $x^2$ | $x^2$ | $x^2$ | $x^2$ | $x^2$ |
|---|---|---|---|---|---|---|
| $x$ | $x^3$ | $x^3$ | $x^3$ | $x^3$ | $x^3$ | $x^3$ |
| $x$ | $x^3$ | $x^3$ | $x^3$ | $x^3$ | $x^3$ | $x^3$ |
| $x$ | $x^3$ | $x^3$ | $x^3$ | $x^3$ | $x^3$ | $x^3$ |
| $x$ | $x^3$ | $x^3$ | $x^3$ | $x^3$ | $x^3$ | $x^3$ |
| $x$ | $x^3$ | $x^3$ | $x^3$ | $x^3$ | $x^3$ | $x^3$ |

This diagram shows the result of $30x^3$.

One important point to make here is that this representation requires pupils to have a prior understanding of the laws of indices – that $x^2 \times x$ results in $x^3$. Of course, the argument could be made, once again, that pupils with this level of understanding don't need visualisations in order to understand what is happening when we multiply $3x$ by $2x$ and then by $5x$.

We will now move on to explore a further type of multiplication – the multiplication of a sum by a numerical or algebraic factor. This is usually referred to in the classroom as 'expanding'. The next chapter explores expanding and its inverse process, factorisation.

# Chapter 14

# Expanding and factorising algebraic expressions

Expanding and factorising are based around multiplication and multiplicative relationships. For this reason, many of the representations and structures we will use in this chapter will appear similar to those used in the preceding chapter.

What is different when considering expanding and factorising are that they rarely reduce the number of calculation steps. Consider evaluating $3x + 9$ compared to $3(x + 3)$ when, given the value of $x$, both require two calculation steps. Change the $3x$ to a $6x$ and the factorised form has more calculation steps than the expanded form. Keep the $3x$ but include a $6y$ and the factorised form has slightly fewer calculation steps. Clearly, this is not a simplification process – neither expanding nor factorising is guaranteed to simplify the process or reduce the calculation steps required to evaluate an expression.

An obvious question then arises: what is the point? We justified the techniques for simplifying in the last two chapters because of the reduced steps in evaluation. If that is no longer the case, then why bother?

As teachers, we know that these different forms support multiple other concepts in mathematics. Factorising can support equation solving, provide information about key points on a graph, support with logarithmic and exponential work and many other areas of mathematics. Expanded forms provide information about key graphical points, they are easier to differentiate than products and sometimes allow greater manipulation of equations, amongst other things. We know this but our pupils do not. So what do we tell them?

The purist in me wants to say simply 'because it is interesting'. These are different forms of the same expression, different ways of considering and expressing the same relationships, and these different forms have the possibility of revealing different insights about these relationships. That, to me, is interesting, and I often come across pupils in different year groups who will say things like 'Wow!' or 'Mind blown!' or even 'That is so cool!' when I highlight certain connections and relationships that they previously hadn't appreciated.

There are also a significant number of pupils who do not find this interesting, so what about them? Well, there is the pragmatic approach: 'You need this for your exams', but

I am never happy to employ this. Whilst I am aware that many pupils are only in a maths classroom because their future aspirations depend on them doing well in it, for this to be the primary reason for their learning seems shallow to say the least. A third approach is simply 'because we can'. There is something to be learned here, a relationship to explore. Why would anyone want to shy away from increasing their knowledge and understanding of the world? Admittedly, this doesn't always work either, but it is the best I have.

We will leave for now the question of why, and focus on the how and what – as in, how do we expand and factorise, and what do our representations show us about the underlying structure of these different forms and processes?

$3(x + 1)$

These counters show $x + 1$ repeated three times. Once this has been presented, then the process becomes one of simplification – collecting together the '$x$' counters and the '1' counters, which results in the expression $3x + 3$.

Precisely the same approach can be used with a vector representation:

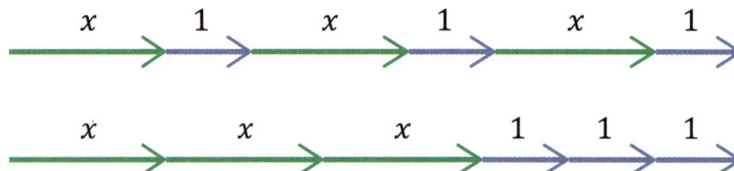

It also applies with algebra tiles:

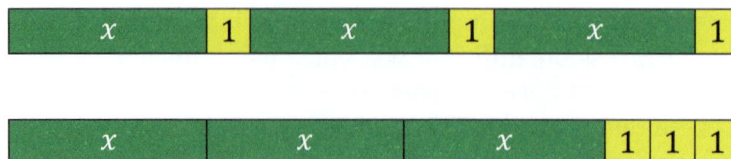

An alternative approach that can be taken with algebra tiles (and also counters) is to use the area model with '$x$' tiles and '1' tiles:

| $x$ | 1 |
|---|---|
| $x$ | 1 |
| $x$ | 1 |

In the diagram above we have $x + 1$ repeated three times, but the repeat now creates an array rather than a long strip of tiles. There are multiple benefits to this approach. The first is simply in terms of the length – although repeating $x$ and 1 only three times doesn't produce an overly long strip, the example below illustrates the complications with a larger expansion:

$5(3x + 7)$

| $x$ | $x$ | $x$ | 1 | 1 | 1 | 1 | 1 | 1 | 1 |
|---|---|---|---|---|---|---|---|---|---|
| $x$ | $x$ | $x$ | 1 | 1 | 1 | 1 | 1 | 1 | 1 |
| $x$ | $x$ | $x$ | 1 | 1 | 1 | 1 | 1 | 1 | 1 |
| $x$ | $x$ | $x$ | 1 | 1 | 1 | 1 | 1 | 1 | 1 |
| $x$ | $x$ | $x$ | 1 | 1 | 1 | 1 | 1 | 1 | 1 |

Here the $x$ tiles have had to be shortened just to make the diagram fit.

The second benefit (and the main reason why I prefer the area model representation) is that it allows us to view both forms of the expressions simultaneously. In the earlier counter and vector representations, we had to rearrange the counters/vectors in order to simplify the expression, and this lost the idea of the original expression inside the bracket. In the array, a single row is $3x + 7$, which is repeated 5 times, but at the same time we can also see 15 '$x$' tiles in a block and 35 '1' tiles in a block. For me, this is probably the best way of showing that $5(3x + 7)$ and $15x + 35$ are the same expression.

Similar approaches can be used when there are negative values inside the bracket:

$5(3x - 7)$

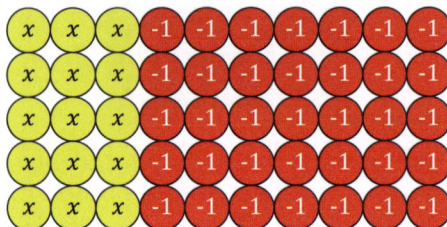

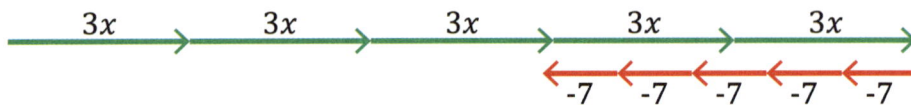

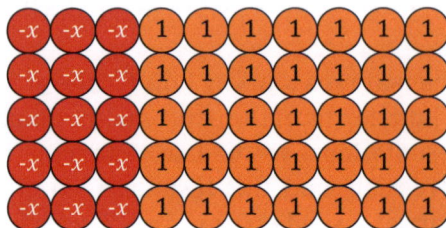

$5(-3x + 7)$ or $5(7 - 3x)$

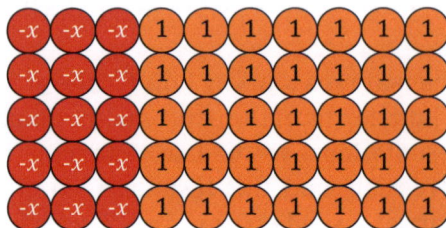

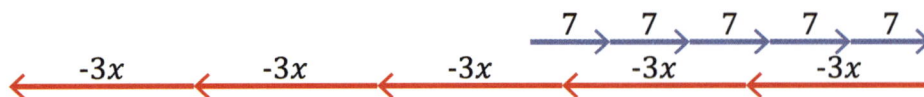

| -x | -x | -x | 1 | 1 | 1 | 1 | 1 | 1 | 1 |
|----|----|----|---|---|---|---|---|---|---|
| -x | -x | -x | 1 | 1 | 1 | 1 | 1 | 1 | 1 |
| -x | -x | -x | 1 | 1 | 1 | 1 | 1 | 1 | 1 |
| -x | -x | -x | 1 | 1 | 1 | 1 | 1 | 1 | 1 |
| -x | -x | -x | 1 | 1 | 1 | 1 | 1 | 1 | 1 |

This includes when there are more than two algebraic terms inside the bracket:

$5(3x + 2y + 7)$

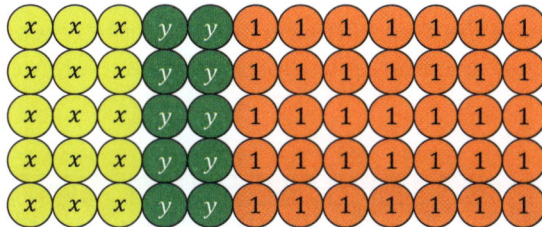

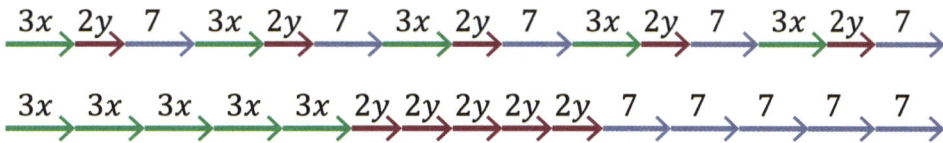

| x | x | x | y | y | 1 | 1 | 1 | 1 | 1 | 1 | 1 |
|---|---|---|---|---|---|---|---|---|---|---|---|
| x | x | x | y | y | 1 | 1 | 1 | 1 | 1 | 1 | 1 |
| x | x | x | y | y | 1 | 1 | 1 | 1 | 1 | 1 | 1 |
| x | x | x | y | y | 1 | 1 | 1 | 1 | 1 | 1 | 1 |
| x | x | x | y | y | 1 | 1 | 1 | 1 | 1 | 1 | 1 |

Whilst the representation of a negative value within the bracketed factor is easy enough to represent and manipulate, more thought is required if the factor leading the bracket is negative. The ideas and approaches are similar to those we saw in the last chapter, which once again may suggest that this might be better done as a purely numerical exercise after having fully secured the concept using positive values.

-5(3*x* – 7)

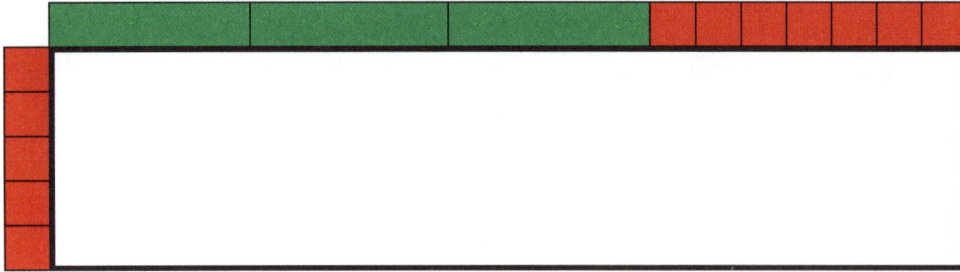

The rectangle above shows the area in question, with a length of 3*x* – 7 and a width of -5. In order to evaluate the area of the rectangle correctly we again have to bring in an understanding of negative multiplication – in particular, recognising that -1 × *x* = -*x* and -1 × -1 = 1:

| | *x* | *x* | *x* | -1 | -1 | -1 | -1 | -1 | -1 | -1 |
|---|---|---|---|---|---|---|---|---|---|---|
| -1 | -*x* | -*x* | -*x* | 1 | 1 | 1 | 1 | 1 | 1 | 1 |
| -1 | -*x* | -*x* | -*x* | 1 | 1 | 1 | 1 | 1 | 1 | 1 |
| -1 | -*x* | -*x* | -*x* | 1 | 1 | 1 | 1 | 1 | 1 | 1 |
| -1 | -*x* | -*x* | -*x* | 1 | 1 | 1 | 1 | 1 | 1 | 1 |
| -1 | -*x* | -*x* | -*x* | 1 | 1 | 1 | 1 | 1 | 1 | 1 |

This diagram shows the result of -15*x* + 35 (or alternatively 35 – 15*x*).

A third benefit of the area model is that it allows the modelling of expansions where both of the factors involve algebraic terms. These can be of the same variables or different variables:

$2x(3x + 7)$

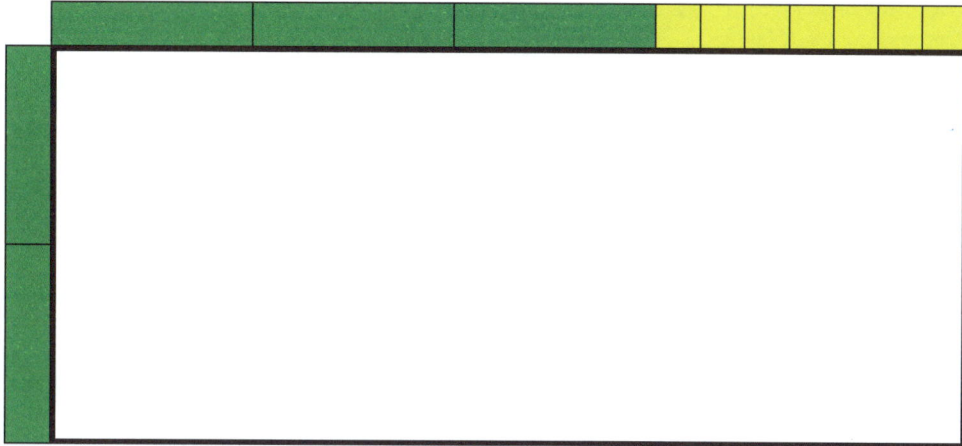

Here we see the length of the rectangle as $3x + 7$ and the width as $2x$. The area can now be tiled as follows:

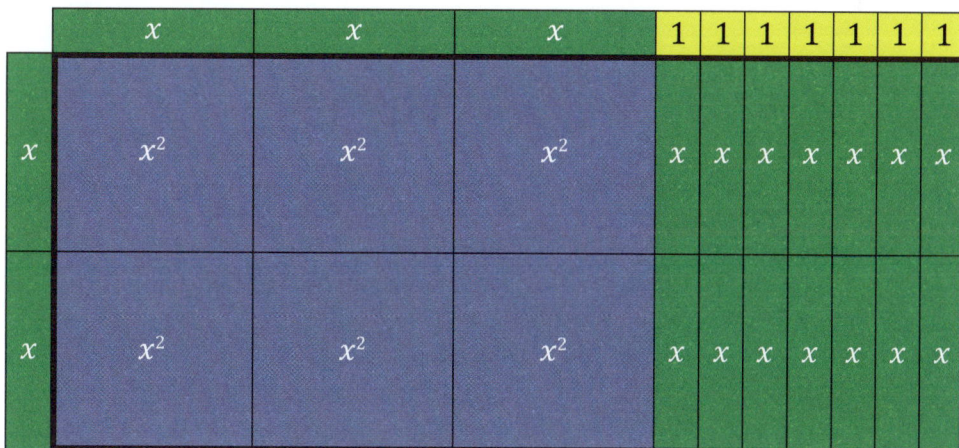

This shows that the final expansion is $6x^2 + 14x$.

$2y(3x + 7)$

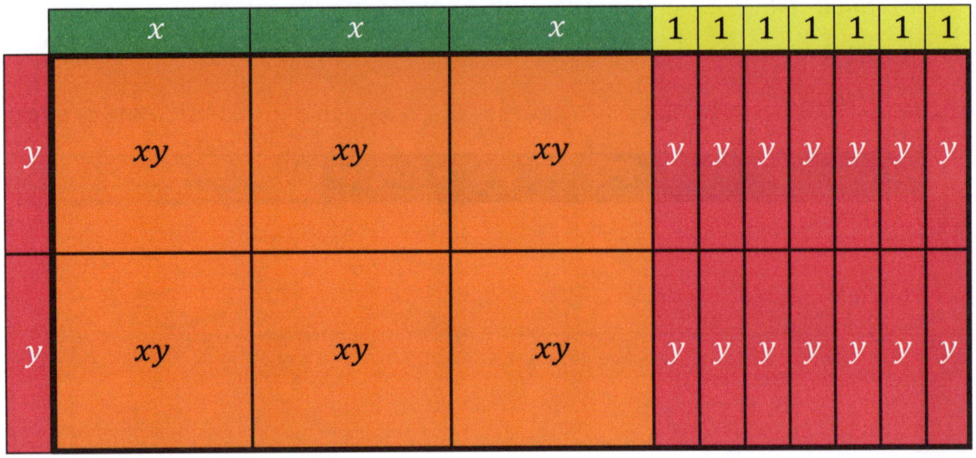

In the diagram above we see that the length is still $3x + 7$, but now the width is $2y$. This means the area can be tiled as $6xy + 14y$.

A further benefit to the area model is that we can represent the result of multiplying two linear expressions in brackets. Again, this can be with factors of the same variable or different variables:

$(x + 3)(x + 5)$

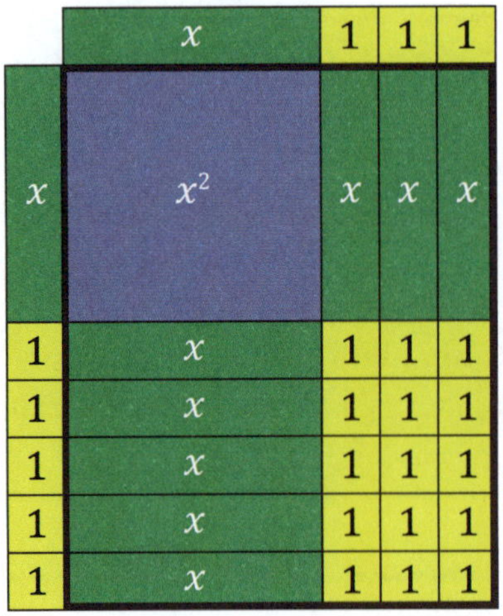

The length now is $x + 3$ with a width of $x + 5$ (these are obviously interchangeable). The resulting rectangular area can be tiled by multiplying the separate parts – the $x$ by $x$ part is tiled using an '$x^2$' tile, the 1 by $x$ part is tiled using '$x$' tiles and the 1 by 1 part is tiled using '1' tiles. This gives the result of the expansion as $x^2 + 8x + 15$.

The same approach can be used for linear factors where the $x$ coefficients are greater than 1:

$(2x + 3)(3x + 5)$

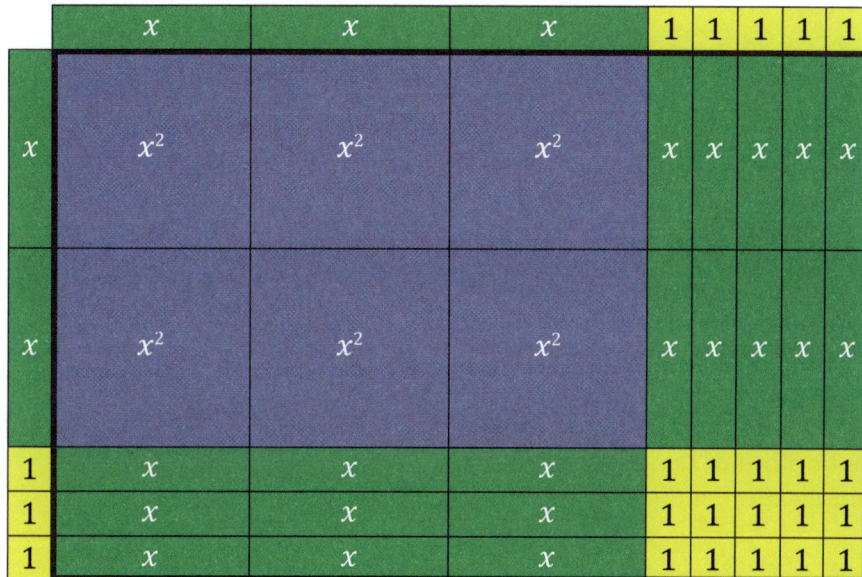

In the diagram above the length of $3x + 5$ and the width of $2x + 3$ give an area tiled as $6x^2 + 19x + 15$.

There are a couple of things worth mentioning explicitly at this point. Firstly, in common with the multiplication of integers, this area model is a precursor to the grid method of multiplication as applied to algebra. This is a common approach for supporting pupils to expand brackets and usually appears something like this:

|      | $3x$    | $7$   |
|------|---------|-------|
| $2x$ | $6x^2$  | $14x$ |

|      | $3x$    | $5$    |
|------|---------|--------|
| $2x$ | $6x^2$  | $10x$  |
| $3$  | $9x$    | $15$   |

If we compare the results in these two diagrams to the area models in the examples above them, then the parallels become clear. This suggests that the grid method could be a useful approach for pupils to begin to move from concrete/pictorial approaches towards more abstract/symbolic representations.

The second point worth noting are the continuing links to the laws of arithmetic, particularly the distributive law applied to multiplication over addition. When we consider something like $2x(3x + 7)$, application of the distributive law gives $2x \times 3x + 2x \times 7 = 6x^2 + 14x$. Even with two linear factors, the result can be seen as multiple applications of the distributive law – for example, $(2x + 3)(3x + 5)$ can be seen as $(2x + 3) \times 3x + (2x + 3) \times 5$. If needed, we can apply the commutative law to each multiplication to give $3x \times (2x + 3) + 5 \times (2x + 3)$, although this is not strictly required to apply the distributive law to both separate multiplications. This results in $3x \times 2x + 3x \times 3 + 5 \times 2x + 5 \times 3 = 6x^2 + 9x + 10x + 15$, which can then be simplified to give $6x^2 + 19x + 15$.

Many teachers use the grid method, which can be very useful when pupils are ready to completely move away from anything resembling a pictorial approach. However, I am not sure how many teachers make it explicit that this links back to the distributive law and so reinforces the role of algebra in generalising the relationships we see with numbers.

We can use the area model to work with expressions which have two linear factors where one or more of the terms is negative, providing pupils have an understanding of the multiplication of directed numbers:

$(x - 3)(x + 5)$ $(x - 3)(x - 5)$

$(3 - x)(x - 5)$ $\qquad\qquad\qquad\qquad$ $(3 - x)(5 - x)$

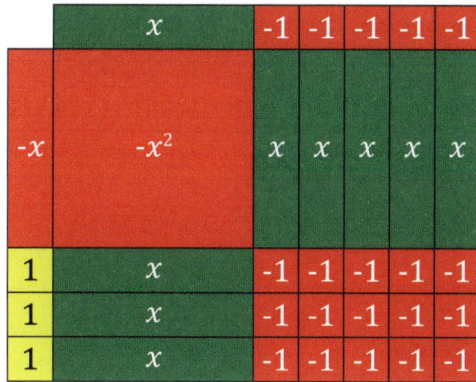 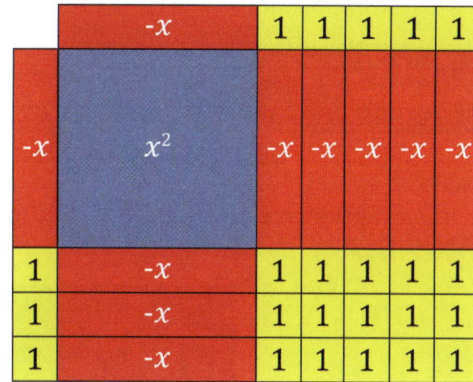

Some teachers may not agree that this is worthwhile, preferring to secure the concept using concrete and pictorial representations with positive terms only. However, these representations do allow for some interesting insights – for example, noting that the areas in the examples $(x - 3)(x - 5)$ and $(3 - x)(5 - x)$ are identical and providing a structure for pupils to consider why this happens.

The final reason that the area model wins out in terms of representing the expansion of algebraic expressions is that it provides a structure to allow the introduction of factorisation. We have seen that expansion can be about tiling a rectangular area, so factorisation can be considered as being about finding the length and width when a set of tiles are arranged as a rectangle – and in particular, for a proper factorisation, finding out which possible rectangle maximises the width.

Consider the expression $8x + 12$:

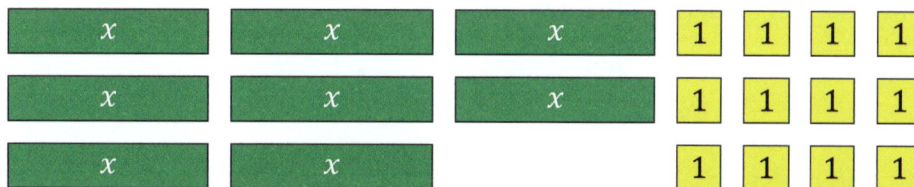

There are many ways to arrange these tiles as a rectangle. The obvious way is to simply place them together as one long strip. However, there are alternatives such as:

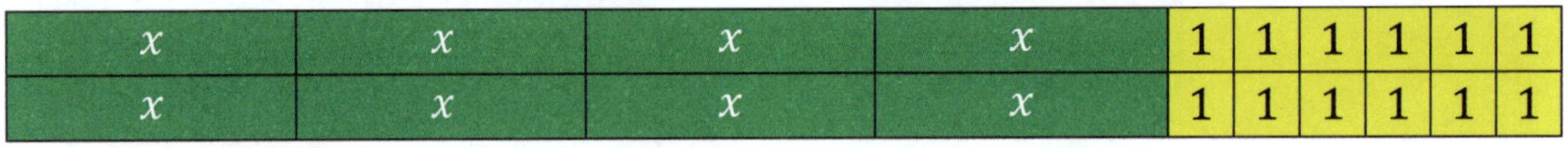
x x x x 1 1 1 1 1 1
x x x x 1 1 1 1 1 1

Or this one which has the largest width:

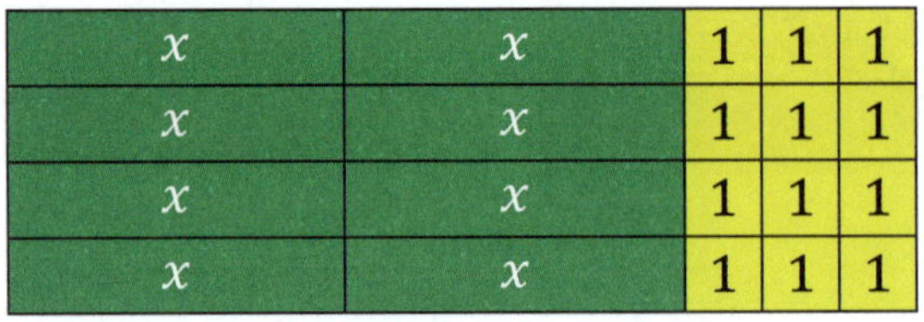
x x 1 1 1
x x 1 1 1
x x 1 1 1
x x 1 1 1

The length and width of this rectangle are $2x + 3$ and 4, as shown below:

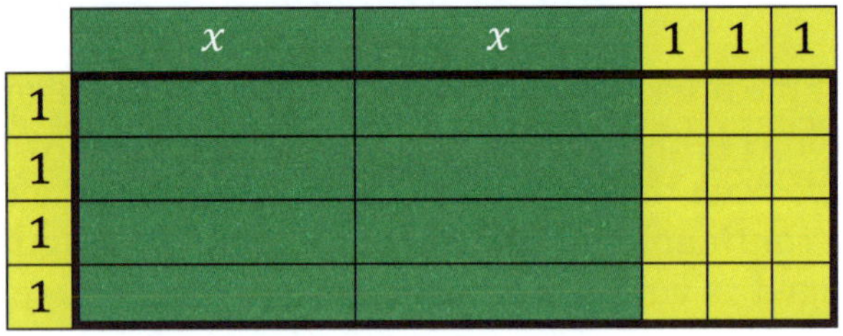
x x 1 1 1
1
1
1
1

This shows that the factorisation is $4(2x + 3)$.

The same idea can be applied to quadratic expressions:

$x^2 + 5x$

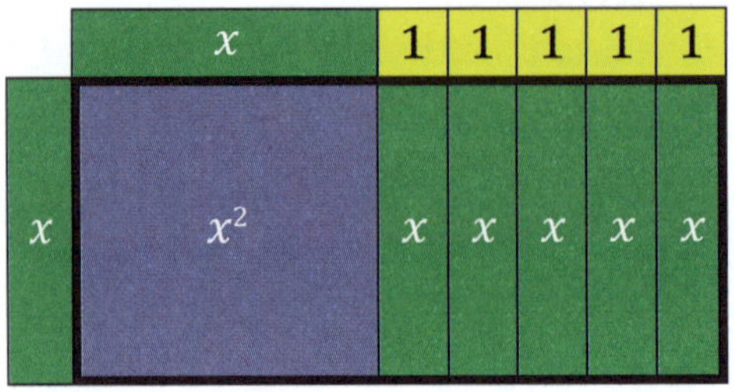
x 1 1 1 1 1
x
x2
x x x x x

In this diagram we see the area of $x^2 + 5x$ arranged to create a rectangle. The rectangle has a width of $x$ and a length of $x + 5$, giving the factorisation of $x(x + 5)$.

$x^2 + 5x + 6$

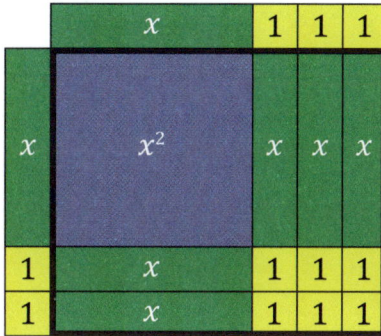

In the diagram above we see the area of $x^2 + 5x + 6$ arranged as a rectangular area. This time, the rectangular area has a length of $x + 3$ and a width of $x + 2$, giving a factorisation of $(x + 3)(x + 2)$.

There is a strong parallel here with the multiplication and division of numbers (as we would expect). In earlier chapters, we saw that the area model allows us to see both multiplication and division – for example, the diagram below shows $3 \times 4 = 12$, but it can also be interpreted as $12 \div 3 = 4$ or even $12 \div 4 = 3$. In other words, it shows that a factorisation of 12 is $3 \times 4$:

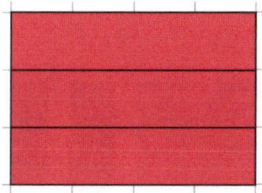

The factorisation of $x^2 + 5x + 6$ can be thought of in the same way – that $(x + 3)(x + 2)$ = $x^2 + 5x + 6$, that $(x^2 + 5x + 6) \div (x + 3) = (x + 2)$, and also that $(x^2 + 5x + 6) \div (x + 2)$ = $(x + 3)$.

249

The same approach can even be taken with mixed variable expressions:

$6xy + 3x + 2y + 1$

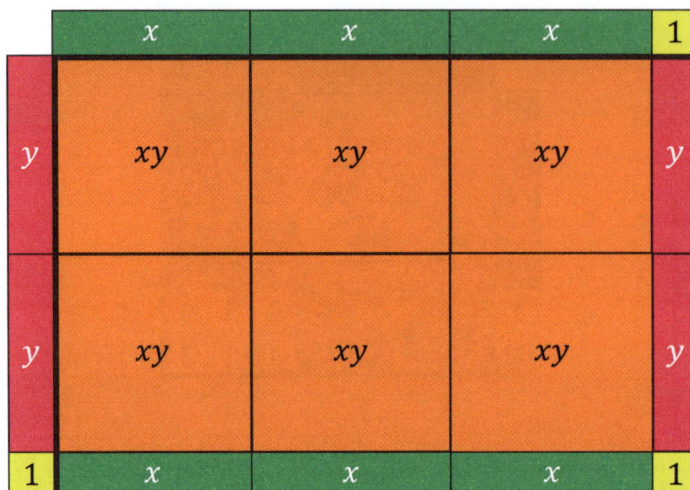

In the diagram above, the rectangular area of $6xy + 3x + 2y + 1$ has a length of $3x + 1$ and a width of $2y + 1$, giving a factorisation of $(3x + 1)(2y + 1)$.

When we consider expressions with negative coefficients, there are two interpretations, both of which have their advantages and drawbacks. We will start with a simple example:

$x^2 - 2x + 1$

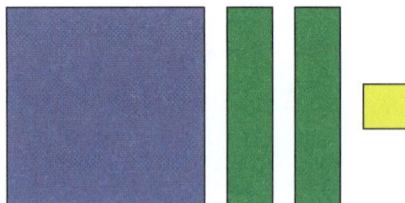

The first interpretation sees the $2x$ remaining positive, as in the diagram above. The subtraction is then seen as the difference between the area of the $x^2 + 1$ and the $2x$

– that is, the $2x$ has to be placed inside the '$x^2$' tile. The diagram below shows the area as a rectangle, allowing us to see the factorisation of $(x - 1)^2$:

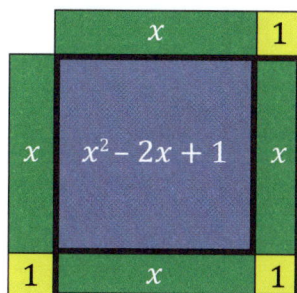

This diagram perhaps needs a bit of interpretation. The blue shaded space is an '$x^2$' tile with two '$x$' tiles overlapped to create an area of $x^2 - 2x$. The problem is that the two '$x$' tiles also overlap each other, actually subtracting an extra 1 from the area. This is why the '1' tile is placed in the bottom right corner. The gives the length and width of the blue shaded space as an '$x$' tile with a '1' tile overlapping the end, or $(x - 1)^2$.

In addition to being difficult to interpret, the other problem with this approach is that the '$x$' tiles can completely cover the '$x^2$' tile. This is an unfortunate side effect of the static nature of the representation ($x$ cannot actually be of variable length), but in some ways it is also accurate – there are certain values of $x$ that will result in the total area of the $x$ tiles being greater than the area of $x^2$.

An alternative approach comes from using negative tiles to create the area. Below is the same expression using negative tiles:

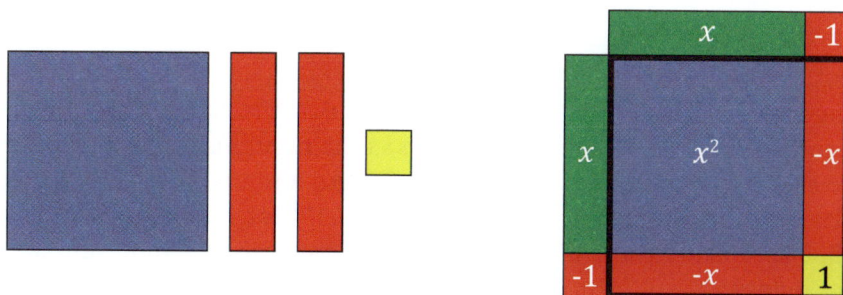

This time we see the '$x^2$' tile, two '$-x$' tiles and the '1' tile. These can be arranged as a rectangle, as in the right-hand diagram, which has both a length and width of an '$x$' tile with a '-1' tile, giving the factorisation as $(x - 1)^2$.

One problem with this approach is that expressions that do not factorise can appear to do so. Take, for example, $x^2 - 2x - 1$:

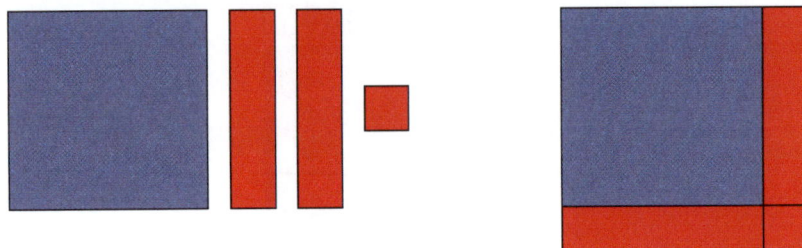

These tiles can clearly still be arranged as a rectangle, and so superficially the expression would appear to factorise. The issue comes when we try to determine the length and width of the rectangle. There is no combination of tiles that can form the length and width of this rectangle that can produce the $-x$ and the $-1$ simultaneously.

A second problem with the use of negative tiles is that they can make expressions that do factorise appear as if they don't. Take, for example, $x^2 - 5x - 6$:

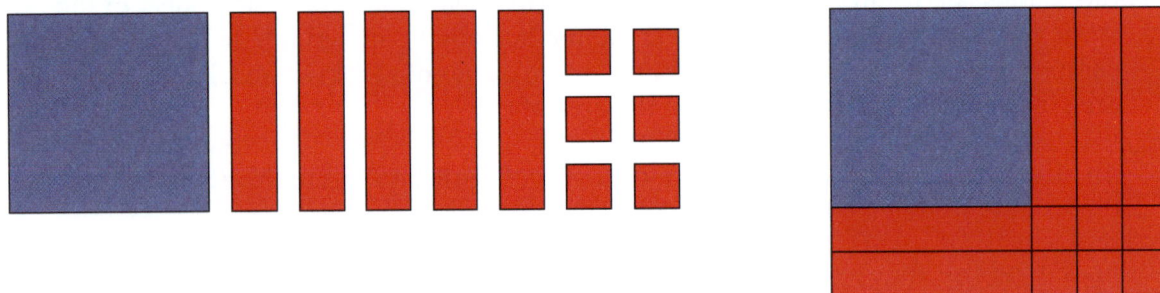

At first glance this can be arranged as the rectangle on the right of the diagram above. However, this suffers from the same problem as the previous example when we try to determine the length and width – there is no length and width for this rectangle that will simultaneously produce the '-$x$' tiles and the '-1' tiles. This might lead to the conclusion that this expression doesn't factorise; however, the diagram that follows shows that it does:

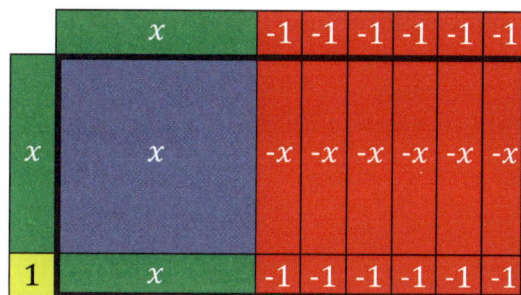

The key here is the introduction of the extra '-$x$' tile and the positive '$x$' tile as a zero-pair. This allows the formation of a rectangle with a length of $x - 6$ and a width of $x + 1$, giving the factorisation as $(x - 6)(x + 1)$.

Of course, as I am sure many readers are thinking, the spontaneous introduction of this zero-pair is not something that pupils will think of for themselves; it will need to be modelled through careful teacher explanation. This can also lead to some pupils pursuing attempts to factorise expressions that cannot be factorised by trying to introduce more and more zero-pairs in an effort to search for factorisations that don't exist. This might be desirable if we want pupils to create their own meaning and insight from the experience, but it will need to be carefully managed to ensure that pupils actually learn from the process and don't develop misconceptions.

This management could include selecting expressions for pupils to work on that will definitely factorise, telling them the number of zero-pairs they will need to introduce or setting limits on the number of zero-pairs allowed. For example, we could ask pupils to show the factorisation of given expressions (perhaps mixing in some that won't factorise) which have been carefully selected so that they do not require any more than five zero-pair introductions.

Other teachers may prefer to simply develop the concept well using manipulatives and visual representations with expressions that have only positive coefficients, using this to support pupils to the point where they can work purely symbolically, and only then moving on to factorisations involving negative values.

The other minor problem with the diagram above is that at first glance the length looks larger than the width. Pupils need to appreciate that whilst this may be the case physically, it is not true numerically. We may need to remind pupils that the red '-1' tiles actually reduce the value of the expression, even though they increase the length.

Over the last three chapters, we have investigated the representations that can support virtually all the manipulations of algebraic expressions required up until the end of secondary school. We will explore some final factors in Chapter 16, but first we will switch from manipulating expressions to solving equations.

# Chapter 15

# Equations and representations

It is actually much easier to represent equations pictorially than to use concrete materials. Consider, for example, the simple equation $x + 4 = 9$. If we try to represent this using algebra tiles, the result is this:

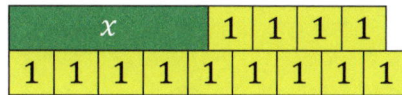

Due to the static nature of the '$x$' tile, it is impossible to make $x + 4$ equal to 9. If we switch to Cuisenaire rods the result looks like this:

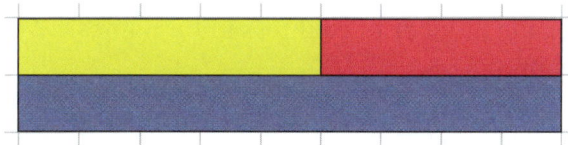

The problem here is that in order to model the equation, we almost need to know the solution before we can begin modelling it (in this case that $x = 5$). Some teachers may find this helpful as it forces pupils to engage their reasoning in order to work out the missing bar. This might work for simple equations, but for more complicated equations it is the model that we need in order to engage with the reasoning, not using reasoning to build the model.

Rather than using a concrete representation, $x + 4 = 9$ can be modelled visually using bars:

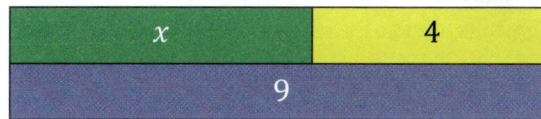

Technically, this can be interpreted as using the difference approach to the subtraction of numbers – what we are solving here could be considered as $x + 4 - 9 = 0$ (i.e. the difference between $x + 4$ and 9 is 0). Either way, we can model the equation solving process like this:

Before moving on to more complicated equations, it is worth noting that there is one concrete representation still available to us that can support the solving of equations – counters:

The approach now becomes, 'How many counters do we need to exchange each $x$ for in order to have the same number of counters in both lines?' We can then model the solving process as follows:

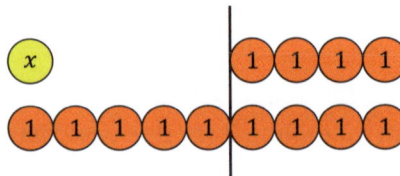

The counters that are equal can be separated and discarded – in this case the four '1' counters from the top line can be paired with four '1' counters on the bottom line, and these can then be discarded (this is akin to the 'subtracting 4 from both sides' step in equation solving). This leaves the single $x$ with 5 counters, indicating that $x = 5$.

Returning to visual representations, it is also possible to represent the same equation using vectors – the result is virtually identical to the bars on this page and the one previous:

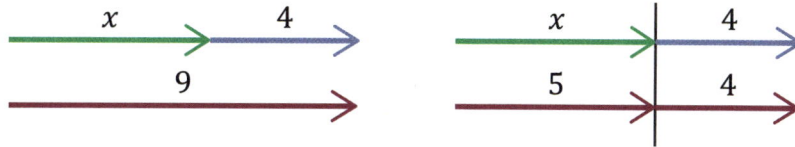

All of these representations can be used for more difficult linear equations; however, each has its own advantages and disadvantages. We will explore each of these in more detail below.

*2x* + 5 = 11

All of the aforementioned representations can be used to model this equation quite straightforwardly:

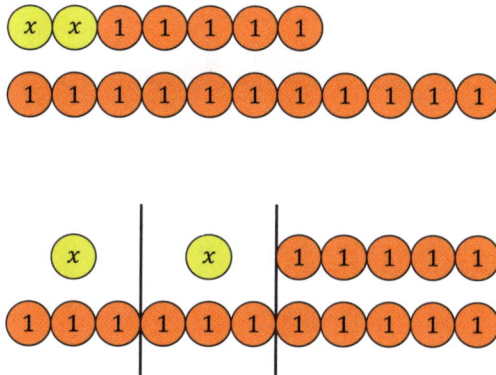

The pair of diagrams above shows the pairing off of the 5 counters from the top row with 5 of the 11 from the bottom row. This leaves 6 counters that are equivalent to *2x*, and so splitting the 6 counters into 2 shares shows that each *x* = 3.

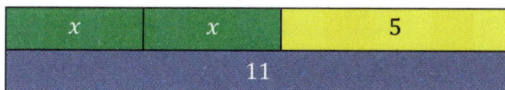

Here the same equation is modelled with bars, and then the same splitting process is modelled, resulting in *x* = 3.

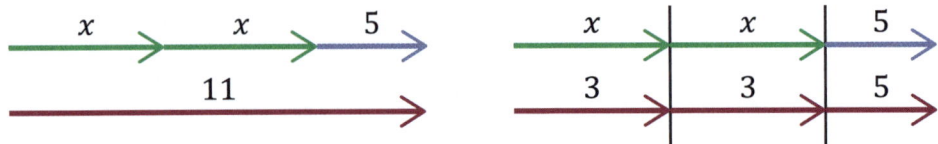

Again, the vector approach is vertically identical to the bars in modelling this equation, with the solution being arrived at in the same way.

The representations are equally useful when a constant is subtracted from the variables rather than added:

$2x - 5 = 11$

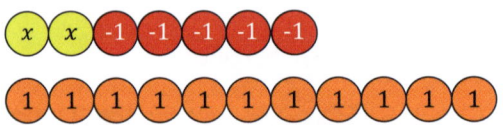

The approach here is to use zero-pairs to eliminate the '-1' counters in the top row. However, pupils will need to have an understanding that if the top row suddenly increases by 5, then the bottom row also has to increase by 5 in order to maintain the equality:

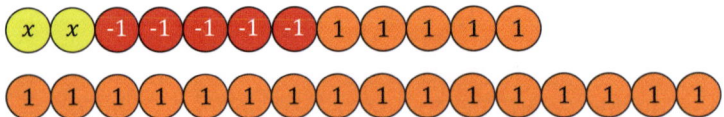

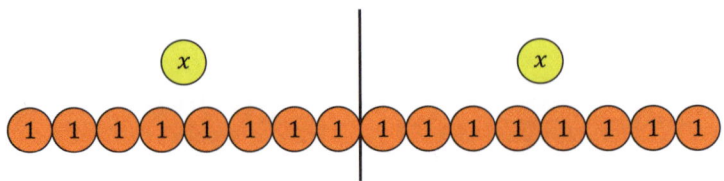

An alternative is to add 5 zero-pairs to the bottom line (i.e. add 5 counters and 5 negative counters), which allows the negative counters to be separated and discarded. This again leaves the two '$x$' counters in the top line, and 16 counters on the bottom line, leading to the conclusion that $x = 8$.

Similar approaches can be taken with bars, again with two possible representations:

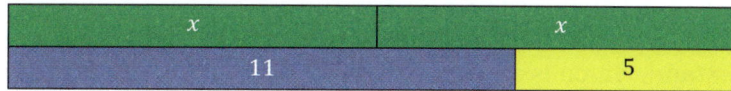

This is perhaps the more usual way to represent the equation. This utilises the count back version of subtraction (although by switching the '5' and '11' bars the difference interpretation could equally well be employed). We see the two '*x*' bars, then count back 5, leaving the result of 11. An alternate way of viewing the same model is that 2*x* is the sum of 11 and 5 – that is, 2*x* = 16. This leads to the logical conclusion that each '*x*' bar is worth 8:

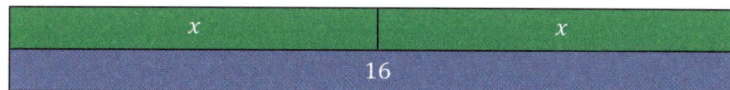

The alternative approach is to use a negative tile and employ strategies similar to those used with counters by eliminating the negatives using zero-pairs:

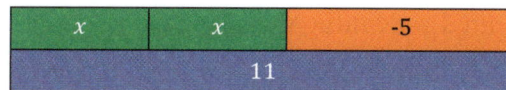

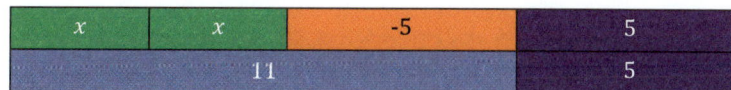

The obvious issue with this approach is that, in the second diagram, the 'x' bars have to physically change size in order to encompass all of the 16, plus in the first diagram it looks as if the 2x is smaller than 11. As with using negative tiles for factorisation, this dichotomy of being numerically smaller but physically longer can be hard for pupils to understand, which is at least part of the reason for favouring the count back approach.

The vector representation doesn't have the same drawbacks, as the subtraction and negative vectors both force the 11 to be shorter than the 2x:

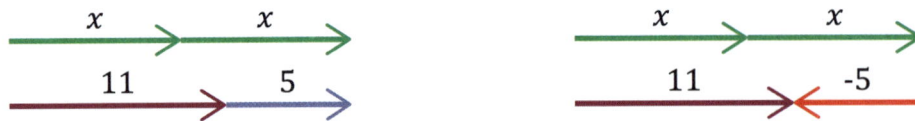

In the left-hand diagram we see 2x then subtract 5 using the standard head-to-head subtraction of vectors. This produces the resultant vector of 11. As with the first approach using bars, this can also be read as $2x = 11 + 5$, which leads to the $2x = 16$ and then to the $x = 8$.

In the right-hand diagram we again see 2x followed by -5. The resultant is still 11. This time, the purple and red vectors can be read alternatively as 11 – (-5), as the 11 and -5 meet head to head. This is the same as 11 + 5, of course, so this still gives $2x = 16$, and therefore $x = 8$.

Where the advantages and disadvantages really start to show are when the value of $x$ is either negative or fractional:

$2x + 11 = 5$

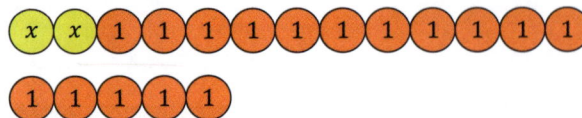

We begin with the same approach, separating and discarding the counters we can match together:

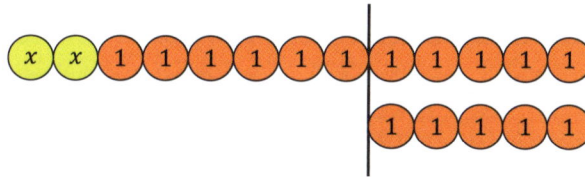

This time we still have 6 counters left with the $x$ counters, and nothing left on the bottom line. This can be rectified by introducing negative counters to create zero-pairs:

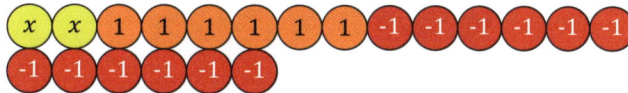

The zero-pairs eliminate all but the $x$ tiles on the top line, which then allows us to show the value of $x$:

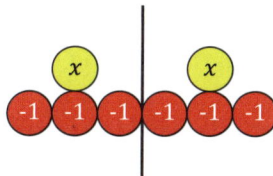

Having $2x$ on the top line and -6 on the bottom line enables us to split the $x$ counters, leading to $x = -3$.

If we try to use bars to show the same equation, we begin to run into difficulties:

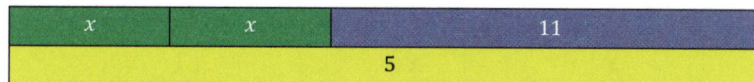

The problem is immediately apparent: the '5' bar has to be much bigger than the '11' bar. In some ways this can be regarded as a positive effect, as it is a clear indicator that $x$ is a negative value. However, if pupils do not recognise this then it can be hard for them to know where to begin.

Even with this apparent issue, we can proceed with the solution. The first step generally would be to use a '-11' bar to create a zero-pair on the top line:

| $x$ | $x$ | 11 | -11 |
|---|---|---|---|
| 5 | | | -11 |

Of course, it is somewhat misleading that the -11 is smaller in size than the 5, but nonetheless the result is that the bottom line becomes -6:

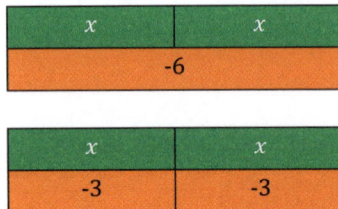

| $x$ | $x$ |
|---|---|
| -6 | |

| $x$ | $x$ |
|---|---|
| -3 | -3 |

This shows that $2x = -6$, which can then lead us to the result that $x = -3$.

The major difficulty with this representation is its failure to lead to greater understanding of the relationships and structures underpinning the equation. It would be very easy to simply treat this as a process – add the negative to create the zero-pair, subtract this value from the bottom, then divide. I suspect that many teachers would once again prefer to use the representations with values of $x$ that are positive until such point that pupils are comfortable working purely symbolically, and then begin to introduce negative values of $x$.

The use of vectors brings with it similar issues:

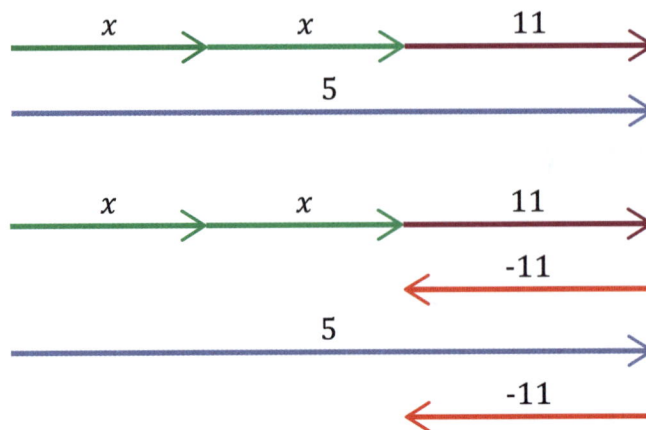

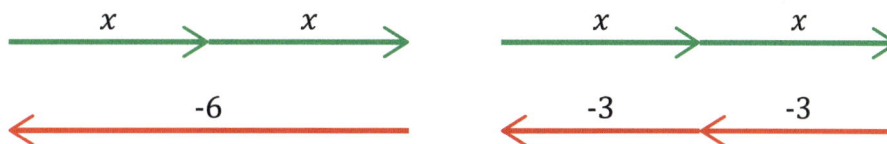

If we consider equations where the value of *x* is a positive fractional value, we find that we begin to encounter difficulties with counters:

$3x + 5 = 12$

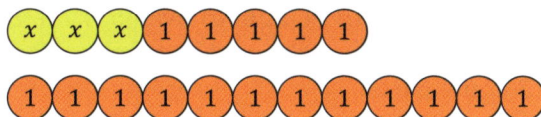

Initially, the same idea of separating and discarding counters from the top and bottom lines appears to work:

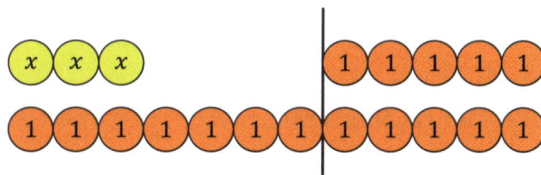

The problem, of course, is that this now leaves 7 counters to be split into 3 shares. When we met this in Chapter 2, we noted that this type of division was only able to show the remainder – this can only be viewed as 2 remainder 1 because the denominator is seen in the number of shares rather than in the number of counters in each group:

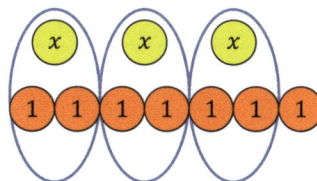

As before, we could argue that if pupils understand that $3x = 7$ implies that we need to divide 7 by 3 in order to find the value of *x*, then they don't need the representation as they already have a well-developed understanding of division.

With these sorts of equations, bars and vectors allow us to handle the division much more smoothly:

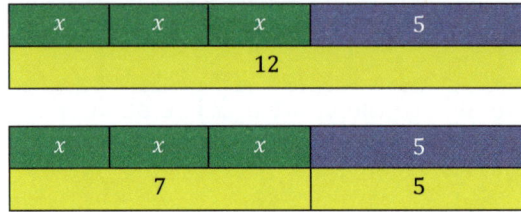

Admittedly, pupils will either have to be able to evaluate 7 ÷ 3 or they will need to redraw the bar onto an appropriate square grid or number line to allow the physical breaking of the 7 into 3 equal parts:

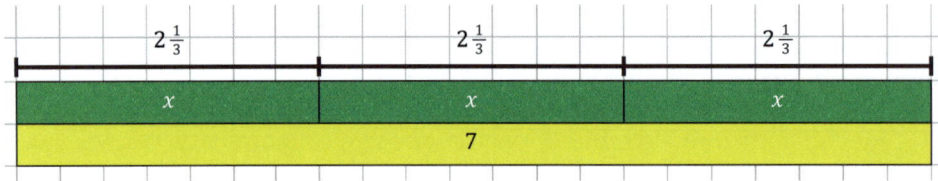

The vector representation works in a similar way:

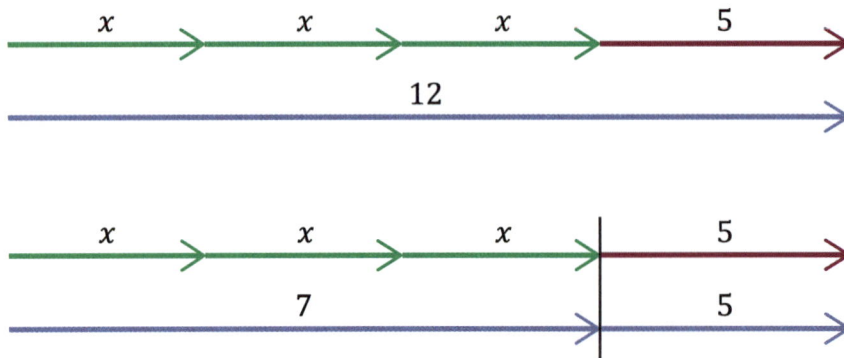

Again, the division can be handled either using pupils' prior understanding of division or by superimposing the vectors onto a suitable square grid or number line:

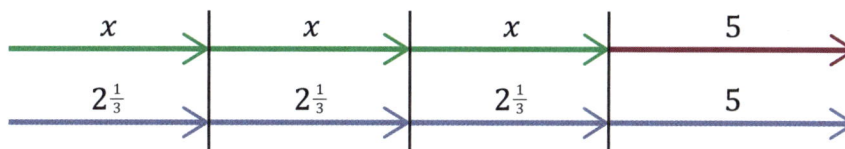

So far, all of the equations we have considered have been simple linear equations that only involve multiplication and addition/subtraction. There are several other types of equations that we may wish to model and explore with pupils. These include:

- Equations involving brackets.

- Equations with unknowns on both sides.

- Equations where the coefficient of $x$ is negative.

- Equations where the coefficient of $x$ is a fraction.

We will now consider one example of each of these. For simplicity, we will keep the value of $x$ as a positive integer.

$3(2x + 1) = 27$

Symbolically, this equation would usually be solved in one of two ways:

1  Expand the bracket and then proceed as a simple linear equation.

2  Divide by 3 first, and then solve the resulting equation.

Both of these can be modelled using our representations. As before, we will start with counters:

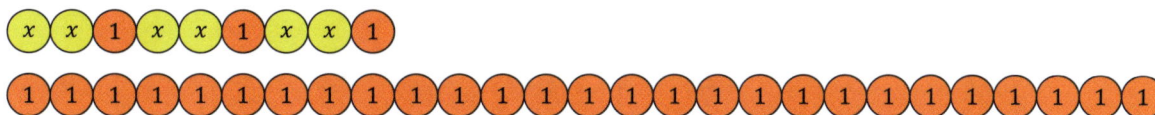

In the first approach, the expansion requires the simplification of the top line, leading to this:

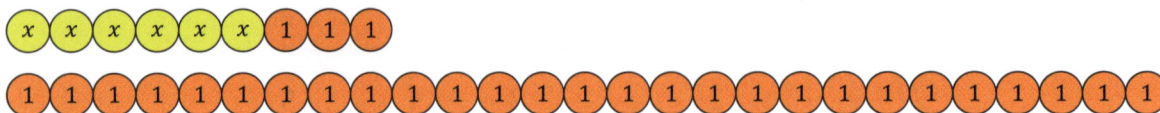

We can then proceed as we would with the previous equations, separating and discarding counters that appear in both the top and bottom lines, and then equating the remaining counters to each *x*.

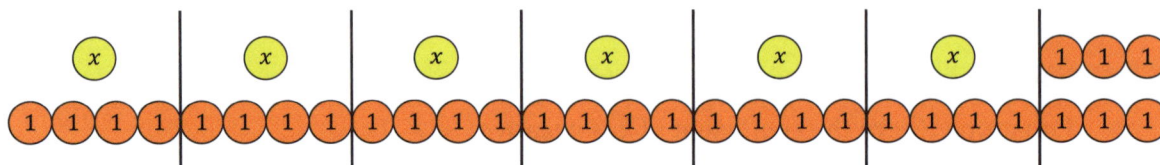

The second approach would start in the same way, but then rather than rearrange the counters in the top line, we would take each group and equate it to a number of counters:

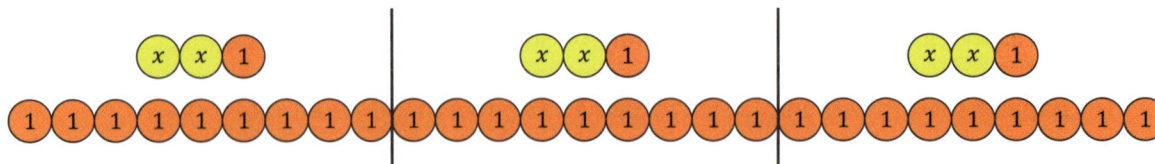

We can then just concentrate on one partition, solving *x* in the same way as we did before:

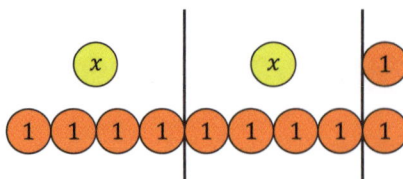

The same two approaches can also be used with vectors and bars:

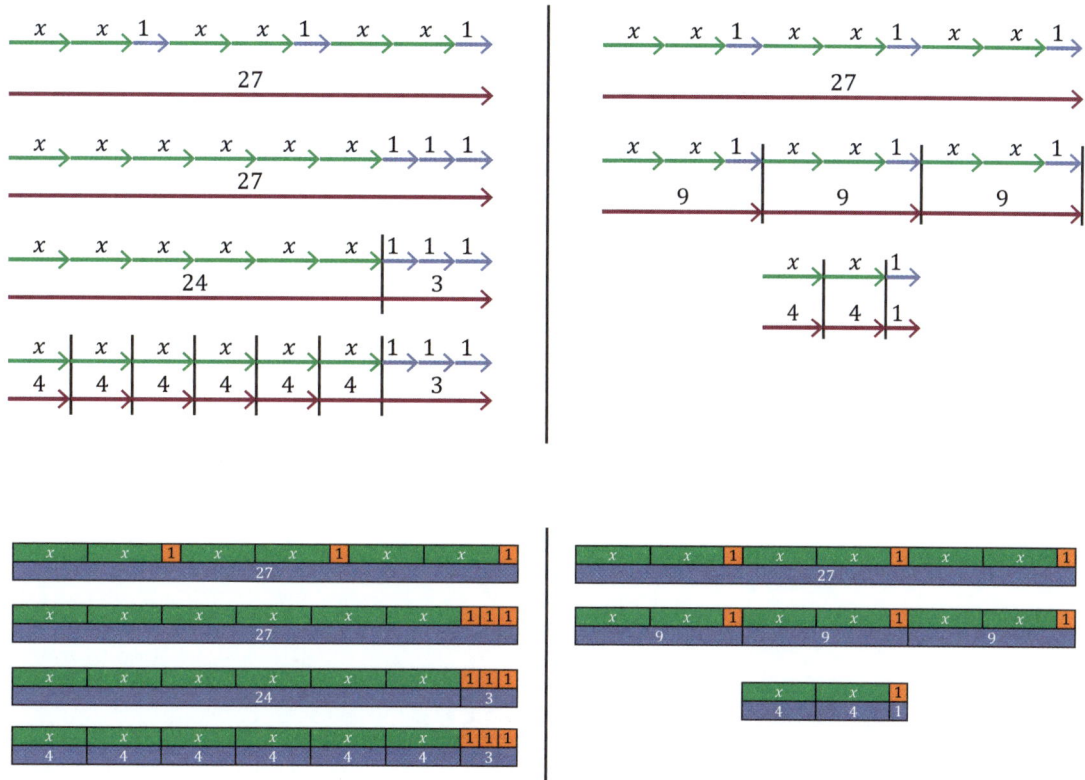

When there is a variable on both sides of the equation, all three representations (counters, vectors and bars) can support the development of understanding of these relationships:

$3x + 5 = x + 13$

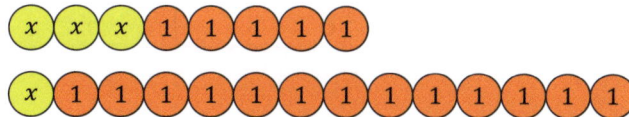

We adopt the same approach that we have taken with counters up to this point – separating and discarding, then equating:

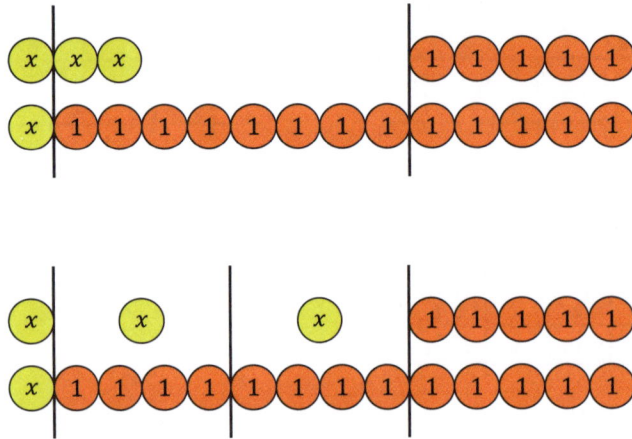

This shows that the result is $x = 4$.

An identical approach can be taken with vectors:

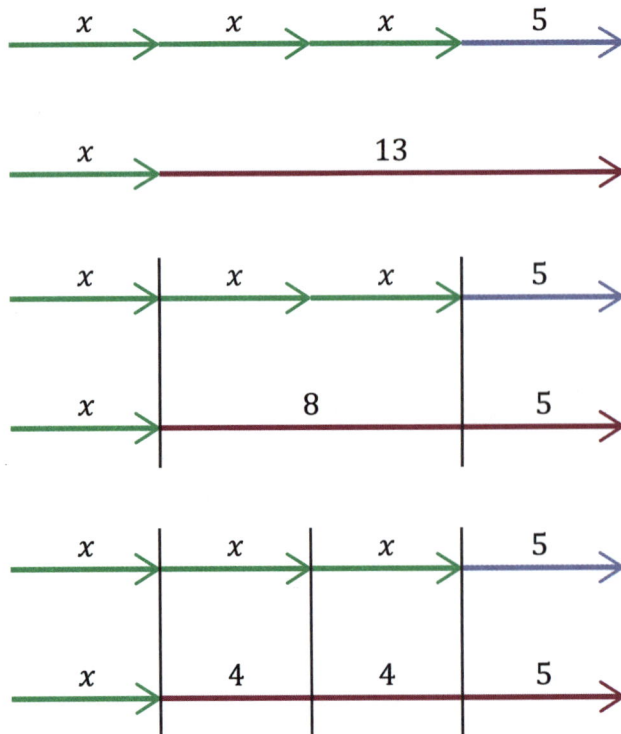

The same approach can also be used with bars:

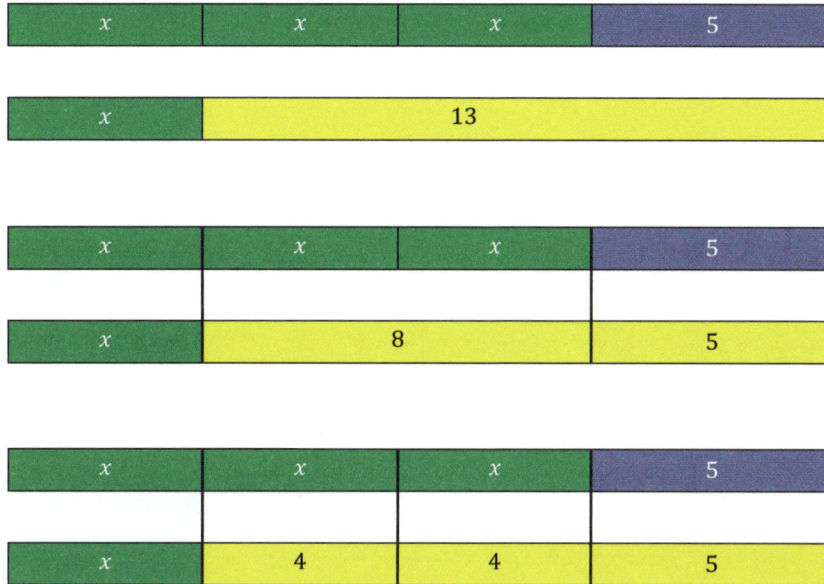

When working with equations where the coefficient of $x$ is negative, the best approach is to use negative counters/vectors/bars:

$3x + 5 = 13 - x$

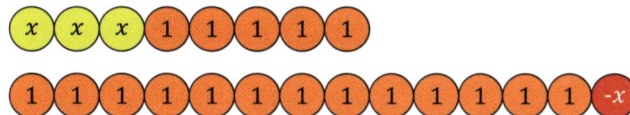

Initially, we can proceed as we would normally, separating and discarding counters:

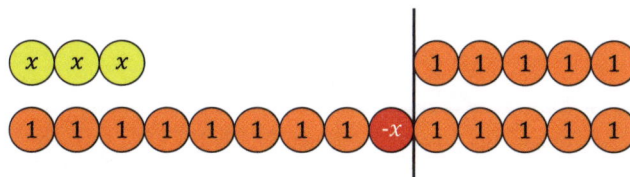

At this point we can proceed in two ways. We can add an extra '$x$' counter to both lines, which forms a zero-pair with the '-$x$' counter, which leaves 4 '$x$' counters on the top line and 8 on the bottom line (as shown in the left-hand diagrams below). Alternatively, we can add both an '*x*' counter and '-*x*' counter to the top line, as this is a zero-pair (as shown in the right-hand diagrams). This allows us to separate and discard the '-*x*' counter, which again leaves 4 '*x* 'counters on the top line and 8 on the bottom:

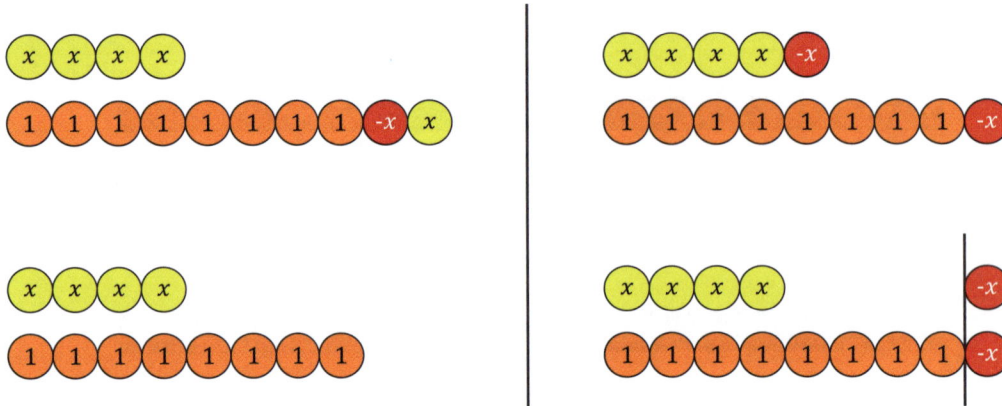

However we arrive at 4 '*x*' counters on the top line and 8 on the bottom, once there we can equate sets of counters to each *x*:

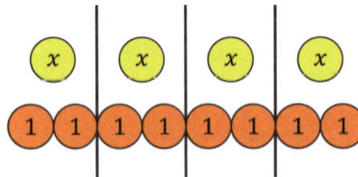

The approach for the vector representation is very similar:

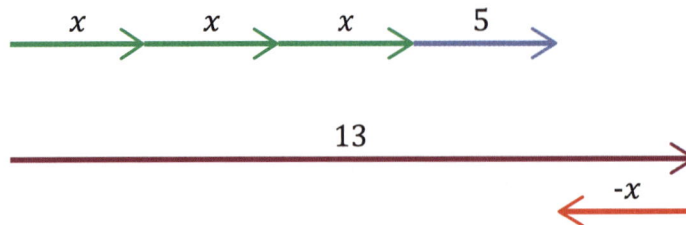

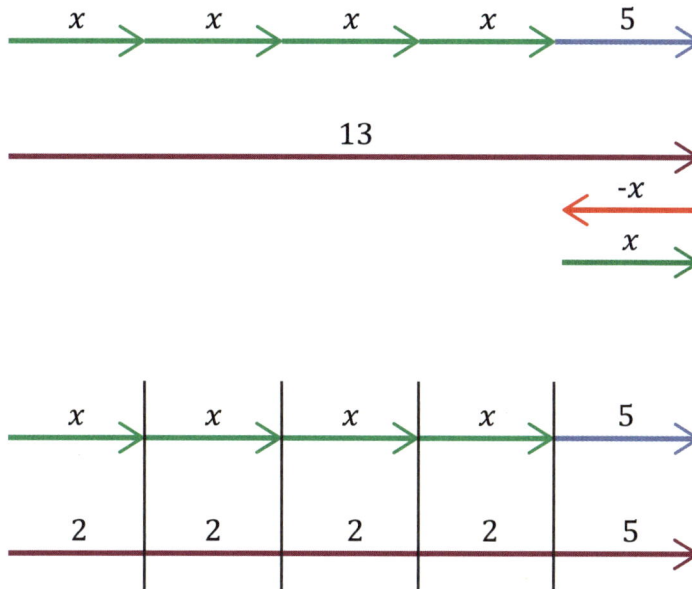

In this sequence we notice that the end of the $3x + 5$ vectors line up with the end of the '$-x$' vector, as this is $13 - x$. We then introduce the extra '$x$' vector to both lines, creating a zero-pair at the bottom. This allows us to equate the 5s, and then split the remaining 8 into 4, giving $x = 2$.

When using bars, it is better to use a subtraction approach rather than negative bars. This avoids the problem of having bars that are longer in length but smaller in value. This means the equation $3x + 5 = 13 - x$ is best represented like this:

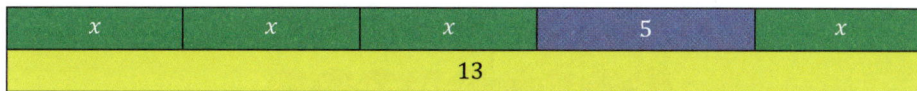

This can be interpreted as 13 count back $x$ is equal to $3x + 5$. However, a small rearrangement of the top line can produce the equation $4x + 5 = 13$:

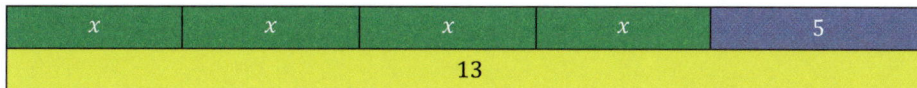

This can then be solved in the same way as the simple linear equations from earlier in the chapter:

| $x$ | $x$ | $x$ | $x$ | 5 |
|---|---|---|---|---|
| 2 | 2 | 2 | 2 | 5 |

Before we consider other types of equations, we will conclude by examining equations where the coefficient of $x$ is a fraction. These can be harder to represent, so an effective approach is to not represent the whole of $x$ immediately but to represent the fraction of $x$:

$\frac{2}{3}x + 5 = 9$

In the diagram above we see that, rather than defining a counter to have the value $x$, we instead give it a value of $\frac{1}{3}x$. This allows us to apply the same approaches we have used in solving the earlier equations. The important understanding here is that to solve the equation we have to find out the value of 3 yellow counters, as it is three-thirds that make a whole:

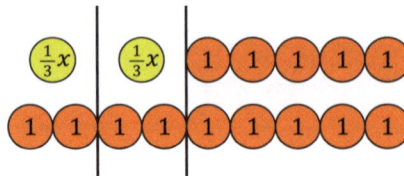

Here we see the 5 counters paired off and discarded, with 5 of the 9 on the second line. This leaves 4 counters on the second line which are split equally between the two-thirds. The final step is to *add* an extra yellow counter to create three-thirds:

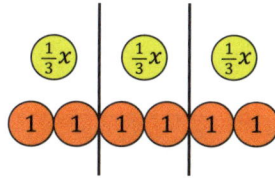

This allows us to see that $x = 6$ is the solution to the equation.

The same approach works equally well with vectors or bars:

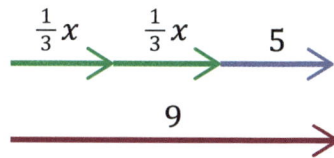

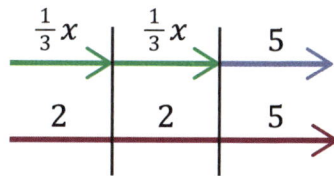

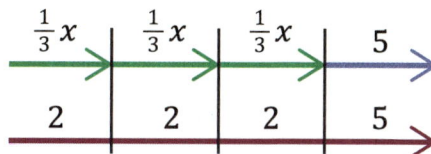

Here we see the vector set up for $\frac{1}{3}x$. The '9' vector is then partitioned in line with the vectors above, showing that $\frac{1}{3}x = 2$. The extra '$\frac{1}{3}x$' vector is then added into the third diagram, illustrating that the whole of $x = 6$.

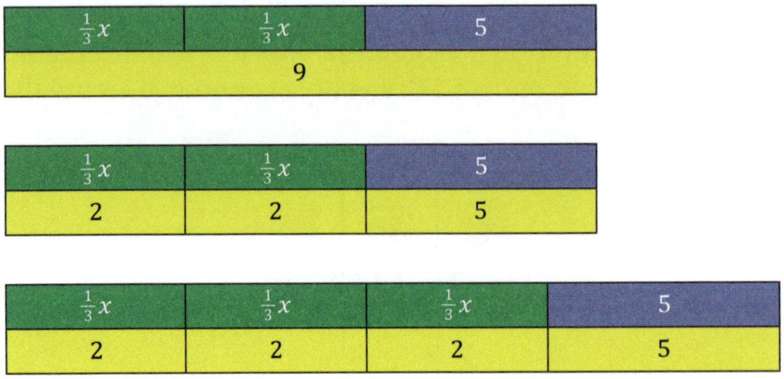

In a virtually identical approach to that used with the vectors, the green bar is now defined to be $\frac{1}{3}x$ and the '9' bar is partitioned to reveal $\frac{1}{3}x = 2$, which leads to $x = 6$.

In addition to linear equations in one variable, our representations can also support the introduction of simultaneous linear equations. We will start with some very simple simultaneous equations.

## Simultaneous equations

$x + 2y = 8$

$x + 5y = 17$

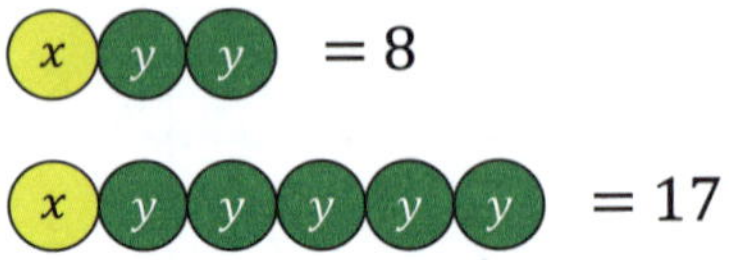

When working with simultaneous equations, the value of the counters is not shown using a second line of counters (as with equations in one variable). Instead, the values are written numerically or shown visually. Counters can be used to support the reasoning as follows:

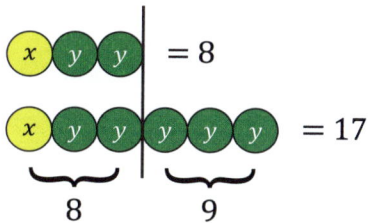

This leads to the conclusion that $y = 3$, and so it follows that $x = 2$.

Vectors can also be used in a very similar way, although it is generally more useful to impose the vectors on an unscaled number line:

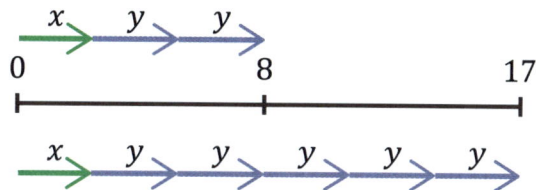

The same reasoning can then be used to solve the equations:

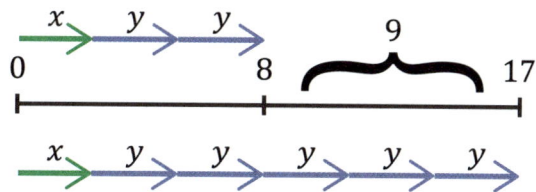

Again, we see that $3y = 9$, implying $y = 3$ and therefore $x = 2$.

Bars work in a comparable way:

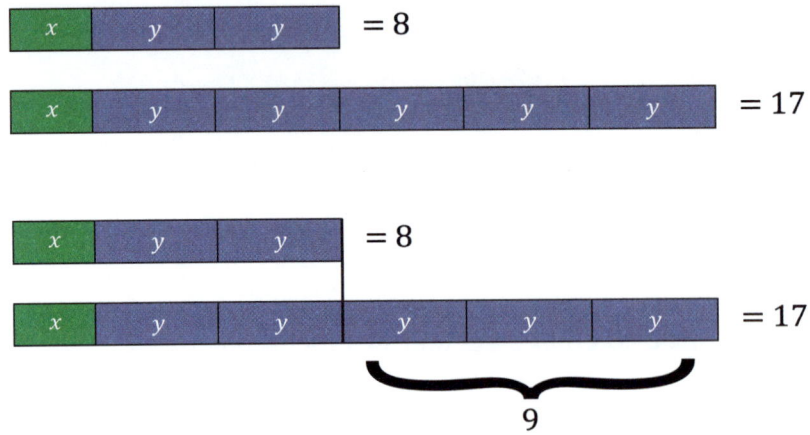

The same logic then follows: $3y = 9$, so $y = 3$ and $x = 2$.

If coefficients are negative, they are best represented using negative counters/vectors/bars:

$3x + 2y = 12$

$4x - 2y = 2$

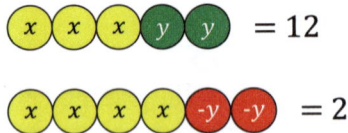

There are a few possible choices when working with this pair of equations, although the most straightforward approach is simply to add the two sets together. This allows the formation of the zero-pairs with the '$y$' and '$-y$' counters, leaving just the '$x$' counters:

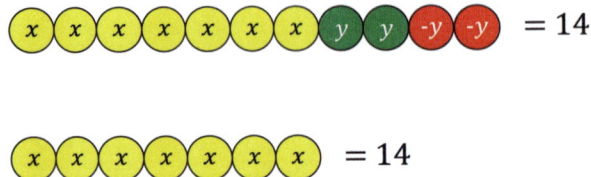

It then follows that $x = 2$, which leads to $y = 3$.

Vectors work in the same way:

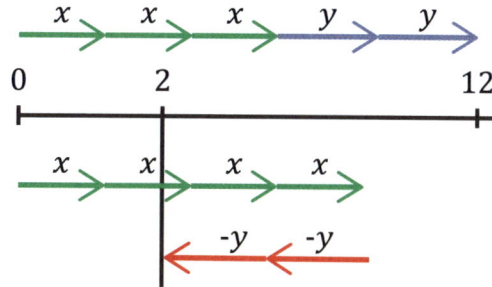

The initial set-up is a bit messier with vectors than with counters. However, once the addition of the two equations is completed, the diagram simplifies somewhat:

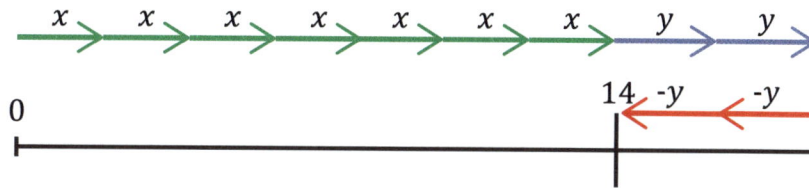

This leads to the same conclusion – that $x = 2$ and therefore $y = 3$.

The same equations can be represented using bars, although this once again introduces the problem of a bar being physically longer but having a smaller numerical value:

We could also represent this using the count back or difference approach, although difficulties can arise when then combining the equations:

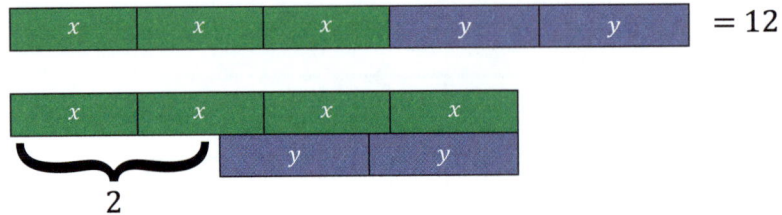

$$= 12$$

The issue with the second arrangement is that it is difficult to see how to combine the two equations, or even where to begin solving. Eventually we might arrive at something like this:

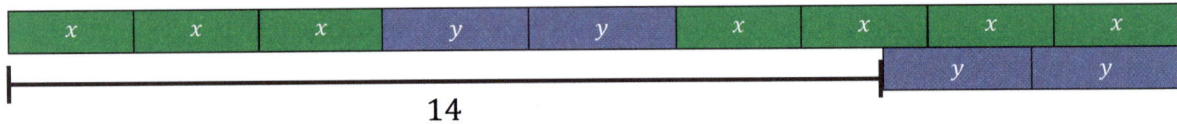

Which can then be rearranged to this:

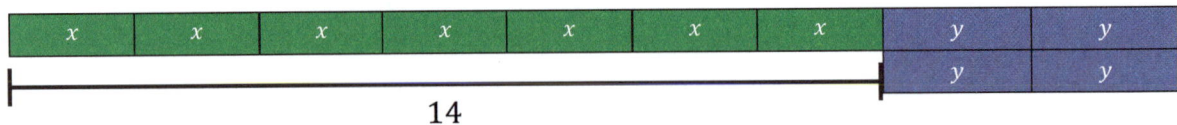

This leads to the conclusion that $x = 2$, so it then follows that $y = 3$.

The process becomes a little more straightforward with the use of negative bars:

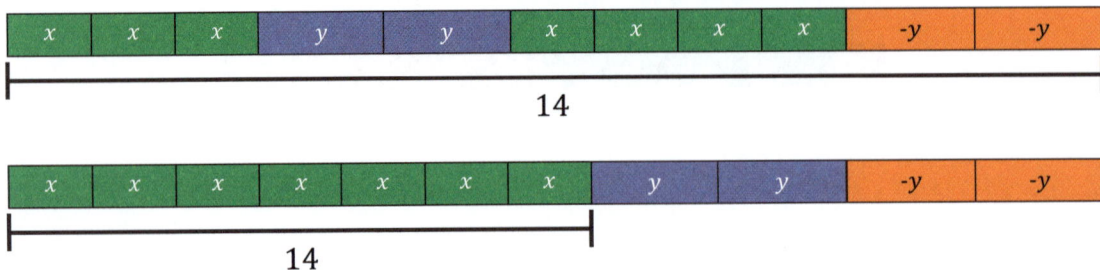

Once again, the problem with this representation is that the 14 physically changes size because 0 has an actual length in the diagram, which obviously doesn't reflect the reality of numbers. Due to the recurrent difficulties of representing negatives using bar models, it is not uncommon for teachers to use a different representation or to limit the use of bars to those equations with positive coefficients until pupils no longer need the support of the representation, and then return to negative coefficients when pupils are comfortable working purely symbolically.

These simultaneous equations are made somewhat easier to solve by the fact that the coefficients have been chosen so that there is at least one variable with the same coefficient – that is, additive inverse coefficients (e.g. 2 and -2). In practice, however, we often work with equations that do not have any coefficients in common, so it is worth taking some time to explore how we can model the solution of these equations.

$3x + 2y = 12$

$4x + 3y = 17$

We can again represent these equations using counters, vectors and bars:

The standard approach, symbolically, is to multiply one or both equations in order to force the coefficients of one of the variables to be either the same or the additive inverse. In this case, if we repeat the first set of counters three times and the second set of counters twice, we get this:

If we then simplify each individual row of counters, the result looks like this:

 = 36

 = 34

We then separate and discard the counters that feature in both rows, leaving the difference as the difference in the two totals:

 = 36

2  = 34

This clearly illustrates that $x = 2$, and from there it follows that $y = 3$.

The same equation can be solved in an identical way using vectors:

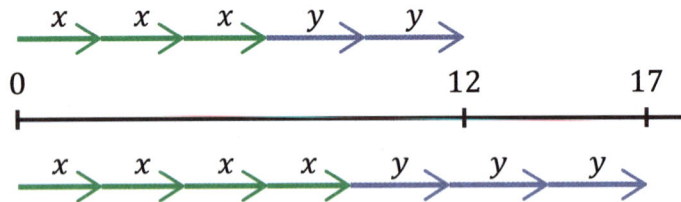

The same process of repeating the top row three times and the bottom row twice can again be employed:

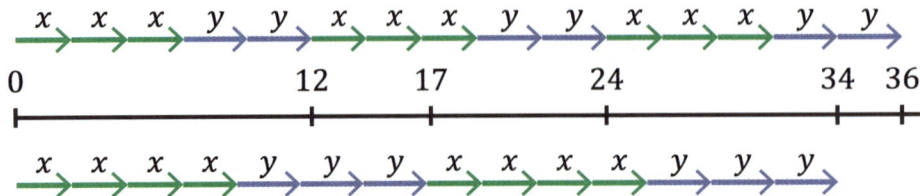

The same simplification of each line that we saw with the counters then follows:

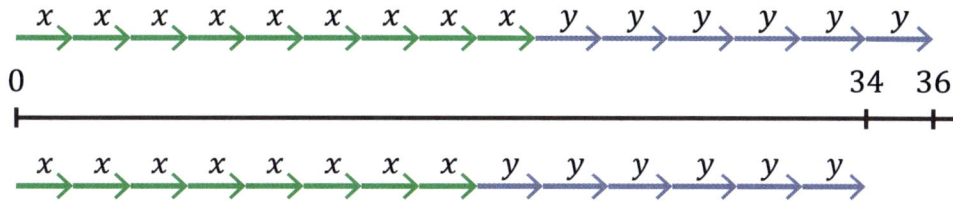

Resulting in the same conclusion:

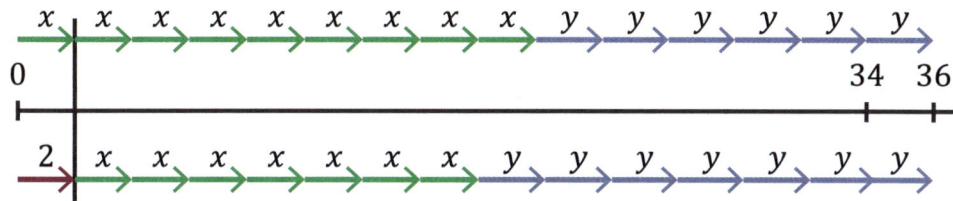

Once the fact is established that $x = 2$, it follows that $y = 3$.

The same approach can be modelled with bars:

The final type of equation that we ask pupils to work with before they finish secondary school is the quadratic equation. We will take a brief look at these to finish the chapter.

# Quadratic equations

There is not much more to add on quadratic equations that we didn't explore in the previous chapter when looking at factorisation. The standard approach for quadratics that do factorise is to factorise, and then when set equal to 0 to solve each separate bracket. It is this approach that we will explore using the algebra tiles that were so useful in modelling the factorisation process:

$x^2 + 5x + 6 = 0$

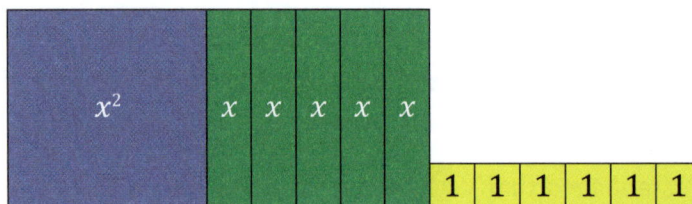

In the diagram above we see the tiles indicated by the expression on the left of the equation. We recall that we can factorise this expression by creating a rectangular area:

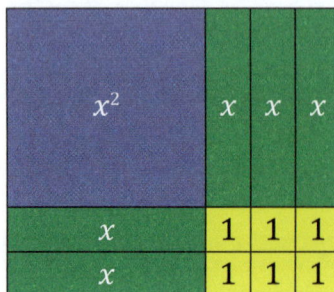

Once arranged in a rectangle, the length and width of the rectangle informs us as to the separate factors that make up the factorisation:

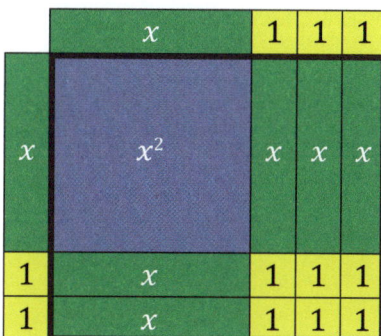

The length is $x + 3$ and the width $x + 2$, giving the factorisation $(x + 3)(x + 2)$. The logic now goes that if we want this area to be equal to 0, then we need to reduce either the length or width to 0. This means that $x$ will need to be either -3 or -2 in order to form the necessary zero-pairs with the '1' tiles that are added to the $x$. This can be seen below:

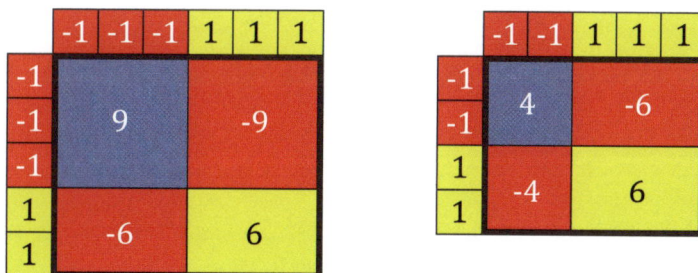

There are two more approaches to solving quadratic equations (beyond simple numerical methods): completing the square and the quadratic formula. The second of these is not possible to represent – as a general formula we would need a variable number of '$x^2$' and '$x$' tiles, which we simply cannot capture pictorially. However, we can represent the process of completing the square in both a concrete and pictorial fashion. The next chapter looks at this along with further algebraic manipulations.

# Chapter 16

# Further algebraic manipulations

In addition to the algebraic manipulation and equation solving that we considered in the previous chapter, there are some particular relationships that we explore with pupils in the secondary classroom, so we will spend a little time examining these separately.

The first of these is the difference of two squares factorisation. You will recall from Chapter 14 that we looked at two ways of working with factorisations when one of the coefficients is negative. Both had their issues, and indeed many teachers avoid using concrete or pictorial representations altogether when factorising with negative coefficients. One place where I feel it is certainly worthwhile is when considering the difference of two squares, as the concept and process has so much more meaning when seen visually.

## Factorising the difference of two squares

$x^2 - y^2$

Algebra tiles can be useful here. Instead of defining the small square to be a 1 by 1 square, we define it to be a $y$ by $y$ square. This allows us to use a positive '$x^2$' tile and a negative '$y^2$' tile to show the difference of two squares:

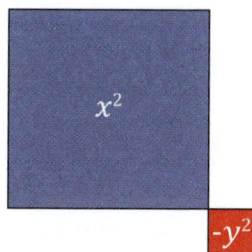

So how does this lead to the factorisation? Well, if we fill in the blank spaces with a positive and negative '*xy*' tile then we get this diagram:

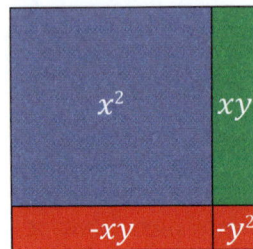

This area is the same as the previous area, as the *xy* and the *-xy* are a zero-pair. The area is now written as $x^2 + xy - xy - y^2$. Some readers may recognise this as the expansion of $(x + y)(x - y)$; however, we can see this properly if we examine the length and width of the area:

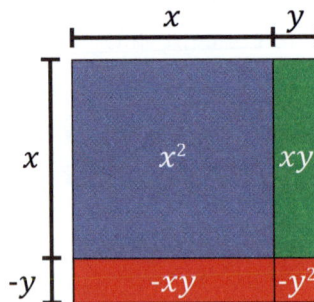

This shows that the factorisation is $(x + y)(x - y)$.

Although this representation does show the factorisation, the spontaneous introduction of the zero-pair can cause problems and does seem like a bit of a trick (even though I argued earlier, when looking at the subtraction of negatives, that it isn't).

My preferred approach to demonstrating the difference of two squares visually is to use the alternative approach that we saw when we explored factorisation with negative coefficients. You may recall that this involved overlapping the areas to find the physical difference; for me, this resonates much more strongly with the idea of 'the difference of two squares'.

We start with a smaller square overlapping the larger square:

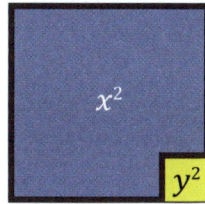

The difference between the area of the two squares is outlined in black. This area can be broken up into two rectangular parts:

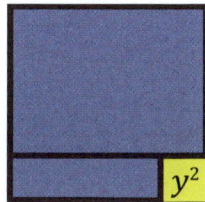

If we detach the bottom rectangle, rotate it and place it next to the larger rectangle, we can reconfigure the area into a complete rectangle:

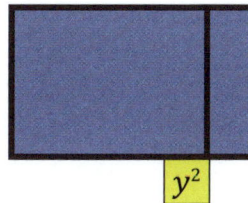

By examining the length and width of this rectangular area, we can determine that the length is $x + y$ and the width is $x - y$, demonstrating that the factorisation is $(x + y)$ $(x - y)$:

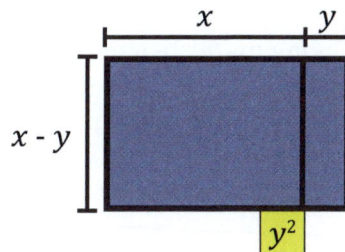

Whilst this is a really interesting algebraic relationship, one of its most brilliant applications is when the relationship is applied back to particular values. Consider, for example, the calculation $87^2 - 13^2$. If we represent this is in the same way, the diagram looks like this:

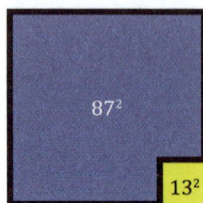

When this area is rearranged in the same way as the general case on page 287, we end up with this diagram:

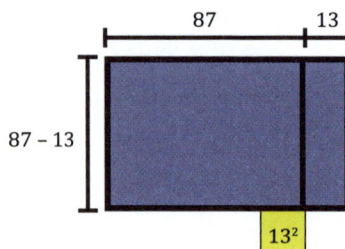

This gives the area as $(87 + 13) \times (87 - 13) = 100 \times 74$. This means that $87^2 - 13^2 = 7400$. Of course, this also tells us that $87^2 = 7400 + 169 = 7569$. I really like this application of the difference of two squares, both in terms of finding the difference between two square numbers but also in finding the squares of large numbers.

Whilst on the subject of squares, we will now explore the last algebraic manipulation we are going to look at in this book – completing the square.

## Completing the square

Like many pupils who end up being maths teachers, I was adept at algebraic manipulation when I was at school. I could factorise expressions, I could work with surds and I could complete the square. But, also like many pupils, I had no sense of what I was doing beyond following processes – a teacher showed me how to do something and I replicated it. I believed I understood everything I needed to about these things.

A number of years ago, I watched the *Story of Maths* with Marcus du Sautoy on the BBC and I experienced something that completely changed my perspective of maths.[*] It is probably what sparked my interest in representation and structure in mathematics teaching, as well as teaching for real understanding rather than just teaching pupils how to follow a process. Approximately 30 minutes into the episode is a demonstration of an Ancient Babylonian problem about land area, which utilises a geometric approach to completing the square and using it to solve equations. This was a revelation to me – for the first time, I truly understood what it meant to complete the square. I also truly understood why the coefficient of $x$ has to be halved and why the square is important. I won't recreate the exact example here, but I will create a similar example below.

$x^2 + 4x + 1$

The understanding of the underlying structure can be supported with the use of algebra tiles:

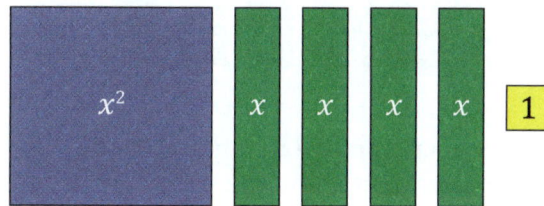

In this diagram we see the tiles used to create the expression. The idea here is not just to try to create a rectangular area from these tiles (which in this case is impossible), but to attempt to get as close as possible to a perfect square. There are two possible ways to achieve this:

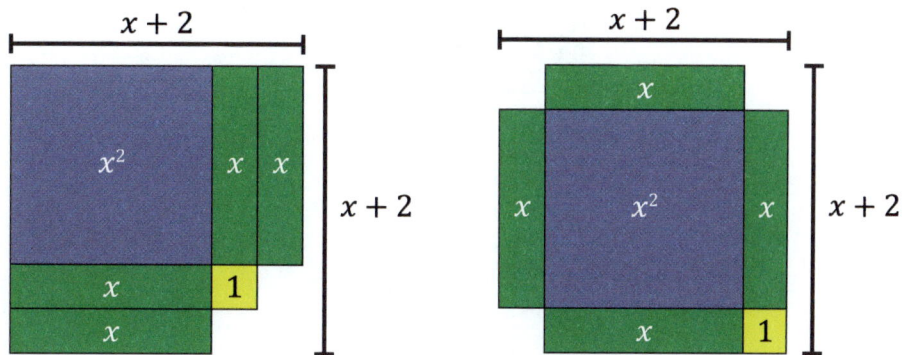

[*]   M. du Sautoy, The Language of the Universe (Episode 1), *The Story of Maths* [TV series]. BBC Four (6 October 2008).

What this diagram shows is that we are three '1' tiles short of being able to form a complete square, but if we had those three tiles we would be able to form a square of the length $x + 2$. So the result of completing the square is $(x + 2)^2 - 3$.

This also explains why the coefficient of $x$ gets split in half when completing the square. Half of the '$x$' tiles are attached to the side(s) of $x^2$, whilst the other half are attached to the top or bottom (or both). This creates a problem when trying to represent an expression where the coefficient of $x$ is not an even integer: if we are using algebra tiles as a concrete resource then we cannot physically split tiles in half. It is possible to do this pictorially, but it can be rather challenging.

$x^2 + 3x + 1$

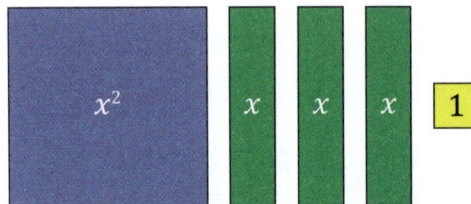

We have a dilemma when we have an odd number of '$x$' tiles. We can attach one to the side and one to the bottom, but what about the third? The correct approach is to split the third in half as in the diagram below:

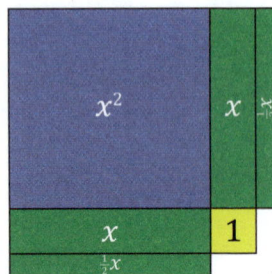

This shows that the correct completed square form of $x^2 + 3x + 1$ is $(x + 1\frac{1}{2})^2 - 1\frac{1}{4}$. However, pupils could be forgiven for trying to arrange the tiles like this:

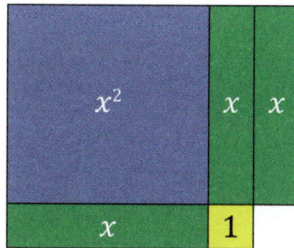

This could mean that they mistakenly believe that the completed square form is $(x + 2)^2 - x - 3$. Whilst this expression is equal to $x^2 + 3x + 1$, it is clearly not in the completed square form, and is not as close to a square as the previous diagram. Pupils need to understand that if we are as close to a square as possible, we will only ever have a numerical difference from the square and not an algebraic one. Whilst this is difficult ground, it may be useful to use these visual representations to support pupils in reaching this understanding.

As we saw in the last chapter, the completed square form is another approach that we can take to solving quadratic equations, and again the algebra tile can help to support pupils in understanding how and why this works.

$x^2 + 4x + 1 = 0$

The expression on the left of the equation has already appeared in the completed square form:

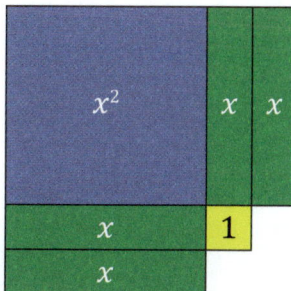

The equation suggests that this area has a numerical value of 0, and prompts us to find out the value of *x* which makes that happen. The approach we will take is to fill in the missing parts of the square, which produces the diagram below:

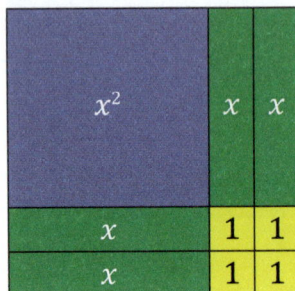

This is a perfect square which we created by increasing the area by 3. So the area of this square is now 3. This implies that the length of the square is $\pm\sqrt{3}$. However, the length of the square is $x + 2$. This means that $x + 2 = \pm\sqrt{3}$, and therefore that $x = \pm\sqrt{3} - 2$.

What is interesting about solving quadratic equations using the completed square form is that many teachers insist on equations being in the form $f(x) = 0$. This is almost certainly influenced by the fact that it must be in this form to solve quadratic equations by factorising or using the quadratic formula. I suspect that teachers do not want to add a layer of confusion when pupils are tackling quadratic equations which must be equal to 0 before they can attempt a solution, whilst with other quadratics there is no such restriction.

In my opinion, however, if the completed square form is going to be used to solve a quadratic equation, then the optimum form is to have the equation in the form $x^2 + px = q$. Indeed, readers may well recognise this as the beginnings of a proof of the quadratic formula, where $p = \frac{b}{a}$ and $q = \frac{q}{c}$, where *a*, *b* and *c* are the coefficients when the quadratic is expressed in the form $ax^2 + bx + c$.

Consider the example $x^2 + 4x = 32$:

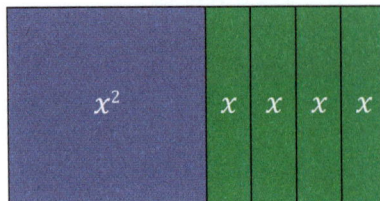

In this diagram we see the $x^2 + 4x$ arranged as a rectangle. The equation implies that the area of this rectangle is equal to 32 and prompts us to find the value of $x$ that makes this true.

We can approach this by rearranging the rectangle into a shape as close to a square as possible:

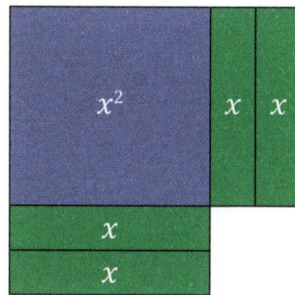

The area of this rearranged shape is still 32, so we fill in the remaining space to complete the square, which produces the following diagram:

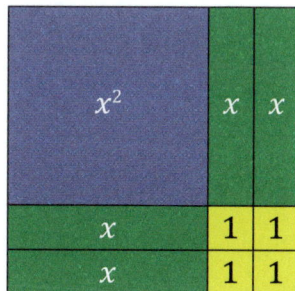

Given that the area of the original shape was 32, and we have added 4 to the area, the area of the complete square is now 36. This implies that the length is 6. However, the length of the square in the diagram is actually $x + 2$. This therefore implies that $x + 2 = 6$, or that $x = 4$.

Symbolically this appears as follows:

$x^2 + 4x = 32$

$(x + 2)^2 - 4 = 32$

$(x + 2)^2 = 36$

$x + 2 = 6$

$x = 4$

However, because the length is positive, pupils can be blinded to the negative solution. In order to give the full solution, the final lines should read:

$x + 2 = \pm 6$

$x = 6 - 2 \ \& \ \text{-}6 - 2$

$x = 4 \ \& \ \text{-}8$

The fact that the length appears positive must not preclude negative solutions, unless the context of the question makes it clear that only positive solutions are appropriate. This is an important point that we need to make sure is secure when pupils are using representations. In order to do this, we need to be explicit that pupils must consider the negative values of $x$, even when using a positive '$x$' tile. This applies both when they are using a visual representation and also when moving from pictorial to abstract representations.

This concludes our review of different representations that can support pupils' understanding of the underlying structures behind everything from a basic familiarity with our number system and the operations that form it, to the higher algebra that pupils study at GCSE. My sincere hope is that this work will support teachers in using multiple representations to help develop pupil understanding, that it will enable teachers to arm pupils with the proper tools for them to reason and think mathematically, and that this will assist pupils in being able to apply mathematics to new and unfamiliar situations because they recognise the similarity in the underlying structures that underpin the mathematics they are studying.

I am aware that I may have raised questions as well as answering them, however, so I have devoted the final chapter to frequently asked questions.

# Chapter 17

# Frequently asked and anticipated questions

The ideas and approaches set out in this book have never, to my knowledge, appeared in one place. There have been individual books and papers written about nearly all of these representations (although I have yet to find one about the use of vector notation to explore number and algebra or the use of ordered-pair graphs), but I have never seen them collected together and compared. I am privileged that I have occasionally been invited to speak at conferences where I have discussed some of the ideas and representations that appear in this book, but as I am sure you will appreciate, to describe them all would take a session lasting many hours, if not days.

In writing this book, I hope that teachers will acquire a greater understanding of the strengths and drawbacks of each representation (downsides are often notably lacking from texts on the individual representations), and so make informed decisions about which representations they will use to help develop their pupils' understanding. Due to the fact that these ideas have never been collected together in this way, there hasn't really been an opportunity for teachers to ask many questions about them. The answers that follow are my responses to questions that have been asked when I have talked with individuals or groups about these representations, as well as queries that I anticipate will arise from some of the ideas put forward.

## 1. Are these all of the manipulatives/ representations I should be using in the classroom, or that other teachers use in the classroom?

This book is by no means a complete collection of every representation that is used or can be used in the classroom. There are some notable exceptions, such as the dual number line which is used for exploring proportional relationships, as well as the multitude of representations used to develop understanding in the primary classroom. When first looking at number and operations, particularly with questions set in context, many primary teachers will use representations that engage directly with the context. For example, if an addition question is about people getting onto a bus, the teacher will model this with actual toy people and a toy bus. Some teachers use

Lego blocks. Some use Multilink cubes. I know at least one teacher who uses paper folding to teach children about fractions. I even know of teachers who use sweets to model different mathematical ideas.

What I have tried to do in this book is to capture the core representations that many of these tools devolve to – sweets and toy people can, at an appropriate point, be replaced with counters. Lego blocks can become bar models or vectors. Multilink can become bars or counters (or both). The aim is to provide teachers with both (a) a starting point from which to explore representation and structure and (b) enough understanding that there should be little in the realms of number or algebra that teachers cannot approach in a concrete or pictorial way, should they wish.

## 2. Should I use all of these representations with my pupils? I am not sure I have the time!

I am a strong believer in the idea that teachers are the people best placed to make decisions about the learning of their pupils, and the approaches, explanations and activities that will best support their learning. If you, as a teacher, believe that all of the representations in this book will benefit your pupils in understanding the concept(s) or process(es) you wish them to understand, then use them all. If you feel that two or three are enough to provide them with the understanding you wish them to have, or for them to develop this understanding for themselves, then choose those you feel will best support this goal.

Being aware of multiple representations and their strengths/weaknesses gives teachers a toolkit to support their pupils, so if one representation doesn't make the concept clear then you can try another, or another, until a representation is found that can illuminate the concept. You will also notice that as the book progresses, the number of active representations diminishes – in the final chapters I have limited the representations to basically counters, vectors and bars/algebra tiles.

Many of the representations have a natural shelf life beyond which they fail to properly clarify concepts. Number lines, for example, are difficult to employ with algebra, particularly when more than one variable is required. Teachers should bear this in mind when choosing representations, because we need them to support pupil understanding both now and in related concepts they might encounter in their future learning.

One thing I would like to stress is that it is definitely not necessary to introduce all of the representations at once. In the scheme of work that my department works to, we concentrate on three representations to begin with – counters, bars and number lines. Later on, we introduce the ordered-pair graphs and vectors when we work with negative integers, and then the proportion diagram, particularly when working on proportion problems. I want to reiterate that it is crucial for pupils to be comfortable with the representation prior to it being used with a new concept. So, if you want to use number lines to explore rounding, then ensure your pupils are given enough time to become familiar with number lines graduated in different units before you use them to look at rounding.

## 3. Pupils can't use these concrete and visual approaches in their exams, so what is the point?

Admittedly, pupils will not have access to concrete manipulatives, but I understand that exam boards are happy to credit the use of visual approaches to problem solving in GCSE exams. Many mark schemes now have lines in such as '3 × 4 or 12 seen' for awarding marks, and they are prepared to award marks for this shown on a diagram. Key Stage 2 exams only credit certain approved methods if the answer is incorrect – although, if the answer is correct then any method is allowed.

My response here is two-fold: firstly, these representations should be complicit in their own demise. The point of any representation is to make itself redundant – they allow pupils to develop the necessary understanding of the underlying structures such that they achieve the fluency to work purely symbolically (i.e. just with numerical or algebraic symbols). If teachers approach the representations as just a new process to learn, then pupils will be no better off in their understanding. However, if they are used skilfully by teachers to reveal aspects of the concept that would otherwise pass them by, then pupils can quickly move beyond the need for them.

Secondly, if the representations are used skilfully, then pupils will be much better prepared for their exams than if they see mathematics as a series of disparate processes and techniques that they are expected to learn in order to find the right answer to a question. Therefore, the point of these representations is to enable pupils to understand the structures of mathematics and the connections between them, which will ultimately result in them performing better in examinations.

# 4. I just use … with my pupils. What is wrong with that?

Nothing at all, provided it equips your pupils with the understanding necessary to approach the concepts that you are currently trying to support them in, and also allows them to develop an insight into the connected concepts they may meet in the future.

I first faced this question after speaking in Essex about approaching negatives using counters and zero-pairs. The questioner was talking about using temperature. My response highlighted two key problems. Firstly, temperature is not a good model for using negatives beyond basic addition and subtraction. Creating a situation where a positive temperature needs to be multiplied by a negative value is challenging, to put it lightly. I cannot envisage a scenario in the context of temperature where this would be necessary, never mind illuminating the underlying structure of multiplication and how it applies to negative integers.

The second problem is that of reach: teachers have been using temperature to teach negative numbers for years, and yet many pupils continue to make basic mistakes when it comes to calculating with negative numbers. Clearly, temperature works for some pupils, but not all. These other pupils require a different model if they are to succeed, and as teachers we should have a wealth of approaches to call on to support pupils in developing this understanding. As a model for negative values, temperature does not allow pupils to achieve the 'mastery' that Bloom talked about – where over 90% of pupils, given enough time, can secure a concept.[*] This teacher felt comfortable with the idea of temperature as a model for negatives, but it is not for us to pass on our biases to our pupils. Just because we are at ease with a model, this does not mean that it will necessarily do the job for our pupils, so it is important we have a number of approaches at our disposal.

---

[*] B. S. Bloom, Learning for Mastery, *Evaluation Comment*, 1(2) (1968). Available at: https://programs.honolulu.hawaii.edu/intranet/sites/programs.honolulu.hawaii.edu.intranet/files/upstf-student-success-bloom-1968.pdf.

## 5. If you had to pick just one manipulative/representation, which one would you pick?

I wouldn't. Don't get me wrong, I have representations that are my 'go to' models – in particular, bars and counters. These are usually the first representations I will try in order to support a pupil who is struggling to make the necessary connections or develop the required understanding. But when they don't work, I need others. Any teacher who reads this book and tries to focus on just one representation has missed a fundamental point: it is the flexibility of using multiple representations that compensate for the others' weaknesses that make them powerful. I want my pupils to understand what I understand about mathematics, but that doesn't mean I need them to think like me. I need to provide them with the models and structures that they require in order to reach this level of understanding, and so the more ways of thinking about the mathematics they are studying pupils have, the better.

## 6. My school/department doesn't have these manipulatives for use in the classroom. What can I do?

The United States Marine Corps has an official motto: 'Improvise, Adapt and Overcome'. In the absence of concrete manipulatives, adapt other things. I have used coloured pencils in place of bars and vectors. I have already mentioned teachers using sweets. Algebra tiles can be cut out of card (there are lots of templates available online). Failing all of that, there are virtual manipulatives which can be used either to model with pupils or for pupils to use if they have access to the appropriate technology. One of the best is the excellent www.mathsbot.com, created by Jonathan Hall (@ StudyMaths) – indeed, this is the source which provided the basis of most of the diagrams in this book. Given time, if your school/department can see that these approaches are working for pupils, they might be convinced to invest in some manipulatives for pupils to use.

# 7. Whenever I try to use these manipulatives, pupils just end up distracted by the manipulative and don't focus on the learning. How can I prevent this?

This is something I hear from teachers a lot. Unfortunately, there is no easy answer – as with any new approach in the classroom, pupils need time to get used to it and feel comfortable with it. There are many factors that will influence this, including the school culture and how this promotes pupils valuing their learning opportunities, the peer relationships and dynamics in the classroom, the prior understanding of pupils (both in terms of use of the representation and the concept) – the list goes on.

All I can say is that there are primary pupils up and down the country using these manipulatives to support the development of their own understanding, and therefore there is no reason why pupils of all ages shouldn't be able to achieve the same. The best advice I can give is to persevere – try to get to the point where the use of the manipulatives is a normal part of classroom practice, and eventually this should settle down.

# 8. My head of department/maths lead doesn't believe these approaches are worth bothering about, and insists I do things their way. What can I do?

This is always a tricky one to negotiate. Ultimately, I believe that the leader of an area should set the tone for how that area goes about its work, and the staff should take their cue from the head. But I also believe that leaders should listen to the viewpoints of their team and engage with new ideas, so if a leader isn't doing that, then it is legitimate to ask why. I would be tempted to talk with them, understand where their resistance comes from and see if I could get them to agree to allowing a trial of small changes in certain approaches. Then, if this works, I would take that back to them as a motivator for further change.

I am aware that this assumes a lot about how confident a teacher is in having this sort of conversation with their maths lead, which will be affected by their experience, how long they have worked in the department/school and so on. Ultimately, if it got to the point where I felt there was no way that I could use some classroom autonomy to introduce these approaches to support my pupils, if I felt the representations would benefit them, then I would have to consider moving on and finding an environment in which I would be more comfortable. But I appreciate this may not be an option for everyone.

# 9. How does this fit in with all the talk of 'mastery' that is being used in maths education?

We have to be careful when we talk about mastery in education, as it has come to mean certain things that it wasn't originally intended to mean. When it was first used in the early 20th century, mastery spoke of a curriculum model that could be applied to any subject, so the vast majority of learners could attain a high level of understanding in whatever was being taught. Mark McCourt provides an excellent outline of the history of the mastery curriculum.[*]

In addition to a mastery curriculum, we can talk about mathematics teaching for mastery approaches. This is a more recent development and is perhaps what most people mean when they talk about mastery in English schools. Different people have put forward different views, but they generally agree on the importance of the use of concrete and pictorial models to support progress in pupil understanding. Therefore, the approaches and concepts set out in this book can be considered fairly central to teaching for mastery in the mathematics classroom.

# 10. I am nervous about employing these approaches in the classroom. Is there somewhere I can go to see them being used in practice?

Absolutely. If you are in a secondary school, the first thing I would do is to contact some of your local primary schools – the use of representations seems to be much stronger in primaries than secondaries (in England anyway). There are also local Maths Hubs (www.mathshubs.org.uk), most of which will have teaching for mastery specialists at both primary and secondary level, who will have engaged with representation and structure and can share their practice with you. They may even have

---

[*] See Mark McCourt, Teaching for Mastery – Part 1, *Emaths* [blog] (2 October 2016). Available at: https://markmccourt.blogspot. co.uk/2016/10/teaching-for-mastery-part-1.html and Teaching for Mastery – Part 2, *Emaths* [blog] (21 October 2016). Available at: https://markmccourt.blogspot.co.uk/2016/10/teaching-for-mastery-part-2.html.

work groups around representation and structure or the use of manipulatives that you could get involved in, which would enable you to develop these approaches with the support of others in the work group. If not, the NCETM (www.ncetm.org.uk), which has oversight of the Maths Hub programme, has a large collection of materials – including videos and case studies – that may be helpful.

There are also a number of hands-on training opportunities in using manipulatives and representations. Some of the best are offered by La Salle Education, run by the great Mark McCourt. They include courses on mastery, bar modelling, and the concrete, pictorial, abstract and language approach. Details of these can be found on their website (http://completemaths.com).

I hope this chapter answers any questions you might have about the ideas and approaches discussed in the book. If they didn't, you can always contact the organisations I mention in question 10 above, or tweet them to me (@MrMattock) or to the maths community in general on Twitter – someone will have the answer. My sincere thanks for reading!

# Glossary

**Addend** – A number that is added to another.

**Argand diagram** – A representation that plots complex numbers on a two-dimensional plane using one axis to represent the real part and the other axis to represent the irrational part.

**Algorithm** – A process or a set of instructions that are followed to produce a result.

**Array** – An arrangement of objects in two dimensions using columns and rows.

**Base (of a number system)** – The number of unique digits used to represent numbers in that system. The most well-known are binary (base 2), denary/decimal (base 10) and hexadecimal (base 16).

**Cardinal numbers (cardinality)** – Broadly speaking, numbers used to represent a count of how many objects make up a number or set – for example, one, two, three.

**Chunking** – An approach to division that involves removing large multiples of the **divisor** until zero is reached.

**Continuous numbers** – Numbers that can take all values and can be considered as connected to each other without a break.

**Denominator** – The value at the bottom of a fraction.

**Discrete numbers** – Numbers that can only take certain values and can be considered as separate objects to each other.

**Dividend** – In a division calculation, the number to be divided by another number (the **divisor**).

**Divisor** – In a division calculation, the number to be divided into another number (the **dividend**).

**Equation** – A mathematical statement showing that two things are equal. Often used specifically to describe problems where a variable is unknown and the values can be found using analytical or numerical approaches.

**Exchange** – The act of changing something for another, or others, of total equal value.

**Expand** – The process of applying the distributive law by multiplying a value over a sum or difference.

**Factor** – A positive whole number that divides into another number to produce a whole number answer.

**Factorise** – The process of writing a value or expression as the product of two or more **factors**.

**Formula** – A relationship between two or more variables.

**Hypotenuse** – The label given to the longest side in a right-angled triangle.

**Identity element** – The value that produces no effect when combined with any other under a given operation. The identity element of addition is 0, because 0 added to anything doesn't affect the thing. The identity element of multiplication is 1, because multiplying anything by 1 doesn't affect the thing.

**Index (pl. indices)** – An alternative word for the power to which a number is raised.

**Integer** – A whole number that can be positive, negative or zero.

**Inverse (operation)** – The operation that when applied to a value reverses the effect of a different operation applied to the same value. Subtraction is the inverse operation of addition because subtracting 4 (say) from a value reverses the effect of adding 4 to a value. Division is the inverse operation of multiplication because dividing a number by 4 reverses the effect of multiplying a number by 4.

**Inverse (value)** – A value that when combined with another under a given operation produces the **identity element** under that operation.

**Irrational number** – A number that cannot be expressed as the ratio of two **integers** (i.e. as a fraction).

**Numerator** – The value at the top of a fraction.

**Ordered-pair** – Two numbers grouped so that a change of order changes the meaning. Fractions and coordinates are both examples of ordered-pairs of **integers**.

**Ordinal numbers (ordinality)** – Numbers used to indicate position in a series (order) – for example, first, second, third.

**Proportion** – A relationship between quantities based on one quantity being a constant multiple of another.

**Quotient** – In a division calculation, the result of dividing a **dividend** by a **divisor**.

**Rational number** – A number that can be expressed as the fraction of two **integers** – for example, $\frac{1}{2}$, $\frac{2}{3}$ and 5.

**Rounding** – Reducing the accuracy of a given value due to physical requirements (i.e. rounding 42.2 pence as it is impossible to have 0.2 pence) or to reflect the accuracy of a measurement.

**Standard index form** – A way of writing numbers, usually very large or very small numbers, by indicating the size of the highest place in the number, with the size of smaller places given after a decimal point. Also called scientific notation.

**Surd** – An **irrational number**, usually used to mean the irrational root of a positive **integer** value.

**Vector** – A quantity that has a size (magnitude) and acts in a certain direction. Common examples include force and acceleration. The opposite of a vector is a scalar, which has size only (such as mass, area, etc.).

# Bibliography

Ainsworth, C. (2016). Consistency of Imagery. *Mathematics Teaching: Journal of the Association of Teachers of Mathematics*, 253, 15–18. Available at: https://www.atm.org.uk/write/MediaUploads/Journals/MT253/MT253-16-05.pdf.

Bloom, B. S. (1968). Learning for Mastery, *Evaluation Comment*, 1(2). Available at: https://programs.honolulu.hawaii.edu/intranet/sites/programs.honolulu.hawaii.edu.intranet/files/upstf-student-success-bloom-1968.pdf.

Boulton, K. (2013). Why Is It That Students Always Seem to Understand, But Then Never Remember? ... *To the Real* [blog] (6 May). Available at: https://tothereal.wordpress.com/2013/05/06/why-is-it-that-students-always-seem-to-understand-but-then-never-remember/.

Boulton, K. (2015). The Stories of Mathematics – Part 1. Presentation at the Complete Mathematics Conference 5, Sheffield, 26 September.

Cockcroft, W. H. (chair) (1982). *Mathematics Counts: Report of the Committee of Inquiry into the Teaching of Mathematics in Schools* [Cockcroft Report] (London: HMSO). Available at: http://www.educationengland.org.uk/documents/cockcroft/cockcroft1982.html.

Department for Education (2014). National Curriculum in England: Mathematics Programmes of Study. Statutory Guidance (July). Available at: https://www.gov.uk/government/publications/national-curriculum-in-england-mathematics-programmes-of-study/national-curriculum-in-england-mathematics-programmes-of-study.

Department for Education (2017). *Statutory Framework for the Early Years Foundation Stage: Setting the Standards for Learning, Development and Care for Children from Birth to Five* (March). Available at: https://www.gov.uk/government/publications/early-years-foundation-stage-framework--2.

du Sautoy, M. (2008). The Language of the Universe (Episode 1), *The Story of Maths* [TV series]. BBC Four (6 October).

EE Times (2006). An Introduction to Different Rounding Algorithms (1 April). Available at: https://www.eetimes.com/document.asp?doc_id=1274485.

Hawking, S. (1975). Particle Creation By Black Holes, *Communications in Mathematical Physics*, 43(3), 199–220.

Henderson, P., Hodgen, J., Foster, C. and Kuchemann, D. (2017). *Improving Mathematics in Key Stages Two and Three: Guidance Report* (London: Education Endowment Foundation). Available at: https://educationendowmentfoundation.org.uk/public/files/Publications/Campaigns/Maths/KS2_KS3_Maths_Guidance_2017.pdf.

Hewitt, D. (1999). Arbitrary and Necessary: Part 1, A Way of Viewing the Mathematics Curriculum, *For the Learning of Mathematics: An International Journal of Mathematics Education*, 19(3), 2–9.

Killian, S. (2017). Hattie's 2017 Updated List of Factors Influencing Student Achievement, *Australian Society for Evidence Based Teaching* (24 September). Available at: http://www. evidencebasedteaching.org.au/hatties-2017-updated-list/.

McCourt, M. (2016). Teaching for Mastery – Part 1, *Emaths* [blog] (2 October). Available at: https://markmccourt.blogspot.co.uk/2016/10/teaching-for-mastery-part-1.html.

McCourt, M. (2016) Teaching for Mastery – Part 2, *Emaths* [blog] (21 October). Available at: https://markmccourt.blogspot.co.uk/2016/10/teaching-for-mastery-part-2.html.

McCourt, M. (2017). Algebra Tiles. CPD session at the Association of School and College Leaders Conference for Heads of English, Maths and Science, Birmingham.

Mason, D. (2015). The Physics of Everything: Understanding Superstring Theory, *Futurism* (10 September). Available at: https://futurism.com/brane-science-complex-notions-of-superstring-theory/.

Moyer-Packenham, P. S. (2001). Are We Having Fun Yet? How Teachers Use Manipulatives to Teach Mathematics. Available at: https://digitalcommons.usu.edu/cgi/viewcontent. cgi?article=1054&context=teal_facpub

Ofsted (2012). *Mathematics: Made to Measure* (May). Ref: 110159. Available at: https:// www.gov.uk/government/publications/mathematics-made-to-measure.

Ollerton, M. and Cooper, K. (2017). Learning to Teach and Teaching to Learn, *Mathematics Teaching: Journal of the Association of Teachers of Mathematics*, 255, 12–16. Available at: https://www.atm.org.uk/write/MediaUploads/Journals/MT255/MT255-17-04.pdf.

Singh, S. (1997). *Fermat's Last Theorem* (London: Fourth Estate).

Sowell, E. J. (1989). Effects of Manipulative Materials in Mathematics Instruction, *Journal for Research in Mathematics Education*, 20(5), 498–505. Available at: http://www.jstor.org/ stable/749423?read-now=1&seq=7#references_tab_contents.

Swan, M. (2005). Improving Learning in Mathematics: Challenges and Strategies (London: Department for Education and Skills Standards Unit). Available at: https://www.ncetm.org. uk/files/224/improving_learning_in_mathematicsi.pdf.

Weinstein, Y. and Smith, M. (2016). Learn How to Study Using … Spaced Practice, *Learning Scientists* [blog] (21 July). Available at: http://www.learningscientists.org/blog/2016/ 7/21-1.